Microsoft® Office PowerPoint® 2003: Essentials Course

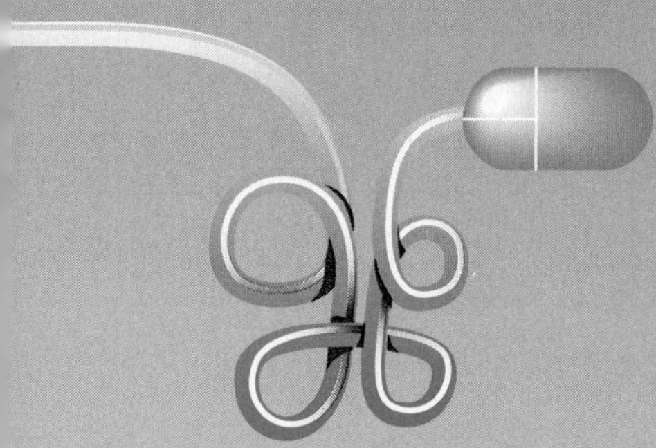

Microsoft Office PowerPoint 2003: Essentials Course

SANDRA CALDWELL
Community College of Allegheny County

JUDY MARDAR
Community College Workforce Alliance

LABYRINTH
PUBLICATIONS®

Microsoft Office PowerPoint 2003: Essentials Course
by Sandra Caldwell and Judy Mardar

LABYRINTH PUBLICATIONS®

Labyrinth Publications
3314 Morningside Drive
El Sobrante, California 94803
800.522.9746
On the Web at labpub.com

Cover and Interior Design:
Seventeenth Street Studios

Series Editor:
Russel Stolins

Managing Editor:
Laura A. Lionello

Production Manager:
Rad Proctor

Editorial/Production Team:
Holly Hammond, Nancy Logan,
Barbara Luck, Nancy Roberts

Indexing: Joanne Sprott

Printer: Courier, Kendallville

ISBN 1-59136-031-5

Manufactured in the United States of America.

10 9 8 7 6 5 4 3 2 1

Microsoft Office Specialist Program

What Does This Logo Mean?

NOTE! Microsoft Office PowerPoint 2003: Essentials Course *will prepare you to take the Microsoft Office PowerPoint 2003 exam.*

It means this courseware has been approved by the Microsoft Office Specialist program to be among the finest available for learning PowerPoint 2003. It also means that upon completion of this courseware, you may be prepared to become a Microsoft Office Specialist.

What Is a Microsoft Office Specialist?

A Microsoft Office Specialist is an individual who has certified skills in one or more Microsoft Office desktop applications such as Microsoft Word, Microsoft Excel, Microsoft Outlook®, Microsoft PowerPoint, or Microsoft Project. The Microsoft Office Specialist program typically offers certification exams at different skill levels.* The Microsoft Office Specialist program is the only Microsoft-approved program in the world for certifying proficiency in Microsoft Office desktop applications and Microsoft Project. This certification can be a valuable asset in any job search or career advancement.

Which Exam(s) Will This Publication Prepare You to Take?

Microsoft Office PowerPoint 2003: Essentials Course is approved by Microsoft as courseware for the Microsoft Office Specialist program. After completing this course, students will be prepared to take the Microsoft Office PowerPoint 2003 exam.

For more information:

- To learn more about becoming a Microsoft Office Specialist, visit www.microsoft.com/officespecialist/.
- To purchase a Microsoft Office Specialist certification exam, visit www.microsoft.com/officespecialist/.
- To learn about other Microsoft Office Specialist approved courseware from Labyrinth Publications, visit labpub.com/mos/.

---

* The availability of Microsoft Office Specialist certification exams varies by application, application version, and language. Visit www.microsoft.com/officespecialist/ for exam availability.

Microsoft Office PowerPoint 2003 objectives covered in this book

Objective Number	Skill Sets and Skills	Concept Page References	Exercise Page References
PP03S-1	**Creating Content**		
PP03S-1-1	Create new presentations from templates	20, 25	25–26
PP03S-1-2	Insert and edit text-based content	15, 21, 118, 140	16–17, 21–22, 119, 141–142
PP03S-1-3	Insert tables, charts, and diagrams	143–145, 147–148, 150–151, 154, 161–162	145–152, 154–159, 162–164
PP03S-1-4	Insert pictures, shapes, and graphics	68–69, 73–74	69–70, 74–76
PP03S-1-5	Insert objects	76–77, 257–259	78–79, 259–262
PP03S-2	**Formatting Content**		
PP03S-2-1	Format text-based content	40	41–42
PP03S-2-2	Format pictures, shapes, and graphics	71, 85	72
PP03S-2-3	Format slides	8–9, 13–14, 56, 244–245	10–11, 14–15, 56, 246–249
PP03S-2-4	Apply animation schemes	88	89
PP03S-2-5	Apply slide transitions	85–86	86–87
PP03S-2-6	Customize slide templates	244, 249–250	246–252
PP03S-2-7	Work with masters	18, 113, 253, 255	19, 113, 253–257
PP03S-3	**Collaborating**		
PP03S-3-1	Track, accept, and reject changes in a presentation	220–222, 226–229	222–223, 228–231
PP03S-3-2	Add, edit, and delete comments in a presentation	224	225–226
PP03S-3-3	Compare and merge presentations	231–232, 235	232–235
PP03S-4	**Managing and Delivering Presentations**		
PP03S-4-1	Organize a presentation	17, 52, 77, 110, 182–183	18, 52–53, 110–111, 183–184
PP03S-4-2	Set up slide shows for delivery	98, 110, 263–264	98–99, 264–265
PP03S-4-3	Rehearse timing	96–97	97
PP03S-4-4	Deliver presentations	26–28, 115–116	28–29, 116–117
PP03S-4-5	Prepare presentations for remote delivery	203–206, 276–277, 280	205–206, 277–279, 281
PP03S-4-6	Save and publish presentations	122–123, 189–192, 194–197	192–195, 198–199
PP03S-4-7	Print slides, outlines, handouts, and speaker notes	111	112
PP03S-4-8	Export a presentation to another Microsoft Office program	140	141–142, 164

Contents in Brief

Contents

LESSON 3 MANAGING CLIP ART, DRAWING OBJECTS, AND ANIMATION 66

LESSON 4 MANAGING PRESENTATION TOOLS 108

UNIT 2 BEYOND THE BASICS

LESSON 5 WORKING WITH CHARTS, TABLES, AND OFFICE APPLICATIONS 138

LESSON 6 WORKING WITH ONLINE PRESENTATIONS 180

LESSON 7 WORKING WITH ONLINE COLLABORATION 218

LESSON 8 MANAGING TEMPLATE CUSTOMIZATION AND MULTIMEDIA 242

LESSON 9 ON THE ROAD AGAIN: A CASE STUDY WORKSHOP 274

APPENDIX USING FILE STORAGE MEDIA 298

Index of Quick Reference Tables

List of Keyboard Shortcuts

Document Commands

Ctrl+K to insert a hyperlink

Ctrl+P to display the Print box

Ctrl+S for Save

Shift+F10 to display pop-up menu

Editing Commands

Ctrl+C for Copy

Ctrl+F for Find

Ctrl+H for Replace

Ctrl+V for Paste

Ctrl+X for Cut

Format Font Commands

Ctrl+B for Bold

Ctrl+I for Italics

Ctrl+U for Underline

Presentation Commands

Ctrl+A to change the pen to the pointer tool

Ctrl+P to change the pointer tool to the pen

H to go to the next hidden slide while running a presentation

Preface

Microsoft Office PowerPoint 2003: Essentials Course provides complete coverage of Microsoft PowerPoint 2003. The text prepares students for the Microsoft Office PowerPoint 2003 exam offered through the Microsoft Office Specialist program.

This newest edition of Labyrinth's Microsoft PowerPoint book has been reorganized into two units and includes a significant amount of new subject matter. Unit 1: PowerPoint Basics has students design, create, and deliver a new presentation. Students are engaged with interesting PowerPoint features, including graphics and animation. Unit 2: Beyond the Basics introduces more advanced topics such as outlining, Microsoft Visio, and multimedia effects. This book contains stimulating case studies that engage students as they develop sophisticated presentations that continually build from lesson to lesson. This book assumes that students understand the basic concepts of using a mouse and drop-down menus, saving files to some type of storage media, and other basic skills required to run Windows programs.

Over the last 10 years of writing and publishing Microsoft Office courses, Labyrinth has developed a unique instructional design that makes learning faster and easier for students at all skill levels. Teachers have found that the Labyrinth model provides effective learning for students in both self-paced and instructor-led learning environments. The material is carefully written and built around compelling case studies that demonstrate the relevance of all subject matter. Mastery of subject matter is ensured through the use of multiple levels of carefully crafted exercises. The text includes Concepts Review questions and Hands-On, Skill Builder, Assessment, and Critical Thinking exercises.

Microsoft Office PowerPoint 2003: Essentials Course is also supported on the Labyrinth Website with a comprehensive instructor support package that includes a printable solutions guide, detailed lesson plans, PowerPoint presentations, a course syllabus, extensive test banks, and more.

We are grateful to the many teachers who have used Labyrinth titles and suggested improvements to us during the 10 years we have been writing and publishing Office books. *Microsoft Office PowerPoint 2003: Essentials Course* has benefited from the reviewing and suggestions of Julie Sharrow of Metro College, Youngstown State University, in Youngstown, OH.

About the Authors

Sandra Caldwell (BA, Liberal Arts) has provided corporate training, technical writing, workshop leadership, and consulting to corporate and small businesses in Boston, Chicago, Philadelphia, and Pittsburgh for more than a decade. She is presently a corporate trainer with the Institute for Corporate and Professional Development at the Community College of Allegheny County as well as a Microsoft technologies instructor for the Lifetime Learning division of the college. She is also a computer instructor with Washington & Jefferson College. Sandra is coauthor of *Microsoft Office 2003: Essentials Course*.

Judy Mardar has been an independent computer trainer, technical writer, and consultant for many years. She teaches, writes, and consults at the Community College Workforce Alliance, as well as for private training companies, the state government, and small businesses. She is a certified Microsoft Office Expert and has trained thousands of people to use computers and business software over the last 10 years. Judy is coauthor of *Microsoft Office 2003: Essentials Course* and *Microsoft Office Excel 2003: Comprehensive Course*.

Introduction

Welcome to Labyrinth Publications, where you'll find your course to success. Our real world, project-based approach to education helps students grasp concepts, not just read about them, and prepares them for success in the workplace. Our straightforward, easy-to-follow language is ideal for both instructor-led classes and self-paced labs. At Labyrinth, we're dedicated to one purpose: delivering quality courseware that is comprehensive yet concise, effective, and affordable. It's no wonder that Labyrinth is a recognized leader in Microsoft Office and operating system courseware.

More than a million users have learned Office our way. At Labyrinth, we believe that successful teaching begins with exceptional courseware. That's why we've made it our goal to develop innovative texts that empower both teachers and students. We give educators the necessary resources to deliver clear, relevant instruction and students the power to take their new skills far beyond the classroom.

Labyrinth Series Give You More Choices

Labyrinth offers seven exceptionally priced series to meet your needs:

- Microsoft Office 2003 Series—These full-length, full-featured texts explore applications in the Office 2003 system. All application-specific books in this series are Microsoft Office Specialist approved for the Microsoft Office 2003 certification exams, and the Word and Excel books are also approved for the Microsoft Office 2003 Expert certification exams.
- Silver™ Series—Designed especially for adult learners, seniors, and non-native speakers, this series includes larger fonts and screens, our unmistakable straightforward design, and fun hands-on projects.
- ProStart Foundations™ Series—These full-length, full-featured texts for operating systems and applications include the new Microsoft Windows titles and are designed to lay a solid foundation for students.
- ProStart™ Series for Office XP—These full-length, full-featured texts walk students through the basic and advanced skills of the primary Office XP applications. Most are Microsoft Office Specialist approved. The Office XP Essentials and Comprehensive courses offer surveys of all the primary Office XP applications.
- Briefcase™ Series for Office XP—The popular and inexpensive choice for short classes, self-paced courses, and accelerated workshops (or mix and match for longer classes), these concise texts provide quick access to key concepts. Most are Microsoft Office Specialist approved.
- Off to Work™ Series for Office 2000—Full-length, full-featured texts set the standard for clarity and ease of use in this series. All books in this series are Microsoft Office Specialist approved.
- Briefcase Series for Office 2000—Designed for short classes, self-paced courses, and accelerated workshops, each lesson in this series is broken down into subtopics that provide quick access to key concepts. All books in this series are Microsoft Office Specialist approved.

Microsoft Office 2003 Series Teaching Resources

Instructor Support Material

To help you be more successful, Labyrinth provides a comprehensive instructor support package that includes the following:

Teaching Tools

- Detailed lesson plans, including a topic sequence and suggested classroom demonstrations
- PowerPoint presentations that give an overview of key concepts for each lesson (also available online for students)
- Answer keys for the Concepts Review questions in each lesson
- Comprehensive classroom setup instructions
- A customizable sample syllabus
- A teacher-customizable background knowledge survey to gather information on student needs and experience at the beginning of the course

Testing Tools

- Printer-friendly exercise solution guides and solution files for Hands-On, Skill Builder, Assessment, and Critical Thinking exercises
- Teacher-customizable, project-based Assessment exercises
- Teacher-customizable test banks of objective questions for each lesson and unit
- TestComposer™ test generator for editing test banks with Microsoft Word (and for creating new question banks and online tests)

These resources are available on our Website at labpub.com and on our instructor support CD, which you can obtain by calling our customer service staff at 800.522.9746.

Website

The Website labpub.com/learn/pp03/ features content designed to support the lessons and provide additional learning resources for this book. This main page contains links to individual lesson pages. Some of the items you will find at this site are described below.

PowerPoint Presentations The same presentations available to instructors are accessible online. This makes an excellent tool for review, particularly for students who miss a class session.

WebSim

Web-Based Simulations Some exercises contain topics that have Web-based simulations. These simulations can be accessed through the lesson pages.

Downloads Required course files can be downloaded on the lesson pages.

Student Exercise Files The student files needed to complete certain Hands-On, Skill Builder, Assessment, and Critical Thinking exercises are available for download at labpub.com/students/fdmso2003.asp.

Labyrinth's Successful Instructional Design

In conjunction with our straightforward writing style, Labyrinth books feature a proven instructional design. The following pages point out the carefully crafted design elements that build student confidence and ensure success.

Lesson introductions present clear learning objectives.

LESSON 3

File Management and Online Help

When you begin working with a computer, you will have just a few files to keep track of. But as your use of the computer grows, so will the number of files you must manage. After several months, you can have over a hundred of your own ...

files: folders. With folders, you can group related files together. You can even create folders inside of other folders. As you learn how to use new features such as folders, you should take advantage of the excellent online Help system featured in Windows. Online Help makes ...

IN THIS LESSON

Using Online Help with Windows	86
Browsing through Files	92
Working with Folders	97
Moving and Copying Files	102
Deleting Files ...	

Case studies introduce a practical application that integrates topics presented in each lesson.

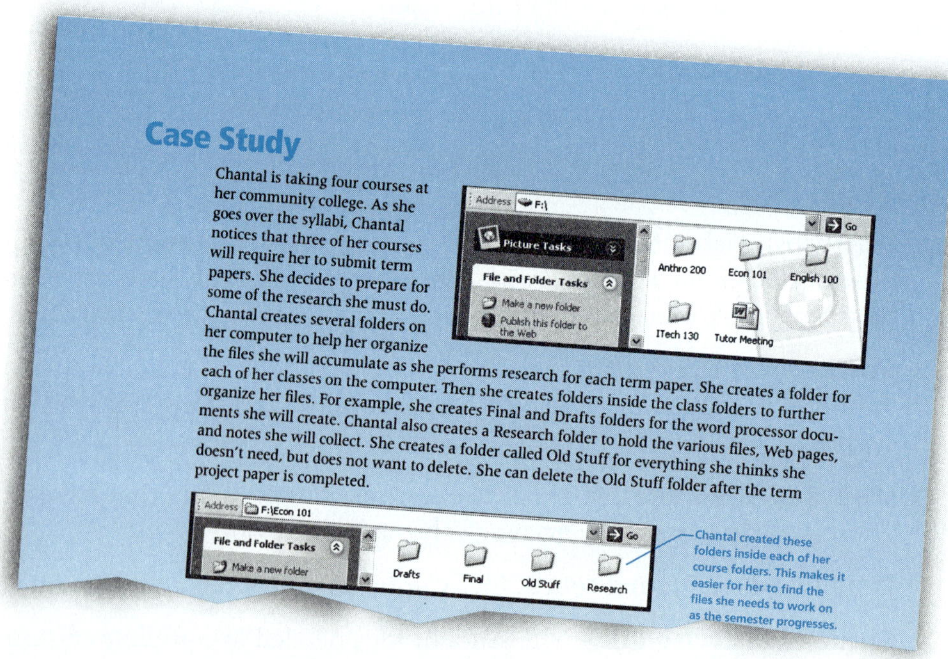

Case Study

Chantal is taking four courses at her community college. As she goes over the syllabi, Chantal notices that three of her courses will require her to submit term papers. She decides to prepare for some of the research she must do. Chantal creates several folders on her computer to help her organize the files she will accumulate as she performs research for each term paper. She creates a folder for each of her classes on the computer. Then she creates folders inside the class folders to further organize her files. For example, she creates Final and Drafts folders for the word processor documents she will create. Chantal also creates a Research folder to hold the various files, Web pages, and notes she will collect. She creates a folder called Old Stuff for everything she thinks she doesn't need, but does not want to delete. She can delete the Old Stuff folder after the term project paper is completed.

Chantal created these folders inside each of her course folders. This makes it easier for her to find the files she needs to work on as the semester progresses.

Concepts discussions are kept concise and use illustrations for added clarity and to help students understand the material introduced.

Quick Reference tables provide generic procedures for key tasks that work outside the context of the lesson.

Hands-On exercises are detailed tutorials that help students master the skills introduced in the concepts discussions. The illustrations provide clear instruction and allow unparalleled ease of use.

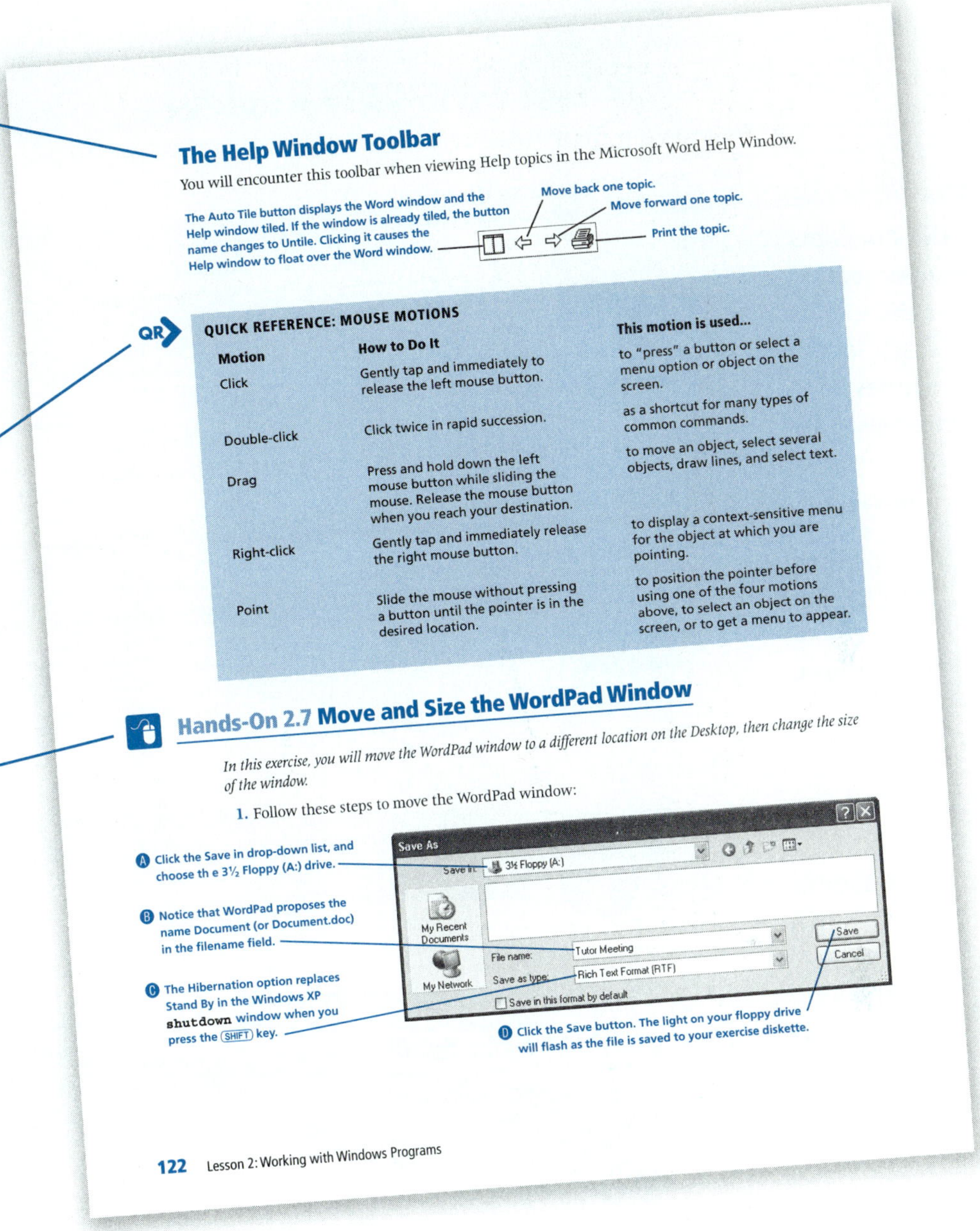

The Help Window Toolbar

You will encounter this toolbar when viewing Help topics in the Microsoft Word Help Window.

QR

QUICK REFERENCE: MOUSE MOTIONS

Motion	How to Do It	This motion is used...
Click	Gently tap and immediately to release the left mouse button.	to "press" a button or select a menu option or object on the screen.
Double-click	Click twice in rapid succession.	as a shortcut for many types of common commands.
Drag	Press and hold down the left mouse button while sliding the mouse. Release the mouse button when you reach your destination.	to move an object, select several objects, draw lines, and select text.
Right-click	Gently tap and immediately release the right mouse button.	to display a context-sensitive menu for the object at which you are pointing.
Point	Slide the mouse without pressing a button until the pointer is in the desired location.	to position the pointer before using one of the four motions above, to select an object on the screen, or to get a menu to appear.

Hands-On 2.7 Move and Size the WordPad Window

In this exercise, you will move the WordPad window to a different location on the Desktop, then change the size of the window.

1. Follow these steps to move the WordPad window:

122 Lesson 2: Working with Windows Programs

The Concepts Review section at the end of each lesson includes both true/false and multiple choice questions.

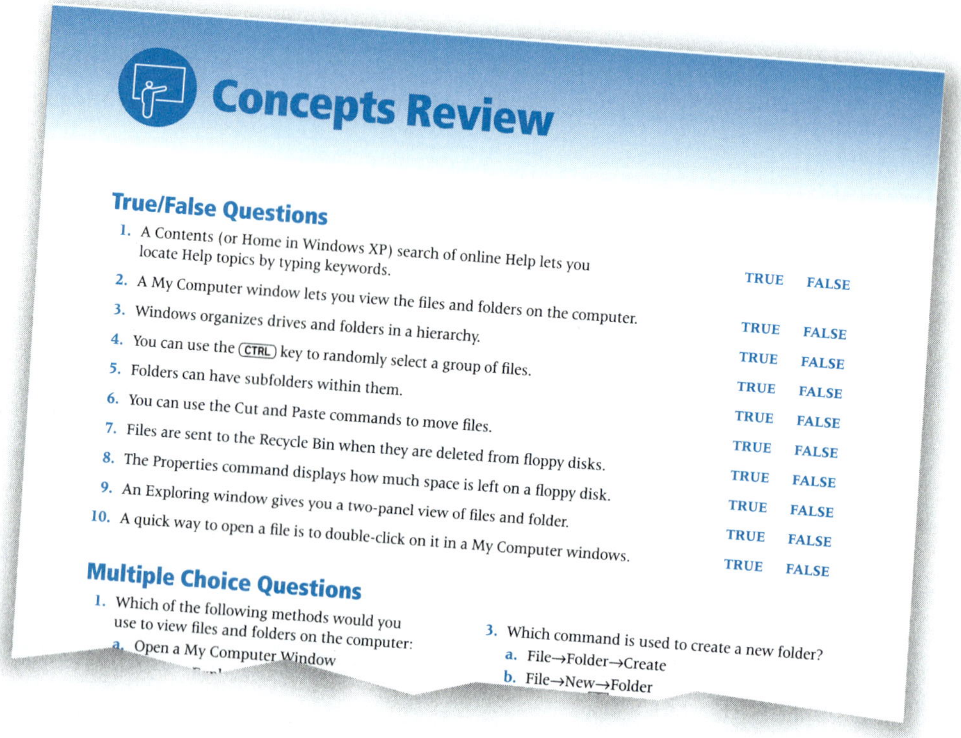

Skill Builders, Assessments, and Critical Thinking exercises provide fun, hands-on projects with reduced levels of detailed instruction so students can develop and test their mastery of the material.

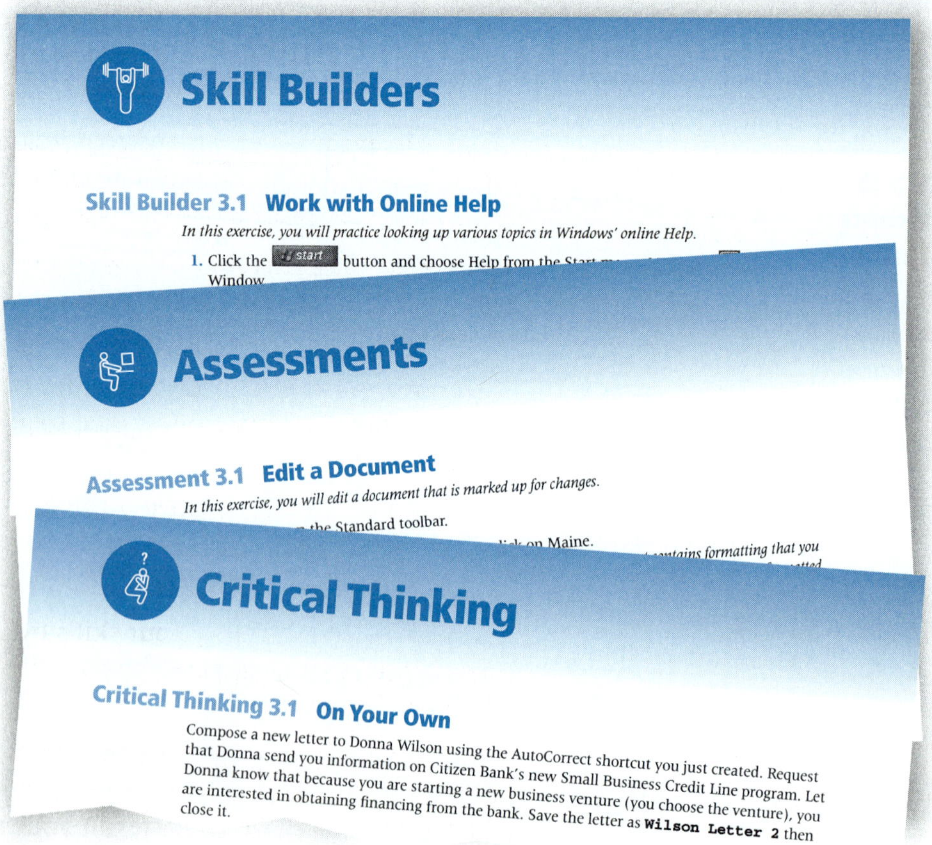

How This Book Is Organized

The information in this text is presented so that you master the fundamental skills first then build on those skills as you work with the more comprehensive topics.

Visual Conventions

This book uses many visual and typographic cues to guide you through the lessons. These pages provide examples and describe the function of each cue.

Cue	Description
`Type this text`	Anything you should type at the keyboard is printed in this typeface.
TIP!	Tips, Notes, and Warnings are used throughout the text to draw attention to certain topics.
Command→Command	This convention indicates multiple selections to be made from a menu bar. For example, File→Save means to select File then select Save.
FROM THE KEYBOARD Ctrl+S to Save	These margin notes indicate shortcut keys for executing a task described in the text.
QR	Quick Reference tables provide generic instructions for key tasks. Only perform these tasks if you are instructed to in an exercise.
WebSim	This icon indicates the availability of a Web-based simulation for an exercise. You may need to use a WebSim if your computer lab is not set up to support particular exercises.
	Hands-On exercises are introduced immediately after concept discussions. They provide detailed, step-by-step tutorials so you can master the skills presented.
Microsoft Office Specialist	Concepts discussions that deal with the Microsoft Office Specialist Program exam objectives are marked with one of these icons.
	The Concepts Review section includes both true/false and multiple choice questions designed to gauge your understanding of concepts.
	Skill Builder exercises provide additional hands-on practice with moderate assistance.
	Assessment exercises test your skills by describing the correct results without providing specific instructions on how to achieve them.
	Critical Thinking exercises are the most challenging. They provide general instructions, allowing you to use your skills and creativity to achieve the result you envision.

Microsoft Office PowerPoint 2003: Essentials Course

Unit 1

PowerPoint Basics

PowerPoint 2003 is Microsoft's powerful multimedia program. From a slide show of your vacation photos to your next big sale's pitch, PowerPoint can help you create dynamic presentations. In this unit, you will be introduced to essential PowerPoint features. You will learn how to work with the task pane, design templates, and wizards. You will also get valuable design and formatting tips, use outlines and the Slide Sorter, and work with clip art and animation. Finally, you will learn about delivery options, editing procedures, and saving your presentations in different formats. By the end of this unit, you will be well prepared to tackle the advanced topics discussed in Unit 2.

Lesson 1: Creating and Delivering a Presentation

Lesson 2: Designing the Presentation

Lesson 3: Managing Clip Art, Drawing Objects, and Animation

Lesson 4: Managing Presentation Tools

LESSON 1

Creating and Delivering a Presentation

In this lesson, you will create a PowerPoint presentation for the Pinnacle Pet Care pet clinic. Throughout the lesson, you will be using many PowerPoint features to develop the presentation. You will be working with design templates, text layout styles, the Master slide, and the Research feature. You will also manage toolbars, choose views, and use the AutoContent Wizard. By the end of the lesson, your presentation will be ready for delivery. Equipped with the tips and techniques of successful presentation delivery, you will practice the delivery of your presentation to the Pet World trade show.

IN THIS LESSON

Microsoft Office PowerPoint 2003 objectives covered in this lesson

Objective Number	Skill Sets and Skills	Concept Page References	Exercise Page References
PP03S-1-1	Create new presentations from templates	20, 25	25–26
PP03S-1-2	Insert and edit text-based content	15, 21	16–17, 21–22
PP03S-2-3	Format slides	8–9, 13–14	10–11, 14–15
PP03S-2-7	Work with masters	18	19
PP03S-4-1	Organize a presentation	17	18
PP03S-4-4	Deliver presentations	26–28	28–29

Additional learning resources are available at labpub.com/learn/pp03/

Case Study

Al Smith, owner of Pinnacle Pet Care, has been invited to make a presentation representing his firm to the Pet World trade show. Al's goal is to introduce Pinnacle Pet Care to trade show attendees and entice them with a promotional offer. Al decides to use PowerPoint to develop and deliver his presentation using his new laptop and video projection system. Al chose PowerPoint because it is easy to learn and seamlessly integrates with his other Microsoft Office applications. Al's dynamic speaking abilities, coupled with PowerPoint's robust presentation features, are sure to win over the trade show attendees.

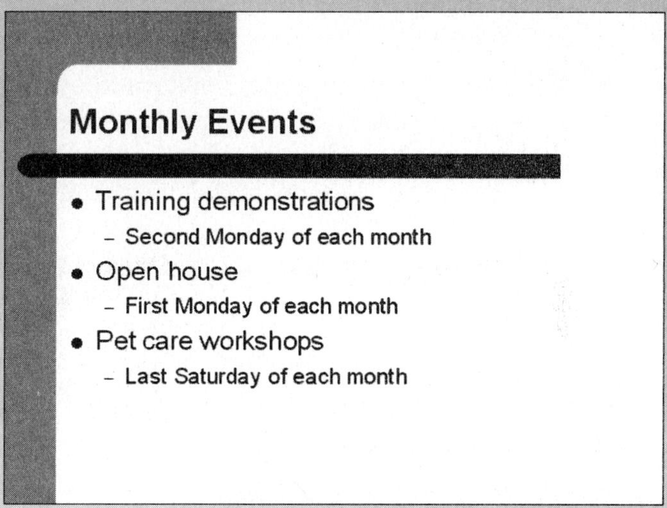

Slides from the Pinnacle Pet Care Presentation

Presenting PowerPoint

PowerPoint 2003 is an intuitive, powerful presentation graphics program that enables you to create dynamic, multimedia presentations for a variety of functions. Whether you are developing a one-on-one presentation for your manager or a sophisticated presentation for a large group, PowerPoint provides the tools to make your presentation a success. PowerPoint allows you to project your presentation in a variety of ways. You can deliver it using transparencies that are projected through an overhead projector, use 35 mm slides, or present your slide show using a liquid crystal display (LCD) device attached to your PC or laptop. With PowerPoint 2003, you can also give your presentation as an online broadcast over the Internet or an intranet.

PowerPoint provides powerful tools that let you concentrate on the content of your presentation instead of focusing on the design details. Using PowerPoint's built-in design templates, you can rapidly create highly effective professional presentations. PowerPoint tools help you to organize, develop, and deliver your presentations with precision, control, and creativity.

Starting PowerPoint

The method you use to start PowerPoint depends in large part on whether you intend to create a new presentation or open an existing presentation. To create a new presentation, use one of the following methods. Once the PowerPoint program has started, you can begin working in the new presentation that appears.

- Click the start button and choose Microsoft PowerPoint from the All Programs menu.

TIP! *In older versions of Windows and the classic view of Windows XP and 2003, the command on the Start Menu is Programs.*

- Click the Microsoft PowerPoint button on the Quick Launch toolbar (near the Taskbar).

Use one of the following methods to open an existing PowerPoint presentation. Once the PowerPoint program has started, the desired presentation will open in a PowerPoint window.

- Navigate to the desired document using Windows Explorer or My Computer and double-click the presentation.
- Click the start button, point to Documents, and choose the desired presentation. The Documents list displays the most recently used Office documents.

Hands-On 1.1 Start PowerPoint

In this exercise, you will start PowerPoint.

1. Start your computer.
2. Click the Start start button.
3. Choose (All) Programs→Microsoft Office→Office PowerPoint.
   PowerPoint will open and the PowerPoint program window will appear.

The Program Window

The PowerPoint 2003 program window has not significantly changed from prior versions of the program. The task pane, introduced in PowerPoint 2002, plays an enhanced role in PowerPoint 2003, providing shortcuts to many basic tasks and options. The following illustration provides an overview of the program window.

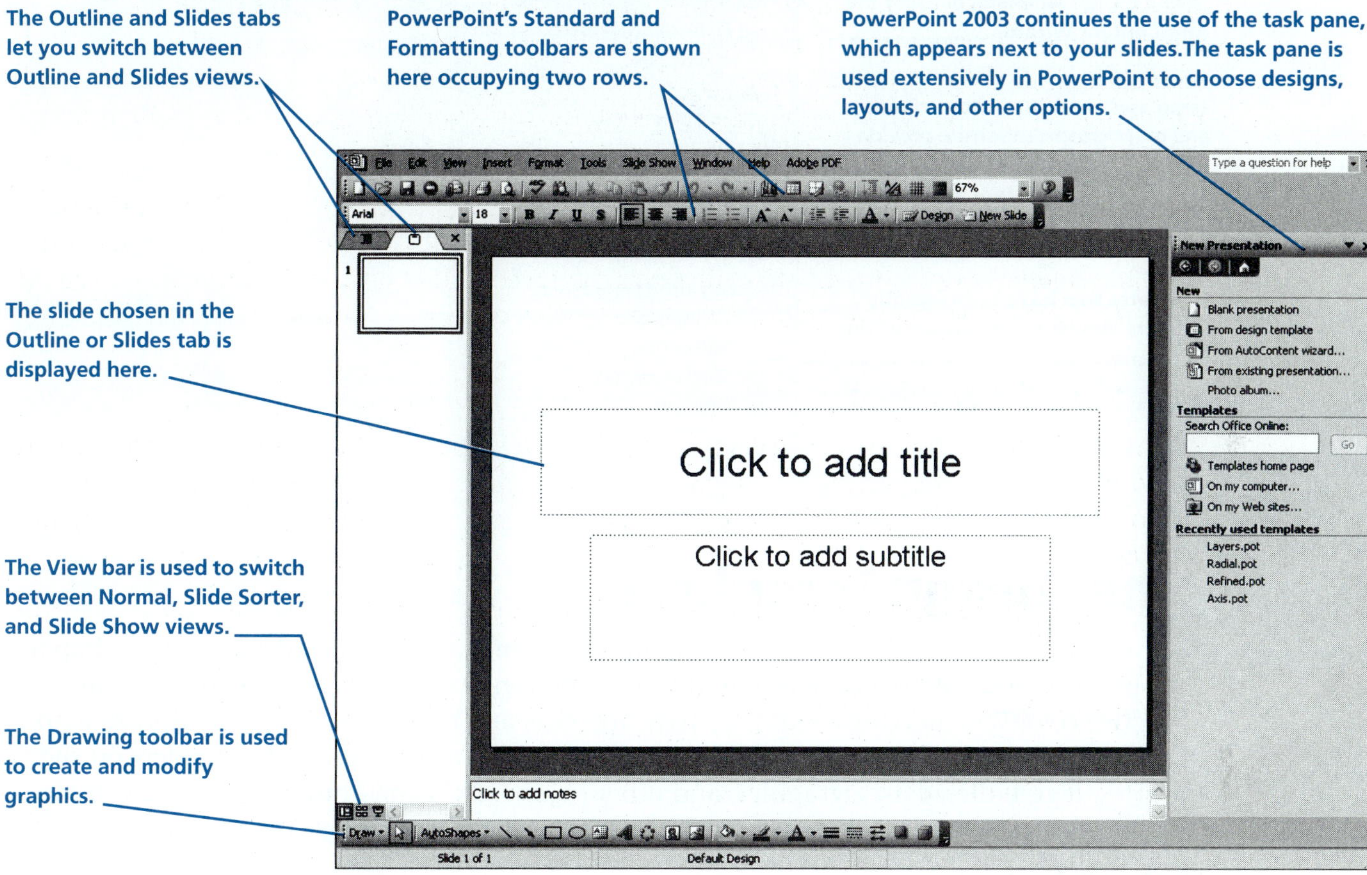

Task Panes

Task panes, which appear on the right side of the program window, contain shortcuts to commonly used, essential tasks needed for creating, developing, and delivering presentations. In PowerPoint 2003, the task pane also incorporates the Research and Shared Workspace features. As you build a presentation, the task pane will dynamically appear to assist you in your development. For example, the Getting Started task pane appears when you first start PowerPoint. This task pane helps you create a new presentation or open an existing one. There is a task pane to help you with every step of your presentation, from creation to delivery. You can display or hide the task pane at any time with the View→Task Pane command. The following illustration describes the options on the New Presentation task pane.

Notice that the task pane's name, New Presentation, is displayed here.

The New Presentation task pane lets you choose among opening a blank presentation, opening a presentation from a design template, or using the AutoContent Wizard.

Templates available in PowerPoint and on Microsoft's Website provide ready-to-use presentations complete with suggested content and formatting.

Templates that have been recently used are shown at the bottom of the task pane.

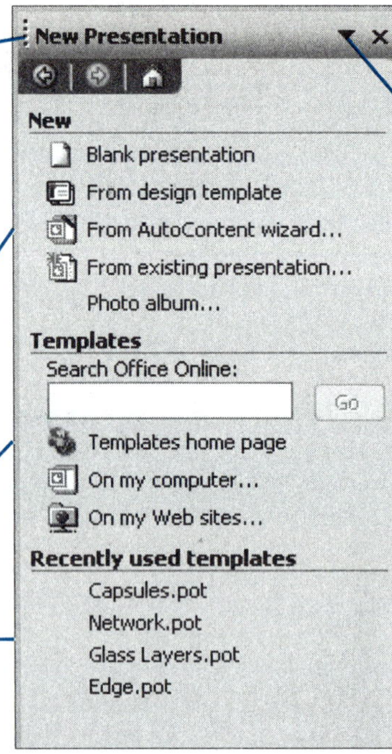

This drop-down button displays a list of all available task panes. You can switch to another task pane at any time by choosing it from the list.

Using the Design Template

Microsoft Office Specialist

You can use PowerPoint's built-in design templates, which provide a ready-made backdrop for your presentations. With a design template, your presentation automatically includes an attractive color scheme, consistent font style and size, and bulleted lists to synchronize with the design and style of the presentation. Design templates also position placeholders on slides for titles, text, bulleted lists, graphics, and other objects. By using design templates, you can focus on the content of the presentation by simply filling in the blanks as you create the presentation.

The 

button on PowerPoint's Formatting toolbar displays the Slide Design task pane. The Slide Design task pane displays previews of the various design templates. You can choose the From Design Template option to replace the New Presentation task pane with the Slide Design task pane. The following illustration describes options available on the Slide Design task pane.

The Slide Design task pane can be used to apply Design Templates, Color Schemes, and Animation Schemes.

A template can be applied to all slides in the presentation or just to selected slides.

When the Design Templates option is chosen, previews of the template Used in this Presentation, the most Recently Used template(s), and the templates Available for Use are displayed.

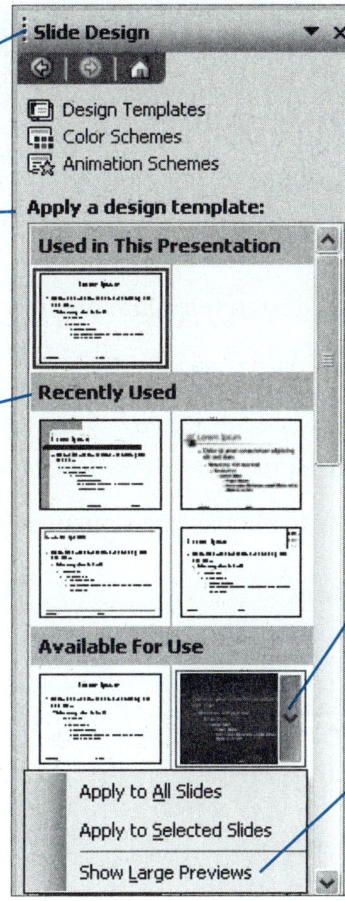

To see a menu of options for each design, hover over the design thumbnail until the drop-down arrow appears. Click this arrow to view the options.

The Show Large Previews option displays the previews in a single column format, allowing larger previews.

Design Tips

Have you ever heard the expression, "A picture is worth a thousand words"? This old adage remains true now even though you are presenting a high-tech electronic PowerPoint presentation. The design of your presentation influences the reaction of your audience. When you are creating a presentation, remember the **SOS** of helpful hints:

- Think **S**hort. Keep your presentation focused, brief, and to the point.
- Think **O**utline. Outline key points, elaborating on those points as you deliver the presentation. As a rule, keep your slides to three to six bullets per page. If there is a lot of information, break the points up over a few slides instead of crowding too much information in one slide. Strive for one line per bullet instead of wrapped text. Remember your purpose and make your case clearly and succinctly.
- Think **S**imple. While animation and special effects are fun, they detract from your message. You should use animation to punctuate a point, never to entertain. Make it work for you, not against you.

Hands-On 1.2 Apply a Design Template

In this exercise, you define the design of your presentation by choosing the Design Template and apply it to all slides.

1. Click the From Design Template option on the task pane.
   The Slide Design task pane will replace the New Presentation task pane. Currently, no design template is applied to the presentation.
2. Point to any of the design template previews on the task pane and a drop-down button will appear.
3. Click the drop-down button and choose Show Large Previews if that option is not currently checked.
   This will make viewing the previews in the following steps easier.
4. Follow these steps to choose the Capsules design template:

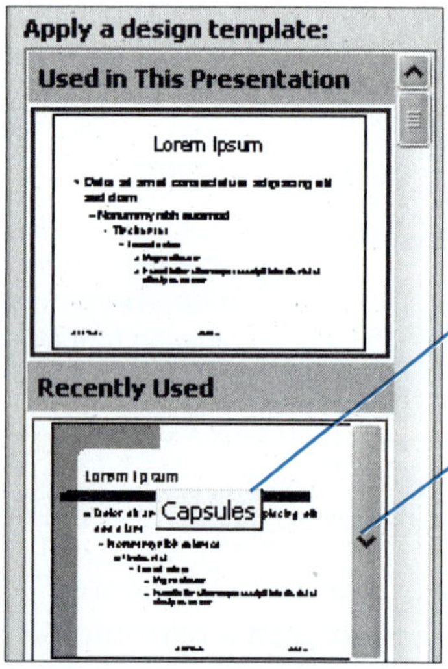

A Scroll through the list until you find the Capsules template. When you point to the template the word Capsules will be displayed.

B Click the drop-down button and choose Apply to All Slides. The title slide in your presentation will be formatted with the Capsules design. The title slide has placeholders for a title and subtitle.

5. Follow these steps to explore the window and enter a title and subtitle in the slide:

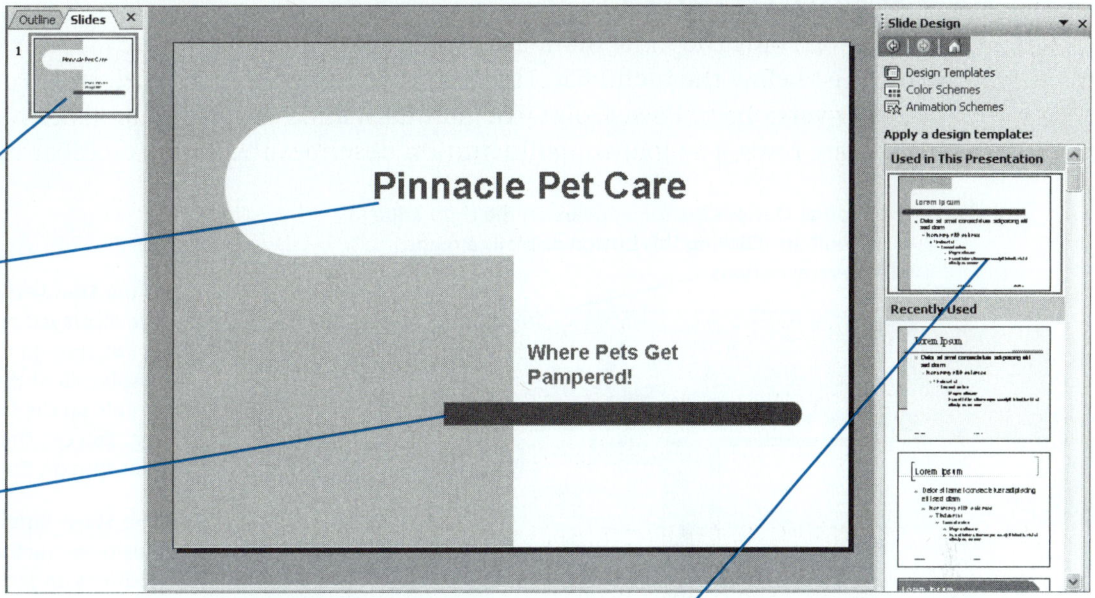

A Thumbnails of all slides in a presentation are displayed on the Slides tab. Display a slide by choosing the thumbnail.

B Click in the title box and type `Pinnacle Pet Care`.

C Click in the subtitle box and type `Where Pets Get Pampered!`

D Notice that the Capsules design template now appears at the top of the template list because it is currently in use.

Managing Toolbars

PowerPoint 2003 features over 10 toolbars to help you create and format presentations. The Standard and Formatting toolbars contain the most frequently used buttons, so they are located at the top of the PowerPoint window just below the menu bar.

Displaying and Hiding Toolbars

You can display or hide toolbars by first displaying the Toolbars list then choosing the desired toolbar(s) from the list. The Toolbars list is displayed with the View→Toolbars command or by right-clicking any displayed toolbar. A checkmark appears on the Toolbars list next to each toolbar that is currently displayed.

Displaying the Standard and Formatting Toolbars on Separate Rows

In PowerPoint 2003, the Standard and Formatting toolbars are placed side by side on a single row just below the menu bar. This arrangement was introduced with PowerPoint 2000. In earlier versions of PowerPoint, the Standard and Formatting toolbars were displayed on separate rows. The following illustration describes the various toolbar options.

The Toolbar Options button appears on the right edge of all toolbars. Clicking this button displays a menu with several options.

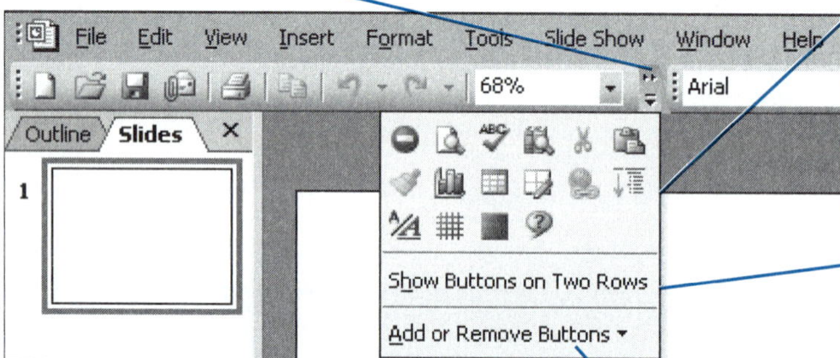

If the Standard and Formatting toolbars are displayed on the same row, then there is not enough room on the toolbars to display all of the buttons. Buttons not visible on the toolbar are displayed on this list. You can choose a command by clicking a button on the list.

The Show Buttons on Two Rows option positions the Standard and Formatting toolbars on separate rows. This option becomes Show Buttons on One Row if the toolbars are displayed on separate rows.

The Add or Remove Buttons option lets you add buttons to or remove buttons from a toolbar. You can also customize toolbars with this option.

Hands-On 1.3 Display the Formatting Toolbar on a Separate Row

In this exercise, you will learn how to separate toolbars if they are positioned on the same row.

1. Follow these steps to display the Standard and Formatting toolbars on separate rows:

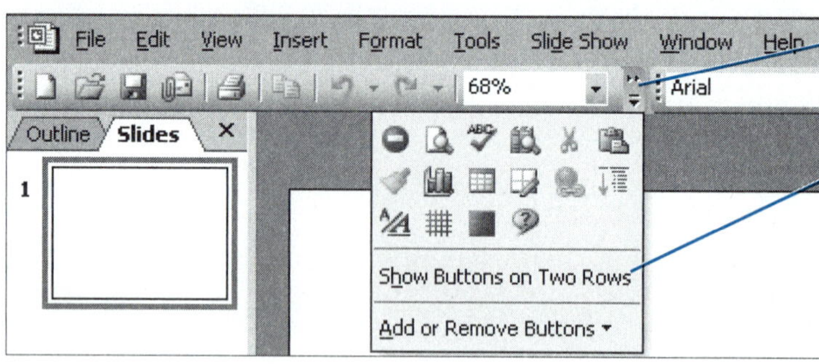

A Click the Toolbar Options button on the right edge of the Standard toolbar.

B If the Show Buttons on Two Rows option is available then choose it to display the Standard and Formatting toolbars on separate rows. If the Show Buttons on One Row option is available then your toolbars are already positioned on separate rows.

IMPORTANT! *From this point forward, the instructions in this text will assume the Standard and Formatting toolbars are displayed on separate rows. Separating the toolbars will make it easier to locate buttons.*

Slide Layout Styles

Microsoft Office Specialist

PowerPoint's preformatted layout styles can be found in the Slide Layout task pane. Layout styles include text formats, content formats, text with content formats, and other format options. Each format option includes a different style of title and body placeholders. A placeholder is a preformatted text or image box designed to hold your data. To add content to your presentation, just click in the placeholder and start typing.

The Bulleted List

With PowerPoint, you can effortlessly create bulleted lists to outline the thrust of your presentation. The bulleted list layout is an outline of five levels. A different bullet character and indentation is used for each level. The following illustration shows the Monthly Events slide you will create in the next exercise.

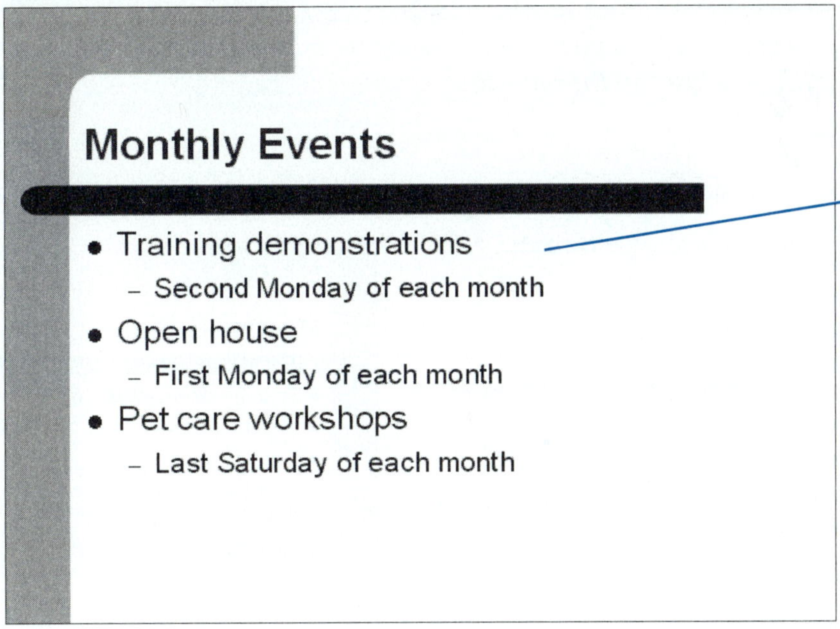

This bulleted list has two levels. A large bullet is used for first-level paragraphs, and a hyphen is used for second-level paragraphs.

Working with Bulleted Lists

When you use a design template, the template automatically formats each paragraph in a bulleted list. The format includes a bullet style, indentation level, font type, and font size for each bulleted paragraph. This outline for the bulleted list is held within a placeholder or text box. The following Quick Reference table describes the various techniques that can be used with bulleted lists.

QR

QUICK REFERENCE: WORKING WITH BULLETED LISTS

Task	Procedure
Turn bullets on and off	Select the desired paragraph(s) and click the Bullets button on the Formatting toolbar.
Promote bullets	Select the desired paragraph and click the Decrease Indent button on the Formatting toolbar. Promoting reduces a paragraph's indentation level and changes the bullet character.
Demote bullets	Select the desired paragraph and click the Increase Indent button on the Formatting toolbar. Demoting increases a paragraph's indentation level and changes the bullet character.

Hands-On 1.4 Use Bulleted Lists

In this exercise, you will enter information in a slide using the bulleted list. The most efficient way to create multilevel bulleted lists is to first type the entire list.

Enter the Data

1. Make sure the Title and Text layout is chosen in the task pane.
2. Click in the title box and type **Monthly Events**.
3. Click in the bulleted list box.
4. Type **Training demonstrations** and tap [Enter].
   PowerPoint formats the new paragraph with the same large bullet. Paragraph formats are carried to new paragraphs when you tap the [Enter] key.
5. Complete the list shown to the right by typing the indicated text and tapping [Enter] at the end of each paragraph. However, do not tap [Enter] after the last paragraph.

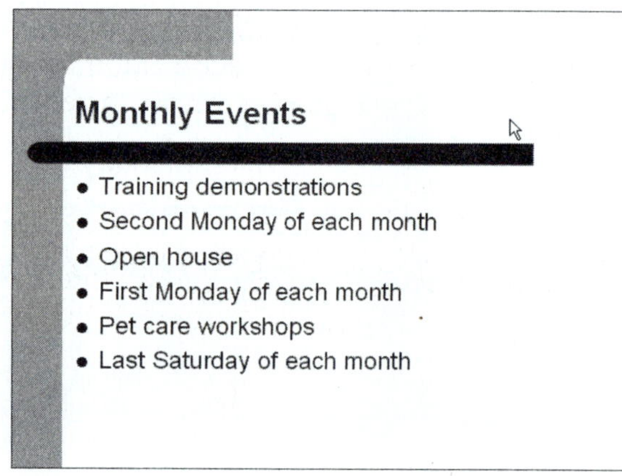

Manipulate the Bullets

Once all of the text has been typed, you can then move the bulleted lists by using the Increase Indent or Decrease Indent buttons on the Formatting toolbar.

6. Click anywhere on the second bulleted paragraph (Second Monday of each month).
   The flashing insertion point should be positioned on the paragraph text.
7. Click the Bullets button on the Formatting toolbar.
   The Bullets button will no longer be highlighted; the bullet will be removed from the paragraph. You can always use this technique to remove bullets from paragraphs.
8. Click the Bullets button again to reapply the bullet.
   The bullet list is a toggle. Clicking it once turns it on, clicking it again turns it off.

9. Click the Increase Indent button on the Formatting toolbar.
The paragraph will be indented and the bullet style will change to a hyphen. Demoting a paragraph makes the paragraph subordinate to the preceding paragraph.

10. Click the Increase Indent button several more times.
The bullet style will change and the indent will increase each time you click the button. Also, the font size and font style will change with each demotion. These formats are determined by the Capsule design template, on which the presentation is based.

11. Click the Decrease Indent button until the bullet reaches the second indentation, the hyphen bullet style.
With each indentation, the bullet style changes.

12. Click anywhere on the fourth paragraph (First Monday of each month).

13. Click the Increase Indent button on the paragraph once.

14. Click the Increase Indent button again on the last paragraph (Last Saturday of each month).

15. Click outside the bulleted list box to view the completed slide.

The Research Feature

Microsoft Office Specialist

As you develop your presentation, you'll want to be meticulous about choosing the right words, spelling them correctly and using them appropriately. To ensure these basic elements of your presentation are correct, use PowerPoint's spelling, grammar, and thesaurus features. In prior versions, these features were separate functions. However, in PowerPoint 2003, they have been combined in the Research feature under the Research task pane. The Research feature offers a quick way to investigate multiple reference guides at once. Research is a powerful tool that you should use to strengthen your presentation.

Hands-On 1.5 Explore Research: Spelling, Grammar, and Thesaurus

In this exercise, you will explore the Research feature of PowerPoint 2003. However, you will not make any changes to the presentation.

Examine the Research Task Pane

1. Follow these steps to explore functions of the new Research feature:

A In the Monthly Events slide, select the word *demonstrations*.

B Open the Research Task Pane by going to Tools→Research on the Standard toolbar. The Research task pane appears to the right of your screen. Notice the three collapsible sections (Thesaurus, Translation, and Help) in the task pane.

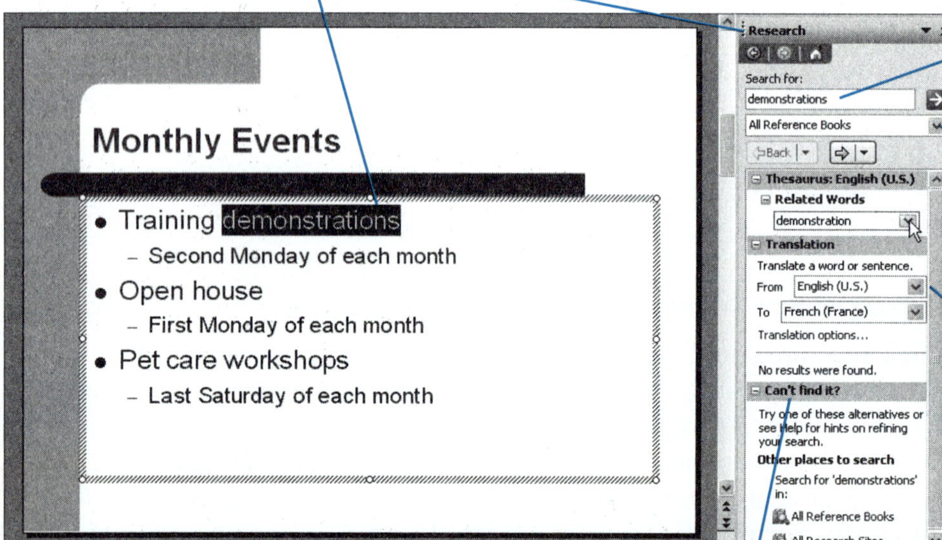

C Notice that the word, *demonstrations* is automatically dropped into the Search For box in the Research pane.

D Use the drop-down arrow to the right of the reference guide box to view all references being indexed. You can search through all reference guides or choose only a few of them.

E The Translation section enables you to translate words or sentences among a variety of languages. When first used, the Translation feature will be installed using Microsoft's Install-on-Demand feature.

F The Can't Find It section offers further assistance to define your word if the search results are unsatisfactory.

Examine the Thesaurus

2. Follow these steps to search for synonyms to the word *demonstrations*:

A Click the Start Searching arrow at the end of the Search For box. After a short pause, all words related to *demonstrations* will appear in the task pane. Note that the synonyms are listed in noun and verb order.

B Point to the word *exhibition*; the drop-down menu appears. Note that you can insert the new word into the slide, copy it or refine your search by looking up the synonym for exhibitions.

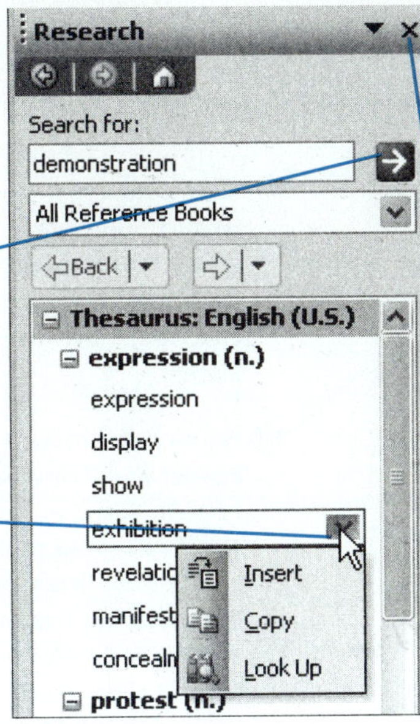

C When you are finished exploring the thesaurus, click the Close button to cancel. Do not make any changes to the Monthly Events slide.

Using PowerPoint Views

Microsoft Office Specialist

As with all Microsoft products, there are many ways to view a file in PowerPoint. We will concentrate, in this section, on the basic views that are easily accessible via the View Bar. The View Bar is located on the bottom-left corner of the Program Window.

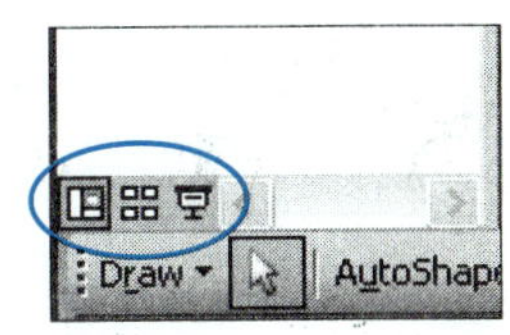

View Bar Options

The three views available in the View Bar include Normal, Slide Sorter, and Slide Show. These views correspond to the different phases of presentation development. To open any of the views, either use the shortcuts provided at the bottom of the Outline/Slide tabs or use the View commands from the Standard toolbar. Each view is described in the following table.

View	Purpose
Normal	The Normal view displays the selected slide in the center of the screen and thumbnails of all the slides in a presentation in the Slides tab. The Normal view is designed to let you focus on the current slide. If desired, the Outline and Slides tabs can be dismissed by clicking the Close button next to the Slides tab. The Outline and Slides tabs can be restored using the View→Normal (Restore Panes) command.
Slide Sorter	Slide Sorter view displays all slides in the presentation. In Slide Sorter view, you can rearrange slides by dragging the desired slide(s) to different positions within the presentation.
Slide Show	The Slide Show button runs the presentation so that all slides are in full-view mode on the screen.

Hands-On 1.6 Explore the Various Views

In this exercise, you will explore the PowerPoint views of the View Bar. The following illustration shows more slides than are currently in your presentation.

1. Follow these steps to explore the various views and the PowerPoint window:

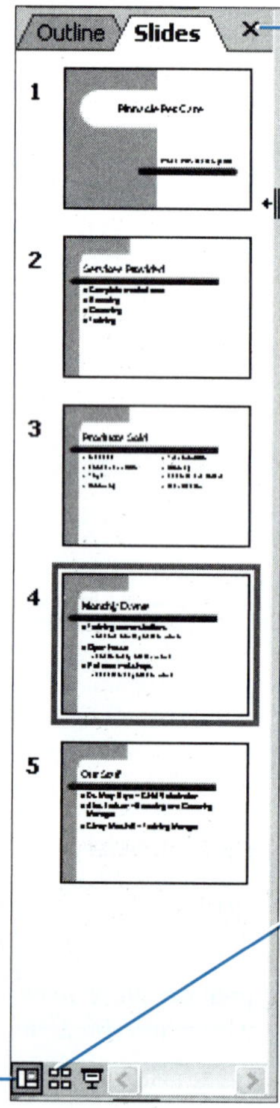

A Notice the Close button (but don't click it). In Normal view, the Outline and Slides tabs can be dismissed by the Close button. They can be restored by choosing View→Normal (Restore Panes).

B Position the mouse pointer on this border and a double-headed arrow will appear. You can change the amount of space allocated to the tabs by dragging this border. Dragging to the right increases the size of the thumbnails or outline and reduces the size of the current slide. This technique can also be used with the task pane and the Notes area below the current slide.

C Click the Slide Sorter button on the view bar. Slide sorter view is useful for changing the order of slides.

D Notice the Slide Show button (but don't click it). The Slide Show button is used to run an electronic slide show.

E Choose Normal to switch back to Normal view.

The Slide Master

Microsoft Office Specialist

Looking at the Slide Master is like looking at an x-ray of your presentation. The Slide Master holds together the structure of the presentation. It does this by organizing the slide into areas, called placeholders, on the slide. Understanding the function of the Slide Master will help you to work more efficiently as you develop your skills in using PowerPoint. We will work extensively with the Slide Master in Lesson 7, Working with Online Collaboration. For right now, it is just important to know that the Slide Master contains all of the elements that make up your slides.

Hands-On 1.7 Explore the Slide Master

In this exercise, you will examine the special features of the Slide Master.

1. Make sure the Monthly Events slide is selected and choose View→Master→Slide Master from the Menu bar.
   This command will display the Slide Master, the backbone of your presentation.

2. Follow these steps to explore the Slide Master window:

(A) Observe that the Slide Master is made up of placeholders. The placeholders contain a Title and Bulleted List. Any text or object that you place in the Slide Master will be placed on each slide of the presentation.

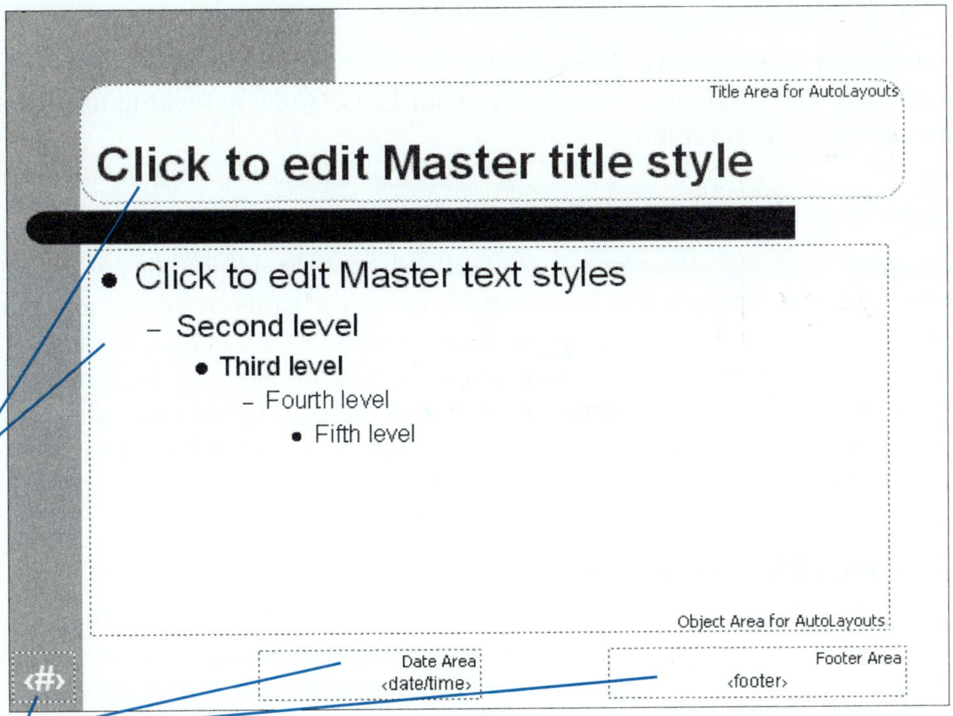

(B) The placeholders at the bottom of the Slide Master, called footers, appear on every design template. The footers can be used to personalize your presentation by inserting the name and date of the event for the presentation along with the page number of the slide. The footers can also be left blank.

TIP! *Think of the Slide Master as the blueprint, the inherent structure of your slides. Each piece of information placed on the underlying structure of the slides is repeated throughout the presentation.*

3. We will work with the Slide Master again in Lesson 7, Working with Online Collaboration. For now, use the Slide Master Toolbar to close the Master view.

Creating a Basic Presentation

There is more to creating a presentation than placing one slide after another. Like Al Smith of Pinnacle Pet Care, you are in the process of creating an image. Choosing the appropriate slide layout, just like choosing the appropriate design, will influence how well your audience understands your message. Use the following guidelines when choosing your slide design and layout:

- Know your audience: Will you be speaking to accountants or artists?
- Know your purpose: Are you introducing a product or giving a report?
- Know your expectations: When the last word of this presentation has been given, how do you want your audience to respond to your facts? Are you looking for approval for a project or customers for a product?

Choosing the Design Template

Microsoft Office Specialist

There are many design templates in PowerPoint 2003. Match the design template to the type of presentation you are giving. For example, using the Crayons design template in a presentation for an annual meeting might be disastrous; however, it's a natural for a presentation created for a PTA group. In short, keep the design appropriate to the function and the audience. Remember that new design templates are sent to Microsoft daily, so if you just can't find the right one, browse the 15 categories of templates available on the Microsoft Office Online Website for new templates.

Choosing the Slide Layout

There are 27 slide layouts in PowerPoint 2003, one for any given situation. Slide layouts are grouped by the type of data they will contain. For example, the Title layout needs only a title and subtitle. The Title and Text layout will hold information on the slide so it has a title and bulleted list for points. Likewise, the Title, Text & Clip Art layout is divided into three sections: title, text to one side, and an area for clip art. The slide layout organizes the information you put into the presentation by giving it a place on the slide. Use the Slide Layout task pane to change the layout of your slides. The new layout is applied to all selected slides. Changing layouts is easy. When you click on the new style, the layout is transferred to the selected slide.

Adding Slides

You can add slides in three ways:

- Click the New Slide button on your Formatting toolbar.
- Use the Insert→New Slide command on the Standard toolbar.
- Right-click a slide on the Slides tab and choose New Slide. PowerPoint always places a new slide after the selected slide.

To see slides, use the Slides Tab in the Normal view or, if your presentation contains more slides than you can see without scrolling, go to the Slide Sorter view to see the entire presentation on a page.

Inserting Text

Microsoft Office Specialist

You click in the desired placeholder to enter text on a slide. For example, to enter the title on a slide, you click in the title placeholder then type the text. Do not press the Enter key; the placeholders are already formatted with word wrap.

To enter text in the bulleted list placeholder, click anywhere in the object and begin typing. At the end of the bullet, tap Enter. If the next line is a sub-bullet of the first line, tap the Tab key to indent to the right then begin typing. You will notice that the bullet changes shape and size when indented. When you have finished typing the sub-bullets and are ready to type the next major bullet, tap Enter at the end of the sub-bullet. Then, tap Shift+Tab to move the insertion point back to the left so you can type another major bullet.

TIP! *You can also enter text in Outline view using the same method: use Tab to indent and Shift+Tab to move the insertion point to the left.*

Editing Text

To change or delete text on a slide, you must first select it. You can select text in either Outline or Slide view by clicking in the placeholder then clicking and dragging over the desired text. Once the text is selected tap the Delete key to delete the text or simply begin typing to replace the selected text. After you click in a placeholder you may also position the insertion point in the text and use the Backspace or Delete key and revise the text.

Using the Slides Tab

You can choose a slide by clicking the desired slide on the Slides tab. However, if a presentation has a large number of slides, the slide you wish to choose may not be visible on the tab. The vertical scroll bar to the right of the slide lets you navigate to the desired slide. The scroll box can be dragged up and down, or the Previous Slide and Next Slide buttons can be used to move from one slide to the next.

Hands-On 1.8 Add a Bulleted Slide and Choose Slides

In this exercise, you will create a slide, add text to the slide, and learn to choose slides using the Slides tab.

Add a Slide

1. Click the New Slide button on the Formatting toolbar and PowerPoint will insert another bulleted list slide after the Monthly Events slide.
   The New Slide button always inserts bulleted list slides.
2. Click the Title placeholder and type the phrase **`Services Provided`**.
3. Click the bulleted list placeholder and type the four bulleted paragraphs shown to the right.

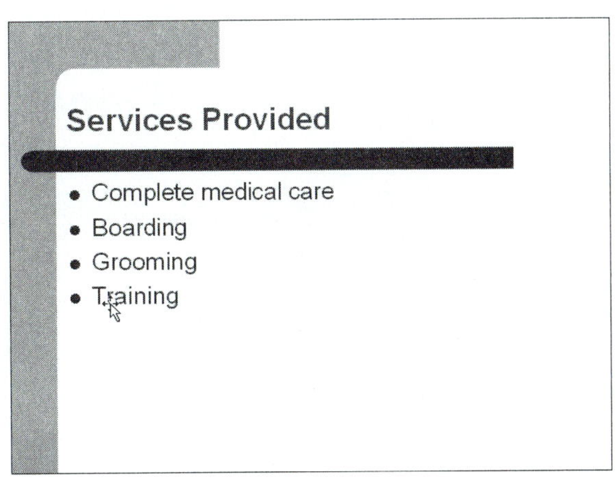

4. Follow these steps to choose slides:

A Click the various slides on the Slides tab.

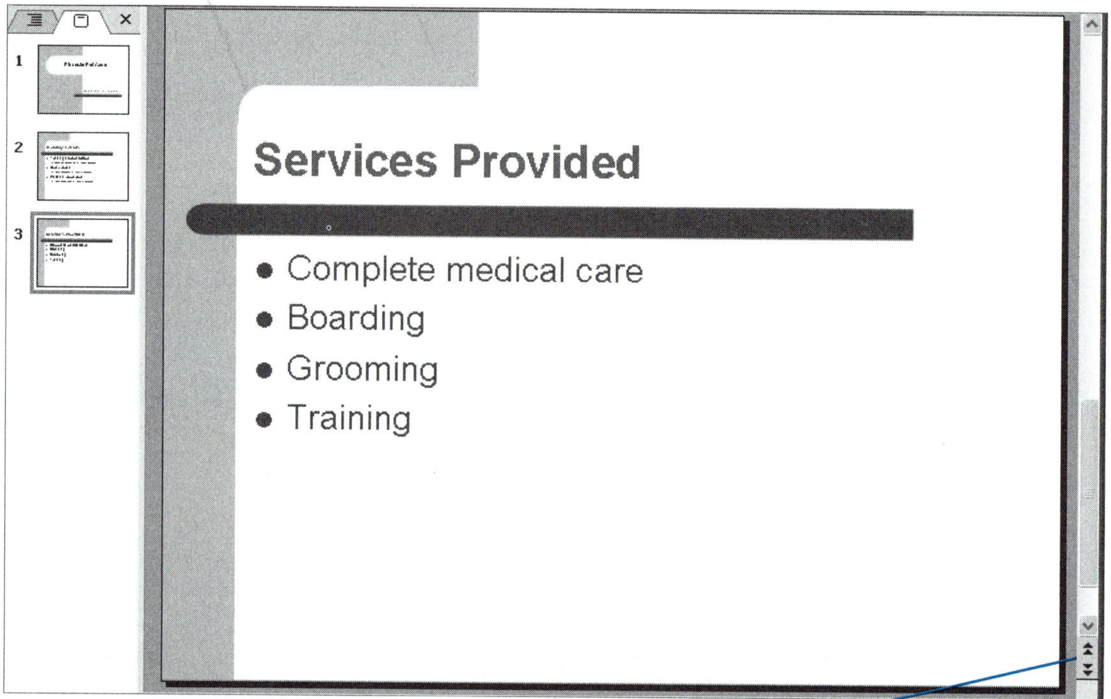

B Use the Previous Slide and Next Slide buttons to move between slides. When a presentation includes only a few slides it is easiest to choose slides from the Slides tab. However, the scroll bar can be useful if a presentation has more slides than can be displayed on the Slides tab.

5. Examine the following illustration, which describes the process of inserting slides and applying slide layouts to selected slides.

A Slide layouts are applied to the slide(s) selected on the Slides tab.

B The New Slide button inserts a new slide and displays the Slide Layout task pane.

C The Slide Layout task pane displays layouts that can be applied to slides.

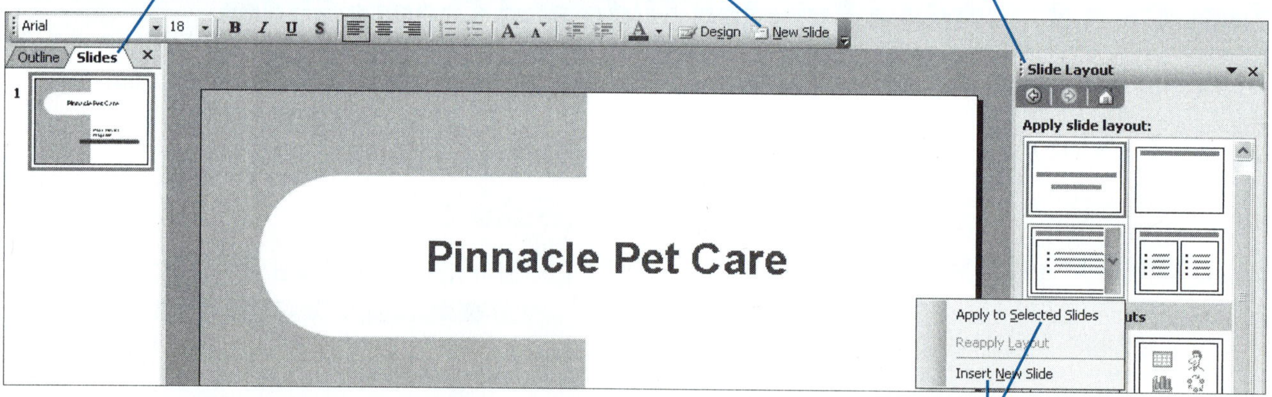

D Layouts can be applied to selected slides, or a new slide can be inserted with a desired layout.

6. Feel free to browse through your slides and make any editing changes you wish.

Saving the Presentation

The byword in PowerPoint is to save early and save often. You can use the Save button on the Standard toolbar or the File→Save command on the Standard toolbar. If it's the first time a presentation has been saved, the Save As dialog box will appear since the file will need a name and location on your computer. You can also use the Save As dialog box to make a copy of a presentation by saving it under a new name or to a different location. If the file has already been saved, PowerPoint replaces the previous version with the new edited version. When saving PowerPoint files, you can use filenames with as many as 255 characters.

FROM THE KEYBOARD

[Ctrl]+[S] for Save

Storing Your Exercise Files

Throughout this book you will be referred to files in your "file storage location." You can store your exercise files on various media such as a floppy disk, a USB flash drive, the My Documents folder, or on a network drive at a school or company. While many figures in the exercises may display files in the 3½ Floppy (A:) drive, it is assumed that you will substitute your own location for that shown in the figure. See the appendix for additional information on alternative file storage media.

The Save In box as it appears in the book

The Save In box as it might appear if you are saving your files to a USB flash drive

Hands-On 1.9 Save the Presentation

In this exercise, you will save the presentation by giving it a name and a location on your computer.

Before You Begin: *If you have not done so already, please turn to Downloading the Student Exercise Files section of the appendix (page 299) for instructions on how to retrieve the student exercise files for this book from the Labyrinth Website, and to copy the files to your file storage location for use in this and future lessons. See also pages 301, 303, and 305 for additional details about using this book with a floppy disk, USB flash drive, the My Documents folder, and a folder on a network drive.*

1. Click the Save button on the Standard toolbar.
2. Follow these steps to save the presentation to your file storage location:

Ⓐ Click here and choose your file storage location. This illustration shows the 3½" Floppy (A:) drive.

Ⓑ Type the name **Pinnacle Pet Care** as shown in the File Name box and click the Save button.

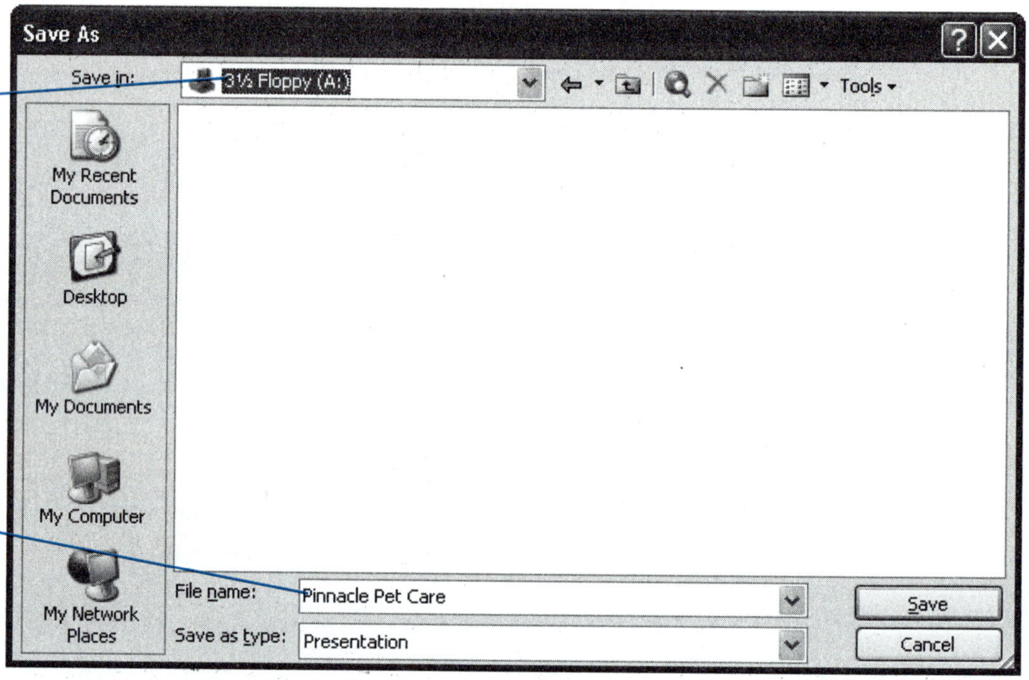

Working with the AutoContent Wizard

Microsoft Office Specialist

Have a presentation to create but don't quite know where to start? Experiment with the AutoContent Wizard. The AutoContent Wizard contains different categories of presentations that are fully outlined for content. For instance, you can use the AutoContent Wizard to create an Employee Orientation. All of the key points for this type of event are outlined in the presentation. Just add your specific information to the framework and you're ready to present!

Hands-On 1.10 Explore the AutoContent Wizard

In this exercise, you will explore options available through the AutoContent Wizard but you won't actually create a new presentation using the wizard.

1. Follow these steps to display the New Presentation task pane:

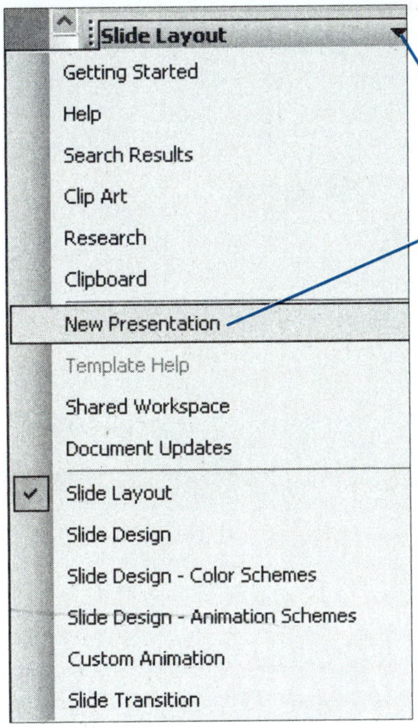

A Click the task pane drop-down button.

B Choose the New Presentation option.

2. Follow this step to open the AutoContent Wizard:

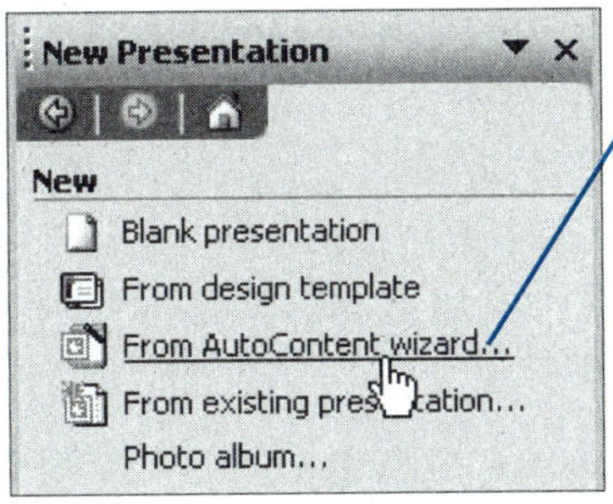

A Choose the From AutoContent Wizard option. The AutoContent Wizard dialog box appears.

3. Follow these steps to explore the AutoContent Wizard:

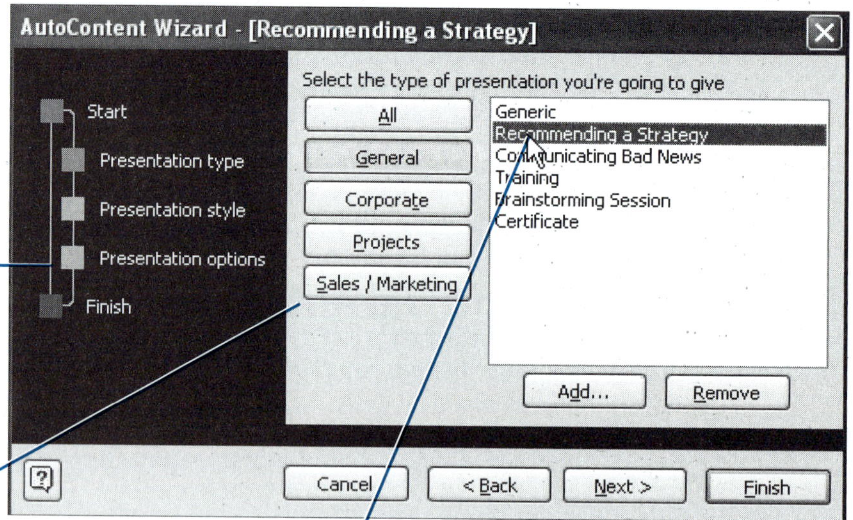

A Notice the three steps available in the AutoContent Wizard (Presentation type, Presentation style, and Presentation options). You can choose a step by clicking it or you can use the Next button to advance through the steps.

B Choose Presentation type.

C Notice various presentation types are available through the AutoContent Wizard.

D Choose the Recommending a Strategy presentation type.

4. Click Presentation Style and choose On-Screen Presentation.
   Examine the other styles that are possible in PowerPoint 2003.

5. Click Presentation Options.
   If you were actually creating a presentation from AutoContent Wizard, it is at this point that the title and footers would be added to the presentation.

6. Cancel the AutoContent Wizard. Do not click Finish or save any changes.

Delivering the Slide Show

Microsoft Office Specialist

The slides are created and the presentation is complete. The first phase of the presentation development is over. The next phase, delivering the presentation, is just beginning. Before you stand before an audience, familiarize yourself with the following tips.

Delivery Tips

It is not only what you say, it is how you say it that makes the difference between an engaging and an unsuccessful presentation. Lead your audience. Help them to focus on the message of your presentation, not on you as the presenter. Give a presentation using the following **PEER** guidelines to deliver an effective presentation:

- Pace. Maintain a moderate pace. Speaking too fast will exhaust your audience, and speaking too slowly may put them to sleep. Carry your audience with you as you talk.
- Emphasis. Pause for emphasis. As you present, use a brief pause to emphasize your point. The pause you take will give your audience time to absorb the message.

- **E**ye Contact. Address your audience. Always face your audience while speaking. A common mistake is to speak while walking or facing the projection screen. Don't waste all of the work you have done in the presentation by losing the interest of your audience now. If you are speaking from a lectern or desk, resist the temptation to lean on them. Stand tall, make eye contact, and look directly at your audience.
- **R**elax. You are enthusiastic and want to convey that tone to the audience. However, when you speak, avoid fast movement, pacing, and rushed talking. Your audience will be drawn to your movements and miss the point. Remember that the audience is listening to you to learn; this material may be old hat to you, but it's new to them. So speak clearly, maintain a steady pace, and stay calm.

Using the Slide Show Toolbar

The Slide Show  toolbar automatically appears in the bottom-left corner of the screen when you launch a slide show. This tool is your control panel for the entire show. Each section provides you with a way to navigate through the slide show. Notice the functions of the Slide Show Toolbar menu in the following illustration.

With these PEER steps in mind, begin the process of delivering the slide show.

Whether you are using a laptop or PC, projecting with an LCD projector, or using transparencies, certain tasks are always completed the same way. The following Quick Reference table describes the options for starting, delivering, and ending a slide show.

FROM THE KEYBOARD

[Shift]+[F10] to display pop-up menu

QR

QUICK REFERENCE: RUNNING A SLIDE SHOW

Task	Procedure
Start a slide show from any slide	■ From Normal view, navigate to the desired slide and click the Slide Show button.
Advance to the next slide	■ Use the Next arrow on the Slide Show toolbar. ■ Right-click on any slide to get the shortcut menu. Choose Next. ■ Click anywhere on the current slide, or tap [Page Down], [N] (for next), [Enter], or [Spacebar].
Go to a specific slide	■ Click Go to Slide on the pop-up menu. ■ Right-click any slide to bring up the shortcut menu and choose Go to Slide.

QR

QUICK REFERENCE: RUNNING A SLIDE SHOW (CONTINUED)

Task	Procedure
Emphasize points on the slide	■ Click the Pointer tool button in the Slide Show Toolbar to use the Pointer tool choices. ■ Right-click on any slide to bring up the Pointer tool menu.
Change the way the screen looks	■ Use the Navigation button on the Slide Sorter toolbar to manipulate the screen by making it black or white, viewing speaker notes, or switching between programs.
Go to a previous slide	■ Use the Previous arrow on the Slide Show toolbar. ■ Tap [Page Up], [P] (for previous) or [Backspace].
End a slide show	■ Using the Navigation button on the Slide Show toolbar, choose End Show. ■ Right-click on any slide and choose End Show. ■ Tap the [Esc] key.

Hands-On 1.11 Run the Slide Show

In this exercise, you will navigate through your slide show.

Run the Slide Show

1. Ensure that the Pinnacle Pet Care presentation is opened in Normal view.
2. Click the Title slide.
   You will start your presentation by displaying the Title slide.
3. Click the Slide Show button on the View bar.
   PowerPoint will display your title slide in full-screen view. All toolbars and other screen objects will be hidden from view.
4. Notice the Slide Show toolbar that appears on your screen when the slides are in full-screen view.
   The Slide Show toolbar is your navigator during the slide show. Notice that the Slide Show toolbar has options to go to the next and previous slides and to end the slide show. The Slide Show toolbar also lets you use a pen tool to draw on the slide and make other enhancements.
5. Click the mouse pointer anywhere on the screen to move to the next slide.
6. Tap the [Page Down] key twice then tap [Page Up] twice using the keys near the main keyboard (not the keys on the numeric keypad).
   PowerPoint displays the next or previous slide each time you tap these keys.

Manipulate the Slide Show Toolbar

7. Click the Slide Options button on the pop-up menu and choose Go to Slide→Services Provided.
   In the Go to Slide menu, your entire presentation is outlined by title. Simply choose the slide you want to see.
8. Then, choose Go to Slide→Pinnacle Pet Care.
   As you can see, there are many ways to navigate slides in an electronic slide show.

End the Slide Show

9. Continue to click anywhere on the screen until the last slide appears (the Services Provided slide).
10. Click the last slide and notice that the slide show will end once the last slide has been shown.
11. Feel free to practice running your slide show.
12. When you have finished, click the Save button to save any changes to your presentation.
13. Choose File→Close from the menu bar to close the presentation.

Concepts Review

True/False Questions

1. Design templates give presentations a consistent format and appearance. TRUE FALSE
2. The Slide Layout task pane appears when the button is clicked. TRUE FALSE
3. You can apply a different slide design template for just one slide. TRUE FALSE
4. A slide's layout cannot be changed once the slide has been created. TRUE FALSE
5. Each slide in a PowerPoint presentation is saved as a separate file. TRUE FALSE
6. The AutoContent Wizard can be found in the New Presentation task pane. TRUE FALSE
7. The Research feature is located under Tools in the Standard toolbar. TRUE FALSE
8. The Slide Master changes one slide at a time. TRUE FALSE
9. You start a slide show by clicking the Slide Show button. TRUE FALSE
10. While delivering a slide show, you can display the Slide Show toolbar by clicking the left mouse button anywhere on a slide. TRUE FALSE

Multiple Choice Questions

1. Which method can you use to change the design of a presentation?
   a. Open the New Presentation Task Pane→Slide Design
   b. Go to AutoContent Wizard→Slide Design
   c. Go to View→Toolbars→Slide Design
   d. Open the Getting Started Task Pane→Research Designs
2. Which technique can be used to turn off bullets for a single paragraph?
   a. Click on the desired paragraph and click the Bullets button.
   b. Click on the desired paragraph and tap the Delete key.
   c. Click the placeholder box that contains the bulleted paragraph and click the Bullets button.
   d. None of the above
3. Which of the following buttons is used to promote a bulleted paragraph?
   a.
   b.
   c.
   d.
4. Which of the following techniques can be used to move to the next slide in a slide show?
   a. Click anywhere on the current slide.
   b. Tap the Page Down key on the keyboard.
   c. Right-click the current slide and choose Next from the pop-up menu.
   d. All of the above

Skill Builders

Skill Builder 1.1 Set Up a Presentation

In this exercise, you will create a presentation for the Tropical Getaways travel service. The presentation will be used to sell potential customers a tropical getaway to paradise. The managers of Tropical Getaways will be delivering the presentation to an audience of more than 40 people.

Apply a Design Template

1. If PowerPoint is still open from the previous exercise, click the New button to begin a new presentation. If PowerPoint is not currently running, then start PowerPoint to open a new presentation.
2. Click the Design button on PowerPoint's Formatting toolbar to display the Slide Design task pane.
   The Slide task pane appears to the right.
3. Scroll through the list of designs and locate the Global design template, as shown to the right.

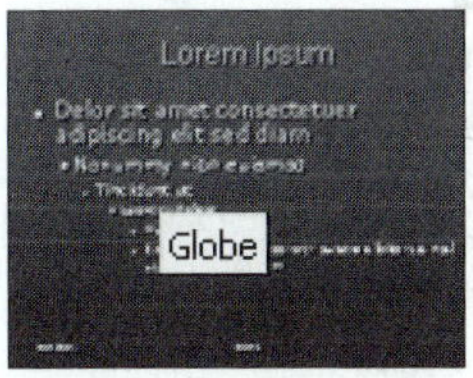

4. Click the Global Design template to select it.
   The design will be transferred to your presentation.
5. Click in the Title placeholder and type the title **`Tropical Getaways`**.
6. Click in the Subtitle placeholder and type the subtitle **`Adventures in Paradise`**.

Set Up another Slide

7. Click the New Slide button on the Formatting toolbar.
   A single-column, bulleted list slide will be added to the presentation and the Slide Layout task pane will appear. Notice that the Global design template is applied to the new slide.
8. In the new slide, select the Title and 2-Column Text layout (as shown to the right) by clicking on it in the Slide Layout task pane.
   The Title and 2-Column layout will be transferred to the new slide.

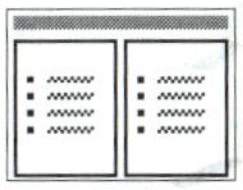

9. Click in the Title placeholder and type the title **`Most Popular Destinations`**.
10. Add the text shown to the right in the bulleted list placeholder.

Set Up the Remaining Slides

11. Add another slide and apply the Title and 2-Column text Layout to it.
    Again, the new layout is transferred to the third slide.
12. In the Title placeholder, enter the phrase **`Complete Packages`**.

13. In the first bullet of the bulleted list, enter the phrase **`Packages Include`** and tap [Enter].

14. Click the Increase Indent button.

    The bullet is indented and a new bullet character is applied by the design template.

15. Type the word **`Airfare`** and tap [Enter].

16. Complete the slide as shown to the right.

17. Add a new slide to your presentation. Leave the layout set to Title and Text.

18. Enter the title and bulleted lists into your new slide as shown to the right. You will need to demote the bulleted paragraphs under the headings Package 1 and Package 2. Also, notice that there is a large space above the Package 2 heading. You can create this space by tapping [Enter] twice after typing the bulleted paragraph with the text $429 per person.

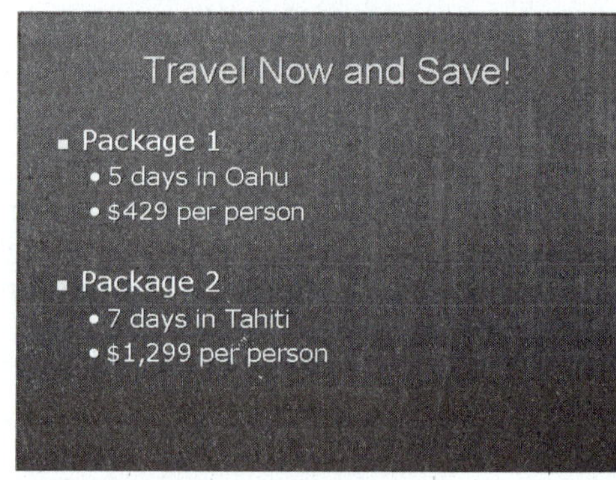

19. Before adding the next slides, be sure to save your presentation as **`Tropical Getaways`**.

20. Add the following slides, using the Title and Text layout for the slide on the left and the Title Slide layout for the one on the right.

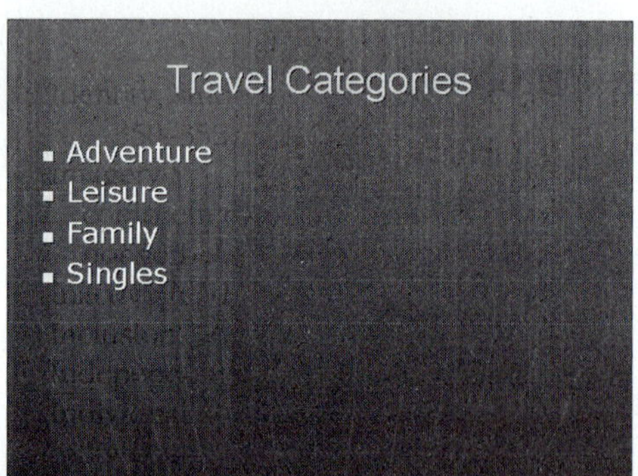

21. When the last two slides are added, save the presentation.

Skill Builder 1.2 Thesaurus Research Feature

In this exercise, you experiment with the Research task pane, replacing one word with another in the Tropical Getaways presentation using the Thesaurus function.

1. In the Travel Categories slide, select the word *Adventure* and go to Tools→Research. The Research task pane appears.
   Notice that the word Adventure *is automatically placed in the Search For box.*
2. Click the Start Searching arrow to the right of the word *Adventure* in the search box to begin the search.
   All reference guides will be searched for a synonym of the word Adventure*; the results will be placed in the task pane.*
3. Point to the word *voyage*. Choose Insert from the drop-down menu to replace *Adventure* with *Voyage*.
   The slide will look like the slide to the right.

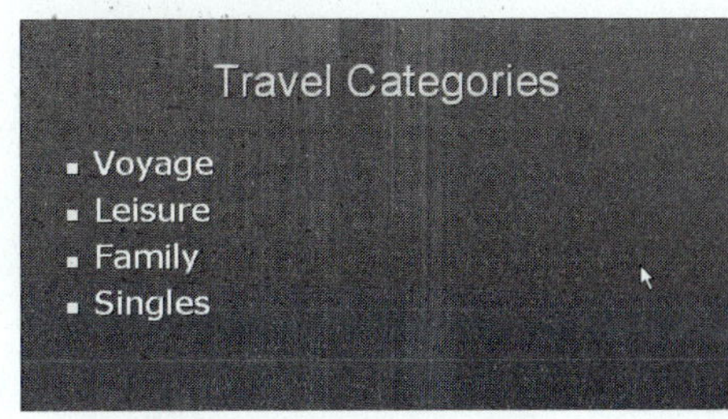

4. Click the Undo button to keep the word *Adventure*.
   The word Adventure *replaces the word* Voyage*. We are done experimenting.*
5. Save the changes and continue with the next exercise.

Skill Builder 1.3 Deliver a Slide Show

In this exercise, you will practice delivering the Tropical Getaways presentation you have been building in the Skill Builder exercises.

1. Click the Title slide then click the Slide Show button.
   The Title slide will occupy your whole screen.
2. Walk through the presentation by clicking each slide until the presentation is ended.
3. Click once more and use the Slide Show button to start the slide show again.
4. Once the slide show begins, position the mouse pointer at the bottom-left corner of the screen to display the Slide Show Toolbar.
5. Click the Navigation button (third button) on the Slide Show Toolbar.
6. Choose Go to Slide→Travel Now and Save.
   Notice that the Go to Slide drop-down menu displays the title of each slide in your presentation.
7. Use the Navigation button on the Slide Show toolbar to end the slide show by choosing Navigation→End Show.
8. Save and close the presentation.

Assessments

Assessment 1.1 Set Up a Presentation

In this exercise, you will create a presentation for Classic Cars. Classic Cars is an organization devoted to tracking, categorizing, and preserving classic automobiles. The presentation will be given to members of the Classic Cars organization at the annual Classic Cars convention.

1. Click the New button to set up a new presentation.
2. Click the Design button to display the Slide Design task pane.
3. Scroll through the design previews and choose the Radial design, as shown to the right.

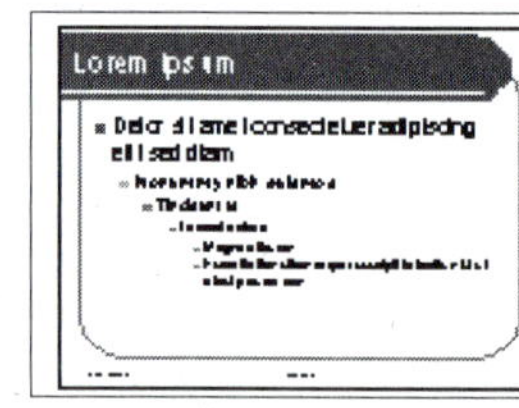

4. Add the following five slides to the Classic Cars presentation. Use the Title Slide layout for the first and last slides.

1

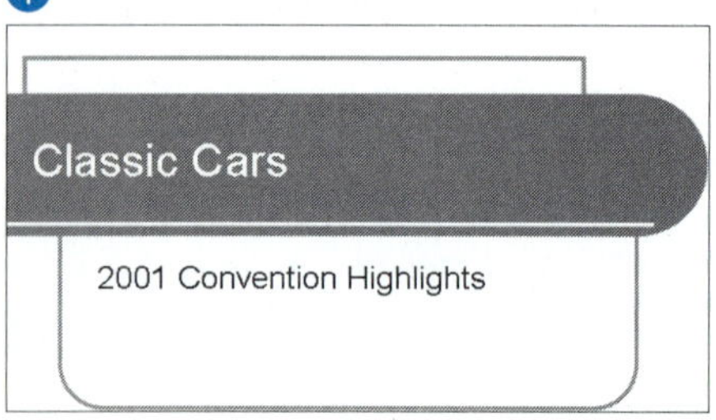

2

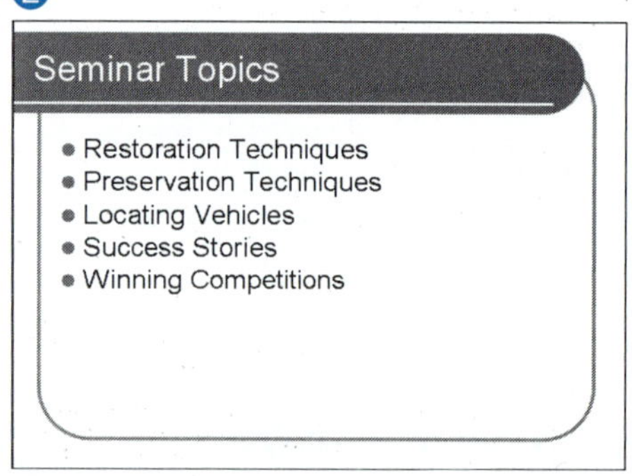

3

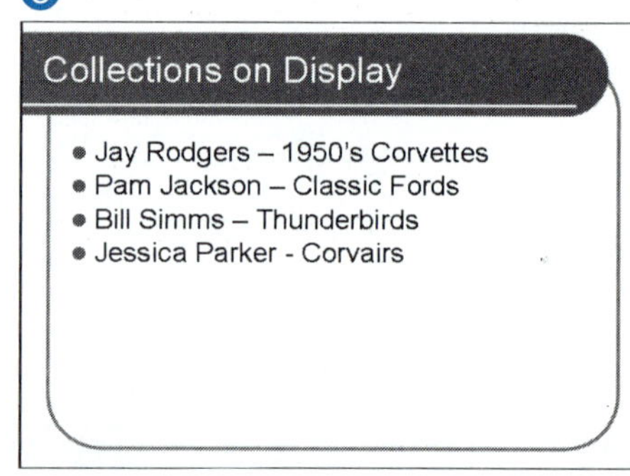

4

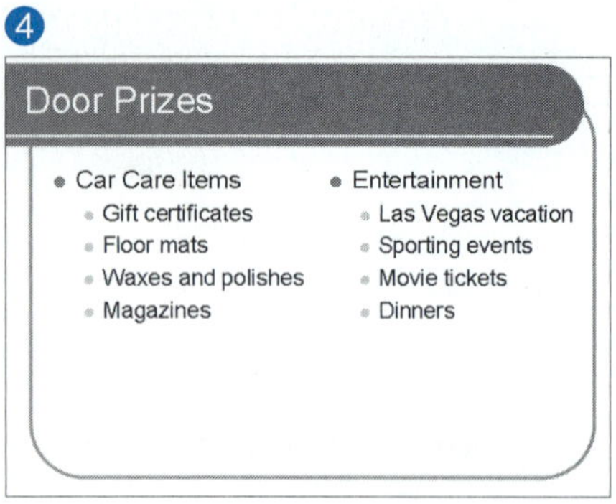

5

5. Save the presentation as **`Classic Cars`**.

Critical Thinking

Critical Thinking 1.1 Create a Presentation

In this exercise, you will set up a presentation for real estate agent Linda Holmes of Homestead Realty. Linda is on a new marketing campaign to get sellers to list their homes with Homestead Realty. She will deliver this presentation to prospective sellers using her laptop.

Follow these guidelines to set up the initial slides in the presentation:

- Design Template—Use the design template that you think fits the function of this presentation.
- Title Slide—Use **`Homestead Reality`** as the title and the tagline, **`Stake Your Claim`** as the subtitle.
- Bulleted List Slides—Using the Title and Text layout, set up five bulleted list slides using the titles and bulleted list text shown in the following table. Notice that some of the slides have two bullet levels. The bullet characters in your presentation may be different than those shown here, depending on the design template you choose.

Slide Title	Bulleted List Text
Follow Up	■ Monthly Reports ◆ Showing Activity ◆ Feedback from Other Agents ◆ Market Activity ◆ Showing Activity ■ Bimonthly Calls ◆ Review Advertising ◆ Review Action Plan ◆ Discuss Concerns
Experienced Staff	■ Linda Holmes—Broker & Primary Listing Agent ■ Joan Barnes—Personal Assistant ■ Chris Bell—Data Entry ■ Karen Rollins—Hearthfire Enterprises contact responsible for the "Feels Like Home" Service.

Slide Title	Bulleted List Text
Satisfied Customers	■ Zebidiah Johanson ◆ Linda was wonderful! She really cared about my home. ■ Maria Mills ◆ I was very pleased. When Linda said she would call, she called. I always felt like I was her most important client. ■ Jack Wilson ◆ The Feels Like Home service increased the appeal of my house. It sold in much less time than I was expecting!
Office Hours	■ Monday through Friday ◆ 9–5 ■ Saturday ◆ 11–3 ■ Closed Sunday

Save the presentation as **`Homestead Realty`**.

Critical Thinking 1.2 Create a Presentation Using the AutoContent Wizard

In this exercise, you will create a presentation using the AutoContent Wizard. Sally Lee, the newest member of the MicroChip, Inc. sales team, has just learned that she will be presenting the new product line to a group of key clients in a few hours. Since she has little time for research, she decides to use the AutoContent Wizard to create and polish her presentation.

Follow these guidelines to create and develop a new presentation using the AutoContent Wizard:

AutoContent Wizard	Option
Presentation Type	■ Choose Sales Category, Selling a Product or Service.
Presentation Style	■ Sally will be presenting the presentation on her laptop.
Presentation Options	■ Ensure that the Company name is included in the Title. ■ Add Sally's name and Department to the footer. ■ Ensure that Page number is visible.

Continue with the next phase of the AutoContent Wizard by adding your own information to the content outline as follows:

Slide Title	Bulleted List Text
Title Slide	MicroChip Sales Product Line 2004 Products
Objective	■ Introduction of 2004 Product Line ◆ Turbo Chip ◆ SST Chip ◆ Value Chip ■ Understanding Product Benefits ◆ Faster Processing Speed
Customer Requirements	■ What are you looking for in a processing speed? ◆ Ways to achieve faster processing ■ How do you want that speed? ◆ With quality, value, and service
Meeting the Needs	■ Product Features ■ Turbo Chip: Premium speed at a reasonable cost ■ SST Chip: Excellent speed at a reasonable cost ■ Value Chip: Better than average speed at a low cost

Save the presentation as **`MicroChip Sales`** and close it. This presentation will be completed in future lessons.

LESSON 2

Designing the Presentation

In this lesson, you will build on the fundamental design of the Pinnacle Pet Care presentation. You will establish a consistent style throughout the presentation, format and organize the text, and work with the Office Clipboard and the Style Checker. Using the Outline view, you will add slides to your presentation and manipulate your completed presentation using the Slide Sorter view. Lastly, working with the printing function of PowerPoint 2003, you will examine page setup, print preview, print setup, and the output formats options.

IN THIS LESSON

Microsoft Office PowerPoint 2003 objectives covered in this lesson

Objective Number	Skill Sets and Skills	Concept Page References	Exercise Page References
PP03S-2-1	Format text-based content	40	41–42
PP03S-2-3	Format slides	56	56
PP03S-4-1	Organize a presentation	52	52–53

Additional learning resources are available at labpub.com/learn/pp03/

Case Study

Now that the initial slides of the Pinnacle Pet Care presentation are complete, Al Smith is wondering how he can polish the presentation for the Pet World Trade Show. Al confers with his administrative assistant, Charlene, who will be formatting the presentation for him. In turning over the presentation to Charlene, Al asks her to make sure that the style is consistent throughout the presentation. He also wants her to check that the slides are in a logical sequence so the presentation is clear. Al knows that Charlene is an expert in PowerPoint. He is confident in her ability to make the presentation shine.

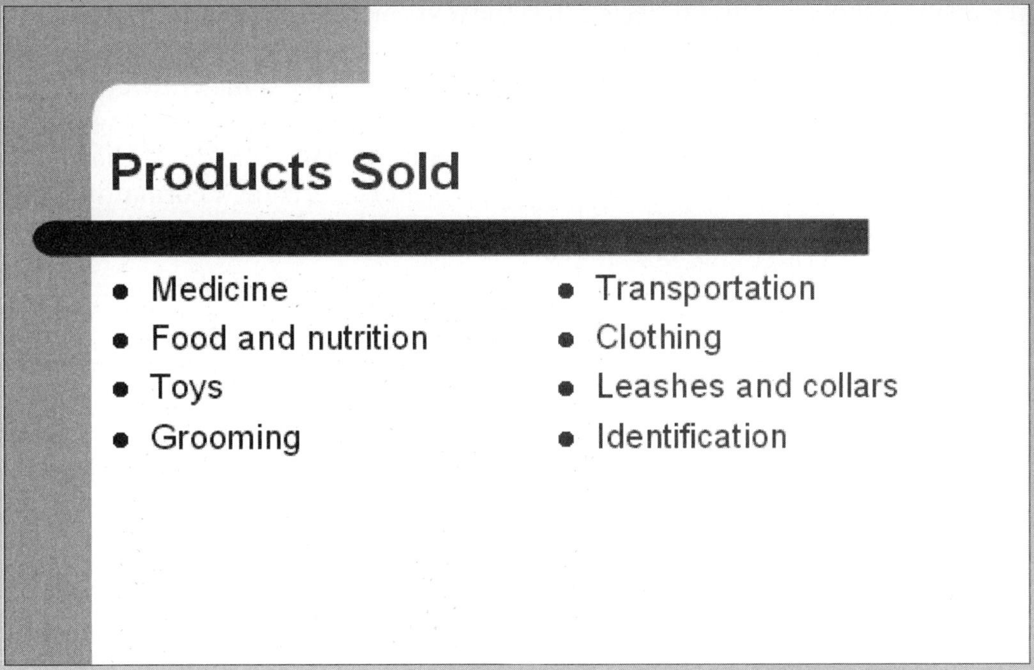

Sample of a slide formatted as a 2-Column Text Layout

Formatting Your Presentation

Microsoft Office **Specialist**

PowerPoint 2003 makes it so easy to create a presentation that the slides you create may not need formatting. After all, the placeholders arrange the text, the bullets are automatic, and the color scheme is preformatted. However, in most cases, you will want to fine-tune your presentation. Formatting your presentation will make a good presentation even better.

Formatting Text

FROM THE KEYBOARD

Ctrl+B for Bold
Ctrl+U for Underline
Ctrl+I for Italics

Formatting text is a common step in the development of a presentation. For instance, when reviewing a slide, you might decide that the text could be emphasized by changing the color of the font. If you had the time, you could change the font color of each piece of text on the slide individually using the Formatting toolbar. However, a more efficient way to change the font color is to first select the placeholder then apply the change of color using the Formatting toolbar. By selecting the placeholder, all text within the placeholder is changed in one swoop. The following illustration describes the buttons on PowerPoint's Formatting toolbar that assist you in formatting.

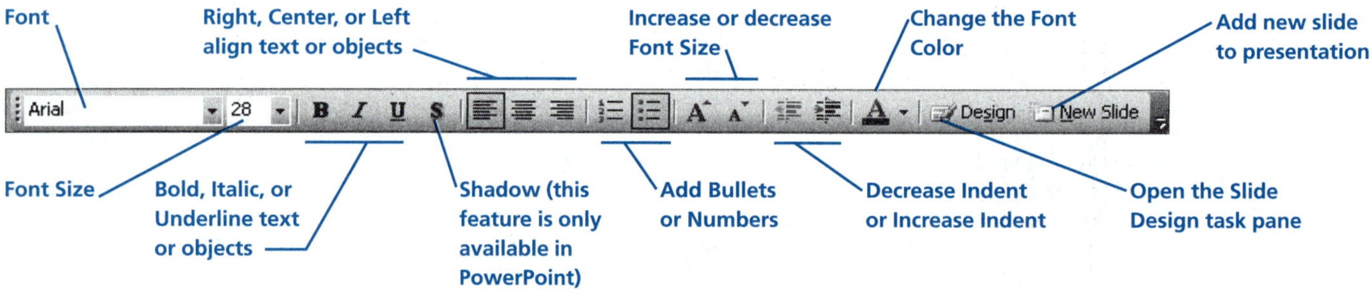

The Office Clipboard

The Office Clipboard works like a magnet to the text you cut and copy. Using the Office Clipboard, you can collect items from any Office document or program and paste them into any other Office document. For example, you can collect data from an Excel table and text from a Word document and paste them into PowerPoint slides. It is the Office Clipboard that holds the items for you while you decide where to paste them. The Office Clipboard can hold up to 24 items.

How It Works

When you use the Cut, Copy, and Paste commands to move text from one point to another, the cut text is placed on the Office Clipboard. You can see what text is being held in the Clipboard by choosing Edit→Office Clipboard from the Standard toolbar or by choosing View→Office Clipboard task pane from the same toolbar. Once the Clipboard task pane is displayed, you can choose an item and paste it into your PowerPoint presentation.

Hands-On 2.1 Format Text

In this exercise, you will change the formatting of the fonts in the Title and Subtitle slides.

Using the Slides Tab

If it is not already opened, open the Pinnacle Pet Care presentation that you created in Lesson 1, Creating and Delivering a Presentation.

1. Choose the Title slide (the first slide) by clicking it on the Slides tab.
   Notice that the subtitle wraps within the box. The slide will look better if the subtitle does not wrap. Also, it may look good to have the title just a little larger.
2. Follow these steps to select the subtitle placeholder box:

(A) Click anywhere on the text to position the insertion point inside the box.

(B) Click any edge of the box and the border pattern will change as shown here. This indicates that the box is selected. Any formatting changes you make now will affect all paragraphs within the box.

3. Notice that the Font Size [28] box is currently set to 28.
   The Capsules design template applied this font size to the subtitle.
4. Click the Decrease Font Size button to reduce the size to 24.
5. Click the Bold **B** button.
   Now the text is easily visible, but the bold format has caused it to wrap within the box again.
6. Click the Decrease Font Size button again.
   The subtitle should fit within the box, but now it is a little too small. The font size buttons let you easily increase or decrease the font size. When you click the button, the font size can change by 2–4 points, depending on the font. Fortunately, you can use the font size box to set the font size with precision.

Continue to Format the Subtitle

7. Click in the Font Size box [28], type **22**, and tap [Enter].
   Now the text is a little smaller, and it fits within the box again. You can always type a size instead of choosing the increase and decrease font size button.

8. Follow these steps to change the box width:

A Position the mouse pointer on this sizing handle, and a double-arrow will appear.

B Drag the border to the left to reduce the box width causing the text to wrap again.

C Now widen the box again until the text no longer wraps. You can always change the size of a placeholder box using this technique. You can also move a box by dragging it to a different location on a slide. Changing the size of the placeholder does not change the size of your text.

Format the Title

9. Click on the border of the Title placeholder.

10. Click the Increase Font Size [A] button once to increase the size to 40.

Copying Text and Objects

FROM THE KEYBOARD
[Ctrl]+[X] for Cut
[Ctrl]+[C] for Copy
[Ctrl]+[V] for Paste

You can move and copy text and objects using Drag and Drop or Cut, Copy, and Paste. It is usually most efficient to use Drag and Drop if you are moving or copying within a slide or to another slide that is visible on the screen. Drag and Drop is also effective for rearranging slides. Cut, Copy, and Paste are most efficient when moving or copying to a location not visible on the current screen.

QR

QUICK REFERENCE: MOVING AND COPYING TEXT AND OBJECTS

Technique	Discussion
Drag and Drop	■ Select the desired text or click an object such as a placeholder box. ■ Drag the text or object to the desired location. Press the [Ctrl] key while dragging if you wish to copy.
Right-Drag and Drop	■ Select the desired text or click an object such as a placeholder box. ■ Use the right mouse button to drag the text or object to the desired location. ■ Release the mouse button at the desired location and choose Move, Copy, or Cancel from the pop-up menu.

QUICK REFERENCE: MOVING AND COPYING TEXT AND OBJECTS (CONTINUED)

Technique	Discussion
Cut, Copy, and Paste	■ Select the desired text or click an object such as a placeholder box. ■ Click the Cut button or press [Ctrl]+[X] to cut the item. Click the Copy button or press [Ctrl]+[C] to copy the item. ■ Navigate to the desired slide and click at the location where you want to paste. ■ Click the Paste button or press [Ctrl]+[V] to paste the item.

Hands-On 2.2 Add a Slide, Change the Slide Layout, and Move Paragraphs

In this exercise, you will add a new slide to the presentation, enter a bulleted list, and change the layout of the slide. You can always change the layout for a slide after the slide has been created.

Add the Slide

1. Make sure the Services Provided slide is selected in the presentation.
   New slides are placed after the selected slide.
2. Click the [New Slide] button.
3. Click in the Title placeholder and type **Products Sold**.
4. Click in the bulleted list placeholder and type the bulleted list shown to the right.
   When you begin typing the last bullet, PowerPoint will reformat all of the bullets with a smaller font size so that all the bullets can fit into the box. Since a long list of bullets is overwhelming, limit the number of bullets to three to six on a slide. If there is more information, consider breaking the list into two columns. In the next two steps, you will use this technique by choosing a different layout for the slide.

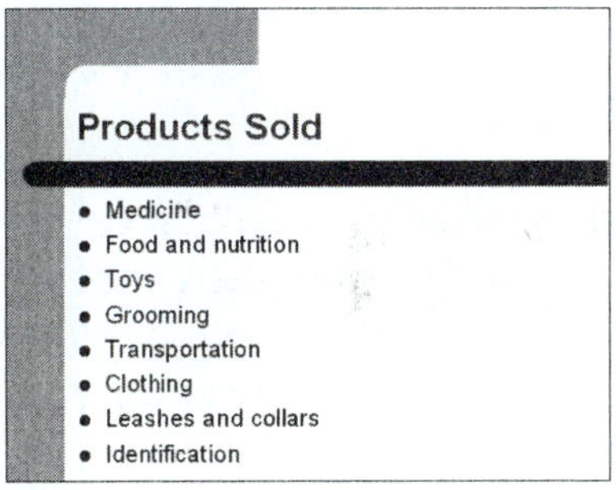

Change the Slide Layout and Move Text

5. Follow this step to change the slide layout:

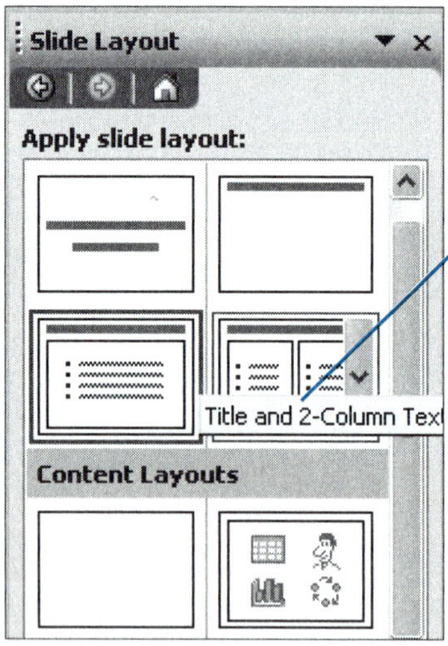

Ⓐ Click the Title and 2-Column Text layout on the task pane. The new layout will be applied to the slide. Notice that you can apply a layout to selected slides by simply clicking the layout on the task pane.

6. Follow these steps to move the last four bullets to the second box:

Ⓐ Select the last four bullets by dragging the mouse over them then release the mouse button.

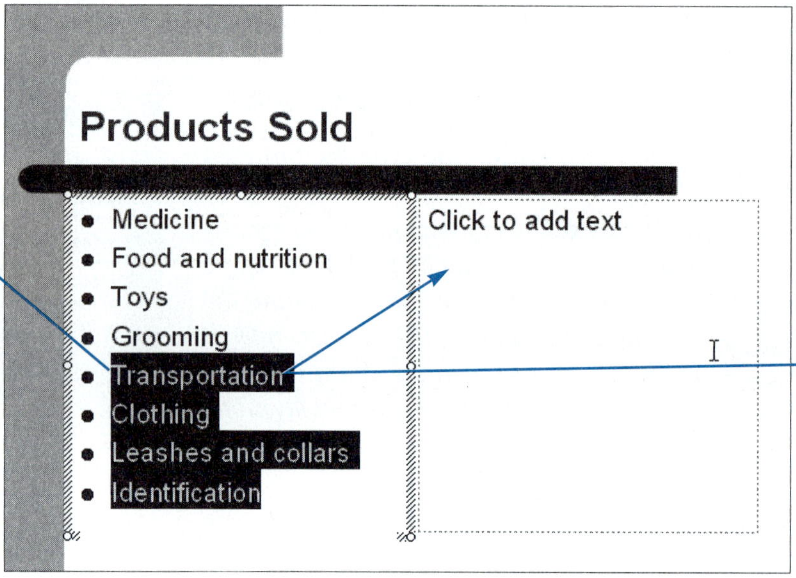

Ⓑ Position the mouse pointer on the selected paragraphs, drag them to the second bulleted column, and release the mouse button. The last four bulleted paragraphs should now be in the second box.

7. Choose File→Save As from the menu bar and save the presentation as **`Pinnacle Pet Care Design`**.

Line and Paragraph Spacing

Sometimes, instead of changing the font size or adding many hard returns, you only need to increase or decrease the spacing between lines to have the proper effect. Line spacing determines the amount of space within and between paragraphs. The Line Spacing dialog box provides line and paragraph settings. The paragraph spacing setting lets you increase the space before and after paragraphs, but does not change the line spacing within paragraphs. These settings are useful if text is wrapping within a placeholder box and you want to change the spacing between paragraphs but not within the wrapped lines. The Format→Line Spacing command displays the Line Spacing dialog box.

Hands-On 2.3 Realign Paragraph and Line Spacing

In this exercise, you will insert a new slide. Also, you will adjust the paragraph spacing to increase the amount of space between the bullets.

1. Choose the last slide in the presentation (Products Sold).
2. Click the New Slide button to add a new bulleted list slide.
3. Click the Title placeholder and type the title **Our Staff**.
4. Click in the bulleted list box and type the three bulleted items shown to the right.
   Notice that the second bullet automatically wraps to a second line. Wrapped lines give a cluttered look. In the next few steps, you will eliminate the wrapping by reducing the font size of the text. You will also increase the paragraph spacing to "open up" the slide. Increasing the spacing will also help balance the slide since it has just three bullets. Finally, notice that PowerPoint's Spelling as You Type feature placed a wavy red line under the name Larkson. *You can correct or ignore a word marked with a wavy red underline by right-clicking the word and choosing a replacement word or Ignore All from the pop-up menu.*

5. Click a border on the bulleted list placeholder.
6. Click the Decrease Font Size button.
   The text should be small enough now so that the second line does not wrap.
7. Choose Format→Line Spacing and follow these steps to set the Before Paragraph spacing:

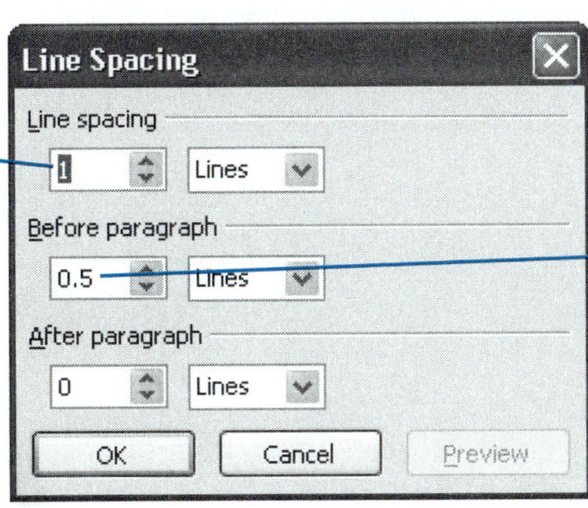

A Notice the Line Spacing option.

B Click in this box, set the Before Paragraph spacing to **0.5**, and click OK. This will set the spacing between paragraphs to ½ of a line. Notice how the change has "opened up" the slide by creating more spacing between the paragraphs.

8. Click the Save button to save the changes to your presentation.

Working with Outlines

While we have been working primarily in the slide to add or format text, the Outline Tab is an alternative way to add, remove, and move text. The Outline Tab is a useful method to organize or structure your presentation.

The Outlining Toolbar

The Outlining toolbar helps you to edit and reorganize your slides when working in Outline view. The Outlining toolbar is normally positioned to the left of the outline. If the Outlining tab is chosen in Normal view and the Outlining toolbar is not visible, you can display it using the View→Toolbars→Outlining command.

You can choose a slide in an outline by clicking the slide icon or by clicking on any text within the slide.

The slide you choose is displayed in the main portion of the window.

The Outlining toolbar can be displayed on the left side of the outline using the View→Toolbars→Outlining command.

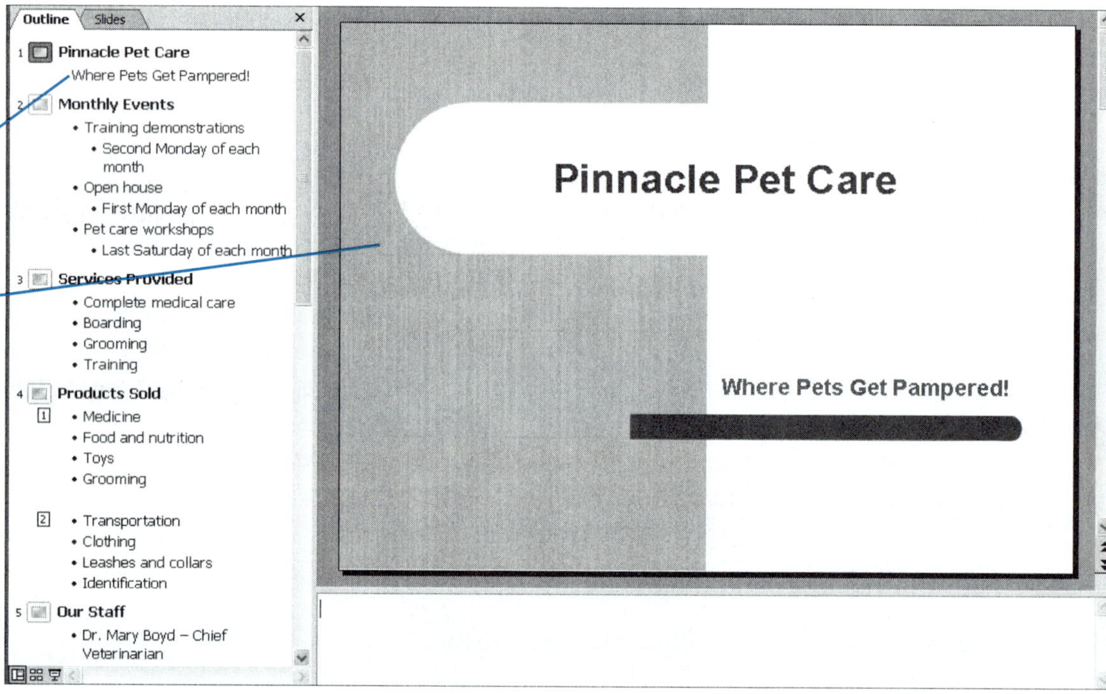

The Promote and Demote buttons let you promote or demote titles and bullets. For example, promoting a first-level bullet would create a new slide. The promoted bullet text would become the title of the new slide.

The Expand and Collapse buttons let you display (expand) additional levels and hide (collapse) levels. For example, you may want to collapse (hide) all bullets so that only the slide titles are displayed.

The Summary Slide button lets you create summary slides that can function as an Agenda. The Summary Slide is made up of each slide title.

The Move Up and Move Down buttons let you rearrange bullets and entire slides.

The Collapse All button displays only the slide titles. The Expand All button displays all levels.

This button is used to display or hide text formatting.

QR

QUICK REFERENCE: WORKING WITH OUTLINES	
Task	**Procedure**
Select text in an outline	Drag over the desired text.
Select an entire slide	Click the slide icon.
Select a bulleted item and all of its sub items	Click the bullet.
Add a new slide	Place the insertion point in a slide and press [Ctrl]+[Enter].

Hands-On 2.4 Add a Slide in Outline Tab

In this exercise, you will work with the Outlining Toolbar to add and move slides.

1. Follow these steps to add a new slide while in the Outline tab:

A Use this scroll bar to scroll down until the Our Staff slide is visible.

B In the Outline tab, click on any bulleted paragraph in the Our Staff slide.

C Press [Ctrl]+[Enter] to add a new slide.

D In the Outline tab, type `Respected Clients` as the title of the new slide, and press [Ctrl]+[Enter].

E Type the three bulleted paragraphs shown here, tapping [Enter] after each paragraph (including the last paragraph).

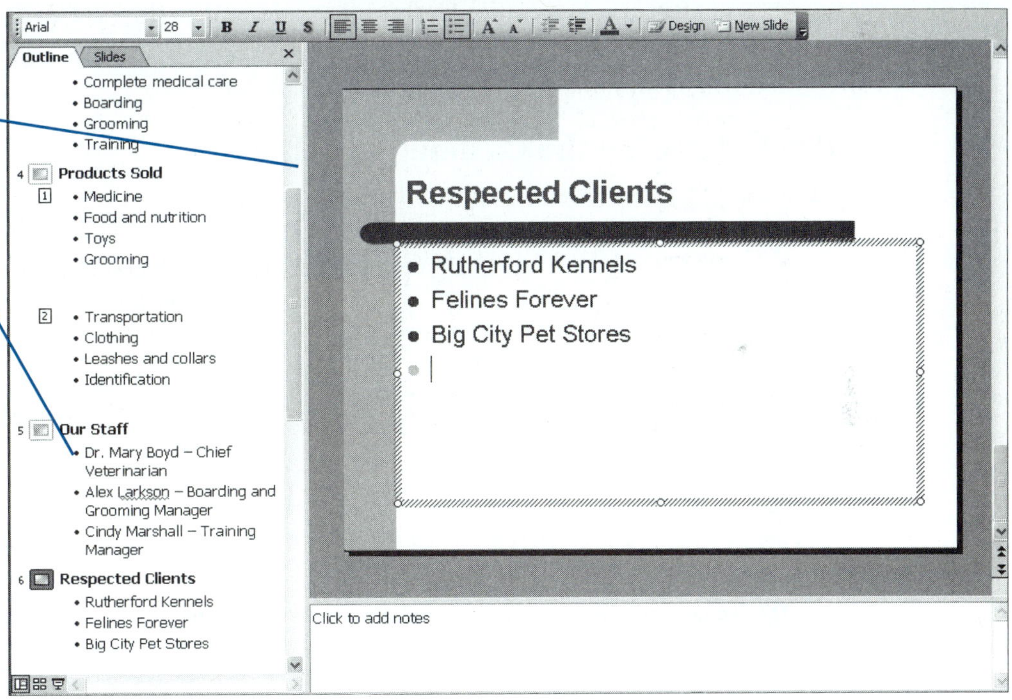

A new slide is added to the presentation whenever the mouse pointer is positioned within a bulleted list and the [Ctrl]+[Enter] keystroke combination is issued.

2. At this point, you should have a new bulleted paragraph visible in the outline below the Big City Pet Stores paragraph. If you don't, tap [Enter] to add the paragraph.

Add Two New Slides

3. Make sure the insertion point is on the blank bulleted paragraph in the Outline.
4. Click the Promote button on the Outlining toolbar. If the Outlining toolbar is not visible, choose View→Toolbars→Outlining to display it.
   The bulleted paragraph will be promoted to a new slide.

5. Type **Welcome Aboard Specials** and tap [Enter].
Notice that tapping [Enter] created a new slide. You must use the [Ctrl]+[Enter] keystroke combination to add a bulleted paragraph after a title slide. However, you will fix this by demoting the new slide in the next step.

6. Click the Demote button on the Outlining toolbar.
The new slide should now be a bullet under the Welcome Aboard Specials title.

7. Complete the new slide in the outline as shown to the right, tapping [Enter] after each paragraph (including the last paragraph).

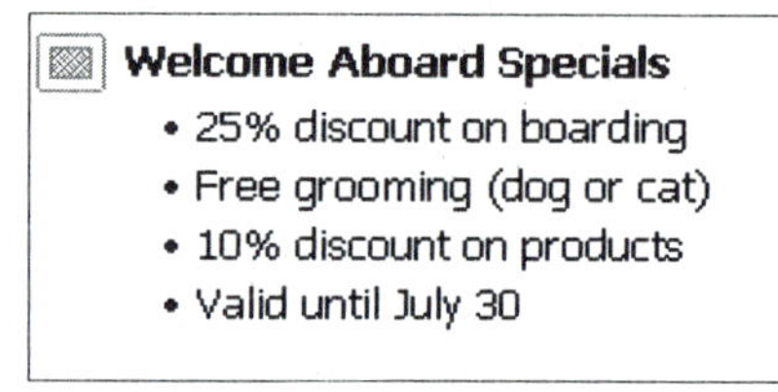

8. Promote the new paragraph that follows the Valid until July 30 paragraph.

9. Type **Pinnacle Pet Care** and press [Ctrl]+[Enter] to create a bullet below the title you just typed.

10. Complete the new slide as shown to the right. Do not tap [Enter] after the last bullet in this slide, since it is the closing slide.
You will format this closing slide in Hands-On 2.6.

Use Buttons on the Outlining Toolbar

11. Follow these steps to explore the Outline tab:

A Scroll up until Slides 4 and 5 are visible.

B Notice that each slide is represented by an icon. If a slide has more than one bulleted list, numbers are used to identify the lists.

C Click any bullet to select the bullet text.

D Click this slide icon to select all text on the slide.

E Click on the Our Staff title to deselect the slide and prepare for the next step.

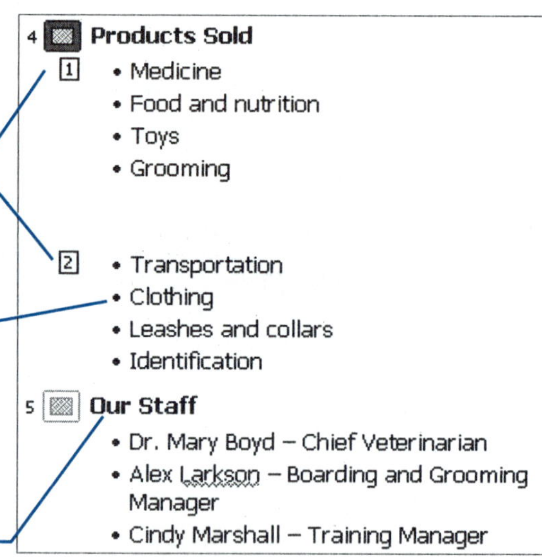

12. Click the Collapse button on the Outlining toolbar.
The Collapse button collapses the bulleted paragraphs beneath the title.

13. Click the Expand button to redisplay the bulleted paragraphs.

14. Click the Collapse All button to display only the slide icons and titles of each slide.

15. Click the Expand All button to expand all of the slides.

Move a Slide

The easiest way to move a slide in an outline is to first collapse all slides. Then you can click on the desired slide title and use the Move Up and/or Move Down buttons on the Outlining toolbar.

16. Click the Collapse All button.
17. If necessary, scroll up until all slide icons and titles are visible in the outline.
18. Click on the Respected Clients title then click the Move Down button.
    The Respected Clients title should now appear below the Welcome Aboard special title.
19. Click the Expand All button.
20. If necessary, scroll down and notice that the subordinate paragraphs (the bullets) below the Respected Clients title were moved along with the title. In other words, the entire slide was moved.

Deleting Slides

You can delete a slide in an outline by clicking the slide icon to select the entire slide then tapping the [Delete] key. Likewise, slides can be deleted in Normal and Slide Sorter views by choosing the desired slide(s) and tapping [Delete]. If you inadvertently delete a slide, you can use the Undo button on the Standard Toolbar to undo the latest action and restore the deleted slide. If you later decide that you want to keep the change, click the Redo button on the Standard Toolbar to go back to the previous action.

Hands-On 2.5 Delete a Slide from the Outline

In this exercise, you will delete a slide using the Outline Tab.

1. If necessary, click the Respected Clients slide icon to select the entire slide.
2. Tap the [Delete] key on the keyboard to delete the slide.
3. Now hide the Outlining toolbar by choosing View→Toolbars→Outlining.

Paragraph Alignment

In time, you will be able to "eye" a presentation by noticing if the paragraph alignment is not balanced. Use the following buttons from the Formatting toolbar to realign paragraphs.

QR **QUICK REFERENCE: WORKING WITH PARAGRAPH ALIGNMENT**

Purpose	Button
Left-Align	
Center-Align	
Right-Align	

This is an easy and immediate way to realign text. Just select the paragraph then click an alignment button to make the change.

Hands-On 2.6 Format the Closing Slide

In this exercise, you will reformat the closing slide, Office Hours.

Format the Closing Slide

1. Click the Slides tab to see thumbnails of the presentation.
2. If necessary, scroll down and click the closing slide at the end of the presentation.
3. Click in the bulleted list placeholder then click a border of the placeholder.
4. Click the Bullets button on the Formatting toolbar to remove bullets from the paragraphs.
5. Click the Center button on the Formatting toolbar to center the paragraphs within the placeholder.
6. Choose Format→Line Spacing from the menu bar.
7. Select the entire telephone number by dragging the mouse pointer over the text.
8. Click the Increase Font Size button to increase the size to 32.
9. Now increase the size of the last line (the Website URL) to 32.

Style Options

As you create slides, you may find that each slide develops its own personality. As changes are made to each slide, the style may begin to vary from slide to slide. A presentation with different styles on each slide is disjointed and suggests carelessness to your audience. An excellent way to guard against inconsistent styling is to use the Style Options in PowerPoint 2003. With Style Options, you can set up the presentation using definite style rules for case, punctuation, or the "white space" for each slide in the presentation. Ensuring that your style is standardized is as easy as checking a box! Once these "rules" are set up, the Style Checker goes into action. If PowerPoint encounters a variation from the established rule, a light bulb appears on your screen to remind you that the rule has been broken. The Style Option dialog box can be displayed by choosing Tools→Options→Spelling & Style tab.

TIP! *One important point to remember is that the Style Option reminders work through the Office Assistant. If the Office Assistant has been hidden or turned off, the Style Option reminders cannot be displayed. Therefore, you will miss any style inconsistencies.*

Examine these illustrations of the Style Option dialog box:

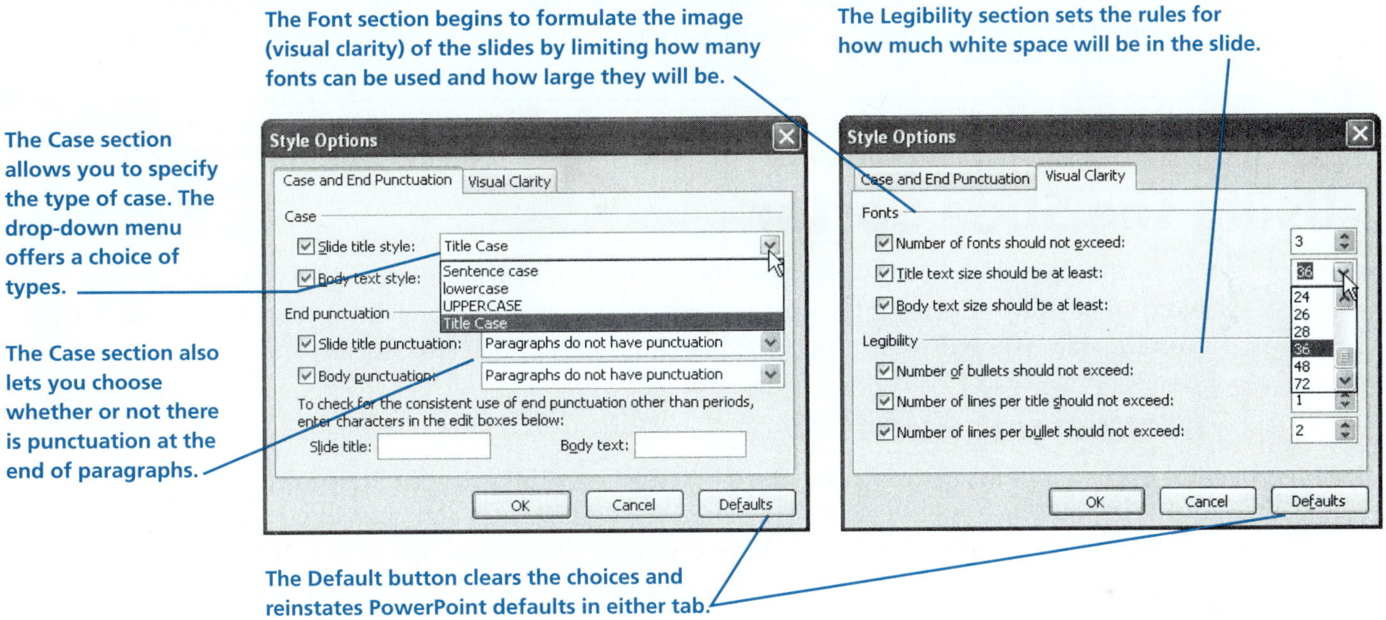

Using the automated features of Style Options will ensure that you create smooth, consistent, and clear presentations for your audience.

Hands-On 2.7 Explore the Style Checker

In this exercise, you will explore the Style checking options of PowerPoint 2003.

1. From any slide, choose Tools→Options.
   Notice the Style section at the bottom of the dialog box.
2. If it is not already enabled, click the Check Style checkbox.
3. Click the [Style Options...] button.
   The Style Options dialog box appears on your screen. It is here that you set the style rules for your presentation.
4. Examine the Case and End Punctuation Tab.
   Notice that this tab regulates how the sentences will look (uppercase, lowercase, etc.) and whether there will be punctuation after each phase. Observe that case and punctuation are broken into two sections: the Title and Body.

5. Examine the Visual Clarity Tab.
Notice that this tab regulates how many fonts will be used throughout the presentation as well as the minimum and maximum sizes of the fonts. The second part of the Visual Clarity dialog box limits the number of bullets permitted per slide, limits the Title slide to one line, and determines whether sentences can be wrapped into two lines.
6. Click the [Defaults] button on either tab.
This button will return the settings to the PowerPoint default settings that were shipped with the software.
7. Click Cancel to get out of the Style Options dialog box without saving any changes.
We are through examining the Style Options. You can practice using this feature in Skill Builder 2.1.

Using the Slide Sorter

Up until now, we've been working in the Normal view, which is good for manipulating a handful of slides. However, as your presentation grows to more slides than are visible in the Normal view, you will want to explore the function of the Slide Sorter view.

Rearranging Slides

Microsoft Office Specialist

PowerPoint's Slide Sorter view is used to rearrange slides. In the Slide Sorter view, each slide is a thumbnail image so the entire presentation is visible at a glance. As your presentation grows, often the order of the slides needs to be changed to create a logical concept flow. Using the Drag and Drop method, you can quickly reorganize your slides by moving them to the correct spot using the Slide Sorter view.

Hands-On 2.8 Use the Slide Sorter View

In this exercise, you will practice using the Slide Sorter View.

1. Click the Slide Sorter view button on the View bar just below the slide thumbnails.

2. Follow these steps to move a slide:

A If necessary, click this drop-down button and change the zoom percentage until all seven slides are visible. Don't be concerned if your slides have a different arrangement than shown in this illustration.

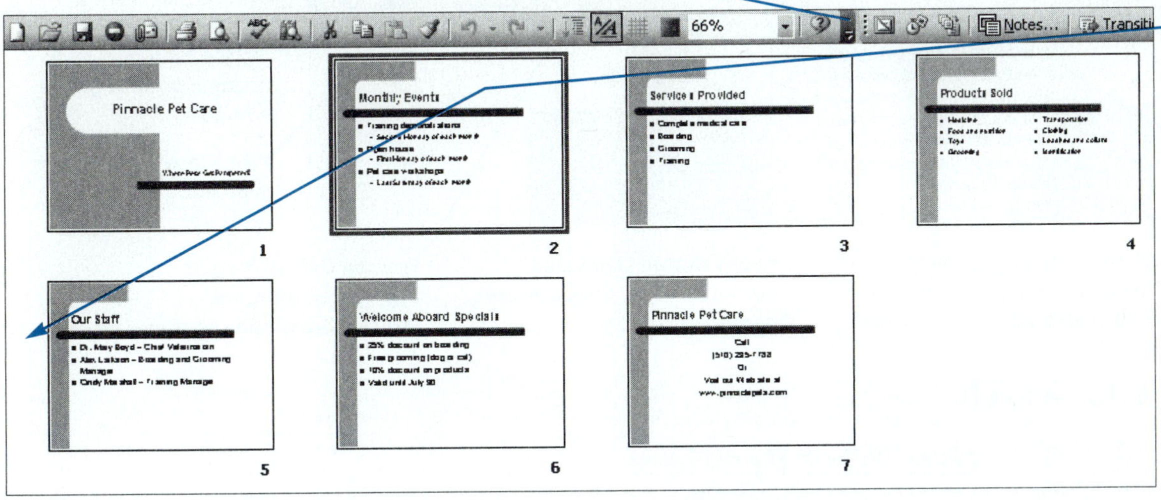

B Drag the Monthly Events slide to the left of the Our Staff slide and a large vertical bar will indicate the eventual position of the slide. Don't be concerned if the Our Staff slide is in a different row or column than shown here.

C Release the mouse button and the Monthly Events slide will become the fourth slide.

3. Click the Normal view button on the View bar to return to Normal view.

Printing Your Presentation

Ninety percent of the time, you will be viewing or projecting the presentations you create from a PC or laptop. However, there may be times when a hard copy of the presentation is needed. It is important to understand that what you are printing is, for the most part, intense graphics and extraordinarily large text. PowerPoint 2003, like prior versions of PowerPoint, provides you with detailed options for printing slides, handouts, speaker notes, or any variation thereof. In this lesson, we will simply explore the options of printing a presentation. In future lessons, we will apply this knowledge to printing handout slides and speaker notes as well.

Print Preview

To discover how your slides translate to print, click the Print Preview button on the Standard toolbar. This will display the Print Preview window. The Print Preview window allows you to see how the slide will be printed. You can then refine the appearance before printing. The following illustration describes the options available on the Print Preview toolbar.

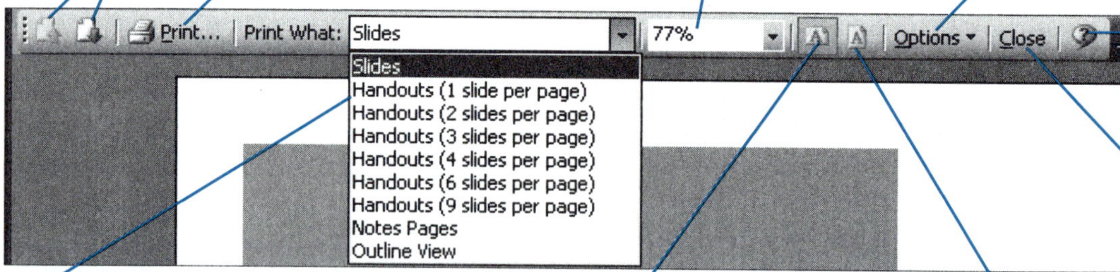

Hands-On 2.9 Use Print Preview

In this exercise, you will work with the Print Preview feature of PowerPoint.

1. Click the Print Preview button on the Standard toolbar.
2. Follow these steps to examine the Print Preview options:

The Print Dialog Box

FROM THE KEYBOARD
Ctrl+P to display the Print box

There are multiple ways of printing a presentation. To view those options, choose File→Print on the Standard toolbar. The Print dialog box allows you to change printers, specify the number of copies to be printed, print a range of slides, and modify the color of the slide for print.

The Name section allows you to choose a printer.

The Print Range section allows you to print all slides, the current slide, or a range of slides. To specify a range of slides, check Slides and type the desired slide numbers in the Slides box.

The Print What section allows you to print slides, meeting handouts, speaker notes, or the outline. This option is also available through Print Preview.

The Color/Grayscale section allows you to print in color, grayscale, or pure black and white. The Color option is only compatible with a color printer.

You are able to set other various options here.

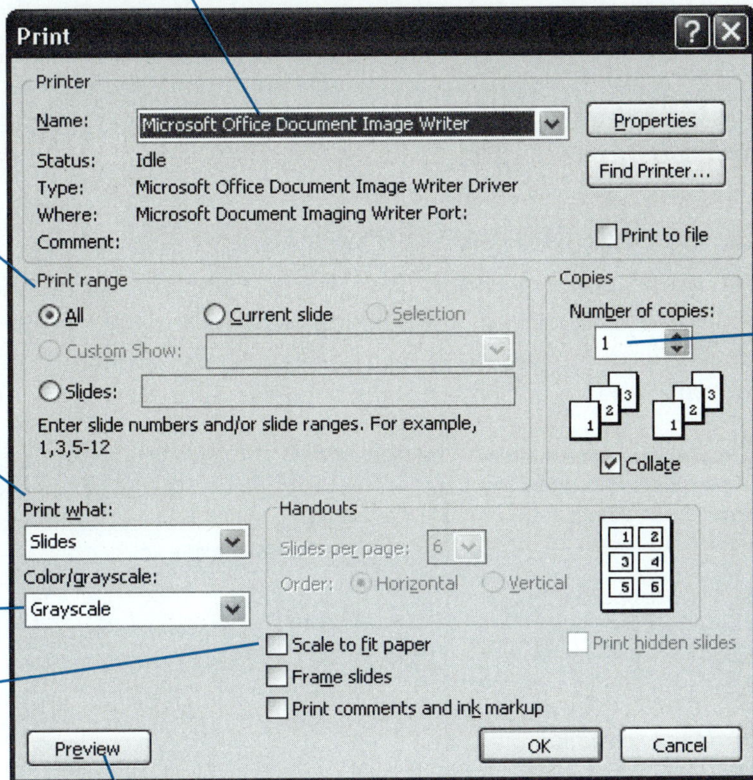

Using the Copies section, specify the number of copies. Check the Collate option to print more than one copy of your slides, handouts, or other print-outs. When Collate is checked, the first copy will print before the second copy begins printing, instead of having two copies of each page print.

Clicking the Preview button displays the appearance of the slides. Click the button if you want to see how your changed settings will look before printing.

Hands-On 2.10 Explore the Print Box

In this exercise, you will explore the Print dialog box.

1. Choose File→Print to display the Print dialog box.
2. Explore the options of the Print What section and other sections of this dialog box.
3. Click the Preview button and the change should be reflected in the Print Preview window. Keep in mind that certain settings, such as the number of copies, do not affect the display in the Print Preview window.
4. Print your presentation.
5. When you have finished, close the Print dialog box or the Print Preview window and make sure your presentation is displayed in Normal view.

The Print Shortcut

It is tempting to just click the Print button on the Standard toolbar. However, before this becomes a habit, know that a click of this button sends the entire presentation to the current printer, whether or not you want to make adjustments. If you are working with a design template that has a colored background, the printing process will not only be painstakingly slow, but may also waste your toner or ink!

Page Setup and Output Formats

Microsoft Office **Specialist**

If you need to print the presentation itself or transparencies for overhead projection, use the Page Setup dialog box. The Page Setup dialog box can be displayed by choosing File→Page Setup on the Standard toolbar. Examine the Page Setup options, along with the different types of output formats you can use by studying the Page Setup dialog box that follows:

Choose an output format from the Slides Sized For list. Available sizes include overhead transparencies, 35mm, and various paper sizes.

PowerPoint sets the size options depending on the output format. However, you can always manually adjust the size.

The orientation options affect the default orientation of the objects in the presentation.

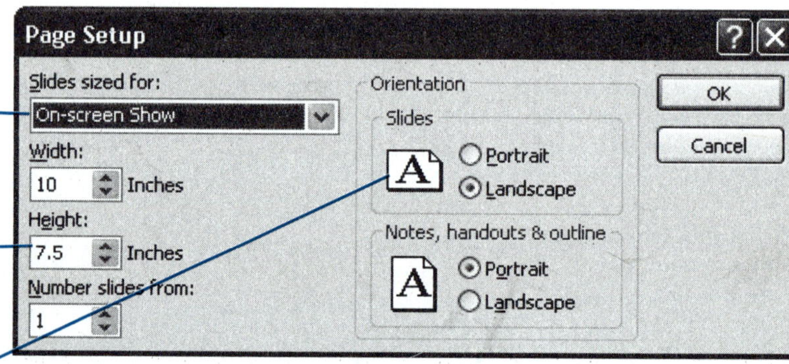

Hands-On 2.11 Explore the Page Setup Box

In this exercise, you will learn about the options provided in the Page Setup dialog box.

1. Choose File→Page Setup to display the Page Setup Box.
2. Click the Slides Sized For drop-down button and examine the various output formats.
3. Notice the Width, Height, and Number of Slide options in this dialog box.
4. Examine the Orientation section of the Page Setup dialog box, noting that the horizontal alignment of the page is located here as well as the orientation of the notes and handout pages.
5. Click the Cancel button when you have finished examining options in the Page Setup box to close the box without applying the settings and close the presentation.

Concepts Review

True/False Questions

1.	Text must be reformatted by changing one word at a time.	TRUE	FALSE
2.	You can copy text from other Office programs to place into PowerPoint.	TRUE	FALSE
3.	The Office Clipboard can hold up to 10 items.	TRUE	FALSE
4.	Line spacing is the same as Paragraph spacing.	TRUE	FALSE
5.	The Outlining Tab in the Normal view can be used to create new slides.	TRUE	FALSE
6.	The Style Option feature changes the background color of your presentation.	TRUE	FALSE
7.	Print Preview is used to examine the presentation before printing.	TRUE	FALSE
8.	Slide Sorter view is most useful for focusing on the development of a single slide.	TRUE	FALSE
9.	Page Setup allows you to choose different output formats for your presentation.	TRUE	FALSE
10.	The Print dialog box is usually used to determine the number of copies to be printed.	TRUE	FALSE

Multiple Choice Questions

1. Where are output formats such as 35mm and overhead transparency chosen?
   a. Page Setup box
   b. Print Preview window
   c. Print box
   d. None of the above

2. The Line Spacing dialog box can be opened by using the __________ command.
   a. Format→Line Spacing
   b. Format→Alignment
   c. Edit→Paste Special
   d. None of the above

3. There are many ways to view the Office Clipboard; they include:
   a. Format→Office Clipboard
   b. Edit→Office Clipboard
   c. Opening the Clipoard task pane
   d. Both b and c

4. The Style Checker can be activated by checking:
   a. Tools→Options→Check Style
   b. Slide Design task pane
   c. View→Style Checker
   d. None of the above

Skill Builders

Skill Builder 2.1 Practice Formatting

In this exercise, you will format some of the slides in the Tropical Getaways presentation created in Lesson 1, Creating and Delivering a Presentation, using the Style Checker.

Format the Presentation

1. Open the Tropical Getaways presentation.
2. If you are not already in Normal view, switch to Normal View now. Then, choose the Slides tab and choose the Title slide.
3. Click the Title placeholder then click again on the edge of the placeholder to select it.
4. Click the Increase Font Size button on the formatting toolbar to increase the font size.
5. With the placeholder still selected, click the Bold **B** button.

Change Paragraph Alignment

6. Using the Slides tab again, go to the Travel Categories slide (second slide).
7. Select the body placeholder by clicking on the border.
8. Click the Bullets button to remove the bullets from all paragraphs.
9. Center the paragraphs in this slide by clicking the Center Alignment button on the Formatting toolbar.
10. Change the line spacing to 1.5 by using the Format→Line Spacing command.

Check Style Options

11. Choose Tools→Options→Style Check.
12. Click the Style Options... button to open the Style Options dialog box.

13. Choose the Case and Punctuation tab. For the Title, select Title Case. For the Body Text style, choose Sentence Case.

14. In the Punctuation section of the Case and Punctuation tab, ensure that neither the title nor body paragraphs have punctuation.
This will allow you to type information without punctuating each fragment or word in a bullet.

15. In the Visual Clarity tab of the Style Options dialog box under the Fonts section, check that the number of fonts does not exceed three; the Title Font size should be at least 36 and the Body Text should be at least 20.
This tab helps you to conform to a consistent style for your presentation.

16. In the Legibility section, check that the number of bullets does not exceed six, number of lines per title does not exceed one, and the number of lines per bullet does not exceed two.
More than six bullets crowds the slide and confuses the viewer. Since you are being brief, notice we've set the lines per title to only one and the word wrap to only two lines. This should help us to keep our data succinct for easy viewing.

17. Now that you've set the style options, click each slide in your presentation to review them.
If the style is different than the rules you've set up, a light bulb will appear on the screen.

18. Each time the light bulb appears to notify you of the inconsistency, click on it and make the changes you think will look best in the presentation.

TIP! *If you choose to ignore the style rule, the light bulb will not appear for the remainder of this presentation.*

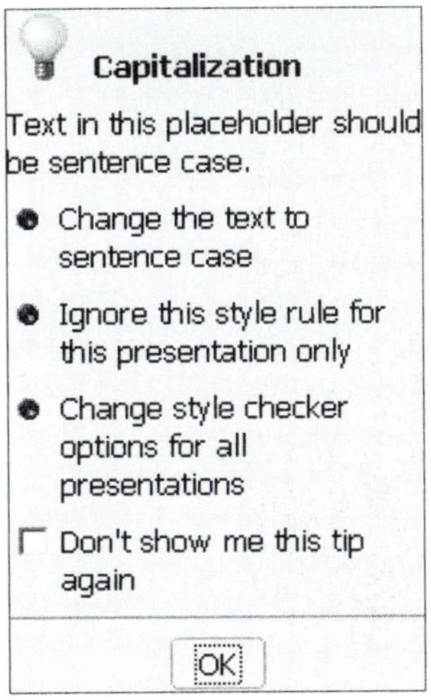

19. Save the changes to the presentation and continue with the next exercise.

Skill Builder 2.2 Rearrange Slides

In this exercise, you will reposition one of the slides in the Tropical Getaways presentation.

1. Click the Slide Sorter view button on the View bar to switch to the Slide Sorter view.
2. Drag the Travel Categories slide from Position 5, and drop it in Position 2 as shown below.

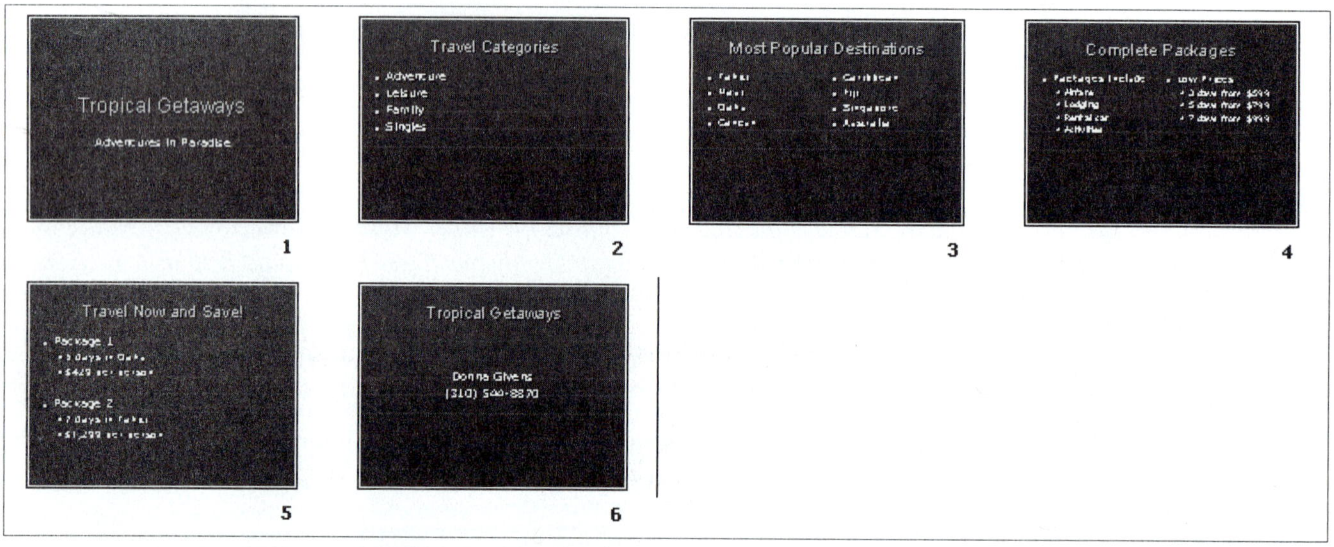

3. Save the change and continue with the next exercise.

Skill Builder 2.3 Print the Presentation

In this exercise, you will print a slide.

1. Open the Tropical Getaways presentation, if necessary, and go to the second slide, Travel Categories.
2. Choose File→Print to display the Print Dialog box.
3. In the Print Dialog box, choose a printer to use for this print job.
   If a printer is already assigned, examine the dialog box.
4. Under Print Range, choose Current Slide to print only the current slide, not the entire presentation.
   This is only a test to see how a slide will look on paper.
5. In the Print What section, choose Slides.
6. Under Color/Grayscale, choose grayscale.
   Save your ink color. Using either grayscale or pure black and white results in a white background with black text, which is acceptable for a draft copy.

7. Save the changes and close Tropical Getaways before moving on to the next exercise.

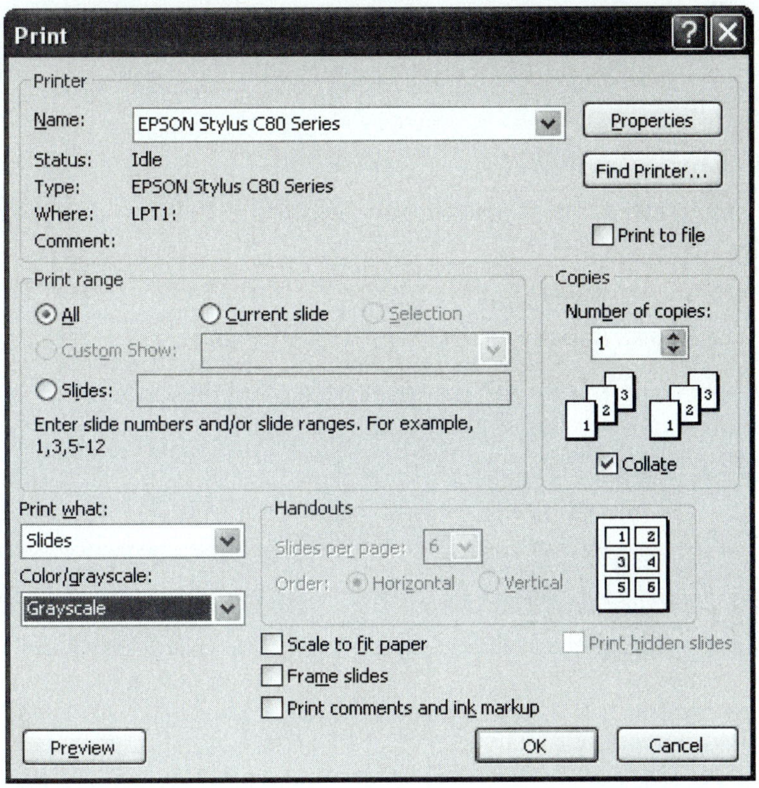

Assessments

Assessment 2.1 Reformat a Presentation

In this exercise, you will add a slide to the Classic Cars presentation, change the format, and print a slide.

1. Open the Classic Cars presentation that was developed in Lesson 1, Creating and Delivering a Presentation.
2. Navigate to the Travel Now and Save slide (fifth slide).
3. Using the Slide Layout task pane, choose the Title and 2-Column text Layout to replace the current layout.
4. Move the last bullet into the second placeholder.
   This will divide the packages into two sections, one per placeholder.
5. Move the last three bullets from the list into the second placeholder.
   This will open up the slide so we can place a graphic there later.
6. Add the following two slides.

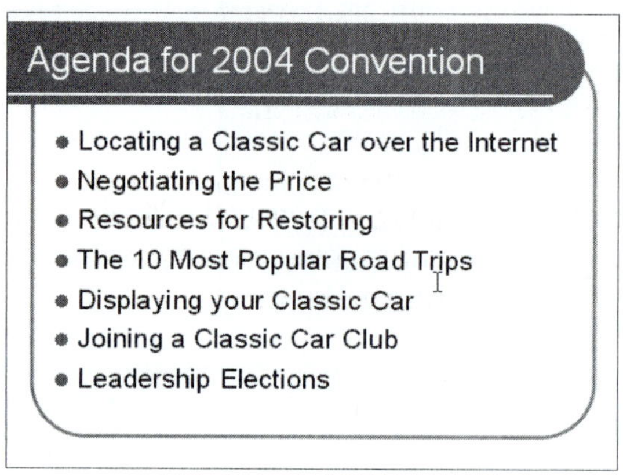

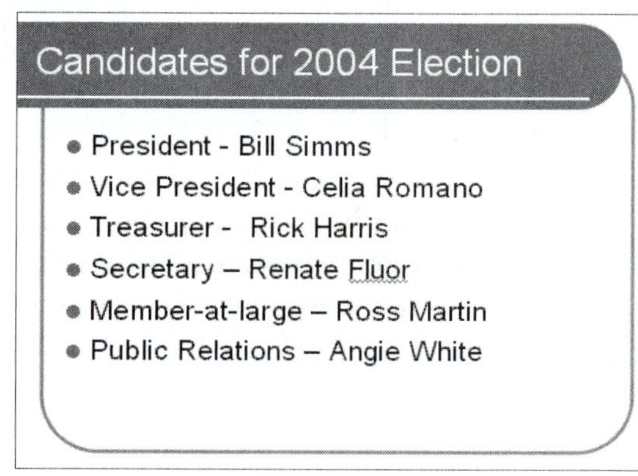

7. The slides look too crowded. Make a few changes to the two slides until they match the following slides. In the second slide, use the Title and Text over Content layout. We are using this layout to prepare for Lesson 3, Managing Clip Art, Drawing Objects, and Animation, in which we will add a graphic to the slide.

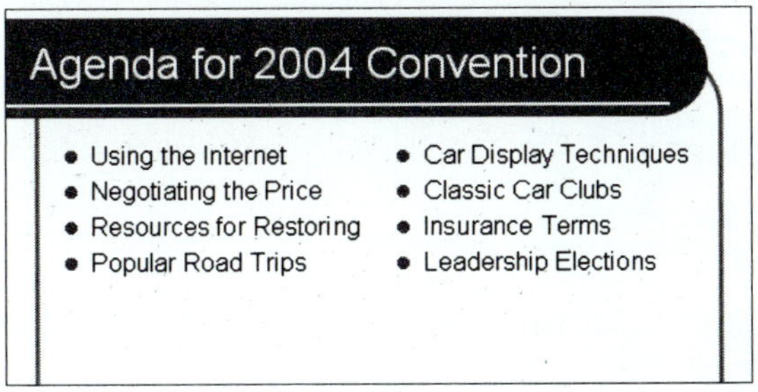

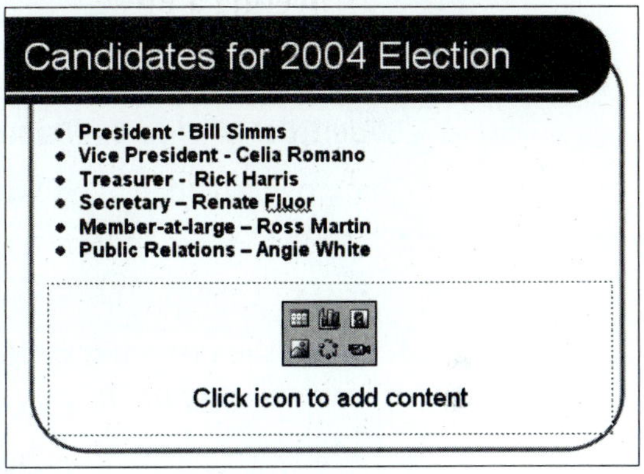

8. When the changes are made, use Print Preview to preview the presentation.

9. Print the slide of your choice, using the Grayscale option.

10. Save the changes to the Classic Cars presentation.
We will enhance the Classic Cars presentation in Lesson 3, Managing Clip Art, Drawing Objects, and Animation.

11. Close the presentation.

Critical Thinking

Critical Thinking 2.1 Format a Presentation

In this exercise, you will add another slide to the Homestead Realty presentation using the Outline Tab. Open the Homestead Realty presentation that was created in Lesson 1, Creating and Delivering a Presentation, and add another slide, using the Outline tab.

Use the following guide to create the new slide:

Slide Title	Bulleted List Text
Targeted Marketing	■ MLS
	■ Web Page
	■ Yard Signs
	■ Flyers
	■ IWANNA
	■ Citizen Times
	■ Real Estate Weekly
	■ Homes and Land

Use the following table to modify other slides in the presentation:

Slide to be Modified	Task
Experienced Staff	Decrease font size to 24
Satisfied Customers	Decrease all paragraphs to 24
	Remove bullets from the quotes
	Decrease font size of quotes to 20
	Apply Italics to all quotes
Office Hours	Print this slide only in Black & White

Save the changes to Homestead Realty and continue.

Critical Thinking 2.2 Add to the Presentation

In this exercise, you will change the look of the Homestead Realty presentation that you created in Critical Thinking 1.1 by changing the layout and rearranging the slides in the Slide Sorter view.

- Change the slide layout of the Targeted Marketing slide to Title and 2-Column Text. Move the last four bullets to the second column.
- Use the Increase Font Size button to increase the font size of the subtitle on the Title slide.

- Rearrange the slides into the following order:

  Slide Title

  Targeted Marketing

  Follow Up

  Experienced Staff

  Satisfied Customers

  Office Hours

- Use the following guide to revise the Office Hours slide:

Slide Title	Bulleted List Text
Title	New Office Hours
Body	Monday, Wednesday, Friday: 9 am – 5 pm
	Tuesday, Thursday: 12 pm – 8 pm
	Saturdays: 12 pm – 6 pm
	Sundays: Closed
	We are here to serve you!

- Change the line spacing of the body text to 1.25 and change the font size to 22pt.
- Remove all bullets.
- Save the presentation and run the slide show. When the slide show ends, do not close the presentation but continue with the next exercise.

Critical Thinking 2.3 Use Print Preview

In this exercise, you will experiment with the Print Preview function in the Homestead Realty presentation.

- Choose the Print Preview view of Homestead Realty.
- Navigate through the Homestead Realty presentation using the Print Preview toolbar.
- Switch to the Outline view and experiment with the different zoom levels.
- Change the orientation of the page.
- Close Print Preview then close the presentation without saving changes.

LESSON 3

Managing Clip Art, Drawing Objects, and Animation

In this lesson, you will enhance the Pinnacle Pet Care presentation that you created in the previous lessons. You will use clip art to add interest to the presentation, a drawing object to add spark, and slide transitions and animation to "bring the presentation to life."

IN THIS LESSON

Microsoft Office PowerPoint 2003 objectives covered in this lesson

Objective Number	Skill Sets and Skills	Concept Page References	Exercise Page References
PP03S-1-4	Insert pictures, shapes, and graphics	68–69, 73–74	69–70, 74–76
PP03S-1-5	Insert objects	76–77	78–79
PP03S-2-2	Format pictures, shapes, and graphics	71, 85	72
PP03S-2-4	Apply animation schemes	88	89
PP03S-2-5	Apply slide transitions	85–86	86–87
PP03S-4-1	Organize a presentation	77	
PP03S-4-2	Set up slide shows for delivery	98	98–99
PP03S-4-3	Rehearse timing	96–97	97

Additional learning resources are available at labpub.com/learn/pp03/

Case Study

The Pinnacle Pet Care presentation is evolving nicely. However, Al Smith returns from the Pet World trade show knowing he will have to add some pizzazz to the presentation if he is to compete with his fellow vendors. While Al and Charlene have created an error-free, technically perfect presentation, he can see that something is definitely missing! Charlene suggests sprinkling clip art and drawing objects to illustrate Al's message. Knowing the robust animation tools in PowerPoint 2003, she also encourages Al to consider using animation to give life to the presentation. They decide that if used sparingly, clip art, drawing objects, and animation will enhance the presentation.

You will animate the paragraphs in the bulleted list by having them "fly in from the left" as they are introduced in the presentation.

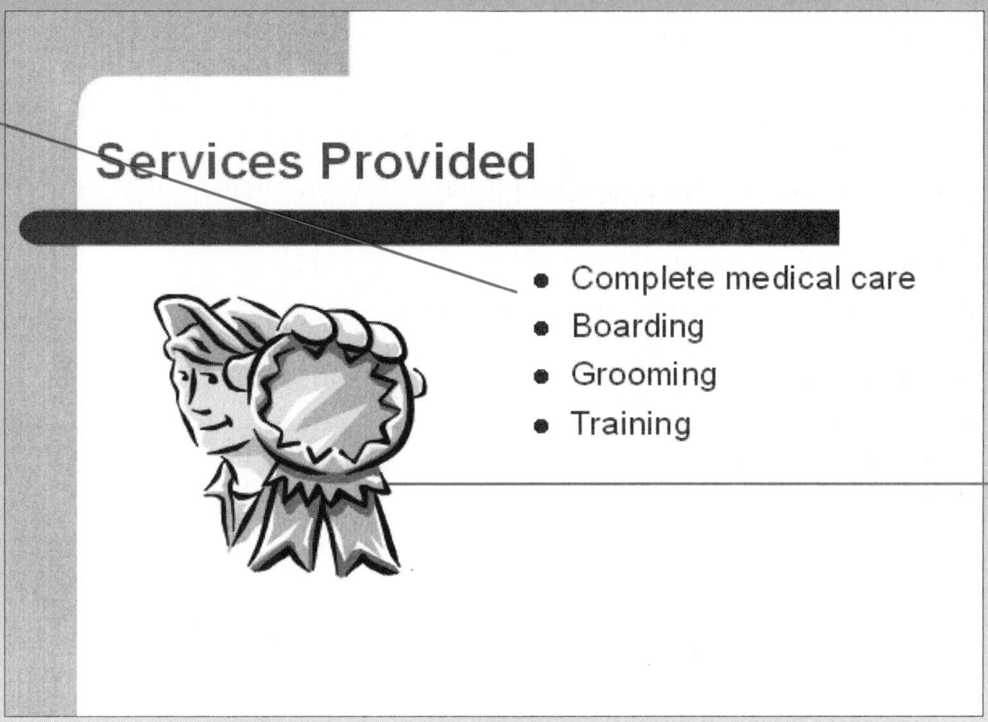

You will insert this clip art image and animate it as well. The picture will "fly in from the left" with a "whoosh" sound as it is introduced.

Working with Clip Art

Microsoft Office Specialist

Adding clip art to your presentations will help you emphasize key points and add polish to the presentation as a whole. Microsoft Office 2003 has a clip art collection of more than 130,000 pieces of art—and it grows daily. There is clip art available for any occasion. In addition to clip art, you can use other media types with PowerPoint slides, including Drawing Object (AutoShapes), photographs, movies, and audio (sound) files.

Content and Clip Art Layouts

In Lesson 2, Designing the Presentation, you worked with layouts that involved a title or title and text combination. These layouts allowed you to easily create slides with a standardized title and bulleted text. PowerPoint's Content Layout and Text and Content Layout categories provide layouts with placeholders for titles, text, and various types of content—including tables, charts, clip art, pictures, diagrams, organization charts, and movies. Using the content layout is effective because content is then automatically positioned within and sized to a placeholder. Likewise, the Other Layouts category on the Slide Layout task pane contains two layouts designed specifically for titles, text, and clip art. Using these clip art layouts greatly simplifies the task of positioning clip art on slides. The placeholder in the Clip Art layout holds the artwork in place. The following illustration describes the clip art layouts.

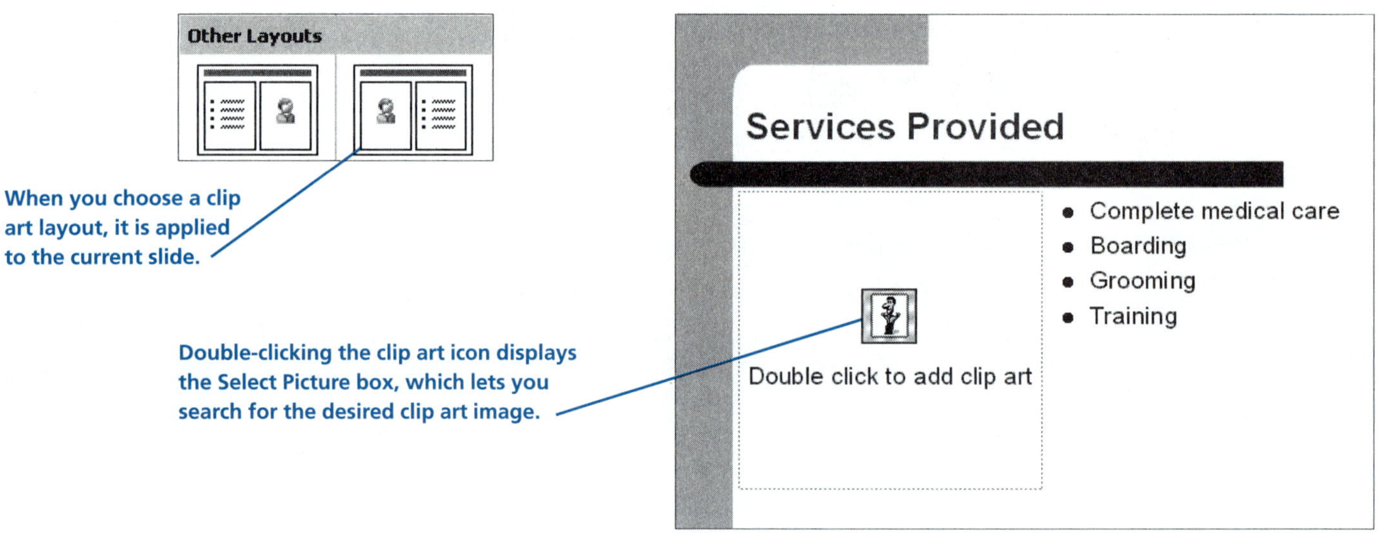

Searching for Clip Art

Finding clip art is easy: Double-click the Clip Art icon in the Title, Text, and Clip Art slide layouts to bring the Select Picture dialog box to your screen. Each piece of clip art is associated with keywords that describe its characteristics. For example, the image shown to the right can be located using the keywords awards, prizes, or ribbons. The following illustration describes the Select Picture box:

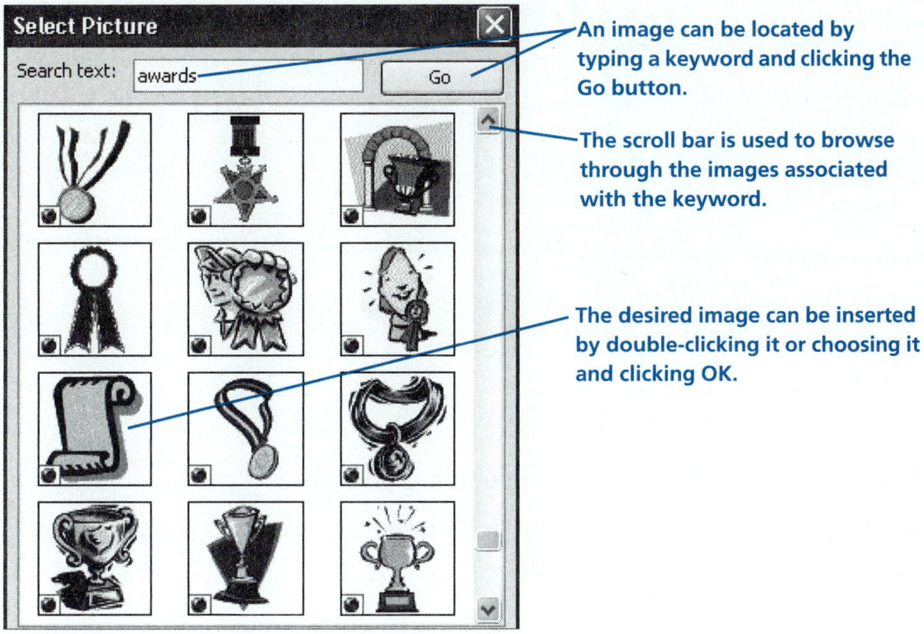

Hands-On 3.1 Insert Clip Art

In this exercise, you will enhance the Pinnacle Pet Care Design presentation using Clip Art.

Open the Presentation and Choose a Slide

1. Start PowerPoint, and the New Presentation task pane should appear.
2. Open the Pinnacle Pet Care Design presentation.
3. If necessary, click the Normal view button to display the presentation in Normal view.
4. Scroll down to the Services Provided slide or choose it on the Slides tab.

Choose a Clip Art Layout

5. Follow these steps to display the Slide Layout task pane. For the remainder of this course, you will simply be instructed to display a particular task pane.

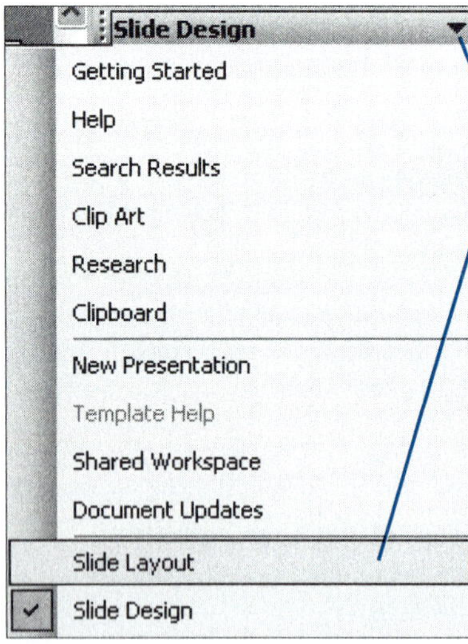

Ⓐ If necessary, choose View→Task Pane to display the task pane.

Ⓑ Click the drop-down button on the task pane and choose Slide Layout.

6. Scroll through the slide layouts until you reach the Other Layouts section.
7. Choose the Title, Clip Art, and Text layout shown to the right and it will be applied to the Services Provided slide.

8. Double-click the clip art icon on the slide to display the Select Picture box.
9. Type **`awards`** in the Search Text box and click the Go button.
   Clip art images associated with the keyword awards *will appear.*
10. Scroll through the list of images and locate the image shown to the right. It should appear in the middle of the list. If the image is not available on your computer then choose any image you like.

11. Double-click the image or choose it and click the OK button.
    The image will be inserted in the slide.

Moving, Sizing, and Rotating Objects

Microsoft Office Specialist

When you click an object (such as a clip art image), sizing handles and a rotate handle appear. You can easily move, size, and rotate selected objects as described in the following illustration.

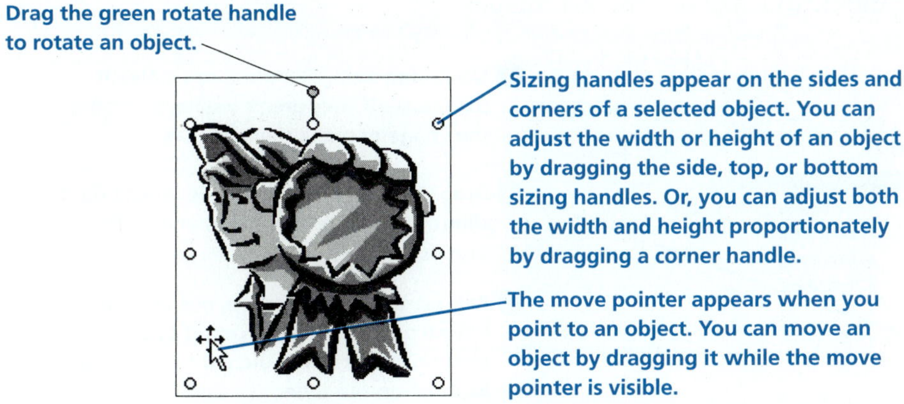

The Format Picture Dialog Box

You can set the size and position of a picture with precision using options on the Format Picture dialog box. The Format Picture dialog box can be displayed by right-clicking a picture and choosing Format Picture from the menu. You can also choose Format→Picture from the menu bar to display the Format Picture box for a selected object. These techniques work with all PowerPoint objects, including placeholders for titles and bulleted lists. The following illustration describes the size and position options on the Format Picture dialog box.

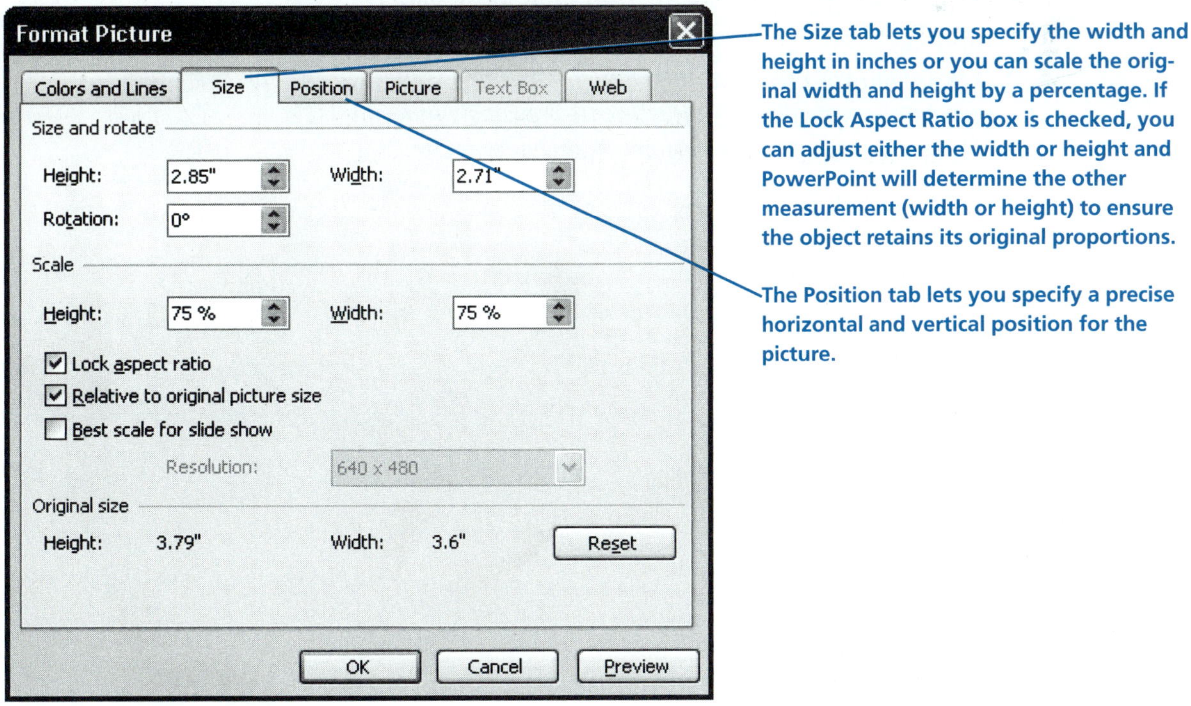

Hands-On 3.2 Move and Size Clip Art

In this exercise, you will manipulate clip art, sizing and moving it to place it on the slide.

1. Follow these steps to move and size the clip art image:

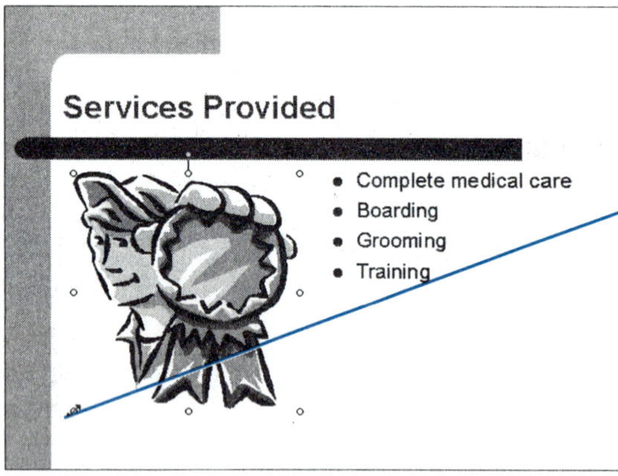

(A) Make sure sizing handles are visible on the image. If they aren't visible, click on the image to make them appear.

(B) Drag this corner sizing handle up and right slightly to reduce the height and width proportionately.

(C) Release the mouse button, position the mouse pointer near the center of the picture, and drag the picture to a different location on the slide.

2. Position the mouse pointer over the picture and click the right mouse button (right-click).
3. Choose Format Picture from the pop-up menu.
4. Click the Size tab in the Format Picture box.
5. Set the Height scaling percentage (not the Height Size and Rotate setting) to 75%.
6. Make sure the Lock Aspect Ratio box is checked and click OK.
   The image will be 75% of its original size. The scaling percentage overrides any adjustments previously made to the size. Because the Lock Aspect Ratio box was checked, it sets the size to 75% of the original size, maintaining both the height and width proportions.
7. Now drag the picture to the approximate position shown to the right.

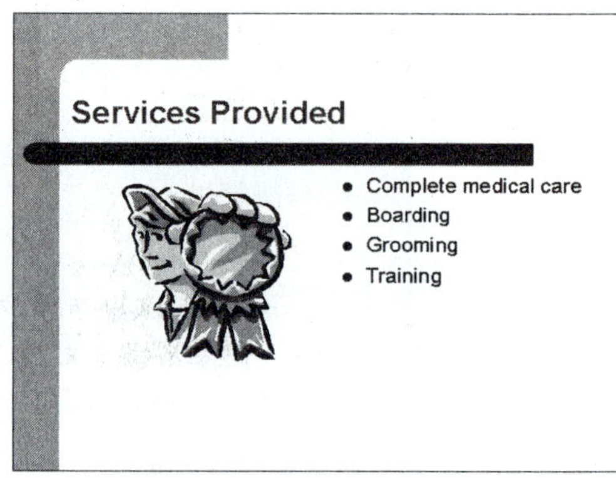

8. Save the presentation as **`Pinnacle Pet Care Art`** and continue with the next topic.

The Clip Art Task Pane

Microsoft Office Specialist

The Clip Art task pane allows you to search for all types of media, including clip art, movies, sounds, and photographs. You can narrow a search by entering a keyword in the Search box. You can also search for an object stored on your computer or online in collections. Collections are explained in the Clip Art Collections section on page 74. The Clip Art task pane also contains the following helpful links:

- **Organize Clips** opens a dialog box in which you can create folders and organize your media objects.
- **Clip Art on Office Online** takes you directly to the Microsoft Office Clip Art and Media Web page.
- **Tips for Finding Clips** opens the Microsoft Office PowerPoint Help window with several links to the tips.

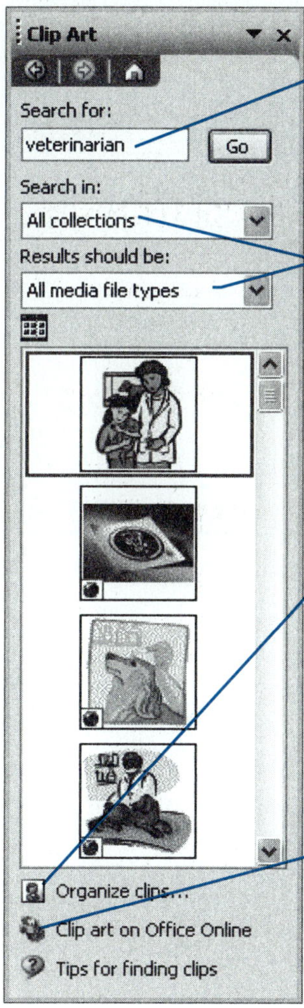

Search for clip art using keywords.

The Search In and Results Should Be lists narrow your search to include only the clip art categories or media types you specify. The Clip Art task pane lets you search for media types other than clip art, including movies, sound files, and pictures.

This option displays the Microsoft Clip Organizer dialog box. The Organizer lets you gather all of the images on your computer, classifying them into categories. Those images become part of the Clip Art collections so when you search for Clip Art, those images are searched as well.

Notice that you can also search for Clip Art through Microsoft Office Online. This site features seasonal clip art, stylized collections, and other media to use as well as offering "clip tips" on how to use clip art.

Clip Art Collections

Each piece of clip art is associated with a group collection. There are three groups of collections available in the Clip Art task pane: My Collections (images on your hard drive), Office Collections (images from PowerPoint), and Web Collections (Microsoft Office Online). One of the advantages of using the Clip Art task pane is that you can search a specific collection instead of browsing more than 130,000 images. The Media File Types section of the Clip Art task pane is also helpful. For example, you can first use the Office Collection then further refine the search by designating only Movies, Animated Gifs to add to your presentation. Examine the following illustration of clip art collections:

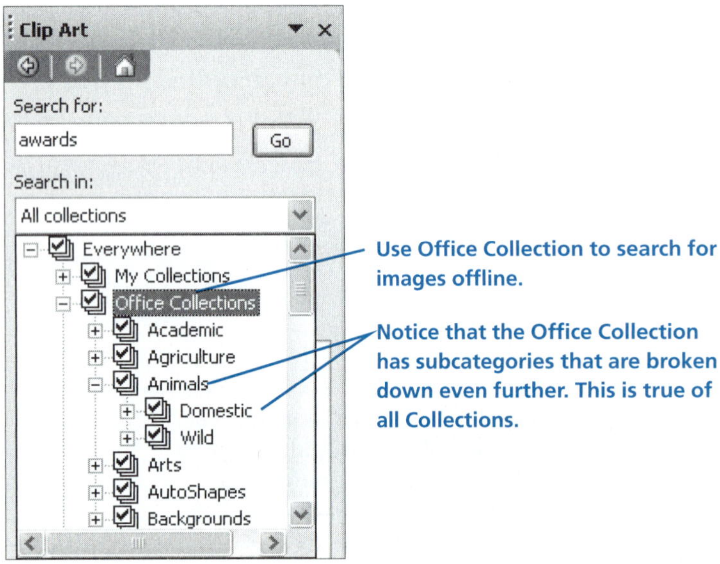

Hands-On 3.3 Use the Clip Art Task Pane

In this exercise, you will work with the Clip Art task pane to insert and position an image into your presentation.

Insert the Image

1. Scroll up to the title slide or click the title slide thumbnail on the Slides tab.
2. Click the Insert Clip Art button on the Drawing toolbar (located at the bottom of the PowerPoint window) or choose Clip Art from the drop-down list at the top of the task pane.
   Whichever button you choose, the Clip Art task pane is displayed.
3. Type **veterinarian** in the Search For box and click the Go button on the task pane.

4. Follow these steps to insert an image:

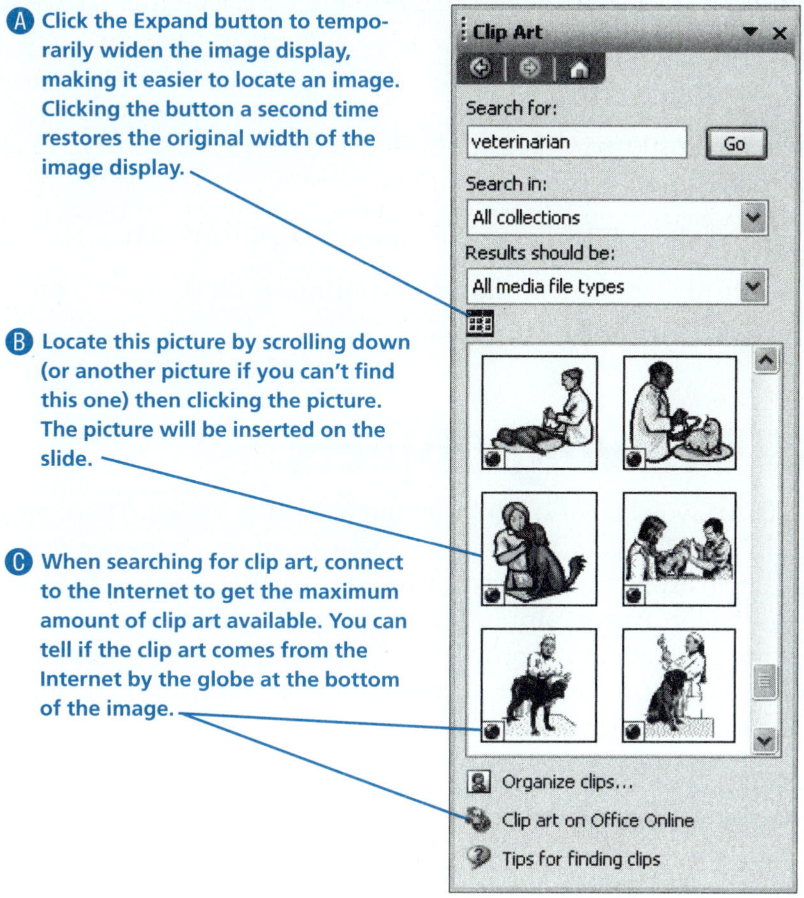

Size and Position the Image

In the next few steps, you will use the Format Picture box to specify a precise size and location for the picture.

5. Right-click the picture and choose Format Picture from the menu.

6. Click the Size tab in the Format Picture box.

7. Set the height to 2.2" (not the height scaling) and make sure the Lock Aspect Ratio box is checked.

8. Click the Position tab.

9. Set the Horizontal position to 1" from the Top Left Corner and the Vertical position to 4.3" from the Top Left Corner.

10. Click OK and your slide should match the preceding illustration.

11. Save the changes to your presentation and continue with the next topic.

Working with Drawing Objects

Microsoft Office **Specialist**

In addition to Clip Art, you can also add drawing objects to a slide. There may be times when Clip Art just doesn't fit with your message. You may want to emphasize the point using something other than a clip art picture. In cases like this, use the Drawing Toolbar to create images that highlight your point. PowerPoint has an excellent set of drawing tools that let you draw lines, arrows, rectangles, callouts, WordArt, and a variety of other objects. The drawing toolbar can be displayed by choosing View→Toolbars→Drawing command. The following illustration describes the buttons on the Drawing toolbar.

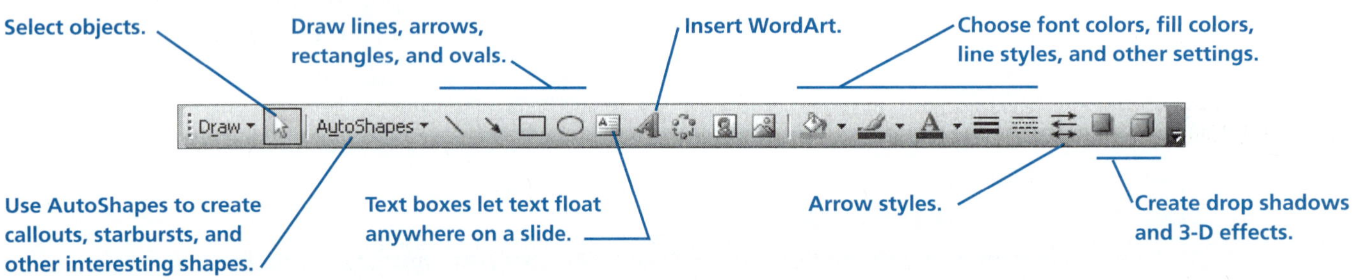

AutoShapes and Other Shapes

You can use AutoShapes to add a variety of fun shapes to your presentations. AutoShapes are predefined shapes organized into categories, such as stars and banners, callouts, and flowchart symbols.

You choose AutoShapes with the [AutoShapes ▾] button on the Drawing toolbar. You can also draw lines, arrows, rectangles, and ovals in your presentations. To draw a shape, click the desired button on the Drawing toolbar then click and drag on a slide.

TIP! *Press the* [Shift] *key while drawing AutoShapes to create symmetrical shapes.*

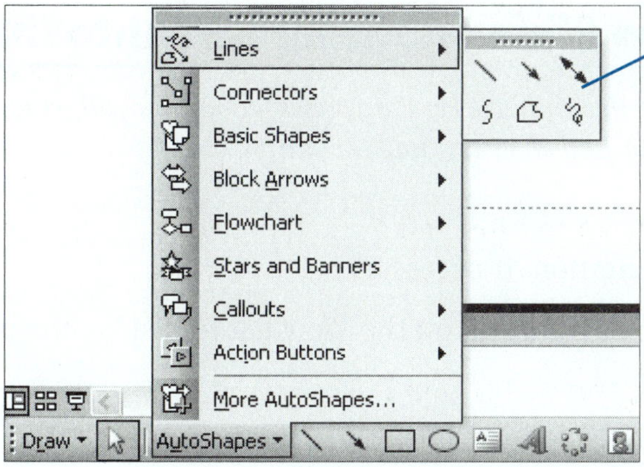

AutoShapes are organized into categories. You choose a shape from a category and click or drag on a slide to draw the shape.

You use these tools to draw lines, arrows, rectangles, and ovals.

Entering and Formatting Text in AutoShapes

You can enter text into an AutoShape by simply typing the desired text while the AutoShape is selected. You can format your AutoShape text by first selecting the text then using the text formatting buttons on the Formatting and Drawing toolbars.

Grids and Guides

Microsoft Office Specialist

As you work with clip art (images) or objects, it will become important to align the graphic with the text associated with it or even with another image or object. Use the Grid and Guide feature to help you to approximate placement of the graphic. The Guide is especially helpful in keeping the message lined up with the appropriate graphic image. The Grid and Guide feature is activated by going to View→Grid and Guide. Examine the Grid and Guide dialog box in the following illustration:

The Snap To section enables you to snap objects to a grid or each other (align them with a grid or with other objects).

Grid Settings allow you to manipulate the spacing and display the grid on the screen.

Guide settings allow you to display the drawing guides on the screen.

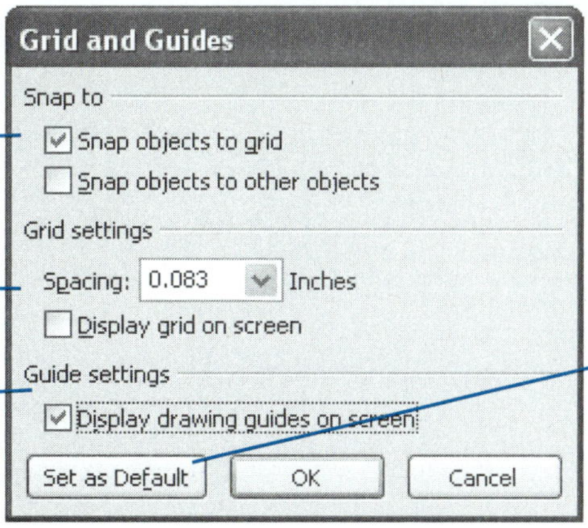

The Set as Default button indicates that the setting you choose will become the default for presentations.

Hands-On 3.4 Set Up a New Slide and Insert an AutoShape

In this exercise, you will add a new slide to the Pinnacle Pet Care presentation. You will set up a bulleted list, position a starburst AutoShape on the slide, and enter text into the starburst.

Set Up a New Slide

1. Open the Pinnacle Pet Care presentation, if necessary.
2. If necessary, click the Normal view button on the View bar to display the presentation in Normal view.
3. Choose the Welcome Aboard Specials slide (sixth slide).
4. Click the New Slide button.
5. Click the Title box and type the phrase **Numerous Awards**.
6. Click the bulleted list box and type the bulleted list to the right.

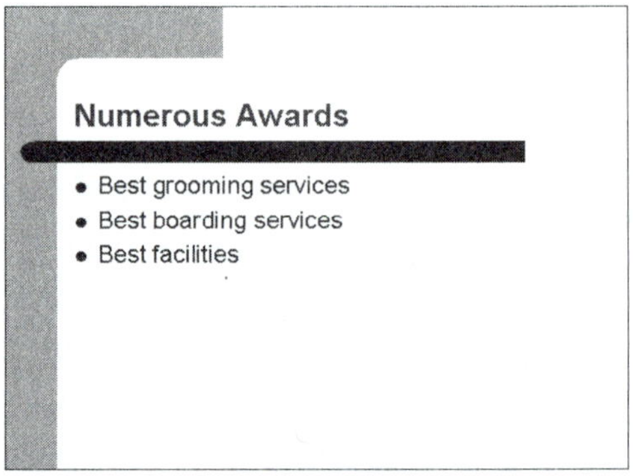

Insert and Format a Starburst AutoShape

7. Click the AutoShapes button on the Drawing toolbar. If the Drawing toolbar is not visible near the bottom of the PowerPoint window, choose View→Toolbars→Drawing to display it.
8. Follow these steps to choose a starburst shape:

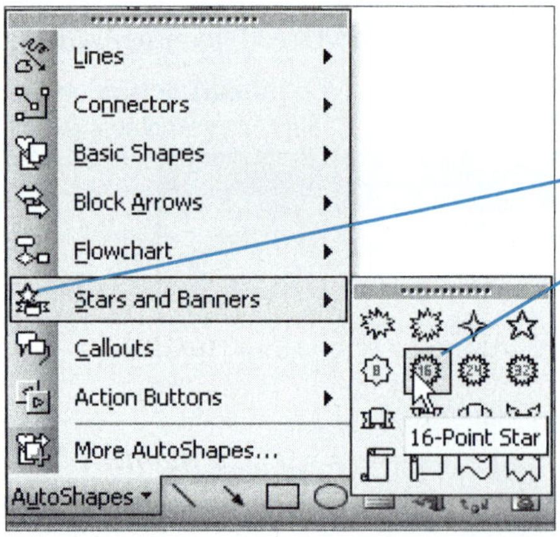

A Slide the mouse pointer up and down this list, noticing the variety of AutoShapes.

B Point to Stars and Banners.

C Choose the 16-Point Star shape.

9. Follow these steps to draw the starburst:

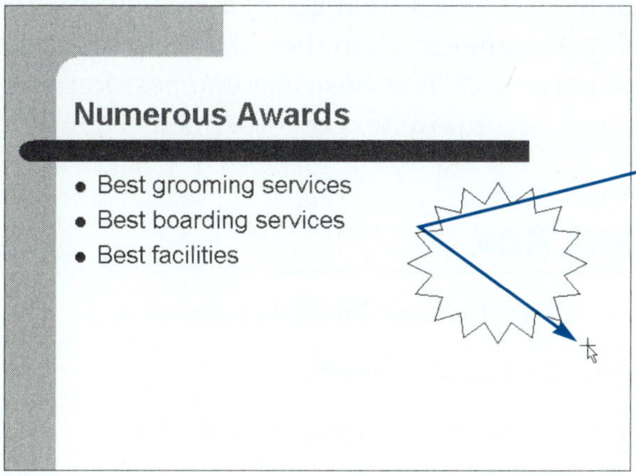

A Position the mouse pointer here and drag down to the right until the starburst has approximately this shape and size. You can press the [Shift] key while dragging to create a symmetrical starburst.

B Release the mouse button then release the [Shift] key to complete the starburst. PowerPoint will format the starburst with a default fill color.

10. Make sure the starburst is selected then type the phrase **`Best Pet Care Award`**.

11. Tap [Enter] and type **`Pets Magazine`**.

12. Follow these steps to format the text:

A Select the text by dragging the mouse over it, as shown here.

B Use the Font Size button on the Formatting toolbar to set the font size to `16`.

C Use the Font Color [A] button on the Drawing toolbar to apply the color of your choice to the text. You can use the More Colors button on the menu that pops up to display a palette with a large number of available colors.

13. Select the phrase *Best Pet Care Award* then click the Bold [B] button.

14. Select the phrase *Pets Magazine* then click the Italics [I] button.
You will adjust the size, position, and formatting of the starburst in a moment.

15. Save the changes to your presentation and continue with the next topic.

Text Boxes

You use the Text Box tool to draw text boxes. Text boxes are one of the most useful drawing objects. Text boxes look like rectangles when they are inserted; however, unlike rectangles, text boxes allow you to enter text. Text boxes let you position text anywhere on a slide. You can also use text boxes to superimpose text on other objects, including AutoShapes.

Hands-On 3.5 Insert a Text Box

In this exercise, a text box will be inserted in the Pinnacle Pet Care presentation.

1. Click the Text Box button on the Drawing toolbar.
2. Follow these steps to position a text box and to enter text within it:

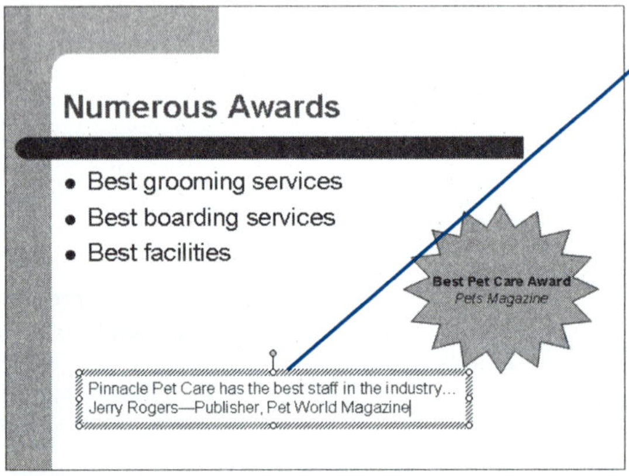

(A) Click the mouse pointer here to place an empty text box on the slide.

(B) Type the phrase `Pinnacle Pet Care has the best staff in the industry.` The text box will widen as you type the text.

(C) Tap [Enter] and type `Jerry Rogers--Publisher, Pet World Magazine.` You can create the em dash symbol between the last name Rogers and the title Publisher by typing two hyphens (without spaces). PowerPoint will convert the hyphens to an em dash when you tap the spacebar before typing the phrase Pet World Magazine.

3. Select the phrase *Jerry Rogers—Publisher, Pet World Magazine*.
4. Change the font size of the selected phrase to 12 and click the Italics button.
5. Save the changes to your presentation and continue with the next topic.

Formatting Objects

You can format text boxes, AutoShapes, clip art, and other objects using options on the Format dialog box associated with each object type. There are many ways to display the Format dialog box. The easiest way is to double-click on the object. You will notice that the title bar of the dialog box reflects the type of object (AutoShape, text box, etc.) as shown in the example to the right. Another way to display the dialog box is to right-click on the object and choose Format… from the pop-up menu. Finally, you can select the object, click Format on the menu bar, and click the bottom item on the drop-down list, which displays the type of object selected.

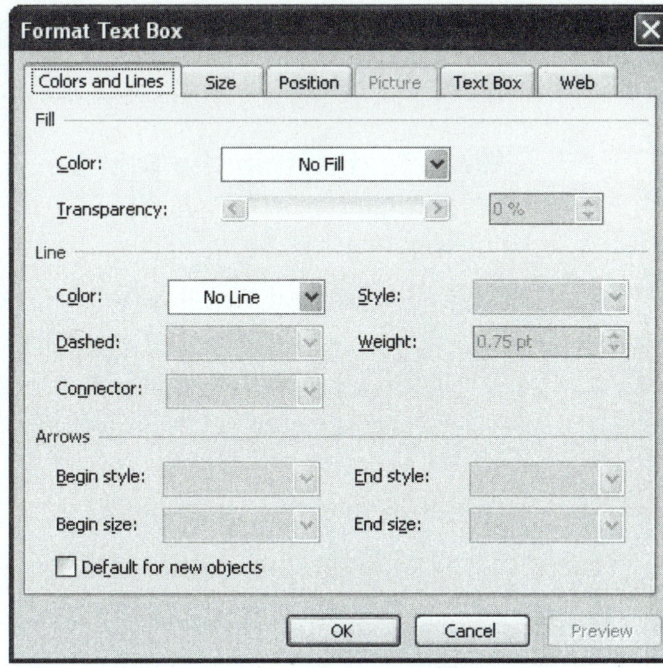

Wrap Text Options

The Text Box tab in the Format Text box contains options that affect the way text behaves within text boxes and AutoShapes. The following illustration describes these options.

This option automatically wraps text within a text box or AutoShape if the box is not wide enough to hold the text. The box height will expand automatically to contain all of the text. The word wrap option is activated when you create a text box by dragging or if you adjust the size of a text box after creating it.

You can change the size of the text box or AutoShape to fit the enclosed text.

You can rotate text 90 degrees.

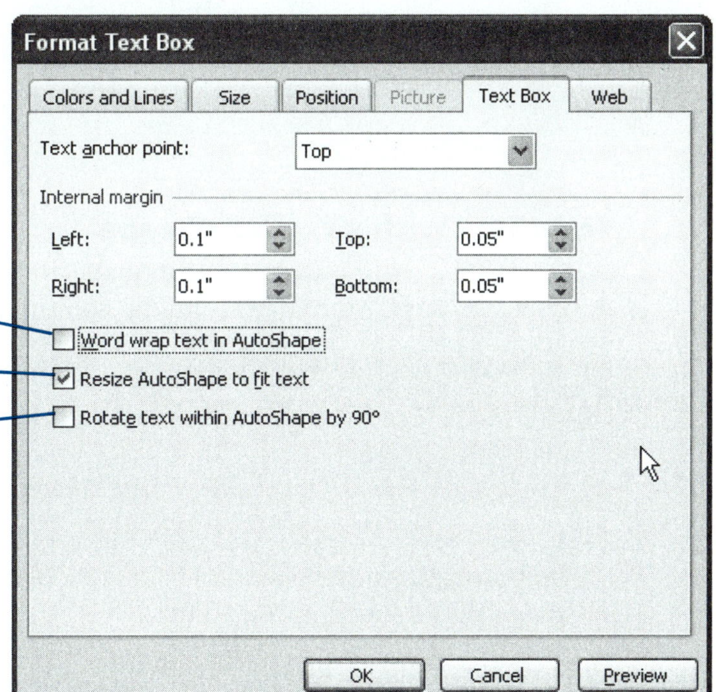

Hands-On 3.6 Use the Wrap Text Feature

In this exercise, you will wrap text within the text box and starburst AutoShapes.

Wrap Text within the Text Box

1. Position the mouse pointer anywhere on the text box and click the right mouse button (right-click).
2. Choose Format Text Box from the pop-up menu.
3. Click the Text Box tab in the dialog box.
   Notice that the Word Wrap Text in AutoShape option is unchecked. This option is unchecked because you created the text box by clicking on the slide. The option would have been checked if you had created the text box by dragging on the slide.
4. Check the Word Wrap Text in AutoShape box and click OK.
5. Follow these steps to adjust the size of the box and to align the text:

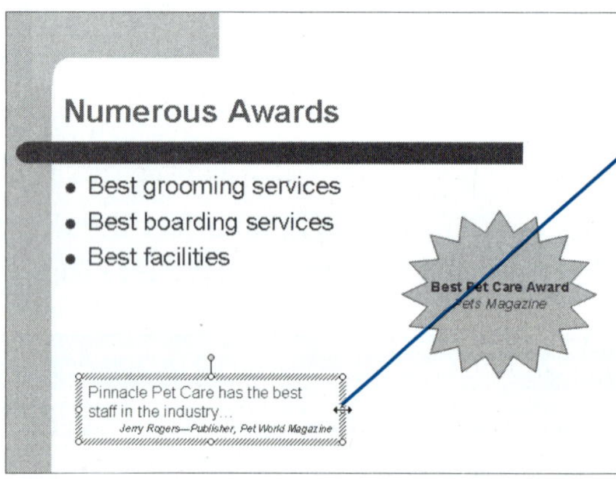

A Position the mouse pointer on this sizing handle and drag to the left until the box has approximately this size. The text will wrap, as shown here, and the box height will expand.

B Click this line then click the Align Right button on the Formatting toolbar.

Wrap Text within the AutoShape

6. Right-click on the starburst AutoShape and choose Format AutoShape from the pop-up menu.
7. If necessary, click the Text Box tab.
8. Check the Word Wrap Text in AutoShape box and click OK.
   The first line should wrap within the AutoShape.
9. If necessary, adjust the size and positions of the text box and AutoShape until your slide matches the example shown to the right.

10. Save the changes to your presentation and continue with the next topic.

Formatting Buttons on the Drawing Toolbar

The Drawing toolbar has several buttons that let you format drawing objects. You can use the Drawing toolbar to format AutoShapes, rectangles, ovals, lines, text boxes, and other drawing objects. To format an object, you must select the object first then apply the desired format(s). You can also select several objects and format them as a group. The following Quick Reference table discusses the formatting buttons on the Drawing toolbar.

QR

QUICK REFERENCE: FORMATTING BUTTONS ON THE DRAWING TOOLBAR

Button	Function
Fill Color	Fills an object with a solid color, pattern, or gradient
Line Color	Changes the color of lines or applies a line pattern
Font Color	Changes the font color of text in a text box or other object
Line Style	Changes the thickness and style of lines and object borders
Dash Style	Formats lines and borders with various dash styles
Arrow Style	Applies arrowheads to lines or changes the arrowhead style of lines
Shadow	Applies a shadow effect to objects
3-D	Applies a 3-D effect to object

Draw Menu Options

The Draw button on the Drawing toolbar displays a menu with a wide range of functions. The following illustration shows the Draw menu and describes several of its options.

You can select multiple objects and use the Group option to mark them as a group. You can then format and manipulate the objects as a group.

Set the Grid options, allowing you to easily align drawing objects.

Align objects with one another or distribute them horizontally or vertically on the slide.

Change AutoShape to a different shape.

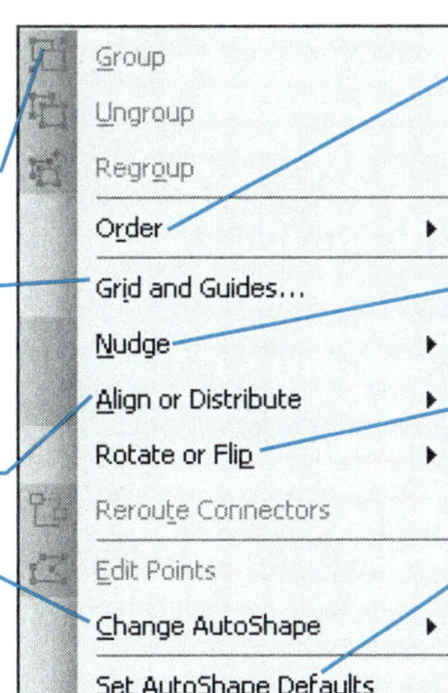

Drawing objects are on invisible layers. You can change the order of the layers to position objects in front of or behind other objects.

Nudge objects up, down, left, or right.

Rotate or flip objects.

Change the default AutoShape settings to the settings used by the currently selected AutoShape.

Bullets and Numbering Styles

While the default styles of the Bullet and Numbering formats may be fine, it is good to know that you can change those styles at any time. To make changes to the Bullets and Numbering style, choose Format→Bullets and Numbering to display the Bullets and Numbering dialog box. The type of bullet or number can be modified by simply choosing a preset style, or by creating your own style using symbols.

Hands-On 3.7 Change Bullet Characters

In this exercise, you will create a new style of bullet for your presentation using Bullets and Numbering.

1. Select the three bulleted paragraphs on the Numerous Awards slide. You can either drag over the paragraphs or click an edge of the placeholder.
2. Choose Format→Bullets and Numbering from the menu bar.
   Notice the several different bullet styles from which you can choose. In the next few steps, you will choose a different character from a character symbol set.
3. Click the [Customize...] button to display the Symbol dialog box.
4. Follow these steps to explore the Symbol dialog box and choose a symbol:

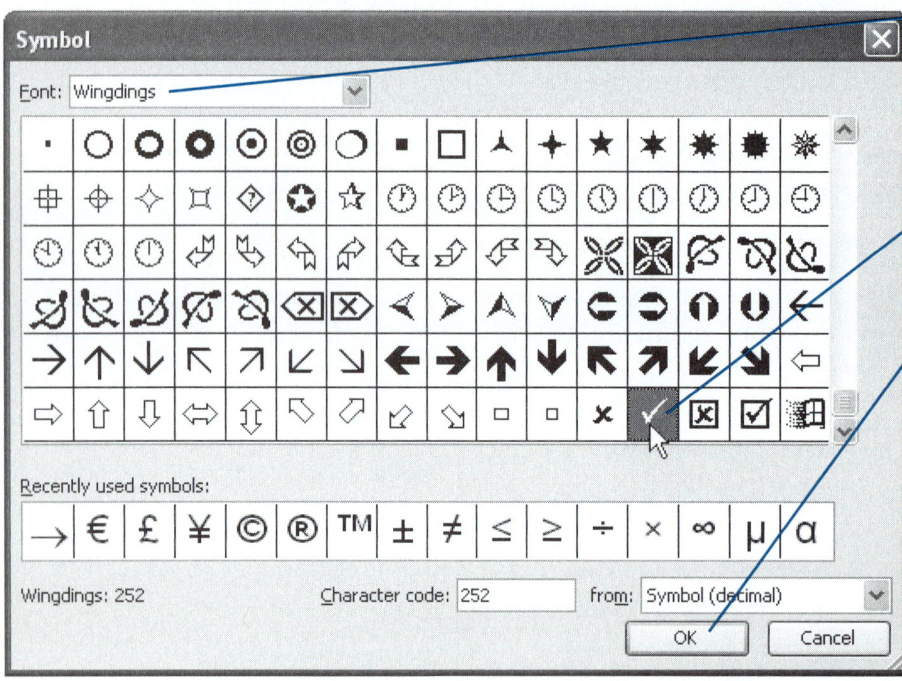

A Make sure the Wingdings character set is selected. You can choose from several character sets.

B Click the various characters to display pop-up previews of them.

C Scroll down and choose the checkmark character or any character of your choice.

D Click OK and the Custom option will be highlighted because you just chose a custom bullet.

E Click OK again to apply the custom checkmark bullet to the paragraphs.

5. Feel free to experiment with any of the drawing object topics discussed in this lesson.
6. Save the changes to your presentation and continue with the next topic.

Working with Animation

Microsoft Office **Specialist**

Animation can add life, energy, and vibrancy to an otherwise static presentation. In PowerPoint 2003, animation comes in many flavors. There are preset animation schemes, transitions, audio clips, and custom animation. You can even time the animation to synchronize with your prepared speech throughout the presentation. Animation, used sparingly, can beautifully accentuate a key point.

Transitions

Microsoft Office **Specialist**

A transition in PowerPoint is the animation between slides. Transitions put zest and excitement in your presentation and provide distinct breaking points between slides. There are more than 40 transition effects available in PowerPoint.

Slide Sorter View and the Slide Transition Task Pane

The majority of time, you will want to create a transition for the entire slide slow. Using the Slide Sorter view is a quick and easy way to accomplish this task. Transitions can be applied to a single slide, multiple slides, or to all slides in a presentation. When a transition is applied, it animates the entire slide, not individual elements of the slide.

The Transition button is displayed on the Slide Sorter toolbar. When you are in the Slide Sorter view, the Slide Sorter toolbar automatically appears. At the click of the Transition button, the Slide Transition task pane is displayed. This task pane allows you to choose transition effects and settings. The following illustration describes the options available on the Slide Transition task pane.

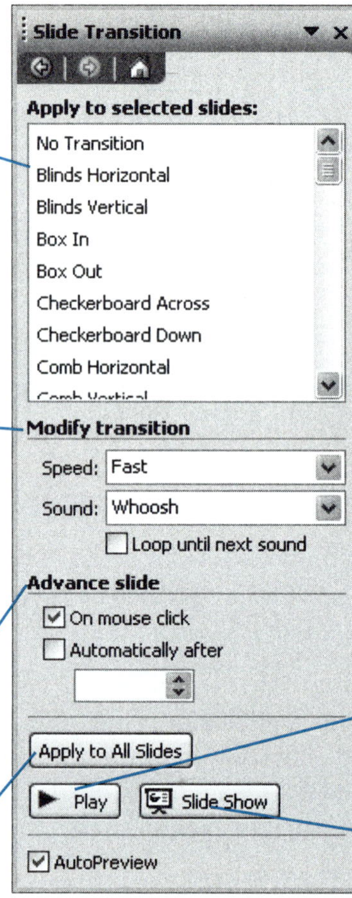

Hands-On 3.8 Apply Transition Effects

In this exercise, you will apply the Dissolve transition to all slides except the title slide. In Hands-On 3.10 and Hands-On 3.11 you will create a more dramatic effect for the title slide.

Choose Transition Effects

1. Click the Slide Sorter button on the View bar.
   The Slide Sorter toolbar will appear, although it may be positioned to the right of the Standard toolbar.
2. Click the Transition button on the Slide Sorter toolbar to display the Slide Transition task pane. If this button is not visible, click the drop-down button at the top of the task pane and choose Slide Transition.

3. Follow these steps to select multiple slides and choose a transition effect:

A Click the Services Provided slide, press and hold the [Shift] key, and click the last slide in the presentation. This selects all slides except the title (opening) slide.

B Scroll through the list of transition effects and choose Dissolve. The effect will briefly be previewed on all selected slides.

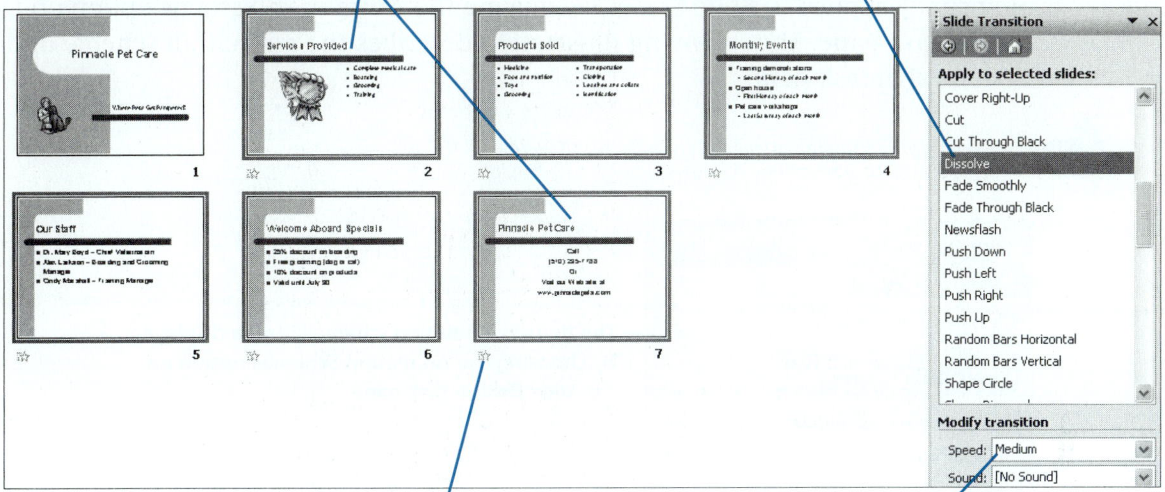

C Notice that all slides except the title slide have an icon indicating that a transition has been applied to them.

D Set the transition speed to Medium.

Run the Presentation

4. Click the title slide.
   At this point, only the title slide should be selected. In the next step, you will run the presentation. Selecting the title slide will force the presentation to begin with that slide.

5. Click the Slide Show button on the View bar.
   The title slide will appear without a transition. The title slide would have opened with the Dissolve transition if you had applied the transition to it.

6. Click the mouse button and the title slide will dissolve into the Services Provided slide.

7. Continue to click the mouse button until the presentation is complete and the Slide Sorter window reappears.

8. Feel free to experiment with the transition effects.

9. Save the changes and continue with the next topic.

Animation Schemes

Microsoft Office Specialist

Animation schemes are preset visual effects applied to text elements on slides. PowerPoint provides a large number of animation schemes that can easily be applied to a single slide, a group of slides, or an entire presentation. An animation scheme usually includes effects for slide titles and additional effects for the bullets or paragraphs on a slide. Animation schemes are usually applied in Slide Sorter view using the Animation Scheme option on the Slide Design task pane. The following illustration describes the animation scheme options on the Slide Design task pane.

TIP! *Animation schemes override transition effects.*

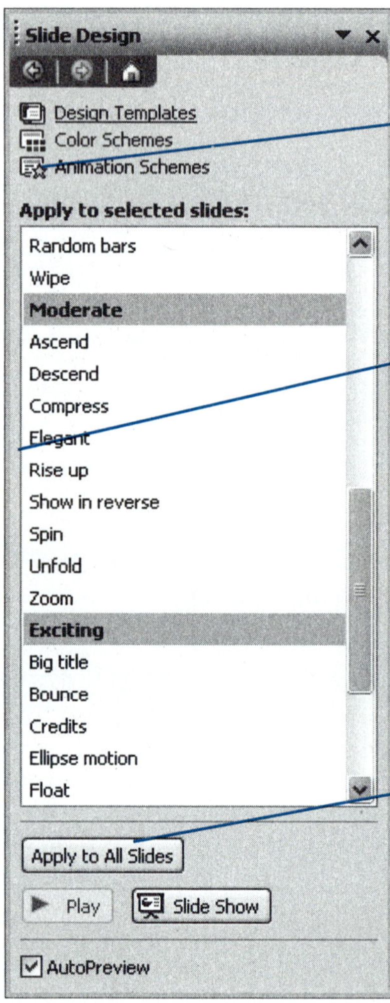

The built-in animation schemes can be displayed by choosing the Animation Schemes option on the Slide Design task pane.

The animation schemes are organized into Subtle, Moderate, and Exciting categories depending on the level of effects in the scheme.

A chosen scheme is applied to the selected slides or to all slides in the presentation if the Apply to All Slides button is clicked.

Hands-On 3.9 Apply an Animation Scheme

In this exercise, you will apply an animation scheme to the Pinnacle Pet Care presentation.

1. Click the Design button on the Slide Sorter toolbar to display the Slide Design task bar.
2. Choose the Animation Schemes option at the top of the task bar to display the animation schemes.
3. Click the Services Provided slide.
   You will test the various animation effects on this slide. Once you choose an effect, you will apply it to all of the slides in the presentation.
4. Click an animation effect; it will be previewed on the slide.
5. Scroll through the list of animation effects, clicking any effects that interest you.
6. Now scroll through the list of effects until the Exciting category is visible.
7. Try some of the exciting effects—such as Big Title, Ellipse Motion, and Neutron.
8. Choose the Float effect when you have finished experimenting.
9. Click the Apply to All Slides button to apply the effect to all slides in the presentation.
10. Click the title slide then click the Slide Show button at the bottom of the task pane.
11. Work through the presentation by clicking the mouse to introduce objects and advance from slide to slide.
    Notice that the animation effects have replaced the transition effects.
12. Complete the presentation and return to slide sorter view.

Custom Animation

With custom animation, you can individually set the animation for each element of a slide. For example, you can apply animation effects to individual titles, bulleted paragraphs, clip art images, and other objects. With custom animation, you can control the visual effects, timing, and sequencing of the animation process.

Applying Custom Animation Effects

Custom animation requires intense work in which you specify how each element on your slide is to be animated. When you apply custom animation effects, each object must first be selected. To do this, work in the Normal view. Using the Custom Animation task pane, apply the custom animation effects throughout your slide show. Customizing the animation of your presentation is a laborious and time-consuming task. If your presentation is large, it is wise to use Animation Schemes. The following illustration describes the options on the Custom Animation task pane.

Animation effects are applied to the selected object.

The Start option specifies whether the animation starts on a mouse click or after the previous event (the introduction of the subtitle), as in this example.

The desired effect is chosen from the Add Effect list. In this example, the Fly In effect is chosen.

Removes an animation effect.

You can specify the direction and speed of the Fly In effect.

Change the sequence in which custom animation occurs here.

Animation effects are listed here. In this example, the text effects set up by the animation scheme are listed first, followed by this custom animation effect. You can choose an effect from the list and make modifications as desired. You can also remove the effect here. Clicking the drop-down button displays a menu of effect options, including sound effects.

Hands-On 3.10 Apply Custom Animation

In this exercise, you will apply custom animation to the Title and Services Provided slides.

Animate Clip Art on the Title Slide

1. Click the Normal view button on the View bar.
   Custom animation is applied to individual objects on slides, so you will work in Normal view.
2. Choose the title slide to display it in the main part of the window.
3. Click the clip art image to select it.

4. Follow these steps to specify the custom animation settings for the clip art object:

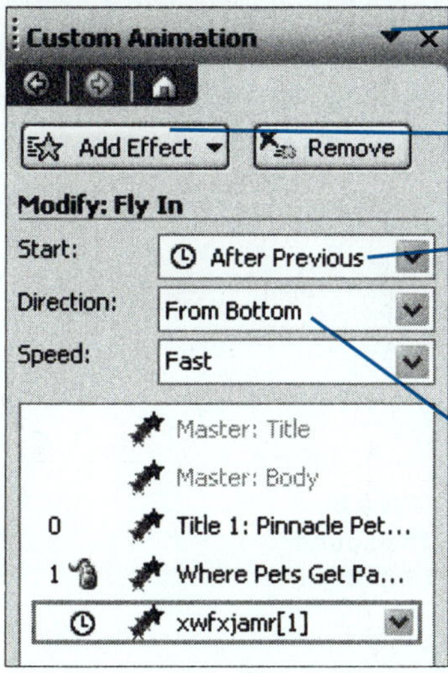

A Click the task bar drop-down button and choose Custom Animation.

B Click the Add Effect button and choose Entrance→Fly In.

C Set the Start option to After Previous. This instructs the clip art animation to begin immediately after the previous event completes. In this case, the previous event is the subtitle introduction.

D Set the direction of the entrance to From Bottom and the speed to Fast.

E Now click the Play button at the bottom of the task bar to preview the animation.

Animate Clip Art on the Services Provided Slide

5. Choose the Services Provided slide.
6. Click the clip art object to select it.
7. Click the Add Effect button and choose Entrance→More Effects.
   This displays a list of additional entrance effects.
8. Choose the Spiral In effect from the Exciting section and click OK.
9. Set the Start option to After Previous.
   Once again, this instructs the animation to begin immediately after the previous event ends. The previous event is the introduction of the last bullet.
10. Click the Play button at the bottom of the task pane to preview the animation.
11. Now click the title slide and then click the [Slide Show] button.
12. Click the mouse repeatedly to initiate the various animation events. You can end the presentation by tapping [Esc] after the clip art is animated on the Services Provided slide.

Sound Effects

PowerPoint 2003 provides audio clips and sound effects to accompany or accentuate your slide elements. For example, in Hands-On 3.11 you will attach the "whoosh" sound effect to the clip art objects. As the objects are introduced in a presentation, the "whoosh" sound effect will play. The following illustration describes the steps used to apply sound effects.

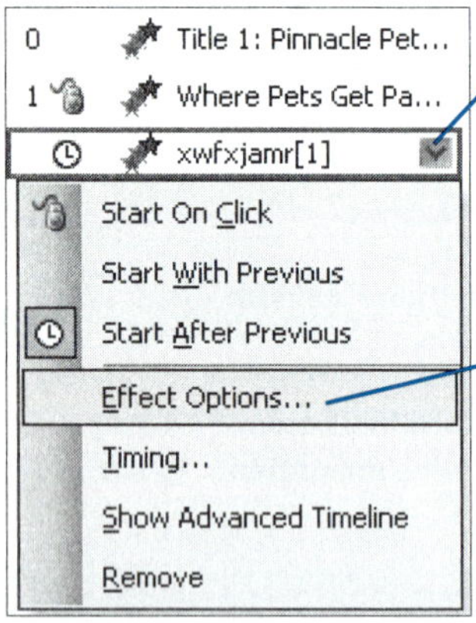

Clicking the drop-down button on a selected animation effect displays a menu of advanced options.

Choosing Effect Options displays a box with Effect and Timing tabs. The Sound option is used to choose a sound effect for the selected object.

Hands-On 3.11 Apply Sound Effects and Modify Animation

In this exercise, you will apply sound to the presentation, run through the slide show with animation, and remove an animation scheme.

Apply Sound Effects

1. Choose the title slide then choose the clip art object.
2. Click the drop-down button for the clip art animation in the task pane and choose Effect Options.
3. Click the Sound drop-down button in the Effect tab, scroll through the list, and choose the Whoosh sound effect.
4. Click OK and the animation and sound will be previewed.
5. Now choose the Services Provided slide and apply the Whoosh sound effect to the clip art object.

Test the Slides

6. Click the title slide then click the [Slide Show] button at the bottom of the Task pane.
7. Click the mouse repeatedly to work through the first two slides in the presentation.
8. Tap the [Esc] key to end the presentation.
9. Now choose the last slide in the presentation and click the [Slide Show] button.

10. Click the mouse to work through the slide. Notice that the introduction of the name, telephone, and Website information is cumbersome.
This information should be introduced as a block. In the remainder of this exercise, you will remove the animation scheme on this slide and replace it with custom animation that introduces the text as you desire.

Remove the Animation Scheme from the Closing Slide

11. End the presentation and make sure the closing slide is visible.

12. Follow these steps to remove the animation scheme from the slide:

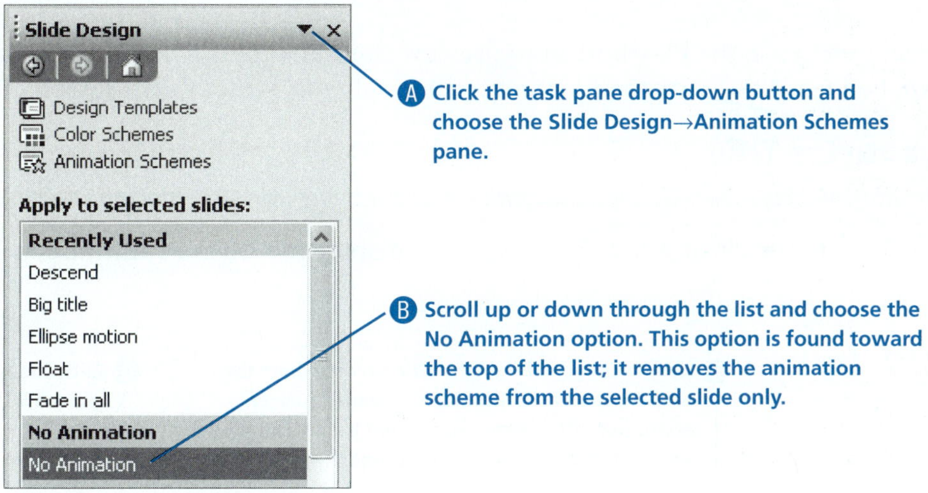

13. Notice that the Play button at the bottom of the task pane is not available.
This is because the animation scheme has been removed from the slide.

Apply a Transition Effect

Animation schemes apply transition effects and animation to slides. In the next few steps, you will do a little detective work to identify the transition effect that was applied to slides by the Float animation scheme in Hands-On 3.9. Then, you will apply the same transition effect to the closing slide to create consistent transitions between all slides.

14. Click the Welcome Aboard Specials slide.

15. Click the Play button at the bottom of the task pane and notice the transition effect that introduces the slide. Click the button several times, if necessary, until you recognize the effect.

16. Now click the Slide Show button to begin the slide show on the sixth slide. Work through the slide by clicking the mouse and notice that when the closing slide is introduced, no transition effect occurs (nor animation for that matter).

17. End the slide show and make sure the closing slide is visible.

18. Follow these steps to apply a transition:

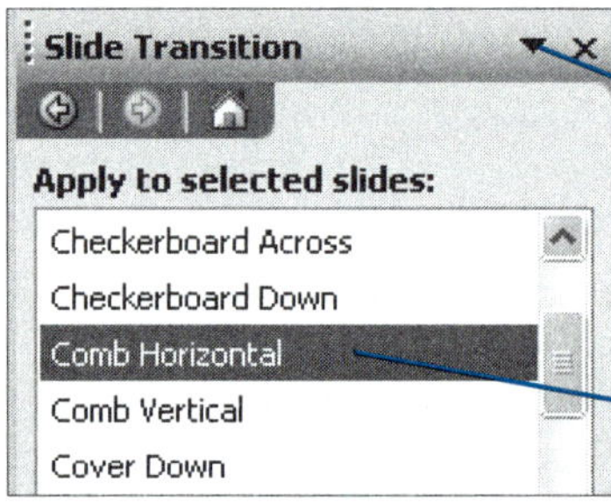

A Click the task pane drop-down button and choose the Slide Transition pane. Normally, transitions are applied to multiple slides using Slide Sorter view. However, you will remain in Normal view since you are applying the transition to just one slide.

B Scroll down and choose the Comb Horizontal transition.

19. Feel free to use the Play button to preview the transition. This is the transition that was applied to all slides by the Float animation scheme earlier in the lesson.

Animate the Title

In the next few steps, you will apply custom animation to the title and information block.

20. Make sure the closing slide is chosen and display the Custom Animation task pane.

21. Follow these steps to animate the title:

A Click the title and the insertion point will be positioned within the title text.

B Now click a border of the title box to select the entire box. This is important because custom animation effects can be applied to individual words or letters within a text object.

C Click the Add Effect button and choose Entrance→More Effects.

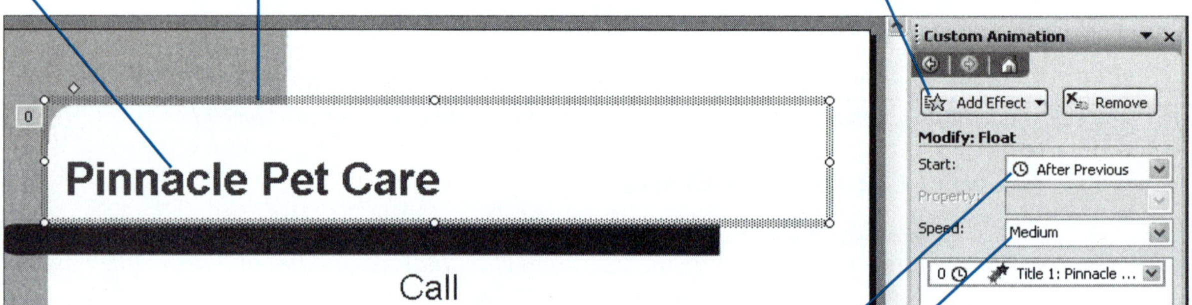

D Choose the Float effect from the Exciting section. This is the same text effect applied to other slides in the presentation by the Float animation scheme.

E Set the Start option to After Previous. This will introduce the title immediately after the previous slide is completed.

F Set the Speed option to Medium. This setting is also used for other slides.

22. Click the Play button at the bottom of the task pane to preview the slide.
Notice that the information block is not animated. You will animate it in the next few steps, and apply the Whoosh sound effect.

Animate the Information Block

23. Click on the telephone number or some other part of the information block.

24. Now click a border of the information block to select the placeholder.

25. Follow these steps to apply animation to the object:

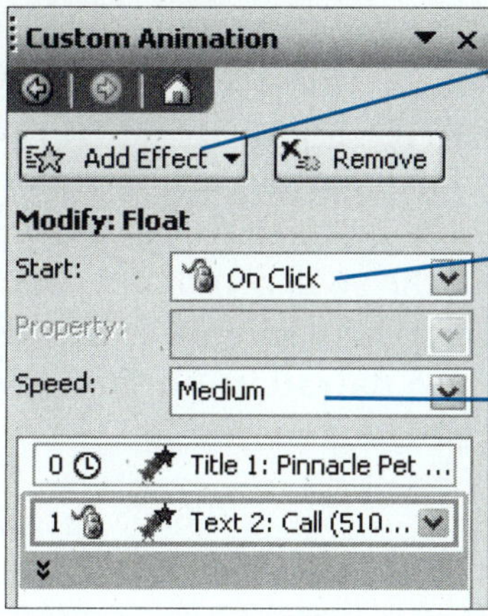

A Click the Add Effect button, choose Entrance, and choose Wipe. If it's not displayed, choose More Effects. And look in the Basic category to find Wipe.

B Leave the Start option set to On Click. We don't want this information presented until the speaker is ready to introduce it.

C Set the Speed option to Medium.

26. Click the Play button at the bottom of the task pane and notice that the individual lines are introduced one at time.
    In this case, introducing the entire block at once with a sound effect will be more dynamic.

27. Make sure the text block is still selected (click the border if it isn't).

28. Click the drop-down button for the information block (the second object on the animation list) and choose Effect Options.

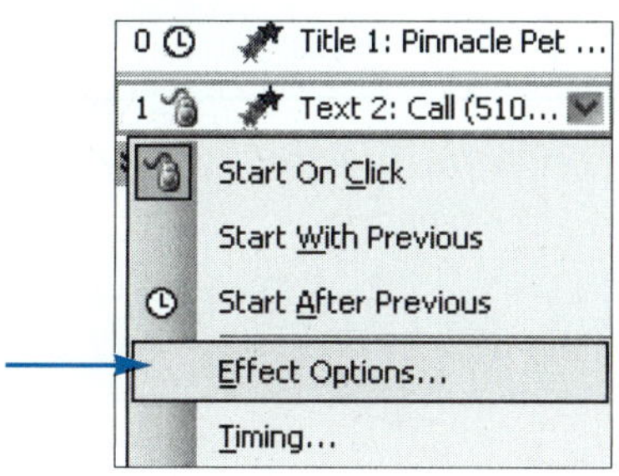

29. Click Effect Options from the drop-down menu and choose the Whoosh effect from the Sounds list.

30. Click the Text Animation tab and choose the As One Object option from the Group Text list.

31. Click OK and the animation will be previewed.

32. Now click the Title slide then click the Slide Show button.

33. Work through the slide show until it is complete.

Creating Timed Animation

You can give momentum to your presentation by automating the movement of slides through the Advance Slide section of the Slide Transitions task pane in PowerPoint 2003. For the most part, when you are presenting to a group manually advancing each slide is preferable since it gives you more control over the flow of the delivery. For example, if a question comes up on a particular slide, you can easily go back and reiterate the point that was missed or just give more detail to the viewer. With a timed presentation, the swiftly moving slides make it awkward to interact with the group or give a smooth presentation. Use the Slide Show→ Rehearse Timings command to add movement (or even narration) to the presentation which will, in effect, deliver the slide show for you.

Setting Timings Manually

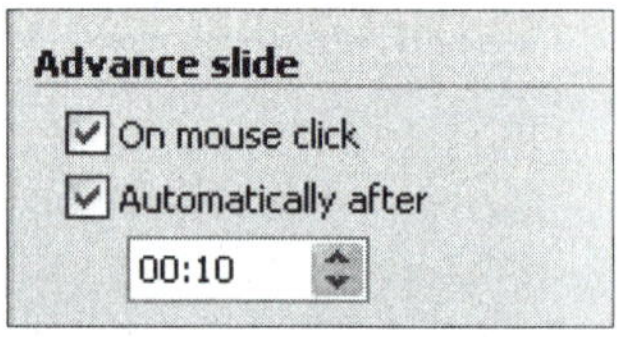

To set up the timing for each slide in your presentation, use the Slide Transitions task pane. The Advance Slide section on the Slide Transitions task pane allows you to determine the amount of time that will elapse between slides or animation. The example to the right shows the Advance Slide option with the On Mouse Click option turned on and the Automatically After option set to 10 seconds. This means the slide will advance after 10 seconds or when the mouse is clicked—whichever comes first. Timings can be set individually for each slide in a presentation.

Hands-On 3.12 Set Timings Manually

In this exercise, you will work with the timing function to automate the slide show.

1. Switch to Slide Sorter view.
2. Display the Slide Transition task bar.
3. Set the Automatically After option to 10 seconds.
4. Click the Apply to All Slides button.
   Notice that each slide now has a 00:10 indicator below it, indicating that the automatic timing is set to 10 seconds.
5. Click the title slide then click the Slide Show button at the bottom of the task pane. Now just sit back and watch your presentation.
   Keep in mind that you set the same timing for all slides. You can also set different timings for each slide.

Rehearsing and Recording Animation Timings

Microsoft Office Specialist

The presentation is created, the clip art added, and the animation complete. If you are setting the slide show to run automatically, now is the time to use PowerPoint's Rehearse Timings feature. This function allows you to walk through each slide of the presentation and preset the time each slide will be viewed. You can time a slide to run 10 seconds or minutes. PowerPoint records the time you set for each slide then applies that timing to the presentation the next time you run it. By using the Rehearse Timings feature, you define the importance of each slide by setting the amount of time you want the viewer to see that slide. The following illustration describes the Rehearsal toolbar.

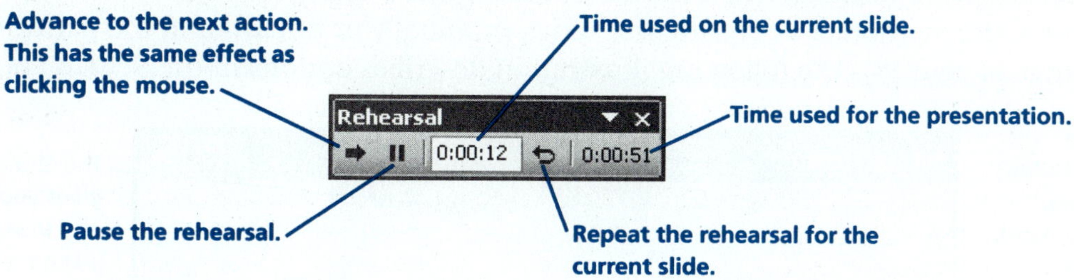

Hands-On 3.13 Record Timings in Rehearsal Mode

In this exercise, you will rehearse the Pinnacle Pet Care slide show, recording the timings per slide.

1. Choose Slide Show→Rehearse Timings and click the Pause button on the Rehearsal toolbar.
   While the rehearsal is paused, take a moment to examine the Rehearsal toolbar. In the next step, you will resume the rehearsal and work through the entire presentation by clicking the mouse. Try to imagine yourself presenting to a group and introduce actions on the various slides as you would in that situation. When you finish the presentation, a message will appear asking if you want to save the timings. You will choose Yes at that point to save the timings.
2. Now, click the Pause button and work through the presentation. When the presentation is finished, choose Yes when PowerPoint asks if you want to save the timings.
3. Look at the various timing indicators under the slides in Slide Sorter view and notice that they differ for each slide.
   PowerPoint replaced the 10 second timings you set earlier with the recorded timings.
4. In the Title slide, click the Slide Show button. Sit back and watch the presentation play with your new recorded timings.
5. Save your changes and continue with the next topic.

Preparing the Slide Show for Delivery

Microsoft Office Specialist

When you prepare the slide show for delivery, you are, in essence, shaping the way the presentation will flow. In the Set Up Show command, you establish the type of show, the show options, the method of delivering the slides (manually or timed), and the performance settings of your PC. The following illustration describes options in the Set Up Show dialog box.

The Show Type section determines the type of slide show, presented by user, viewed by individual or kiosk style. Notice that the menus for each type are dynamic; that is, the choices change depending on the type used.

The Show Options section offers the choice to run the show in a loop (continually), or use voice narration.

The Performance section allows you to tune up the display of the presentation by matching it with your video card. This is an advanced topic that we will not use here.

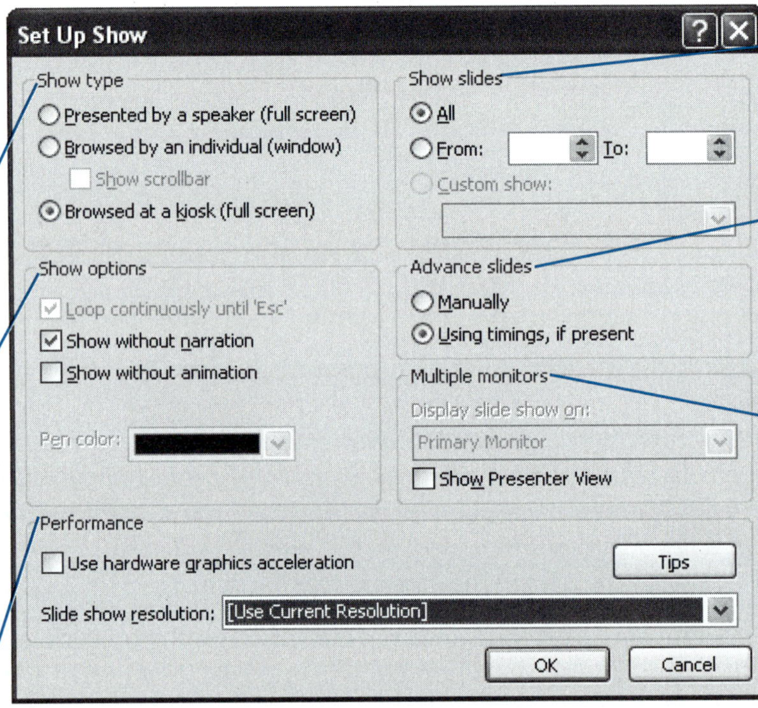

The Show Slides section gives you the opportunity to show all slides or just a few selected slides.

The Advance Slides section sets the show to run manually or with timings.

The Multiple Monitors section offers choices for viewing the slide on multiple monitors.

Hands-On 3.14 Use the Set Up Show Options

In this exercise, you will set up a Kiosk style presentation using the Set up Show Options in PowerPoint.

Run a Kiosk Style Presentation

1. Choose Slide Show→Set up Show from the menu bar.
2. Choose the Browsed at a Kiosk option.
   Notice that the Loop Continuously option is checked and disabled. Kiosk slide shows always loop continuously.
3. Make sure the Using Timings, if Present option is chosen and click OK.
4. Run the slide show. As the slide show runs, move the mouse and try to make the pop-up menu button appear at the bottom-left corner of the slide.
   Notice that the pop-up menu button is not available. Users can tap [Esc] *to end a kiosk style slide show but this is the only command they can execute.*
5. Wait for the slide show to end and watch it restart.
6. Now tap [Esc] to end the slide show.

7. Feel free to experiment with the Set Up Show options.
8. When you have finished, choose Slide Show→Set Up Show from the menu bar.
9. Choose the Presented by a Speaker option.
10. Choose the Manually option to disable the timings and click OK.
11. Save and close the presentation then continue with the end-of-lesson questions and exercises.

Concepts Review

True/False Questions

1.	Clip art can be inserted while working in Normal view.	TRUE	FALSE
2.	Clip art images are associated with keywords that can be used when searching for images.	TRUE	FALSE
3.	Transitions are applied to individual objects on slides.	TRUE	FALSE
4.	Slide Sorter view is the best view to use when setting up transitions.	TRUE	FALSE
5.	You can apply a transition to multiple slides while using Slide Sorter view.	TRUE	FALSE
6.	Animation schemes override transition effects.	TRUE	FALSE
7.	Text objects cannot be animated.	TRUE	FALSE
8.	Clicking the mouse can initiate animation steps and transitions.	TRUE	FALSE
9.	Customized animations are applied to entire slides.	TRUE	FALSE
10.	Animation schemes are used to add clip art to slides.	TRUE	FALSE

Multiple Choice Questions

1. Which of the following actions can be performed on clip art while working in Normal view?
   - a. Rotation
   - b. Sizing
   - c. Moving
   - d. All of the above
2. ________ are affected by animation schemes.
   - a. Titles
   - b. Bulleted lists
   - c. Clip art
   - d. Both a and b
   - e. All of the above
3. Which of the following effects can be controlled through custom animation?
   - a. Timing
   - b. Sound
   - c. Entry effects
   - d. All of the above
4. Custom animation can be applied to ________.
   - a. titles
   - b. bulleted lists
   - c. clip art
   - d. Both a and b
   - e. All of the above

Skill Builders

Skill Builder 3.1 Insert Clip Art

In this exercise, you will add clip art to the Tropical Getaways presentation that you developed in Lesson 2, Designing the Presentation.

1. Open the Tropical Getaways presentation.
2. If necessary, click the Normal view button to switch to Normal view.
3. Choose the Travel Categories slide (the second slide).
4. Display the Slide Layout task pane.
5. Scroll down toward the bottom of the layout list and choose the Title, Text, and Clip Art layout as shown to the right.

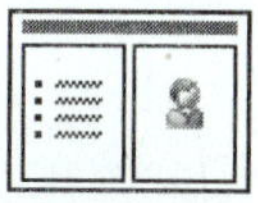

6. Double-click the Insert Clip Art icon to display the Select Picture box.
7. Enter the keyword **`safari`** and click the Go button.
8. Choose a clip art image that appeals to you and click OK.
   If necessary, size and position your clip art image. The example to the right uses the antelope image with the size reduced slightly and the position adjusted slightly.

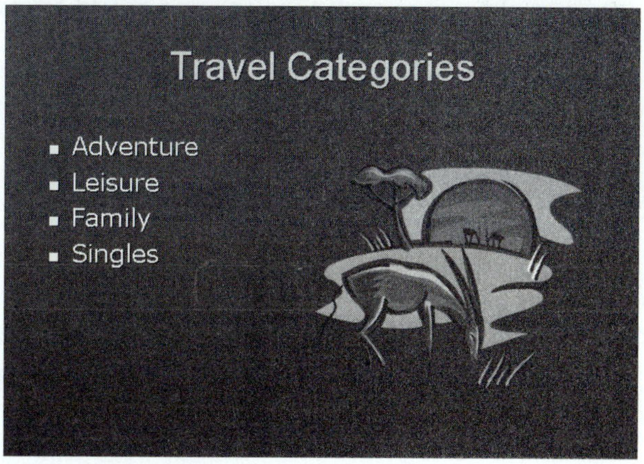

9. Choose the Travel Now and Save slide (the fifth slide).
10. Change the slide layout to Title, Text, and Clip Art.

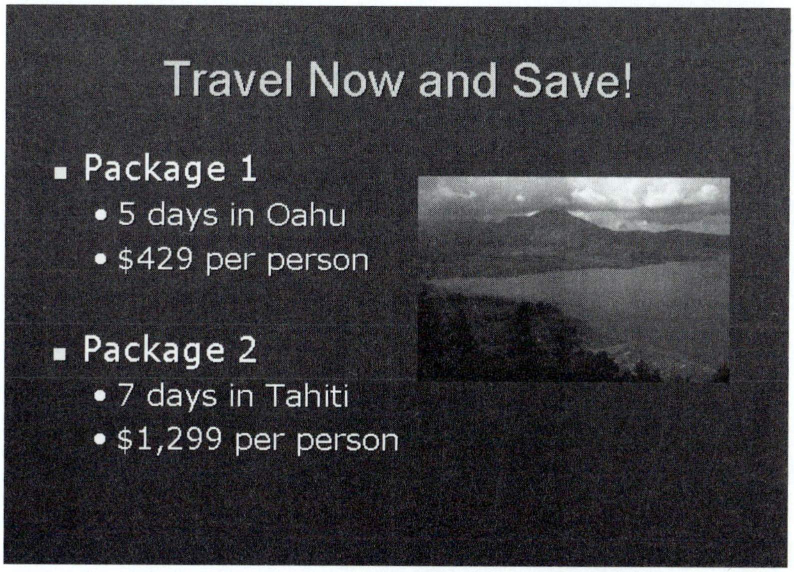

11. Double-click the Insert Clip Art icon and search for clip art using the keyword **`Tropics`**.
12. Choose an image that appeals to you, insert it, and size and position it as needed.
13. Save the changes to your presentation as **`Tropical Getaways Art`** and continue with the next exercise.

Skill Builder 3.2 Apply an Animation Scheme

In this exercise, you will apply an animation scheme to your presentation.

1. Display the Slide Design-Animation Scheme task bar.
2. Scroll through the list of animation schemes and choose Ellipse Motion from the Exciting section.
3. Click the Apply to All Slides button to apply the scheme to all slides in the presentation.
4. Choose the title slide (first slide) and click the Slide Show button at the bottom of the task pane.
5. Work through the presentation and notice the effects introduced by the animation scheme.
   Feel free to choose a different scheme if you don't care for Ellipse Motion. However, if you choose a different scheme, be sure to apply it to all slides.
6. Save your changes and continue with the next exercise.

Skill Builder 3.3 Apply Custom Animation

In this exercise, you will animate clip art images with entry effects and sound.

Animate the Safari Image

1. Make sure you are in Normal view and choose the Travel Categories slide (the second slide).
2. Display the Custom Animation task pane.
3. Click the safari clip art image to select it.
4. Click the Add Effect button and choose Entrance→More Effects.
5. Choose the Grow and Turn effect from the Moderate section and click OK.

6. Set the Start option to After Previous to make the animation begin immediately after the last slide bullet is introduced.

7. Follow these steps to add a sound effect to the animation:

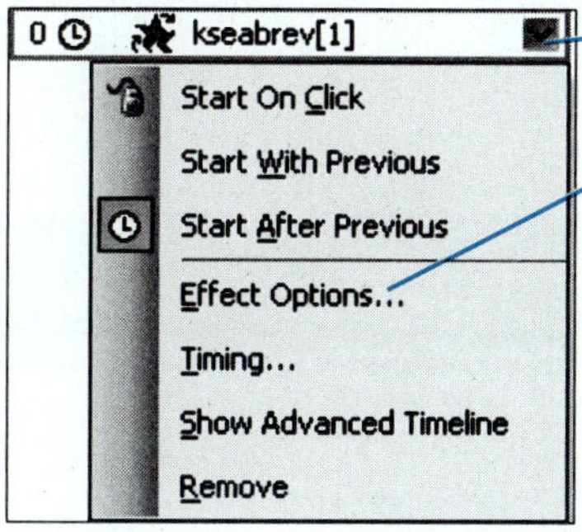

A Click the drop-down button for the custom animation effect.

B Choose Effect Options.

C On the Effect tab, click the Sound drop-down button and choose the Camera effect. This sound effect will compliment the Grow and Turn animation, conveying the feeling of a camera shot.

D Click OK and the animation will be previewed.

Animate the Tropics Image

8. Choose the Travel Now and Save slide (the fifth slide).
9. Click the island image to select it.
10. Click the Add Effects button and choose Entrance→More Effects.
11. Choose the Wedge effect from the Basic category and click OK.
12. Make the animation of the island image start after the previous event has finished.
13. Apply a sound effect you think works well with the island image animation, such as Breeze or Chime effects.
14. Play the slide to make sure the animation functions correctly.
15. Choose the title slide and run the slide show.
16. Work through the presentation, ensuring that the animation functions properly.
17. Feel free to add or modify animation in your presentation.
18. Save the changes to the presentation then close it.

Assessments

Assessment 3.1 Add Animation Effects

In this exercise, you will add animation effects to the Classic Cars presentation you developed in Lesson 2, Designing the Presentation.

1. Open the Classic Cars presentation.

Add Clip Art

2. Add clip art to the second slide as shown to the right. You can locate the picture by doing a search for the keyword phrase **classic cars**. You will need to change the slide layout for the slide and insert the picture in the placeholder box of the new layout. Reduce the size of the picture after inserting it, and adjust the position as shown. If necessary, reduce the font size of the bulleted paragraphs so they no longer wrap.

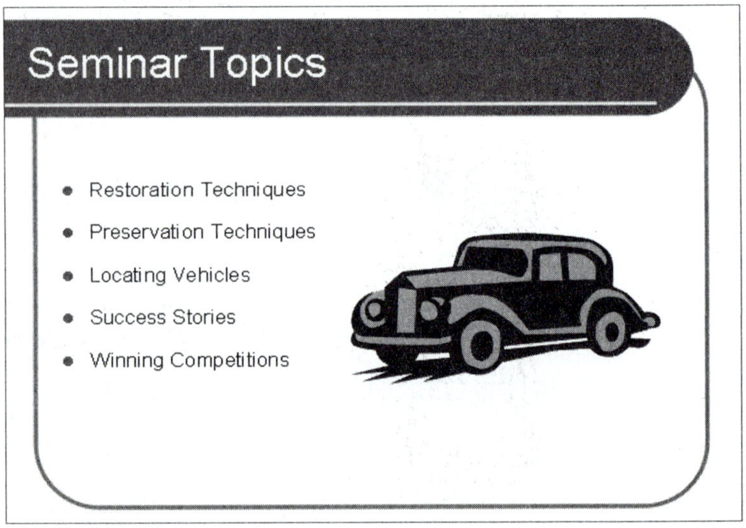

3. Choose the closing slide, and change the subtitle from Enjoy the Ride to **Enjoy the Road Ahead**.
4. Add clip art to the last slide as shown in the following illustration. If you cannot find this image, feel free to choose any clip art image to fit the slide. Don't change the slide layout but use the Clip Art task pane to search for and insert the clip. Use the keyword **road** and size and position the clip as shown.

5. Apply the Big Title animation scheme to all slides in the presentation.
6. Use the following settings to apply custom animation to the car clip on the Seminar Topics slide:
   - Use the Fly In entrance effect.
   - Set the animation to begin after the previous event has finished.
   - Set the direction of the fly in to From Right and the speed to Fast.
   - Apply a Whoosh sound effect or some other effect that you prefer.
7. Use the following settings to apply custom animation to the road clip on the closing slide:
   - Use the Fly In entrance effect.
   - Set the animation to begin after the previous event has finished.
   - Set the direction of the fly in to From Top Left and the speed to Very Fast.
   - Apply a Wind sound effect or another effect that you prefer.
8. Run the presentation when you have finished. If you were able to use the clip art shown, notice the road clip. When it is introduced on the closing slide, the clip itself contains built-in animation that makes the road appear to move.
9. Save the presentation as **`Classic Cars Art`**.

Critical Thinking

Critical Thinking 3.1 Add Clip Art and Animation

Open the Homestead Realty presentation that you developed in Lesson 2, Designing the Presentation. Linda Holmes has been working with her presentation for some time and she now realizes that she needs to liven it up. She asks you to add clip art and animation to the presentation. Follow these guidelines to add clip art:

- Insert a picture of a house on the title slide without changing the slide layout. If necessary, adjust the size of the picture and position it at the bottom-right corner of the slide.
- Apply the Title, Text, and Clip Art layout to the Follow Up slide.
- Insert a picture of a key in the clip art box. Choose any picture of a key you desire. Resize and reposition the picture on the slide as desired.

Follow these guidelines to animate the presentation:

- Add the Descend animation scheme to all slides in the presentation.
- Group the paragraphs on the Office Hours slide so they descend as one object.
- Apply custom animation to the house picture on the title slide as follows:

Entrance Effect	**Spiral In**
Start	After Previous
Speed	Medium
Sound	Whoosh

Apply custom animation to the key picture on the Follow Up slide as follows:

Entrance Effect	**Fly In**
Start	After Previous
Direction	From Top
Speed	Very Fast
Sound	Chime

Save your changes and continue with the next exercise.

Critical Thinking 3.2 Apply Timings

Linda decides to rent a kiosk in the local shopping mall. She wants to set up her presentation to run continuously at the kiosk. Follow these guidelines to prepare the presentation:

- Record timings for the entire slide show and save the timings. Use a moderate pace while recording the timings so individuals viewing the slide show have enough time to read all bullets as they are introduced.
- Set up the show to be browsed at a kiosk. The show should run continuously once it has been started. The timings you recorded should be used while the show is running.
- Now, change the Set Up Show setting to allow the presentation to be Presented by a Speaker (Full Screen).
- Save your presentation as **Homestead Realty Art**.

LESSON 4

Managing Presentation Tools

PowerPoint 2003 supplies you with robust tools for both the development and delivery of your presentation. Throughout this lesson, we will focus on the automatic editing features of PowerPoint 2003 as well as the Slide Show delivery options. All of these tools work together to refine and polish the presentation so that it is visually pleasing, grammatically correct, and effortlessly delivered.

IN THIS LESSON

Microsoft Office PowerPoint 2003 objectives covered in this lesson

Objective Number	Skill Sets and Skills	Concept Page References	Exercise Page References
PP03S-1-2	Insert and edit text-based content	118	119
PP03S-2-7	Work with masters	113	113
PP03S-4-1	Organize a presentation	110	110–111
PP03S-4-2	Set up slide shows for delivery	110	
PP03S-4-4	Deliver presentations	115–116	116–117
PP03S-4-6	Save and publish presentations	122–123	
PP03S-4-7	Print slides, outlines, handouts, and speaker notes	111	112

Additional learning resources are available at labpub.com/learn/pp03/

Case Study

With the style, graphics, and animation in place, Charlene uses PowerPoint's editing tools to check that the spelling is correct. Al uses the enhanced Slide Show toolbar and begins to work on the delivery for the presentation. Knowing that people need to be a part of the presentation to remember it, Al is especially interested in making his presentation interactive. He asks Charlene how he can incorporate a dynamic approach to his presentation. Charlene recommends that they add a Summary Slide now to give the presentation an agenda. Charlene also demonstrates the uses of the Pointer tool that Al can use during the presentation to emphasize points. They both decide that creating handouts will help the audience remember the services of Pinnacle Pet Care. They go back to work on the presentation with renewed enthusiasm.

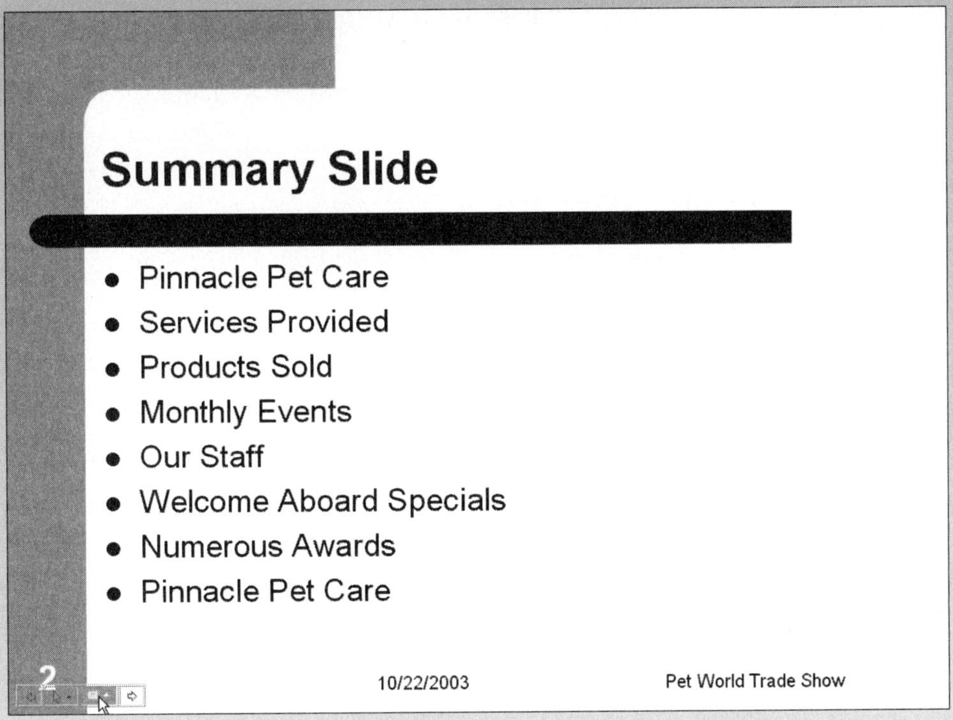

Presenting the Summary Slide in a slide show

Working with Slide Show Delivery Options

PowerPoint 2003 provides you with excellent delivery tools that can be used before, during, and after the presentation to achieve your goals.

Speaker Notes

Microsoft Office Specialist

It's a known fact: Speaking before a group can be intimidating. Even an experienced presenter feels a flurry of anxiety before a presentation. The best way to thwart that anxiety is to be fully prepared. Consider using speaker notes to help you with your delivery. Speaker notes are printable comments you add to slides. They are not visible to the audience. Speaker notes can help you stay on track because if you suddenly freeze, you will be able to scan the notes you carefully prepared to keep your delivery style smooth. Using speaker notes can help you deliver an enthusiastic, informative presentation with confidence. You can add speaker notes in Normal view or use the View→Notes Page command to switch to Notes Page view.

Hands-On 4.1 Add Speaker Notes

In this exercise, you will add speaker notes to a few slides of the Pinnacle Pet Care Art presentation.

1. Open the Pinnacle Pet Care Art presentation.
2. Choose View→Notes Page from the menu bar.
   PowerPoint will display a full screen view that includes the current slide and the notes area. However, notice that the phrase Click to Add Text in the notes area is difficult to read.
3. Adjust the zoom control percentage on the Formatting toolbar to 100%.
4. Use the scroll bar to navigate to the Title slide at the top of the presentation.
5. If necessary, scroll down until the phrase Click to Add Text is visible in the Notes section on the title slide.
6. Click on the phrase Click to Add Text and type **`Don't forget to thank the following people:`** as the replacement phrase.
7. Tap [Enter] to move the insertion point to the next line.
8. Click the Bullets button on the Formatting toolbar.
9. Type the names and titles shown to the right, tapping [Enter] after each line.

   > Don't forget to thank the following people:
   > •Pet World Trade Show Organizing Committee
   > •Donald Johnson – Pet World Vendor Committee
   > •Tanisha Smith – Vendor Support

10. Scroll through the presentation until you reach the Services Provided slide.
11. Click the phrase Click to Add Text and type the speaker note shown to the right.

    > Mention the 1999 Pet World Magazine article ranking us as the most comprehensive pet care facility.

12. Scroll down to the Products Sold slide and add the speaker note shown to the right.

Once again, mention Pet World magazine article.

13. Scroll down to the Our Staff slide and add the speaker notes shown to the right.
    At this point, four slides in your presentation should contain speaker notes.

•Seven other staff members •Combined experience is 63 years

14. Choose View→Normal to switch to Normal view.
15. Notice that the speaker notes are visible in the notes area below the slide.
16. Save the presentation as **`Pinnacle Pet Care Tools`** and continue with the next exercise.

Handouts

You can reinforce the main points of your presentation by providing your participants with handouts. Participants will be able to walk away from your presentation with more than a vague memory of your slide show; all of the facts you presented during the presentation will go with them as a reference. Handouts can be printed in a wide range of layouts, from two to nine slides per page. For example, printing three slides on a page places three small slides on the left side and multiple lines on the right for note-taking.

Handout Masters

Handout sheets have handout masters that control the format of the sheets. As with slide masters, you can change the format of the handout master, which will affect all handouts in the presentation. You display the handout master by choosing View→Master→Handout Master.

Handout Headers and Footers

You can set up a header and footer to print on all pages of a handout. Headers and footers often include the presenter's name, occasion, date, and other information. You can add headers and footers to handout sheets using the Handouts tab on the Header and Footer box. The Header and Footer box is displayed with the View→Header and Footer command.

Printing Handouts

Microsoft Office Specialist

To print handouts, use the Print Preview button to display the Print Preview window. Then, choose the desired handout format from the Print What list. You can also use the File→Print command to display the print box and choose the desired format from the Print What list.

Hands-On 4.2 Print Handouts with a Header and Footer

In this exercise, you will add the date and event to the header and footer of the handout. The handouts will then be printed in a special layout.

Set Up a Handout Header and Footer

1. Choose View→Header and Footer from the menu bar.
2. Click the Notes and Handouts tab in the Header and Footer box.
3. Follow these steps to set up a header and footer for the handout sheets:

A **Choose the Update Automatically option to display the current date.**

B **If necessary, check the Header box and type `Presented by Al Smith` in the box.**

C **If necessary, check the Page Number and Footer boxes and type `Pet World Trade Show` in the footer box.**

D **Click the Apply to All button.**

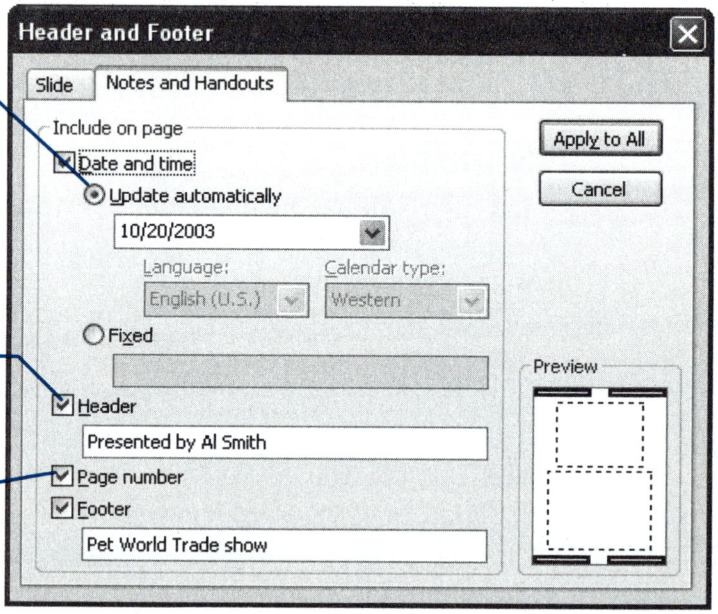

Use Print Preview

4. Click the Print Preview button.
5. Choose Handouts (3 Slides per Page) from the Print What list.
   A handout sheet with three slides and lines for notes will be displayed. Notice that the header and footer you just typed appear at the top and bottom of the sheet.
6. Feel free to browse through the pages.
7. Choose a different handout format from the Print What list, such as the six slides per page format.
   Notice that the three slides per page format is the only one that displays note lines.
8. Close the Print Preview window when you have finished and save the changes to your presentation.

Slide Footers

Microsoft Office Specialist

Just as you can place a header or footer on a handout slide, you can also place footers (information that sits at the foot of the slide) on your presentations. Footers display the date, event name, slide number, or other text that you want visible through the presentation. Now you will learn how to place a footer on your slide using the Header and Footer dialog box.

The Update Automatically option displays the current date and time on the right side of the footer. You can also choose to use the Fixed option to type a desired date and time in the Fixed box.

Use this option to display the Slide Number on the left side of the footer.

If the Footer box is checked, the text you type here is displayed in the center of the footer.

This option prevents the footer from displaying on the title slide.

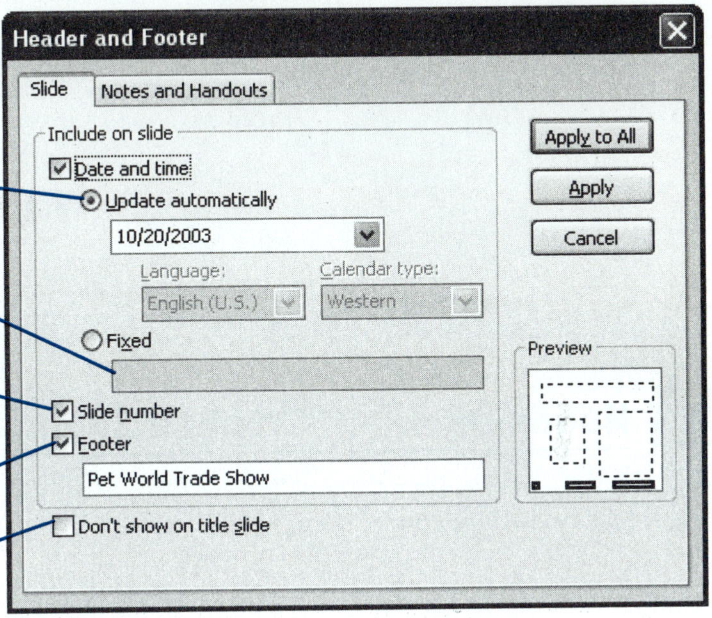

Hands-On 4.3 Set Up a Slide Footer

In this exercise, you will create a slide footer and apply it to all slides in the presentation.

1. Choose the Monthly Events slide (third slide in the presentation).
2. Choose View→Header and Footer from the menu bar.
3. Choose the Update Automatically option, check the Slide Number box, and make sure the Footer box is checked.
4. Type the phrase **`Pet World Trade Show`** in the Footer box as shown in the illustration to the right.
5. Click the Apply to All button to apply the footer to all slides in the presentation.
   The Apply to All button is used to apply a footer to all the pages of the presentation. The Apply button is used to apply a footer to a current page only. The footer should appear at the bottom of the Monthly Events slide as show to the right (note that your date will be different).
6. Browse through the presentation and notice that the footer appears on every slide.

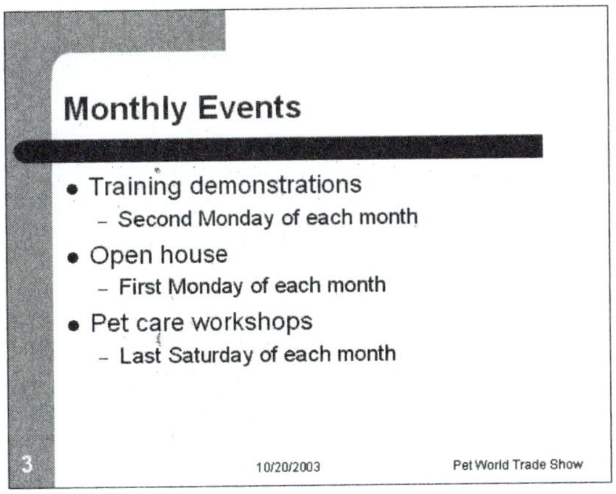

Summary Slides

Many presentations begin with an agenda that outlines the various topics to be covered in the presentation. PowerPoint provides a Summary Slide tool that makes it easy to create a summary or agenda slide. The summary slide displays the titles from each slide in the presentation. The titles comprise the agenda for the presentation. The following Quick Reference table explains how to create a summary slide.

QR

QUICK REFERENCE: CREATING SUMMARY SLIDES

Task	Procedure
Create a summary slide	■ Switch to Slide Sorter view. ■ Press [Ctrl] while clicking the slides you wish to include on the summary slide. ■ Click the Summary Slide button on the slide sorter toolbar.

Hands-On 4.4 Create a Summary Slide

In this exercise, you will create a Summary Slide for the presentation that will automatically be placed at the beginning of the slide show.

1. Click the Slide Sorter button on the View bar.
   In the next step, you will select all of the slides in the presentation. You could accomplish this by pressing and holding the [Ctrl] key while clicking the slides. However, you will use the Edit→Select All command instead, which is an easy way to select all slides.
2. Click Slide 2, hold down the [Shift] key and click Slide 9.
3. Click the Summary Slide button on the Slide Sorter toolbar. The Slide Sorter toolbar will most likely be positioned to the right of the Standard toolbar. You may want to move it below the Standard toolbar.
   A summary slide will appear in front of the Pinnacle Pet Care title slide.
4. Click the Normal view button on the View bar.
   Your summary slide should contain a bullet for each slide title, as shown to the right.

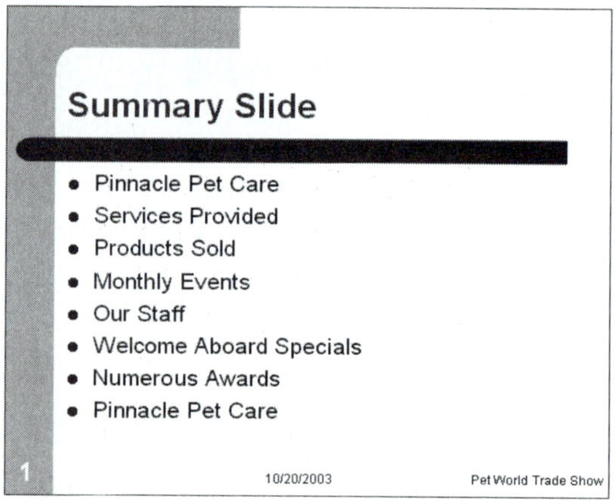

5. Select the phrase Summary Slide in the title box and type **Agenda**.
6. Switch to Slide Sorter view and drag the Agenda slide to the right of the title.
   The title slide should be the first slide in the presentation.

Hiding Slides

The Hide Slide button on the Slide Sorter toolbar lets you hide slides during a presentation. For instance, you can create a generic presentation to use with several different groups. In this case, hiding a slide will allow you to tailor the presentation to the present group without having to recreate the entire slide show. You hide slides by selecting the desired slides in Slide Sorter view and clicking the Hide Slide button. You unhide hidden slides by selecting them in Slide Sorter view and clicking the Hide Slide button.

FROM THE KEYBOARD

[H] to go to the next hidden slide while running a presentation

Hands-On 4.5 Hide the Agenda Slide

In this exercise, you will learn the technique of hiding a slide so it is not displayed during the slide show.

1. Click the Slide Sorter view button on the View bar.
2. Choose the Agenda slide then click the Hide Slide button on the Slide Sorter toolbar.
3. Notice the Hidden Slide icon below the Agenda slide.
   This icon appears below all hidden slides in Slide Sorter view.
4. Click the Title slide (the first slide) in preparation for the slide show.
5. Click the Slide Show button on the View bar to begin the electronic slide show.
6. Click the mouse button after the title slide animation has completed.
   Notice that the Agenda slide is bypassed and the Services Provided slide appears.
7. Leave the slide show as it is and continue with the next topic.

Working with Slide Show Toolbar Options

The Slide Show toolbar is enhanced in PowerPoint 2003. We studied the Slide Show toolbar in Lesson 1, Creating and Delivering a Presentation. Now we will focus on the Pointer tool of the Slide Show toolbar. The Pointer tool enables you to draw, write, and highlight elements of your slides as you deliver the presentation.

The Pointer

Microsoft Office **Specialist**

As you deliver your presentation, the audience may ask for more detail on a key issue. With the Pointer tool, you can immediately respond to the request by using the pen or highlighter to annotate slides, thus emphasizing important information. When the presentation ends you will be asked if you want to keep or discard any annotations. If you choose to keep them, they are saved with the presentation and will be there when you open it again and run the slide show. If you choose to discard the annotations, they disappear immediately and are not saved with the presentation. Examine the features of each Pointer tool in the following table.

FROM THE KEYBOARD

[Ctrl]+[P] to change the pointer tool to the pen

[Ctrl]+[A] to change the pen to the pointer tool

Option	Description
Ballpoint Pen	The Ballpoint Pen allows you to draw and write with a thin line. To open the Ballpoint Pen, click the Pointer and choose Ballpoint Pen.
Felt Tip Pen	The Felt Tip Pen allows you to draw and write with a thick line. To open the Felt Tip Pen, click the Pointer button and choose Felt Tip Pen.
Highlighter	The Highlighter allows you to highlight the text or image with a wide stroke of color.
Eraser	The Eraser removes all lines or highlighting from the slides. To open the Eraser, click the Pointer button and choose Eraser.
Ink	You can choose from the full spectrum of colors available in PowerPoint to change ink color. Click the Pointer button and choose Ink Color.

Hands-On 4.6 Use Pointer Options in a Slide Show

In this exercise, you will use each Pointer tool available in the Pointer menu. Be sure that the slide show is running and the Services Provided slide is visible.

Use the Ballpoint Pen Pointer Tool

1. Activate the Slide Show toolbar.
2. Click the Navigation button and choose Go to Slide→Monthly Events (No. 5).
3. As the Monthly Events slide is introduced, click the Navigation button again and choose Pause to stop the animation.
   With the animation paused, you can now use the pen tool.
4. Click the Pointer button and choose Ballpoint Pen.
   The arrow turns into the point of a ballpoint pen.
5. Click the Pointer button, choose Ink Color, and choose a shade of red for your ballpoint pen.
   Notice the wide range of colors available to you.
6. Use the Ballpoint Pen tool to draw an oval around the Open House bullet, including the phrase First Monday of Each Month in the oval. Use the illustration to the right as a guide. If you make a mistake or want to draw the oval a second time, use the Delete key to undo.
   Drawing an oval around this text will emphasize the open house on the first Monday of each month.

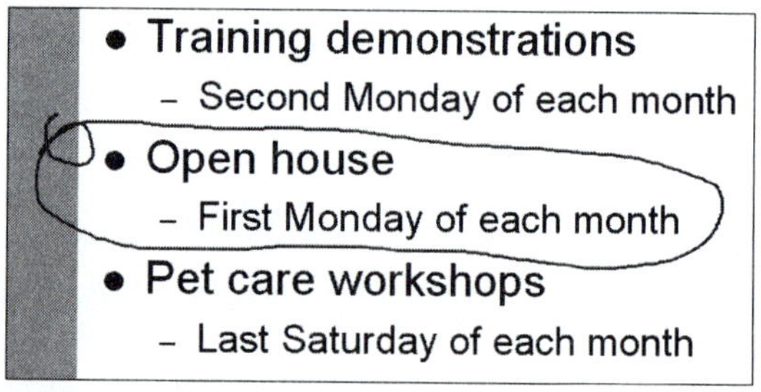

7. Click the Navigation button and choose Go To Slide→Welcome Aboard Specials.
8. Click once to introduce the text then use the Pause button to stop the animation so you can use the Pointer tool.
   Timing the Pause can be tricky; just wait until the last bullet appears.

Use the Highlighter Tool

9. Click the Pointer button and choose the Highlighter.
10. Highlight the paragraph *Valid until July 30*, as shown in the illustration to the right, to emphasize to the audience that the special is only valid for a limited time.
    The Highlighter is really a wide stroke of color. You may need to move it back and forth more than once to cover the text.

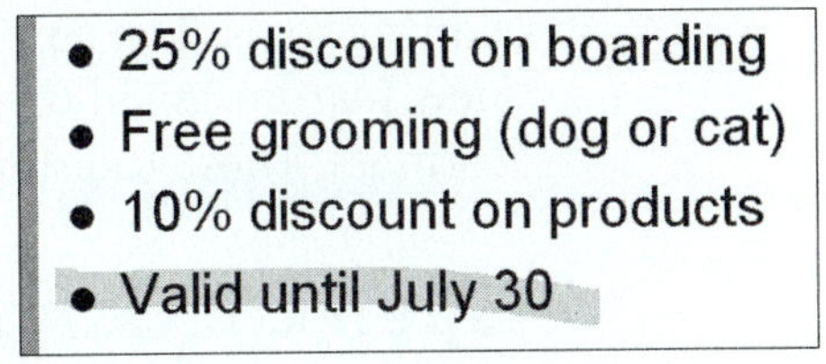

Use the Felt Tip Pen Pointer Tool

11. Click the Navigation button and choose Go to Slide→Numerous Awards (No. 8).
12. Click to introduce the text, then click the Navigation button and choose Pause.
13. Click the Pointer button and choose Felt Tip Pen.
    Notice that this pen has a thicker point.
14. Using the Felt Tip Pen, circle the quote from Jerry Rogers as shown to the right.
    This is another way of saying, look at this!

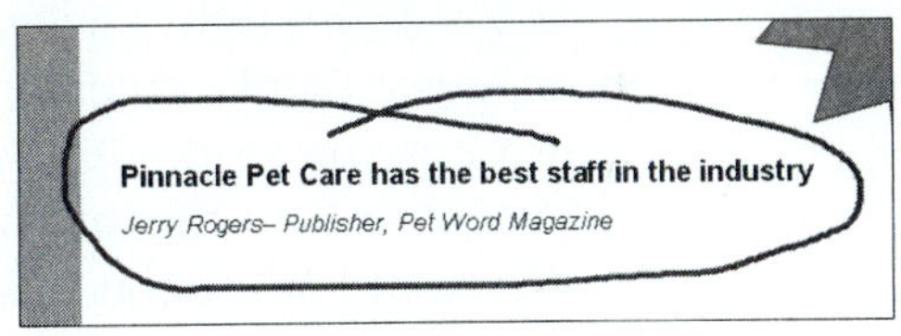

Change the Color of the Highlighter Tool

15. Advance to the last slide, Pinnacle Pet Care, which has the phone number and Website information on it.
16. Click the Pointer button and choose the Highlighter tool.
17. Change the color of the highlighter by choosing Pointer→Ink Color. Choose any shade. Then highlight the phone number for Pinnacle Pet care as show in the illustration to the right.

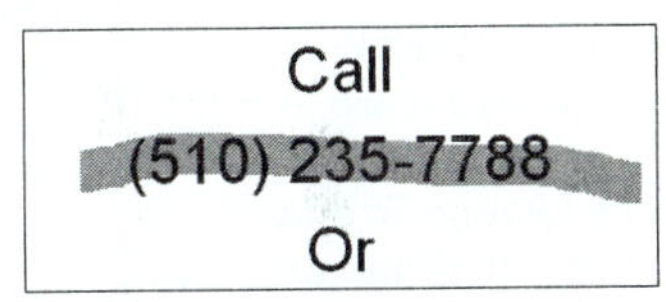

Erase the Pointer Tool Annotations

18. Click the Pointer button and choose Eraser. Click once to erase the highlighting on the slide.
    Notice that the highlighting is erased with one click of the mouse. The highlighting virtually disappears from the slide.
19. Click to end the slide show. When the prompt to save or discard the annotations appears on your screen, choose Discard.
20. Save the changes and continue with the next topic.

Working with Editing Tools

To assist you in editing your presentation, PowerPoint 2003 provides you with a powerful set of editing tools. The editing tools include the Spell Checker, Smart Tags, Find and Replace and a new feature called the Permission option. You can also save your presentation in different formats. These tools are discussed in detail in this section.

Spell Checking

Microsoft Office Specialist

If you are familiar with Microsoft Office, you probably have used the Spell Checker. The Spell Checker automatically checks the entire presentation for misspelled words. To indicate a misspelled word, PowerPoint places a wavy red line under the word. You can set up the Spell Checker to correct as you type (AutoCorrect), manually activate it with each session, or use it both ways. The command to open the Spell Checker is Tools→Spelling. Once opened, the Spell Checker will check not only the slides but also the speaker notes for any incorrectly spelled words.

You can also right-click on a misspelled word, which brings up a shortcut menu with suggested replacements for the word. Choosing a replacement from this menu will correct the error as you work. The Spell Checker uses the same dictionaries used in Word and other Office programs. You can, at any time, add words that you use regularly, creating your customized dictionary or lexicon. Examine the Spelling dialog box in the following illustration:

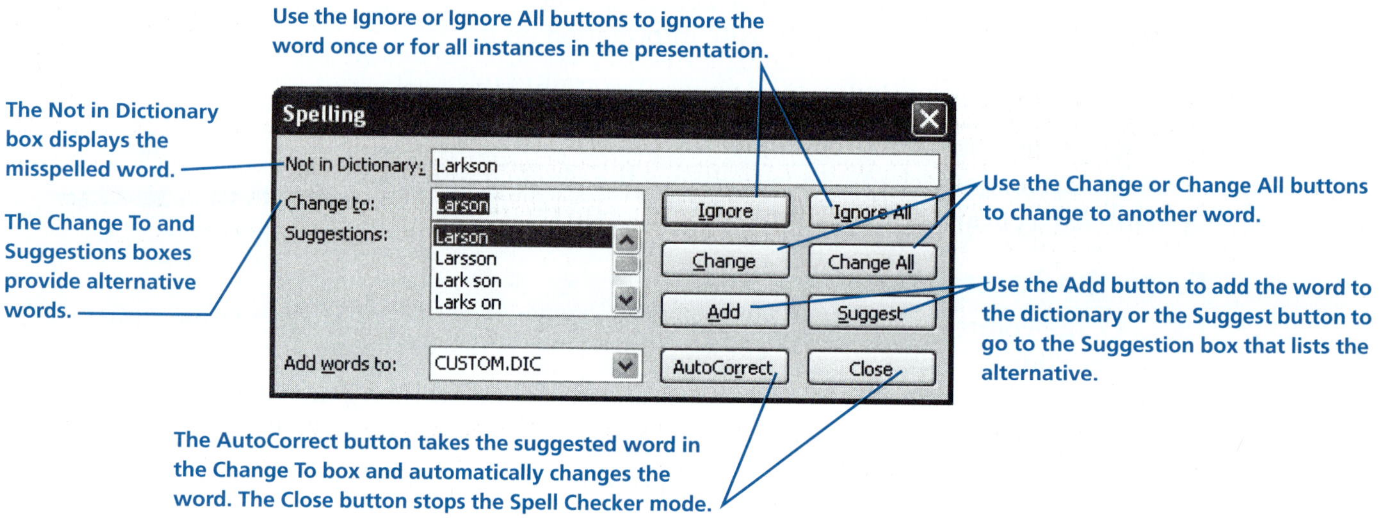

TIP! *Be careful: if you have typed a correctly spelled English word, even if it is not the word you mean, the Spell Checker will not display it.*

Hands-On 4.7 Use Editing Tools

In this exercise, you will explore the features of the Spell Checker.

Spell Check the Presentation

1. Choose the title slide of the presentation.
2. Click the Spelling button on the Standard toolbar.
   The Spelling box will appear and the name Tanisha will most likely be displayed. Tanisha was used in a speaker note on the title slide of the presentation. Although this name is spelled correctly, the spell checker reports it as an error because this name does not appear in the speller's main dictionary. Keep in mind that a different word may appear if you have spelling errors in your presentation that occur prior to the name Tanisha.
3. Click the Ignore button to skip the word Tanisha.
   At this point, the spell checker will continue to display words that it believes are misspelled.
4. Continue spell checking the presentation using your best judgment.
5. Save the changes to your presentation when you have finished.

Smart Tags

Smart Tags recognize types of information such as names, dates, and financial symbols. When a Smart Tag applies to such information, the text is underlined with a purple line. Smart Tags are available in all Microsoft Office programs. Smart Tags enable you to work with other Office programs while still working in PowerPoint. For instance, using the Name Smart Tag, you can add a name to your Microsoft Outlook Contacts folder. You can schedule a meeting in Outlook using the Date Smart Tag. And you can research information in various programs using the Financial Symbol Smart Tag. All of these actions are done while working in PowerPoint.

TIP! *Smart Tags are very volatile. They appear and vanish depending on your actions in PowerPoint.*

Smart Tag Treatment of a Name

The following example of how a Smart Tag reacts to the name *Tim* in your Contacts folder gives you a basic understanding of how a Smart Tag can assist you as you work.

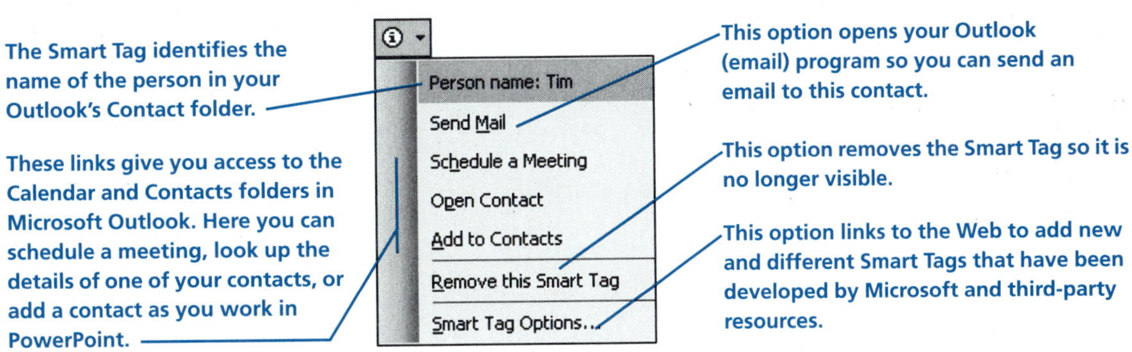

TIP! *The Name Smart Tag only recognizes names exactly as they appear in your Contacts folder in Outlook.*

Smart Tag Treatment of Financial Symbol

The Financial Symbol Smart Tag provides options that may help you obtain information about a company. Examine the following illustration of a Financial Symbols Smart Tag.

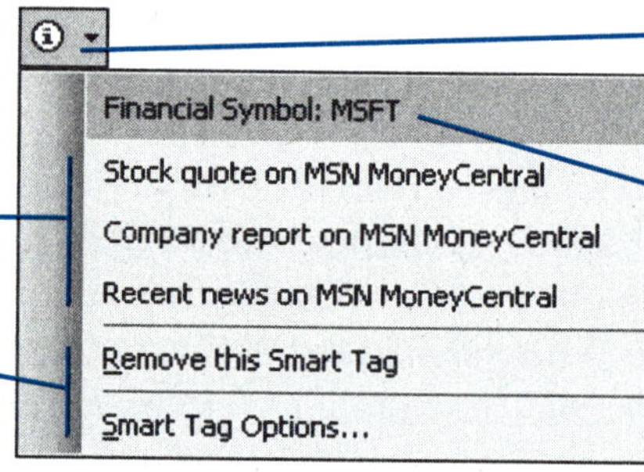

Setting Smart Tag Options

To enable Smart Tags to work in your presentation, choose Tools→AutoCorrect Options then choose the Smart Tags tab. The Smart Tags options are described in detail in the following illustration.

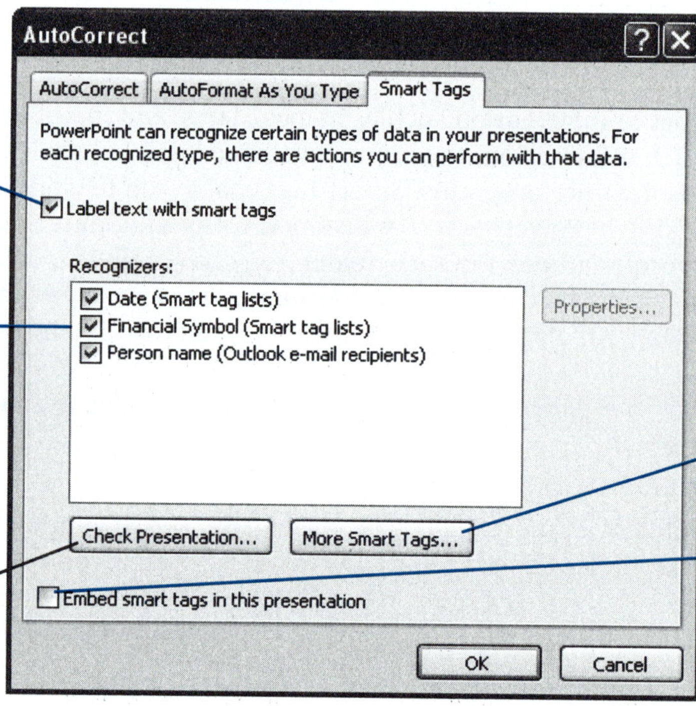

Hands-On 4.8 Use a Smart Tag

In this exercise, you will add a date to a slide and examine the Smart Tag dialog box.

1. Click the Welcome Aboard Specials slide (No. 7) and complete the last bullet so it reads **`July 30, 2004`**.
   Adding the full date will display the Date Smart Tag.

2. Notice that when you point to the Smart Tag ⓘ icon, the menu options are displayed. Examine the menu choices, called Smart Actions, in the illustration to the right.
   Notice that July 30 is set for the meeting date.

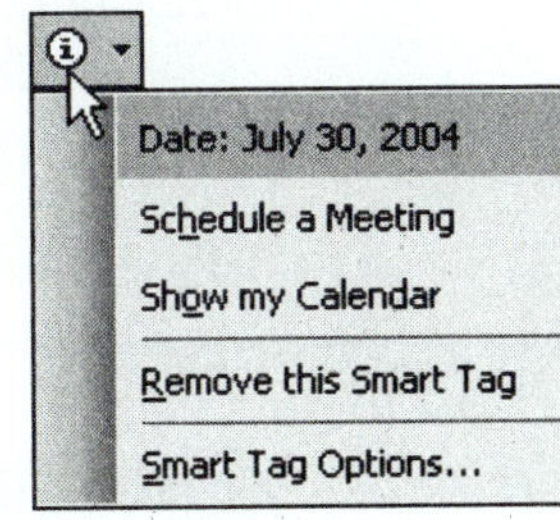

3. Click Schedule a Meeting in the menu options. If you have installed Microsoft Outlook, the Smart Tag icon will link you to the Outlook Calendar to schedule a meeting. Examine the following illustration or click this link to experiment with the folder. When you are finished experimenting, close the Outlook window.

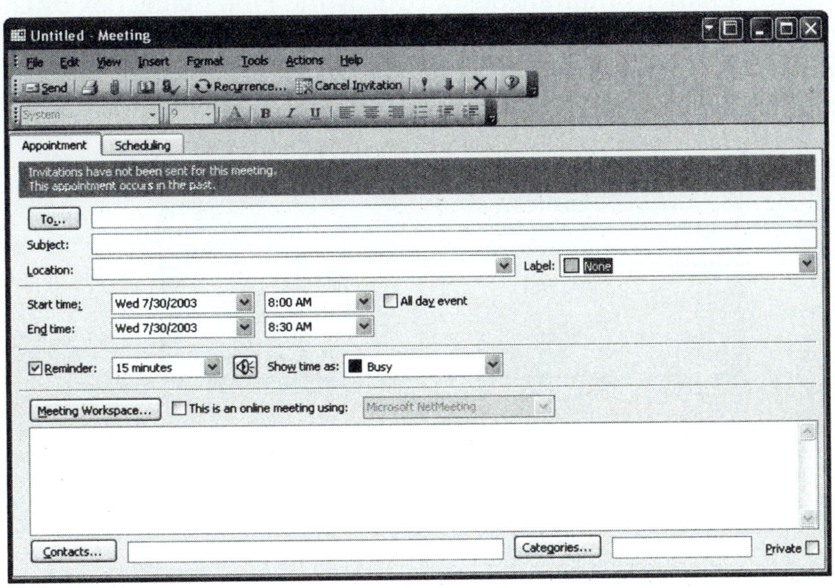

4. Click the Show My Calendar in the menu options. If Outlook is installed, this link will open the Outlook Calendar. Browse the following illustration if Outlook is not installed on your computer. Otherwise, click the link and explore the Calendar. Close the Outlook window when you are finished.

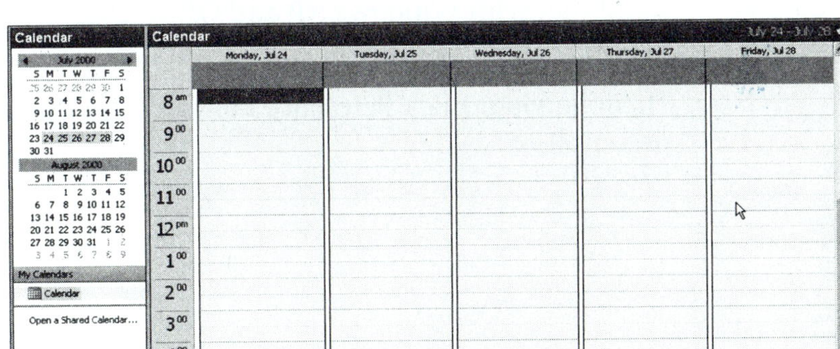

5. Click the Show My Calendar link in the Smart Tag menu. If Outlook is installed, this link will open your Outlook calendar so you can add an appointment in your calendar. When you are finished examining the calendar, close the window to dismiss it.
   You can navigate through the calendar as though you were in Outlook.
6. Click the Smart Tag Options link to open the AutoCorrect dialog box. Here you can reset Smart Tag options.
7. Click the Check Smart Tags button and watch as PowerPoint checks the entire presentation for Smart Tags. When the prompt states that the presentation has been checked, click OK to dismiss the box.
8. Save and close the presentation.

Find and Replace

FROM THE KEYBOARD
Ctrl+F for Find
Ctrl+H for Replace

As you edit the presentation, you may decide to replace one term with a new one. Using the Find and Replace feature, you can quickly search throughout the presentation for one term and replace it with another simultaneously. Display the Find dialog box by choosing Edit→Find or the Replace dialog box by choosing Edit→Replace. Examine the Find dialog box in the following illustration to familiarize yourself with the feature, as you will be working with them in Skill Builder 4.5 and Assessment 4.2.

Saving Presentations in Multiple Formats

Microsoft Office Specialist

Typically, you will save your presentation with the extension, .ppt. However, at some point, you may need to save the presentation as a template, outline, Web page, or other format. Keep in mind that with Windows XP and Office 2003, the extension of the file is not visible but the descriptive word for it will be displayed.

The following Quick Reference table defines the multiple formats that can be used to save your presentation.

QR

QUICK REFERENCE: SAVING A PRESENTATION IN MULTIPLE FORMATS

Format Option	Extension	Description
Presentation	.ppt	Presentation
Windows Meta File	.wmf	Graphic
Graphics Interchange Format	.gif	Graphic to be used on web pages
Joint Portable Enabled Graphic	.jpg	Graphic to be used on web pages
Portable Network Graphics	.png	Graphic to be used on web pages
Outline/RTF	.rtf	Presentation outline in an outline document
Design Template	.pot	Design template
PowerPoint Show	.pps	Slide Show only
Web Page	.html, .htm	Web page folder with supporting files
Web Archive	.mhtml, .mhtm	Single-page web page with supporting files

Concepts Review

True/False Questions

1. A summary slide is composed of titles from various slides in a presentation. TRUE FALSE
2. You do not have to select slides prior to creating a summary slide. TRUE FALSE
3. A footer can appear on every slide in a presentation. TRUE FALSE
4. You can save annotations with a presentation. TRUE FALSE
5. The Smart Tag recognizes names, dates, and financial symbols within a presentation. TRUE FALSE
6. Handouts can have both headers and footers. TRUE FALSE
7. Slides can only be hidden while working in Normal view. TRUE FALSE
8. A presentation can only be saved in two formats. TRUE FALSE
9. Find and Replace searches only slides, not notes. TRUE FALSE
10. Speaker Notes are visible to the audience when you present the slide show. TRUE FALSE

Multiple Choice Questions

1. Which of the following buttons is used to create summary slides?
   a. 
   b. 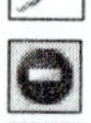
   c. 
   d. 
2. Which command displays the Hide Slide  button?
   a. View→Hide Slide
   b. Slide Show→Hide Slide
   c. Format→Hide Slide
   d. Tools→Hide Slide
3. Speaker Notes are added to the presentation by choosing:
   a. Format→Notes
   b. Inserting the Notes in Normal view
   c. View→Notes Page view
   d. None of the above
4. A summary slide is _________.
   a. A recap at the end of the presentation
   b. An agenda at the beginning of the presentation
   c. Both a and b
   d. Neither a nor b

Skill Builders

Skill Builder 4.1 Add a Summary Slide

In this exercise, you will add a summary slide to the Tropical Getaways Art presentation.

1. Open the Tropical Getaways Art presentation that you developed in Lesson 3, Managing Clip Art, Drawing Objects, and Animation.
2. Switch to Slide Sorter view.
3. Click the Travel Categories slide to select it.
4. Press the Shift key while you click the Most Popular Destinations, Complete Packages, and Travel Now and Save slides.
   The four slides in the middle of the presentation should be selected. Once again, you must select the desired slides prior to creating a summary slide.
5. Click the Summary Slide button on the Slide Sorter toolbar.
   A summary slide will appear in front of the Travel Categories slide.
6. Switch to Normal view to see the summary slide.
7. Select the title of the slide *Summary Slide* and change it to **`Agenda`**.
8. Save the presentation as **`Tropical Getaways Tools`** and continue with the next exercise.

Skill Builder 4.2 Hide a Slide

In this exercise, you will hide the Agenda slide prior to starting the presentation.

1. Click the Slide Sorter button on the View bar to return to the Slide Sorter view.
2. Click the Agenda slide to select it.
3. Click the Hide Slide button on the Slide Sorter toolbar.
   This will prevent the Agenda slide from appearing during the presentation.
4. Click the Tropical Getaways title slide to select it.
5. Click the Slide Show button to begin the presentation.
6. Click the mouse button after the animation has completed on the title slide.
   The Agenda slide will be skipped and the Travel Categories slide will be introduced.
7. Save the file and continue with the next exercise.

Skill Builder 4.3 Print Handouts with a Header and a Footer

In this exercise, you will print handouts for the Tropical Getaways Tools presentation. You will also create a header and a footer for the handouts.

1. Navigate to the second slide.
2. Choose View→Header and Footer and click the Notes and Handouts tab.
3. Follow these steps to set up the handouts header and footer:

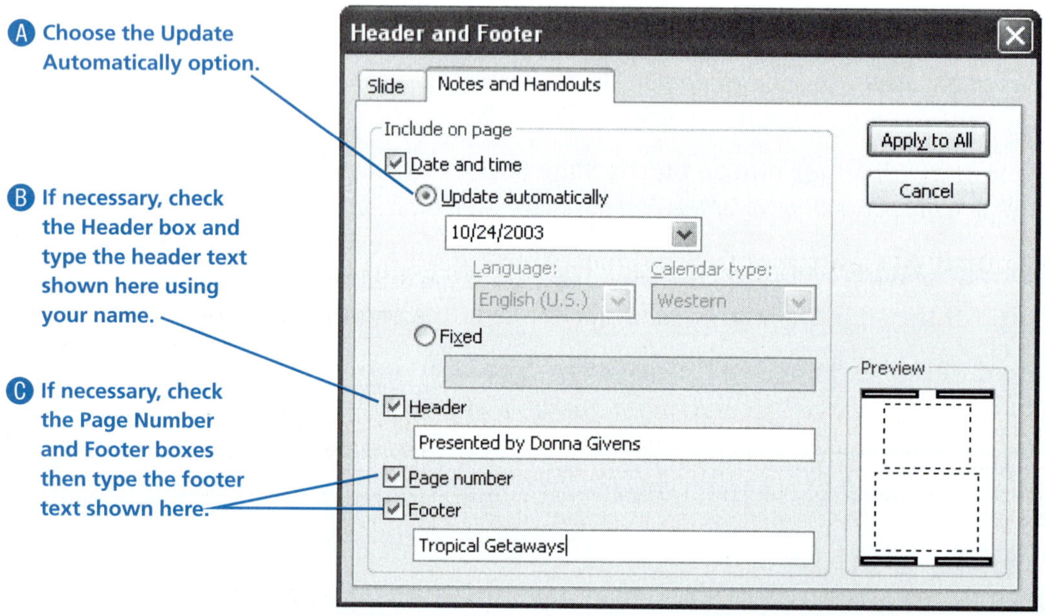

4. Click the Apply to All button.
   Remember that the Apply to All button applies the Header and Footer to all of the slides in the presentation.
5. Click the Print Preview button and click the drop-down menu of the Print What section of the Print Preview toolbar.
6. Place your mouse pointer over the menu choices in the Print What section until you find the handouts (three slides per page).
7. Print the handouts (three slides per page). Take time to explore the other handout options. Print them if desired.
8. Close Print Preview, save the changes to the presentation, and continue with the next exercise.

Skill Builder 4.4 Work with Speaker Notes

In this exercise, you will add speaker notes using the Notes Page View.

1. Still using the Tropical Getaways Tools presentation, navigate to the Title slide and open the Notes Page View.
2. Select the Title slide and insert the text shown to the right on the Notes Page.

   > Welcome the employees to their new travel service
   > Thank Glenda Johnson – Director of Human Resources

3. Next, choose the Most Popular Destinations slide and insert the text shown to the right on the Notes Page.

   > Employees get a 35% discount on all destinations on the Popular Destinations list

4. Navigate to the Travel Now and Save slide and add the text show to the right.

   > •12 preferred discount packages available to employees
   > •No time limit on preferred discount packages
   > •Limit of two packages per employee per year

5. Choose the last slide in the presentation and add the text shown to the right.

   > Add that Donna Givens has won many awards in customer service and is available to talk to them at any time to discuss their travel plans.

6. Save the changes to the presentation and continue with the next exercise.

Skill Builder 4.5 Use the Spell Checker, Find and Replace, and Footers

In this exercise, you will utilize the Spelling feature, find and replace a word, and add footers to further refine the presentation.

1. Navigate to the sixth slide, Travel Now and Save.

Add a Slide

2. Add a slide with the title **`Travel Resources`**. Ensure that the layout is Title and Text. Insert the text in the body as shown in the illustration to the right (including the spelling errors).
   The misspelled words will be corrected shortly.

Work with the Spell Checker

3. In the Travel Resources slide, open the Spell Checker by choosing Tools→Spelling.
   The Spell Checker will automatically find the first misspelled word.
4. Accept each Spell Checker suggestion to correct the word and then click OK to dismiss the PowerPoint prompt stating that the spelling check is complete.
5. The Travel Resources slide should now match the illustration shown to the right.

Use Find and Replace

6. Navigate to the Title slide.
7. Choose Edit→Find and type **`Categories`** in the Find What section of the Find dialog box.
   Notice that the word categories *is highlighted for you on the slide. In the next step, you will open the Replace dialog box and insert a word to replace* categories.

8. Click the Replace button to open the Replace dialog box as shown in the illustration to the right and in the Replace With section, type **`Divisions`**. Notice that the Find dialog box has become the Replace dialog box.

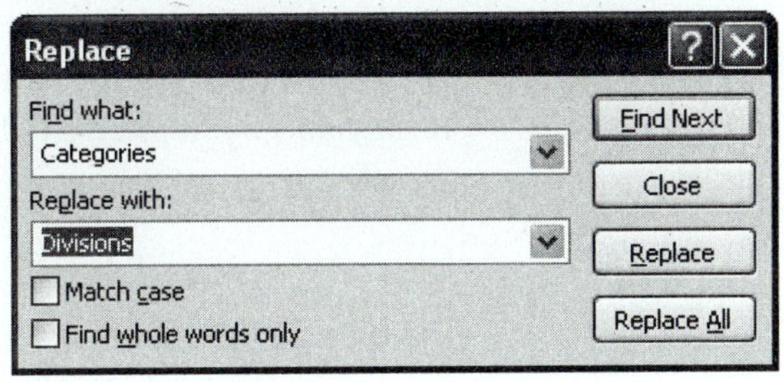

9. Click the Replace button to replace categories with divisions in the Agenda slide.
   The word Categories *is replaced with the word* Divisions.
10. Click the Find Next button to search for other instances of *Categories* in the presentation. The Find feature will go to the third slide, Travel Categories.
11. Click Replace to change the word from *Categories* to *Divisions* on the Travel Categories slide.
12. Click the Find Next button once more. Notice the PowerPoint prompt stating that the search is complete.
13. Click OK to dismiss the prompt then click Close to dismiss the Replace dialog box.
14. Save the changes and continue with the next exercise.

Skill Builder 4.6 Use Pointer Options

In this exercise, you will practice delivering the slides and use the Pointer tools to emphasize key points.

1. Navigate to the Title slide and click the Slide Show button.
2. Advance through the slide show until you reach the fourth slide, Complete Packages.
3. Placing your mouse pointer in the left-hand corner of the screen, choose the Pointer button from the Slide Show Toolbar.
4. Select the Felt Tip Pen tool, choose the white ink color, and circle the paragraph as shown to the right.
   This is a great way to emphasize the low cost of the package.

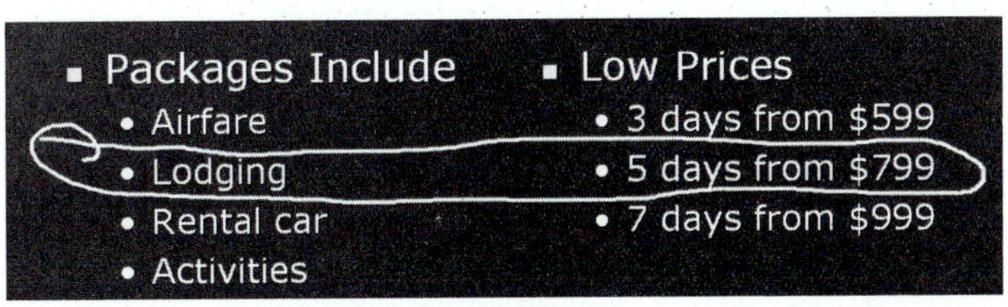

5. Choose the Next arrow on the Slide Show Toolbar and advance to the last slide that shows Donna Givens' phone number.

6. Highlight Donna's phone number in an orange ink color as shown in the illustration to the right.
It may take a few sweeps of the highlighter to cover the phone number.

7. Click Keep to save the annotations you have made to the slide show.
8. Save and close the presentation.

Assessments

Assessment 4.1 Add Speaker Notes and Use Spell Checker

In this exercise, you will add speaker notes and use the Spell Checker.

Add Speaker Notes

1. Open the Classic Cars Art presentation.
2. Use the Bullets button as you add the following speaker notes to each slide:

Slide	Speaker Notes
Classic Cars (title slide)	■ Thank the organizing committee ■ Welcome new members
Collections on Display	■ Thank collectors ■ Most valuable collection of classic cars in one location ■ 110 cars in mint condition
Door Prizes	■ No individual limits on winning ■ Mention the secret grand prize

Use the Spell Checker

3. Navigate to the first page of the presentation and activate the Spell Checker.
4. Use your judgment to correct the spelling of the text. In the Candidates slide, add the name Fluor to the custom dictionary.
5. Dismiss the Spell Checker when you have finished checking the presentation and save the changes.

Assessment 4.2 Use Find and Replace and Pointer Options

In this exercise, you will work with the Find and Replace feature as well as the Pointer Arrow tool in Classic Cars.

Use Find and Replace

1. Navigate to the Title slide.
2. Use the following table to find and replace terms in the presentation:

Find	Replace With
Techniques	Methods
Vehicles	Automobiles
2001	2004

3. Navigate to the Title slide. With the Find dialog box still open, type **2004** in the Find What box. Click the Find Next button.
   You will advance to the fifth slide, Agenda for 2004 Convention.
4. Click the Replace button and, in the Replace With box, type **2005** to change date from 2004 to 2005. Then, click the Replace button to replace the date.
5. Click the Find Next button again.
   You will advance to the sixth slide, Candidates for Election.
6. In the Replace With box, type **2005** to change the date in the title of the slide from 2004 to 2005 and click the Replace button.
7. Close the dialog box and continue.

Use the Pointer Options

8. Run the Slide Show and navigate to the fifth slide, Agenda for 2005 Convention.
9. Using the Pointer options tool, highlight the phrase *Popular Road Trips*.
10. Next, choose the sixth slide, Candidates for 2005 Election, and highlight the *Member-at-Large* bullet. Then use the Ballpoint or Felt Tip pen to circle the name Ross Martin.
11. Save the presentation as **Classic Cars Tools** and continue with the next exercise.

Assessment 4.3 Work with Handouts and Headers and Footers

In this exercise, you will add handouts with headers and footers to the presentation.

1. Switch to Slide Sorter view.
2. Open the Header and Footer dialog box and click the Notes and Handouts tab.
3. Insert a Header and Footer in the Notes and Handouts tab and set up the correct options by using the following table:

Notes and Handout Tab Section	Option to Choose or Type
Date and Time	Enable the Date and Time. Then, set up this section so it is automatically updated.
Header	Classic Cars 2004 Convention
Page Number	Include the page number
Footer	Enjoy the Ride Ahead!

4. Use the Apply to All button to apply the settings to all Handout pages and dismiss the Header and Footer dialog box.
5. Click the Print Preview button and choose the 3-slides per page layout of the Handouts.
6. Take a moment to review your handouts then close Print Preview when you have finished.
7. Save the presentation and continue with the next exercise.

Assessment 4.4 Create and Hide a Summary Slide

In this exercise, you will create a summary slide and practice hiding the slide for future deliveries of the presentation.

1. Switch to Slide Sorter view. Select slides 2–7.
2. Create a Summary Slide using the appropriate button on the Slide Sorter toolbar.
3. Double-click on the Summary slide to switch to Normal view then change the title of the slide to **Agenda**.
4. Return to the Slide Sorter view.
5. Hide the Agenda slide so it cannot be displayed when you deliver the slide show.
6. Check the slide show by running it to make sure the Agenda slide is not visible.
7. Save all changes and close the presentation.

Critical Thinking

Critical Thinking 4.1 Add Speaker Notes, Handouts, and Smart Tag Items

In this exercise, you will add speaker notes to four slides in the Homestead Realty Art presentation. Open the Homestead Realty Art presentation and advance to the Targeted Marketing slide. Now add the following speaker notes to the slides:

Slide	Speaker Notes
Targeted Marketing	MLS has over 1,000 agents Web site updated weekly Color yard signs for easy viewing Professionally designed flyers IWANNA (for smaller homes) Citizen Times (color photo ads) Real Estate Weekly (published every Thursday) Homes and Land (national publication)
Follow Up	Joan makes most of the follow-up calls Clients can call me at any time on my cell phone
Experienced Staff	Over 30 years of combined experience
Satisfied Customers	Additional testimonials on file

Select at least two layouts for the handouts and print them. Save the presentation as **Homestead Realty Tools** and continue with the next exercise.

Critical Thinking 4.2 Use Smart Tags and Hide Slides

In this exercise, you will hide a slide and use the Smart Tag options. In the last slide, Office Hours, add the term **Beginning January 1, 2004** then **New Office Hours** to the slide. If the Smart Tag icon appears, feel free to choose each option available to you.

Now add a slide to the end of the presentation, duplicating the Title slide. Hide the slide, Satisfied Customers. When you are finished working with this presentation, save and close it.

Critical Thinking 4.3 Use the Slide Show Toolbar

In this exercise, you will use the pen and highlighter tools. Run the presentation as a slide show. Using the Pointer tool, use the following table to emphasize points of the slide show:

Name of Slide	Pen or Highlighter Tools
Title	Highlight the subtitle
Targeted Marketing	Circle the Web Page and Real Estate Weekly bullets
Follow Up	Circle the bullet Market Activity then place a checkmark next to each bullet beneath Bimonthly Calls
Office Hours	Highlight the new date.

Save all changes and close the presentation.

Unit 2

Beyond the Basics

All applications in the Microsoft Office suite are designed to work together so you can work more efficiently. In this unit, you will see how PowerPoint can be integrated with Word, Excel, and Microsoft Graph. Armed with the skills you gained in Unit 1, you will now tackle more advanced topics, including outlining, templates, posting your presentations to the Web, and working with online collaboration. As in Unit 1, you will continue to develop and perfect several dynamic presentations. This unit ends with a comprehensive discussion of delivering successful presentations, and a special case study in which you create and deliver a presentation to a live audience.

Lesson 5: Working with Charts, Tables, and Office Applications

Lesson 6: Working with Online Presentations

Lesson 7: Working with Online Collaboration

Lesson 8: Managing Template Customization and Multimedia

Lesson 9: On the Road Again: A Case Study Workshop

LESSON 5

Working with Charts, Tables, and Office Applications

A cornerstone of the Microsoft Office suite of programs is the seamless way programs join together, or integrate, with each other. For example, in this lesson, you will learn how to place an Excel workbook into a PowerPoint presentation to harness the strength of Excel features in PowerPoint. Next you will discover how to set up a Word document so that when it is opened in PowerPoint, it becomes a PowerPoint presentation. And, you will take advantage of the Microsoft Graph charting program to create dynamic and precise charts in your presentation. Lastly, you will use the Diagram Tool to add a beautifully arranged organization chart that is clear, concise and stylish.

IN THIS LESSON

Microsoft Office PowerPoint 2003 objectives covered in this lesson

Objective Number	Skill Sets and Skills	Concept Page References	Exercise Page References
PP03S-1-2	Insert and edit text-based content	140	141–142
PP03S-1-3	Insert tables, charts, and diagrams	143–145, 147–148, 150–151, 154, 161–162	145–152, 154–159, 162–164
PP03S-4-8	Export a presentation to another Microsoft Office program	140	141–142, 164

Additional learning resources are available at labpub.com/learn/pp03/

Case Study

Working as a team, Al and Charlene continue to develop PowerPoint presentations for Pinnacle Pet Care. With the combination of Charlene's skill in fine tuning the presentation and Al's dynamic delivery style, with each presentation they win more customers to Pinnacle Pet Care. Finally, Al decides it is time to expand Pinnacle Pet Care by opening two new branches. He schedules a meeting with the loan committee at Twilight Hollow Bank. Al is concerned that he will have to recreate his best Excel workbook of financial projections until Charlene reminds him that they can simply link the Excel file in the PowerPoint presentation. Charlene uses Word to create an outline of goals for the meeting then imports the outline into PowerPoint. Voila! To Al's surprise, the Word outline is transformed into a PowerPoint presentation. Step by step, they create an integrated, complex presentation for the bank.

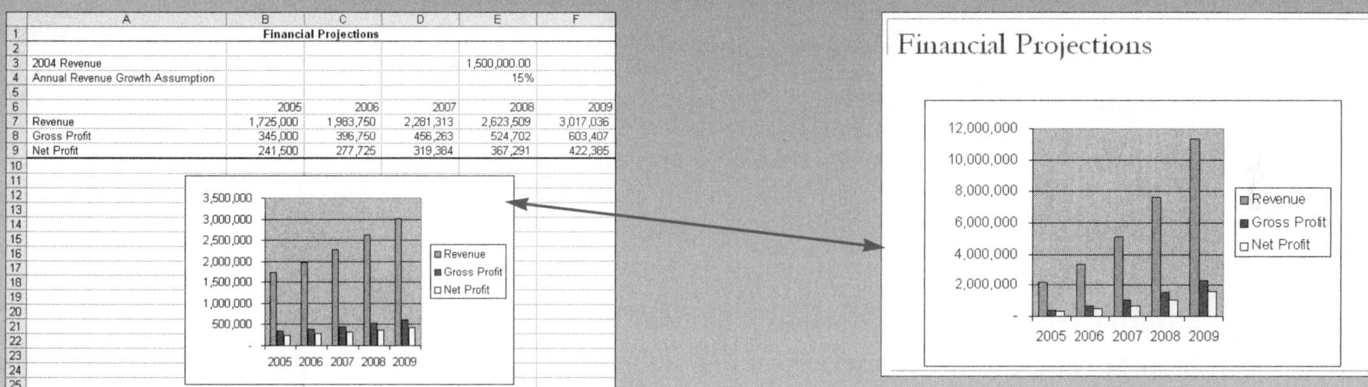

Linking an Excel object to PowerPoint

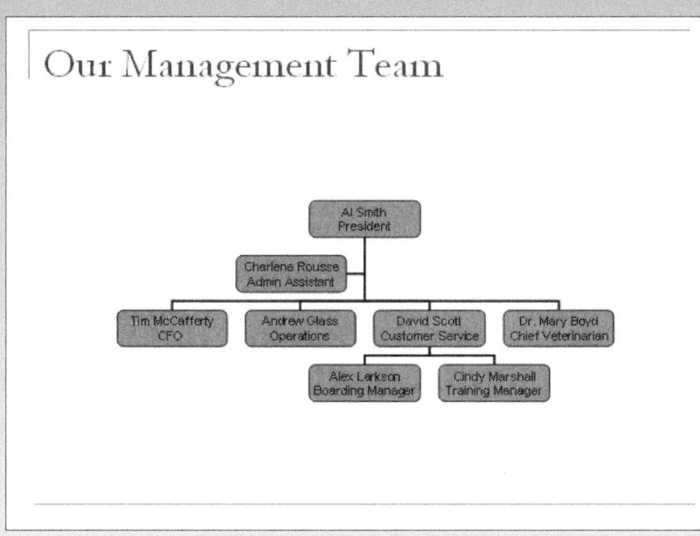

Creating an organization chart in PowerPoint

Working with Word Integration

Microsoft Office Specialist

Microsoft Word is an excellent word processing program that easily integrates with PowerPoint. Word's powerful outlining tool makes setting up and modifying outlines easy. You can create an outline in Word and import it to PowerPoint. Likewise, you can also create a presentation in PowerPoint that will transfer into an outline in Word.

Using Word Outlines

To use Word outlines in PowerPoint, you must apply the appropriate styles to the paragraphs in the Word document prior to importing the outline. PowerPoint converts the Word outline by using these rules:

- All Heading 1 paragraphs translate to Titles in a PowerPoint slide.
- All Heading 2 paragraphs translate to Level 1 Body Bullets in a PowerPoint slide.
- All Heading 3 paragraphs translate to Level 2 Body Bullets in a PowerPoint slide.

Once a Word outline is imported into PowerPoint, you can promote or demote the bullets, apply layouts and a design template, and make other enhancements. To import a Word document, use the Insert→Slides from Outline command.

Exporting PowerPoint Presentations to Word

The File→Send To→Microsoft Word command displays the Send to Microsoft Word dialog box, as shown to the right. The Send to Microsoft Word dialog box gives you the flexibility of sending the presentation to Word in different page layouts. You might recognize some of these layouts from the Handouts section of Lesson 4 (page 111).

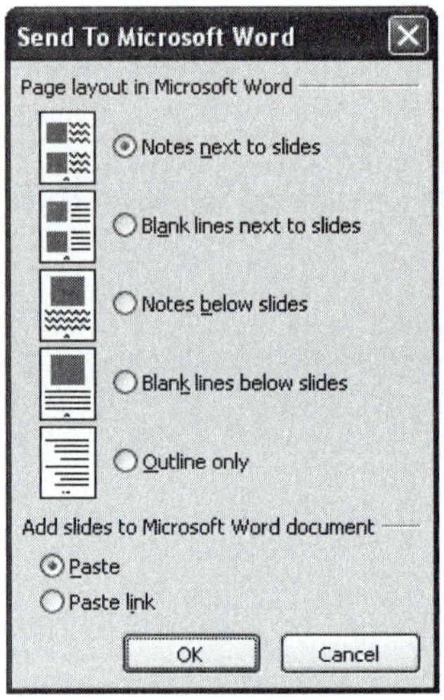

Exporting RTF Outlines

You can export a PowerPoint presentation to Word as an outline in Rich Text Format (RTF). Rich Text Format preserves all text and paragraph level formats. By exporting in RTF format, the new Word outline reflects the organization of the PowerPoint presentation. For example, all slide titles from the PowerPoint presentation are formatted with the Heading 1 style in the new Word outline. All first level bullets from the presentation are formatted with the Heading 2 style, etc. You can export a presentation to Word as an RTF outline by choosing the File→Save As command in PowerPoint, choosing the Outline/RTF option from Save as Type box, and specifying the location and name of the new Word outline.

Hands-On 5.1 Create a Presentation and Import a Word Outline

In this exercise, you will start a new Pinnacle Pet Care presentation, create an outline in Word, and modify the resulting presentation.

1. Open PowerPoint and click the New button to open a blank presentation.
2. Save the presentation as **`Pinnacle Pet Care Loan Statistics`** and minimize PowerPoint.

Create an Outline in Word

3. Start Word and a blank document will be displayed.
   In the next few steps, you will type and apply Word styles to paragraphs.
4. With the blank document opened, choose View→Outline to switch to Outline view then type the outline to the right in Word, tapping [Enter] once after each paragraph.

Pinnacle Pet Care
Twilight Hollow Bank
Our Objectives
Establish a Merchant Visa Account
Establish a $100,000 line of credit
Obtain a $350,000 SBA loan
Our Expansion Plan
Pinnacle Pet Care East
Pinnacle Pet Care West
New Products and Services

Apply Style Headings to the Word Outline

5. Follow these steps to apply the Heading 1 style to the first paragraph:

A Click anywhere in the Pinnacle Pet Care paragraph to position the flashing insertion point on the paragraph.

B Click the Style List drop-down button to display a list of built-in styles.

C Choose the Heading 1 style.

D Notice that the style formats the entire paragraph. This paragraph will become the title of a new slide when the outline is imported into PowerPoint.

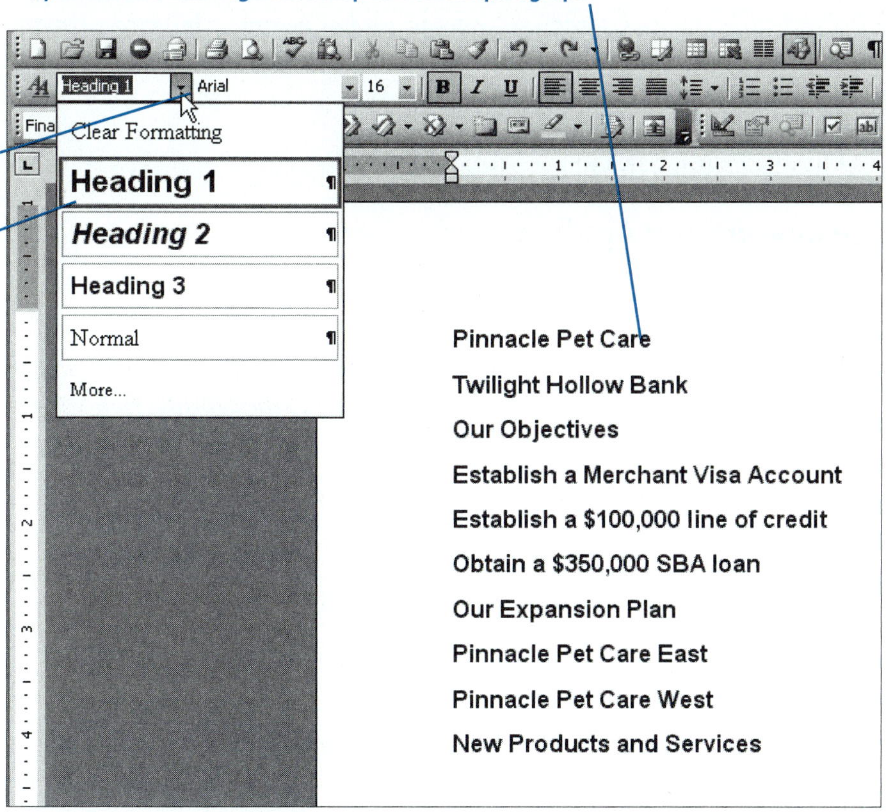

6. Apply the Heading 1 style to the Our Objectives and Our Expansion Plan paragraphs by clicking the paragraphs and choosing the Heading 1 style.

7. Apply the Heading 2 style to all remaining paragraphs. You can apply the style one paragraph at a time or select several paragraphs at once. Your completed outline should match the example shown to the right.

Pinnacle Pet Care

Twilight Hollow Bank

Our Objectives

Establish a Merchant Visa Account

Establish a $100,000 line of credit

Obtain a $350,000 SBA loan

Our Expansion Plan

Pinnacle Pet Care East

Pinnacle Pet Care West

New Products and Services

8. Click the Save button and save the outline to your file storage location as **`Pinnacle Pet Care Statistics Outline`**.

9. Choose File→Exit to close the outline and Word.

Import the Outline

10. Click the Pinnacle Pet Care Loan Statistics presentation that has been minimized on your taskbar to activate it.

11. Choose Insert→Slides from Outline from the menu bar.

12. Use the Insert Outline dialog box to navigate to your file storage location.

13. Choose the Pinnacle Pet Care Statistics Outline file and click the Insert button.
PowerPoint will take a moment to import the outline.

14. Examine the Outline Tab in PowerPoint with the inserted text from Word.
Note that the first slide is blank. Also observe that each Heading 1 paragraph from the outline has become a slide title and each Heading 2 paragraph has become a bulleted paragraph under the appropriate title.

15. Click the Slides tab to view the slide thumbnails.

16. Choose the first slide (the blank slide) and tap Delete to remove it.

Change a Layout and Apply a Design Template

17. Display the Slide Layout task pane.

18. Choose the Title Slide layout (the first layout).
PowerPoint converts the layout of the first slide to a title slide layout. The Pinnacle Pet Care paragraph becomes the slide title and Twilight Hollow Bank becomes the subtitle. Notice that the presentation does not have a design. In the next few steps, you will apply a design template to the presentation.

19. Click the Design button to display the Slide Design task pane.

20. Choose the Edge design template as shown to the right.

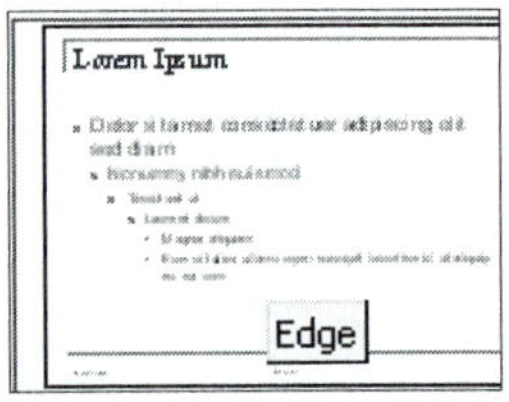

21. Browse through the presentation and notice that the template has been applied to all slides.

22. Choose the second slide, Our Objectives.

23. Select the paragraphs and remove the italic formatting.
The italic formatting was imported because it is part of the Heading 2 formatting in Word.

24. Remove the italic formatting from the bulleted paragraphs on the third slide.

25. Save the changes to your presentation and continue with the next topic.

Working with Microsoft Graph Charts

Microsoft Office Specialist

PowerPoint is an intensely visual application. While it is often the case that you will be creating presentations that represent concepts or goals, there are also times when you will need to present financial statistics or numerical data. To represent numerical data in PowerPoint, take advantage of the impressive charting program used in all Office programs, Microsoft Graph.

Creating Microsoft Graph Charts

Microsoft Graph is a utility that has been integrated into the Office suite. Just as you would apply a slide layout for clip art, you will also apply a slide layout for a chart. PowerPoint supplies you with three different layouts for charts. Each chart layout includes a Chart icon that can activate Microsoft Graph. The following illustration displays the different types of Chart layouts available in PowerPoint.

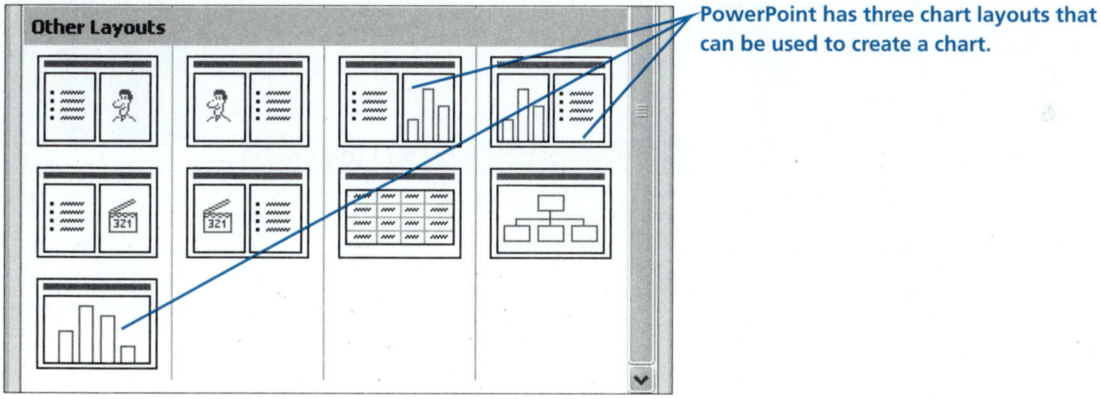

When Microsoft Graph is activated, PowerPoint's toolbars and menus are replaced with Graph's toolbars and menus. You can use Graph's toolbars and menus to create, modify, and format your chart without leaving the PowerPoint window. The following illustration shows the PowerPoint window after Graph has been activated.

Graph displays a sample chart and datasheet with sample data. Use the datasheet to type the information you want represented in the chart.

The Microsoft Graph toolbar replaces PowerPoint's toolbars.

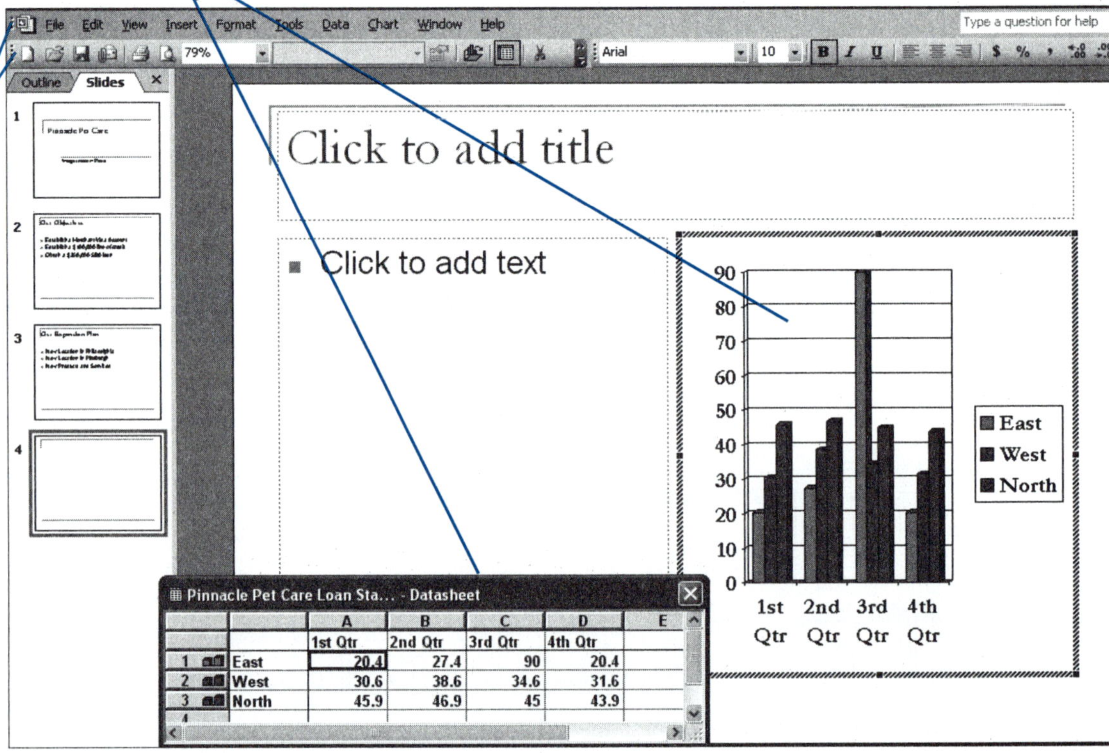

Modifying Charts

To modify a chart, use the commands on Graph's menu bar and toolbar. You can size the chart by dragging the sizing handles then moving the chart by dragging it to a different location. When you have finished editing the chart, click anywhere in the PowerPoint window to hide the chart datasheet and restore the PowerPoint window. Graph can be activated at any time by double-clicking the chart icon.

The Microsoft Graph toolbar is examined in detail in the following illustration.

Hands-On 5.2 Insert and Modify a Chart

In this exercise, you will use Microsoft Graph to create a chart inside your PowerPoint presentation, change the datasheet, and resize the chart.

Insert the Slide and Add Text

1. If necessary, click the Normal icon to make sure the presentation is in Normal view.
2. Click the Our Expansion Plan slide thumbnail (the 3rd slide).
   In the next few steps, you will add a new slide after the Our Expansion Plan slide.
3. Click the New Slide button.
4. Scroll through the layouts and choose the Title, Text, and Chart layout in the Other Layouts category.
   PowerPoint will apply the new layout, which includes a chart placeholder box.
5. As the title, type **`Year-To-Date Results`**.
6. Click in the bulleted list box and add the bullets shown to the right.

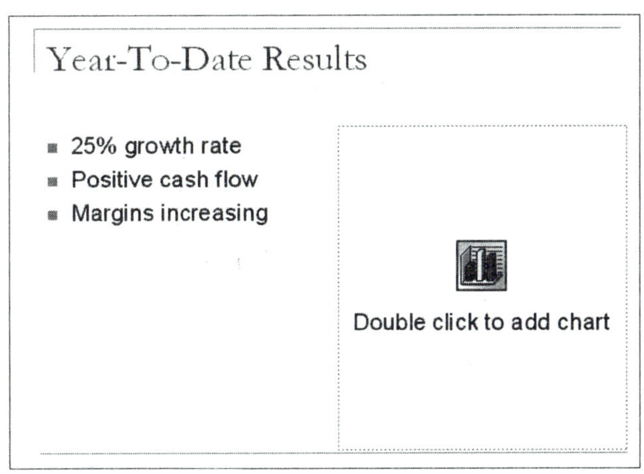

Set Up the Chart

7. Double-click the Chart icon and Microsoft Graph replaces PowerPoint toolbars with Microsoft Graph toolbars.

8. Follow these steps to set up the chart datasheet:

A Click the cell with the word East, type **Revenue**, and tap [Enter]. The word Revenue will replace the word East.

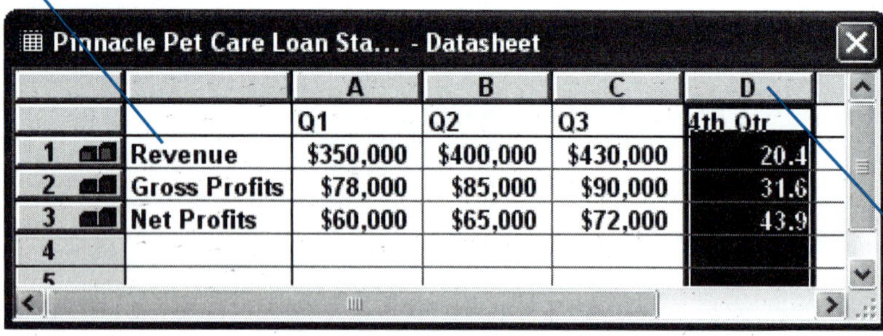

B Enter the remaining data shown here, except for the data in the column labeled 4th Qtr. Click a cell, type the data, then click another cell. Notice that as you replace the data, the new information is displayed in the Chart. The datasheet and the chart are intertwined.

C Select column D by clicking this column heading then tap [Delete]. The chart will no longer include a 4th quarter.

9. Now click outside the datasheet to go back to the PowerPoint window.
   PowerPoint's menu bar and toolbars should appear. The chart datasheet is only visible when Microsoft Graph is activated.

Modify the Chart

10. To modify the chart, just double-click on it. Microsoft Graph will be activated.
    This type of chart is an embedded object. You can always activate an embedded object by double-clicking it.

11. Follow these steps to size the chart:

Ⓐ Drag this sizing handle to the right until the chart has approximately these dimensions.

Ⓑ Click outside the chart to restore the PowerPoint window.

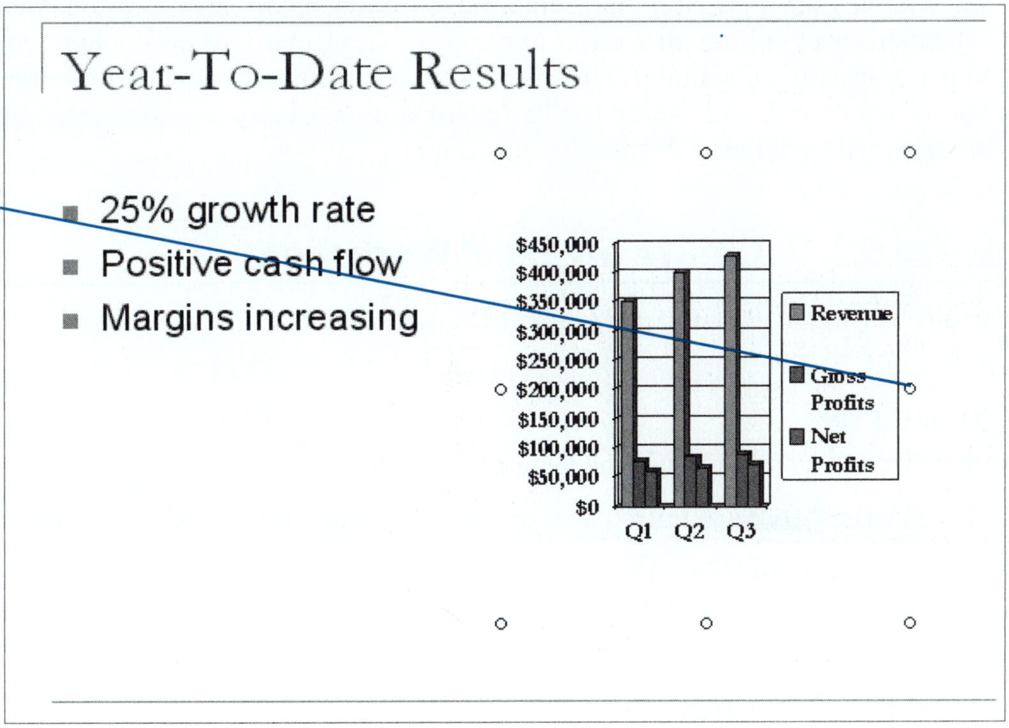

12. Save the changes to your presentation and minimize it on the taskbar.

Working with Excel Integration

Microsoft Office **Specialist**

Office 2003 provides a variety of tools and techniques to let you exchange data between applications. Object Linking and Embedding (OLE) allows you to create links between source documents and destination documents. For example, you may want an Excel chart to appear in a PowerPoint presentation.

Creating a chart in Excel and linking the chart object to PowerPoint gives you the opportunity to use Excel's powerful analysis and charting capabilities. You can integrate an Excel chart into PowerPoint by embedding the chart using the Copy and Paste command. Or, you can link the chart to PowerPoint using the Copy and Paste Special command. If you choose to link the chart, each time the Excel workbook is modified in Excel; the change will be reflected in the presentation. In other words, it is a live link. If you embed the chart, then the data remains static in PowerPoint since the source document is no longer tied to the PowerPoint (destination) slide.

The Paste Special Command

You use the Edit→Paste Special command to establish object linking and embedding. To establish object linking, first select and copy the text, chart, or other object you wish to link to the destination document. Then switch to the destination document, issue the Edit→Paste Special command, and choose the Paste Link option. Changes made in the source document are then reflected in the destination document.

Hands-On 5.3 Create an Excel Worksheet

In this exercise, you will create and save an Excel worksheet. Then you will also copy the Excel data to create a chart in PowerPoint.

Start Excel

1. Start your computer and the Windows Desktop will appear.
2. Click the start button and choose (All) Programs.
3. Choose Microsoft Excel.
   The Excel program will load and the Excel window will appear. Don't be concerned if your window looks different from the following example.

Create an Excel Worksheet

4. Follow these steps to create the Excel worksheet in the following illustration:

A In cell A1, type **`Financial Projections`** then tap [Enter] twice.

	A	B	C	D	E	F
1	Financial Projections					
2		2005	2006	2007	2008	2009
3	Revenue	2,250,000	3,375,000	5,062,500	7,593,750	11,390,625
4	Gross Profit	450,000	675,000	1,012,500	1,518,750	2,278,125
5	Net Profit	315,000	472,500	708,750	1,063,125	1,594,688

B In cell A3, type **`Revenue`**, tap [Enter], and type the remaining text entries in column A.

C Click in cell B2 and enter the data in column B, tapping [Enter] after each entry, then enter the remaining data in the worksheet.

5. Click File→Save As and save the file to your file storage location as **`Pinnacle Pet Care Financial Projections`**.
6. Leave the file open.

Add a New Title and Chart Slide

7. Click the Microsoft PowerPoint button on your taskbar and choose the Year-To-Date Results slide.

8. Click the New Slide button to create a new slide.

9. Scroll down to the bottom of the Slide Layout task pane and choose the Title and Chart layout.

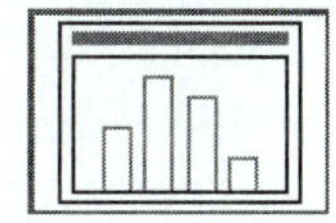

10. Click the title box of the new slide and type **`Financial Projections`**.
You will create a PowerPoint chart using the data from the Excel file you just created.

11. Double-click the chart icon in the body object.
The Microsoft Graph program opens and displays the default chart and datasheet.

Create a Chart with Excel Data

12. Click the Microsoft Excel button on the taskbar to display the Pinnacle Pet Care Financial Projections worksheet.

13. Follow these steps to select the cell range to use for the chart:

	A	B	C	D	E	F
1	Financial Projections					
2		2005	2006	2007	2008	2009
3	Revenue	500,000	3,375,000	5,062,500	7,593,750	11,390,625
4	Gross Profit	450,000	675,000	1,012,500	1,518,750	2,278,125
5	Net Profit	315,000	472,500	708,750	1,063,125	1,594,688

Ⓐ Click and hold the mouse button down in cell A2.

Ⓑ Drag down and across to cell F5 then release the mouse button.

14. Click the Copy button.

15. Click the Microsoft PowerPoint button on the taskbar to redisplay the Pinnacle Pet Care Loan Statistics presentation.

16. Follow these steps to paste the Excel data into the chart's datasheet:

Ⓐ Click in the top-left cell in the datasheet grid.

Ⓑ Hold down the Ctrl key and tap V.

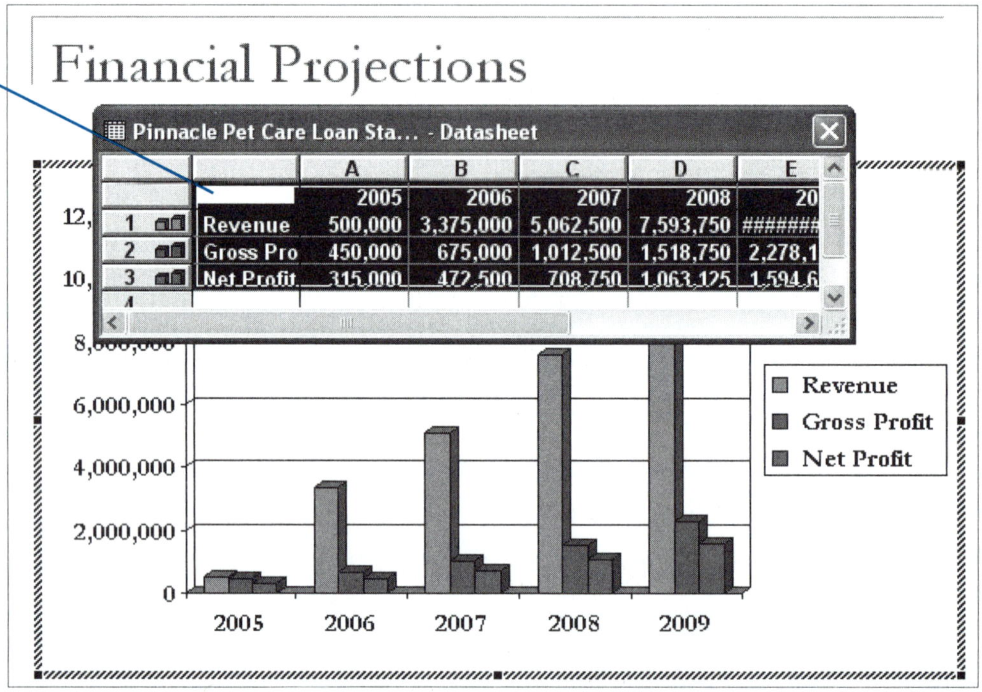

The data is pasted into the datasheet and the chart is updated, reflecting the new Excel data.

17. Click outside the chart.
The Microsoft Graph program closes and you are returned to the PowerPoint presentation.

18. Save and close the Excel file.

19. Save the PowerPoint file but leave it open for the next exercise.

Using PowerPoint Tables

Microsoft Office Specialist

Tables are useful for organizing text and numbers into rows and columns. PowerPoint has a table layout that makes inserting tables into slides easy. You can insert tables into slides with the Table layout using the Insert Tables button on the Standard toolbar or by double-clicking the Table icon on the slide.

The Insert Table button displays a grid so you can choose the number of rows and columns. Drag the mouse pointer across the grid to create a table.

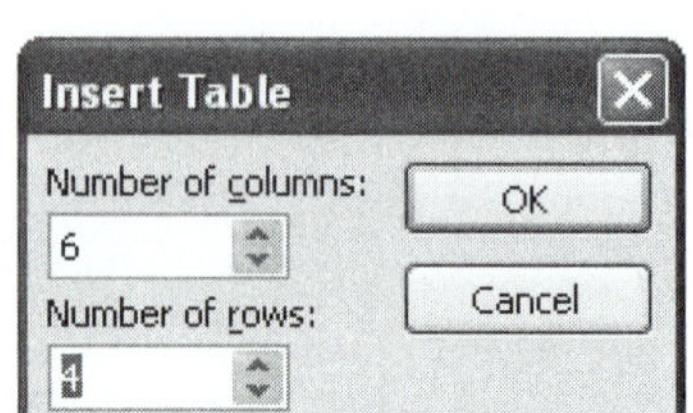

You can also double-click the Table icon in the placeholder to display the Insert Table dialog box. Use this dialog box to determine the number of rows and columns in your table.

Hands-On 5.4 Create a PowerPoint Table

In this exercise, you will create a PowerPoint table.

1. Choose the Year-To-Date Results slide (the fourth slide).
2. Click the New Slide button.
3. Scroll toward the bottom of the Layout list and choose the Title and Table layout, as shown to the right.
4. In the Title placeholder, type **Revenue Details**.
5. Double-click the Table icon on the slide and the Insert Table box will appear.
6. Enter **6** for the number of columns and **4** for the number of rows then click OK.
   A table with 6 columns and 4 rows will be placed in your slide. You will enter data in the table in Hands-On 5.5.

Entering Data in Tables

Microsoft Office Specialist

PowerPoint allows both text and numbers in tables. When text is used, PowerPoint wraps the text to fit the cell. The cell height increases to accommodate the wrapped text. You can also use [Enter] to insert blank lines in a cell and increase the cell height.

Navigating in Tables

You can position the insertion point in a cell by clicking the desired cell. However, it is often more efficient to use the keyboard to move between cells. You use the [Tab] key to move forward one cell and [Shift]+[Tab] to move back one cell. If the insertion point is in the last cell of the table, the [Tab] key will add a new row to the bottom of the table.

Hands-On 5.5 Enter Data into a PowerPoint Table

In this exercise, you will enter data into a PowerPoint table.

1. If your mouse pointer has a pencil shape, click the Draw Table button on the Tables and Borders toolbar to remove it.
2. Click in the second cell of the first row and type the entry **2005**.
3. Tap the [Tab] key to move the insertion point to the next cell.
4. Type **2006** and tap [Tab] again.

5. Continue entering data, using the following table. As you enter data, PowerPoint will wrap many of the entries within the cells. In Hands-On 5.6, you will adjust the font size and column widths to prevent the entries from wrapping.

	2005	2006	2007	2008	2009
Medical Care	$1,121,250	$1,289,500	$1,482,000	$1,705,300	$1,961,000
Services	$431,000	$496,000	$570,000	$656,000	$755,000
Product Sales	$173,000	$198,000	$228,000	$262,000	$302,000

6. Save the changes to your presentation and continue with the next topic.

Selecting Table Cells

To format data in a cell, the cell must be selected. You can select cells by dragging the mouse pointer over the desired cells. Columns can be selected by clicking or dragging above the desired column(s). Rows can be selected by clicking or dragging to the left of the desired row(s).

Aligning and Formatting Cell Entries

Use the Align Left, Center, and Align Right buttons on the Formatting toolbar to align entries horizontally within table cells.

Or use the Table and Borders toolbar, which is displayed when the table is being used to align, fill, or modify the cells. You will learn more about this in The Tables and Borders Toolbar section on page 153.

Adjusting Column Widths and Row Heights

The mouse pointer changes shape whenever it is positioned over a column or row border. Column widths and row heights can be adjusted by dragging the borders. In addition, you can double-click a column's right border to autofit the column width. The column width increases or decreases to accommodate the widest entry in the column.

Hands-On 5.6 Format Table Entries and Adjust Column Widths

Currently, many of the table entries are too wide to fit in the cells. In this exercise, you will reduce the font size of the table text to allow the entries to fit within the cells without wrapping. In addition, you will autofit all column widths to fit the widest entries in the columns.

1. Position the mouse pointer over the first table cell. Press and hold down the left mouse button and drag down and to the right until all cells in the table are selected.
2. Set the font size to 16 using the Font Size 10 button on the Formatting toolbar.
3. Click anywhere in the table to deselect the cells.

4. Follow these steps to autofit the column widths and right-align columns 2–6:

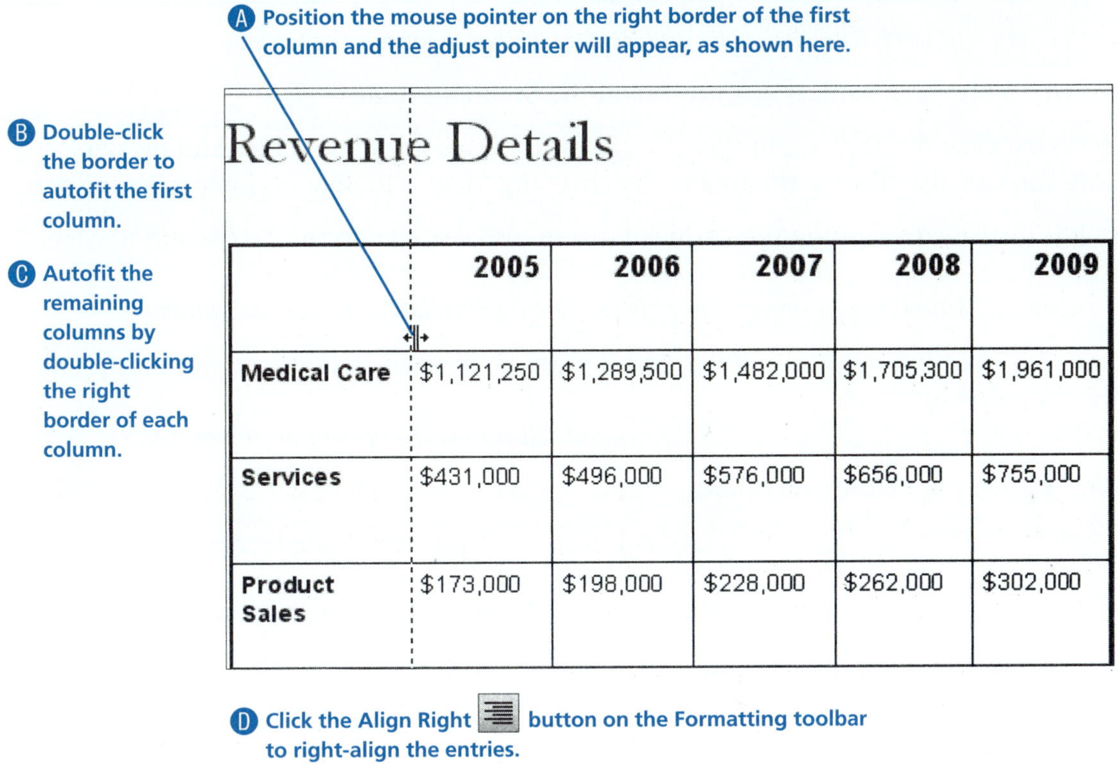

	2005	2006	2007	2008	2009
Medical Care	$1,121,250	$1,289,500	$1,482,000	$1,705,300	$1,961,000
Services	$431,000	$496,000	$576,000	$656,000	$755,000
Product Sales	$173,000	$198,000	$228,000	$262,000	$302,000

5. Feel free to experiment with selection techniques and formatting commands. Your completed table should match the preceding example.

The Tables and Borders Toolbar

The Tables and Borders button on the Standard toolbar displays the Tables and Borders toolbar. Using the Tables and Borders toolbar, you can apply borders and shading to cells in the table, change the alignment of text, add rows or columns, and make many other adjustments. The following illustration describes the buttons on the Tables and Borders toolbar.

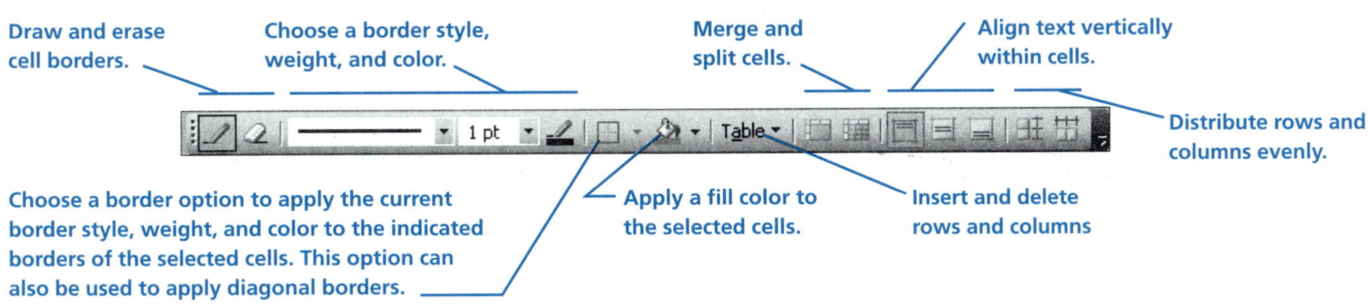

Hands-On 5.7 Experiment with Borders and Shading

In this exercise, you will work with the Tables and Borders toolbar to format the table.

1. Notice the Tables and Borders button on the Standard toolbar.
2. If necessary, click the Tables and Borders button to display the Tables and Borders toolbar. You can also display the toolbar by choosing View→Toolbars→Tables and Borders.
3. Once it is displayed, examine the various buttons and options on the Tables and Borders toolbar.
   The various formatting options are applied only to selected cells when you click the buttons.
4. Choose the Table option on the Tables and Borders toolbar and notice the various options on the drop-down menu.
   Notice that you can insert, delete, and select rows and columns using options on this menu.
5. Tap the [Esc] key to dismiss the menu.
6. Feel free to select various cells, rows, or columns and apply the table formats of your choice.
   You can use Undo after applying formats if you are not satisfied with the results.
7. Save the changes to your presentation and continue with the next topic.

Inserting Microsoft Word Tables

Microsoft Office **Specialist**

Creating a table in Word will give you more flexibility than creating a table in PowerPoint. If you need complex tables, then you may want to develop your tables in Word and insert them into your PowerPoint slides. You use the same techniques for inserting Word objects as you used earlier in this lesson with Excel objects. Word tables and other objects can be embedded in slides using the copy and paste technique or the Insert→Object command. Remember that embedding simply means that the object is in the PowerPoint slide, it is not linked to the original file. Or, you can create dynamic links between Word objects and your PowerPoint slides using the Paste Special technique described in the Working with Excel Integration section of this lesson.

Hands-On 5.8 Insert a Word Table

In this exercise, you will create a table in Word then insert the table in PowerPoint. You will also format and size the table. Finally, you will compare the differences in table features.

Create a Table in Word

1. Start Microsoft Word and a blank document will be displayed.
2. Choose Table→Insert→Table from the Standard toolbar.

3. Follow these steps to construct and insert your table:

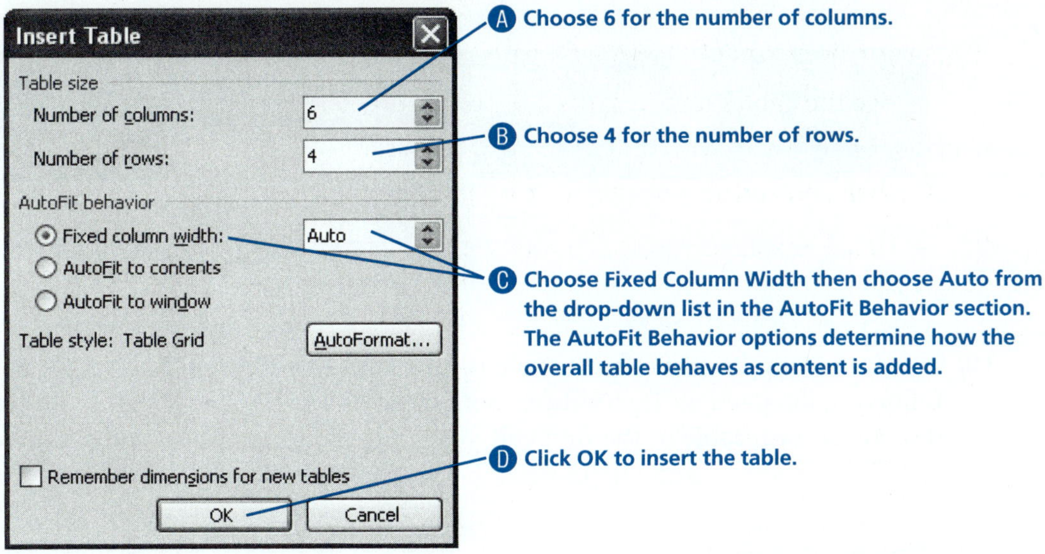

4. Minimize the Word document.

Copy and Paste the Data from PowerPoint

5. Display the PowerPoint window by clicking the Microsoft PowerPoint button on the taskbar.

6. Navigate to the Revenue Details slide.

7. Follow these steps to copy the data from the PowerPoint table:

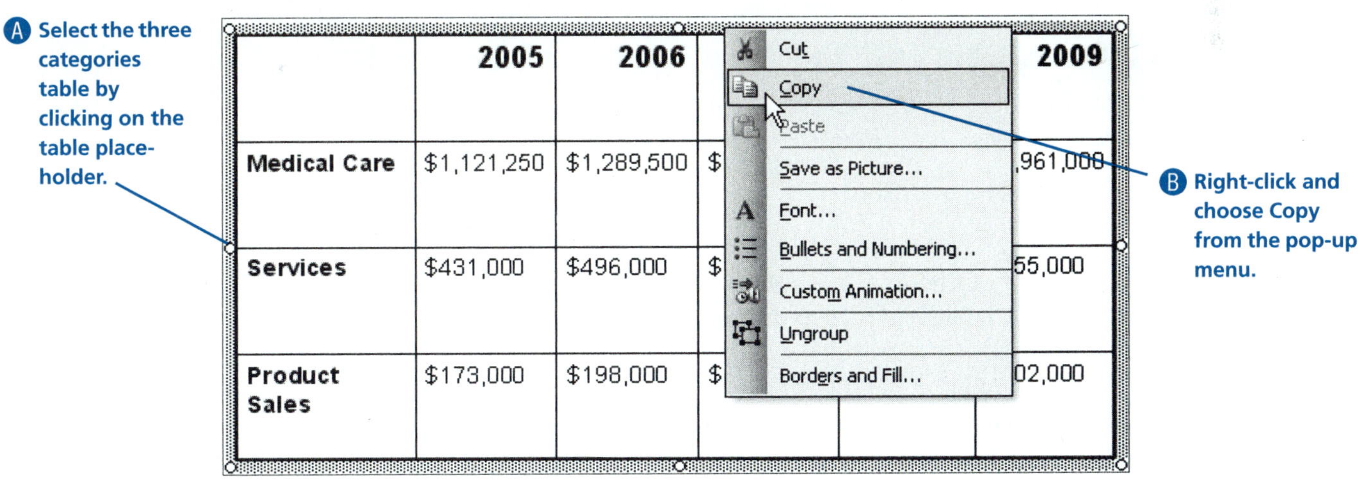

8. Display the Word document by clicking the Microsoft Word button on the Taskbar.

9. Select the Word table then right-click on the cells and choose Paste Cells as shown in the following illustration.

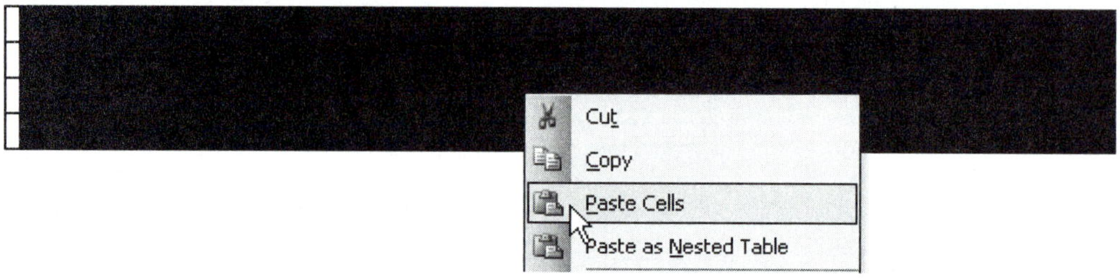

10. The data from the PowerPoint table is now contained in the Word table as shown in the following illustration. In addition, notice the extra characters that were transferred from the PowerPoint table in the first cell of the first column. Select the characters in the first cell of the first row and tap Delete.

[illegible]	2005	2006	2007	2008	2009
Medical Care	$1,121,250	$1,289,500	$1,482,000	$1,705,300	$1,961,000
Services	$431,000	$496,000	$576,000	$656,000	$755,000
Product Sales	$173,000	$198,000	$228,000	$262,000	302,000

Realign the Table with the Word Tables and Borders Toolbar

Notice that the font size is too large for the Word table. You will now format the Word table to improve its appearance.

11. Click the Tables and Borders button on Word's Standard toolbar to display the toolbar in Word.

12. If your insertion point turns into a pencil shape, click the Draw Table button on the Tables and Borders toolbar to dismiss it.

13. Select the entire Word Table.

14. Click the Distribute Rows Evenly button on the Tables and Borders toolbar to format the Word table so all the rows are of equal height.

15. Then click the Distribute Columns Evenly button on the Tables and Borders toolbar to format the Word table so all columns are of equal width.

Change the Page Layout

16. Choose File→Page Setup from the menu bar. In the Page Setup dialog box, click on the Margins tab. In the Orientation section, click the Landscape icon.
Now the Word page and the PowerPoint page have the same page orientation.

AutoFormat the Table in Word

17. Select the entire Word table and click the AutoFormat button on the Tables and Borders toolbar.

18. Choose the Table Contemporary style and make sure that each option is checked. Click Apply to apply the style to the Word table.

19. Follow these steps to widen the first table column:

(A) Position the insertion point on the border between the first and second columns. The insertion point will become a double-headed arrow. Press and hold the left mouse button and drag to the right slightly to widen the column. Continue to adjust the column width until the text in the first column no longer wraps.

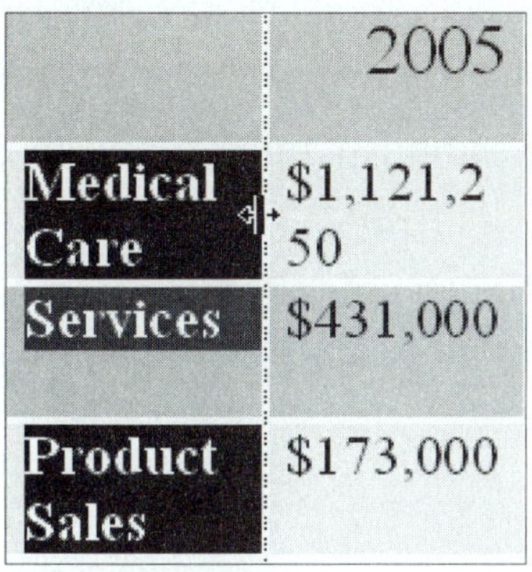

(B) Change each cell of the Word table in the same manner by moving the line of the column to the right until none of the cells wrap.

20. Your table will match the following illustration.

	2005	2006	2007	2008	2009
Medical Care	$1,121,250	$1,289,500	$1,482,000	$1,705,300	$1,961,000
Services	$431,000	$496,000	$576,000	$656,000	$755,000
Product Sales	$173,000	$198,000	$228,000	$262,000	$302,000

21. Save the Word document as **`Pinnacle Pet Care Revenue Details`**.

Insert the Word Table into the PowerPoint Presentation

22. Display PowerPoint and navigate to the Revenue Details slide.
23. Click the New Slide button to add a blank slide below the PowerPoint table.
24. Apply the Title and Content to the slide.
25. In the Title of the new slide, type **`Pinnacle Pet Care Revenue Details`**.
26. Click anywhere in the Content placeholder.
27. Choose Insert→Object from the menu bar to display the Insert Object dialog box.
    This box is similar to the one we used to insert the Excel worksheet.
28. Choose the Create from File option.
29. Click the Browse button and navigate to the Pinnacle Pet Care Revenue Details Word document you just created.
30. Check the Link box beside the Browse button to establish a link between the Word document and PowerPoint slide.
31. Click OK and the Word table should appear in the Revenue Details slide.
    The table is linked to the source file in Word. Thus, any changes made to the table in the Word document will be reflected in the PowerPoint slide.

Format the Table in Word

32. Double-click the PowerPoint table.
    The Word program window will appear with the Word table displayed. Double-clicking a linked object (the PowerPoint table) always opens the associated application and file.
33. Apply Bold formatting to the first row of table text.
34. Change the font size of the first row to 16.
35. Save the Word document and close it.
36. Display PowerPoint by choosing the Microsoft PowerPoint button on the taskbar.
    Notice that the changes have not been reflected in PowerPoint yet.
37. Click the Save button in PowerPoint to save the presentation.
    After the slide is saved, the PowerPoint table reflects the changes you made in the associated Word document!

38. Compare the two tables by clicking the Slide Sorter button to view the two slides. Your slides should match the following two tables.

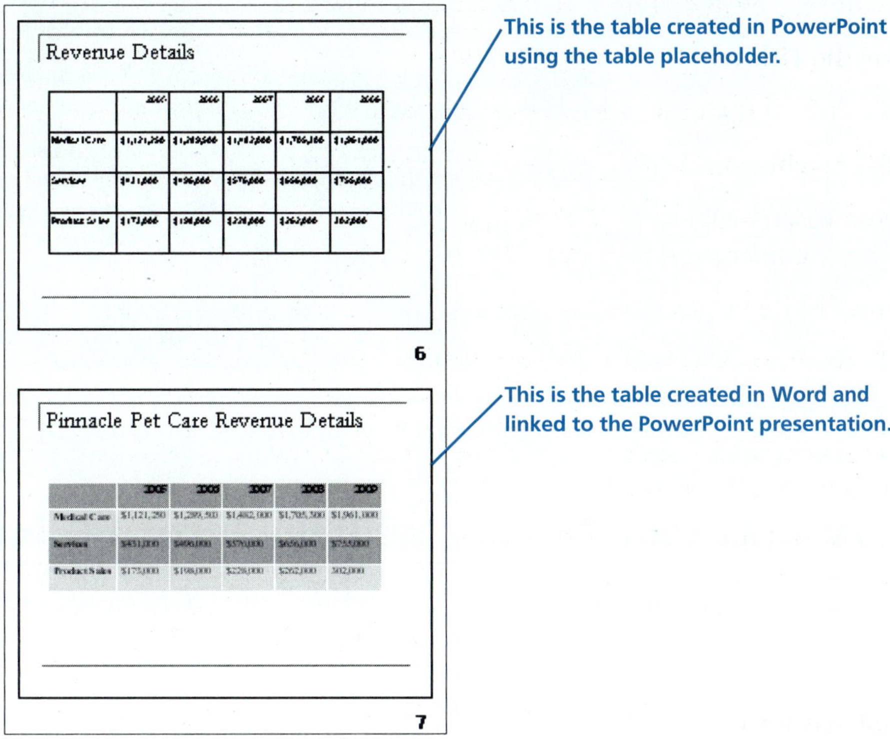

39. When you are finished comparing the slides, save the presentation again and continue with the next topic.
If you were presenting to a bank to obtain a loan, which table would you choose? We will leave both slides in the presentation for right now.

The Format Painter

The Format Painter is a great tool, common to all Office programs, that simplifies the formatting process. For example, we have just worked through an intense process of formatting the table in Word. To simplify the task, we could have copied the formatting using the Format Painter. The Format Painter copies all text formats including the typeface, size, color, and attributes such as bold, italic, and underline. The Format Painter helps you to maintain a standardized, uniform look in your presentation with ease.

QR **QUICK REFERENCE: COPYING TEXT FORMATS WITH THE FORMAT PAINTER**

Task	Procedure
Copy text formats with the Format Painter.	■ Click on the text with the format(s) you wish to copy. ■ Click the Format Painter once to copy formats to only one other location or double-click to copy the formats to more than one location. ■ Select the text at the new location(s) you want to format. If you double-clicked in the previous step, the Format Painter will remain active, allowing you to select text at multiple locations. You can even navigate to various slides in the presentation and select the text you wish to format. ■ If you double-clicked in the second step, click the Format Painter button when you have finished. This will turn off the Format Painter.

TIP! *Using Format Painter, the mouse pointer changes from an arrow to a brush.*

Hands-On 5.9 Change Formats with the Format Painter

In this exercise, you will use the Format Painter to change the format of the top row in the Revenue Details slide and experiment with the categories section of the table.

1. Navigate to the Revenue Details slide.
2. Click on the date 2005 in the second cell and use the Font Size 10 button on the Formatting toolbar to change the font size to 20.
3. Double-click the Format Painter button on the Standard toolbar.
4. Drag the Format Painter over the dates 2006, 2007, 2008, and 2009 to copy the font size to those dates.
   The entire row should now be font size 20 since the Format Painter brushed the formatting onto the other numbers.
5. Use the Slides tab to go to the Title slide.
6. Select the subtitle on the Title slide.
7. Click the Format Painter button.
8. Use the Slides tab to go to the Revenue Details slide.
   Notice that your insertion point has turned into a paint brush to indicate that the Format Painter is ready to copy formats to other locations.
9. Brush the first column of categories in the Revenue Details slide to apply the formatting from the subtitle onto the column categories.
   The font is much too big but the format has been applied!
10. Click Undo to reverse the action.
11. If necessary, click the Format Painter to turn it off or press Esc.
12. Save the presentation and continue with the next topic.

Working with Diagrams

Microsoft Office Specialist

As you create your presentation, you may need to include an organization chart that features the key players in your project or the leadership team of your organization. Organization charts can be created in PowerPoint using the Diagram Tool. The Diagram Tool has been improved in PowerPoint 2003. With the Diagram Tool, creating a diagram is as straightforward as it is effortless. The resulting diagrams will crystallize concepts in your presentation so that the audience will clearly understand your ideas.

The Title and Diagram or Organization Chart layout shown in the following illustration features placeholders for a title and diagram. When you double-click the icon that appears on the slide in the diagram placeholder, the Diagram Gallery is displayed. You can choose a diagram type from the gallery then construct the diagram directly on the slide within the placeholder.

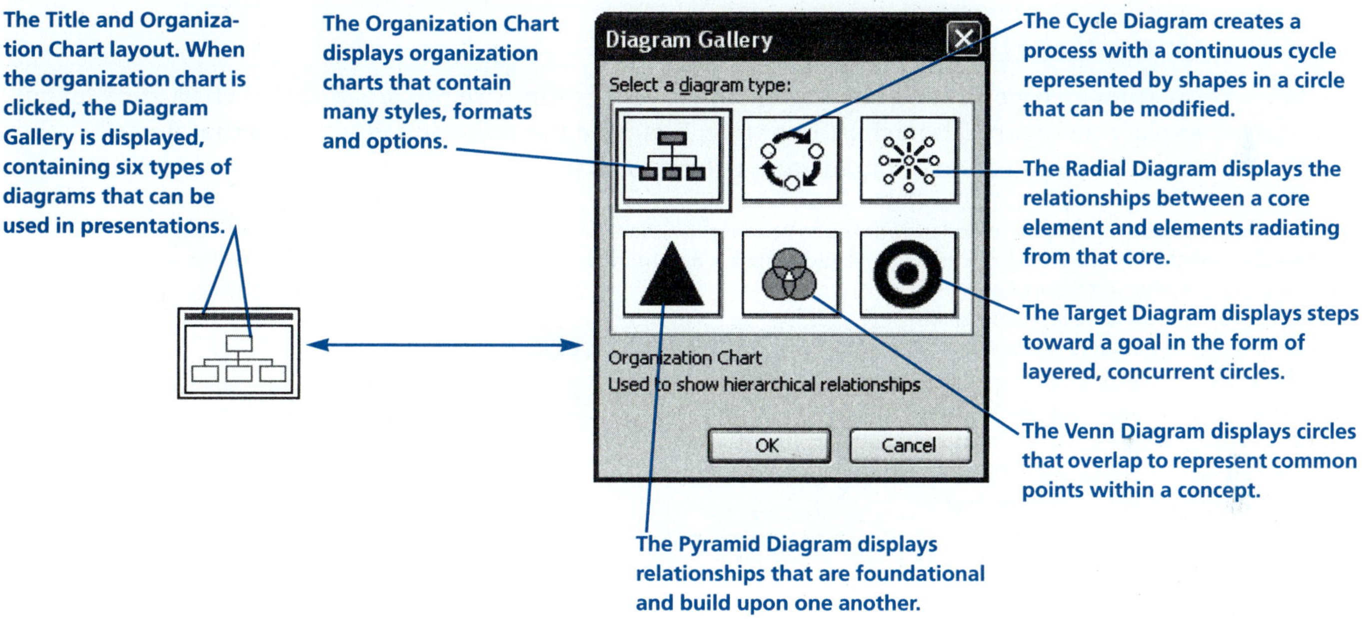

Diagram Toolbars

As you work with PowerPoint diagrams, you will observe that each diagram type has an associated toolbar. These toolbars are comprised of similar buttons that step you through the process of adding, formatting, realigning, and revising the diagram. As a stepping stone to understanding all toolbars, examine the following illustration.

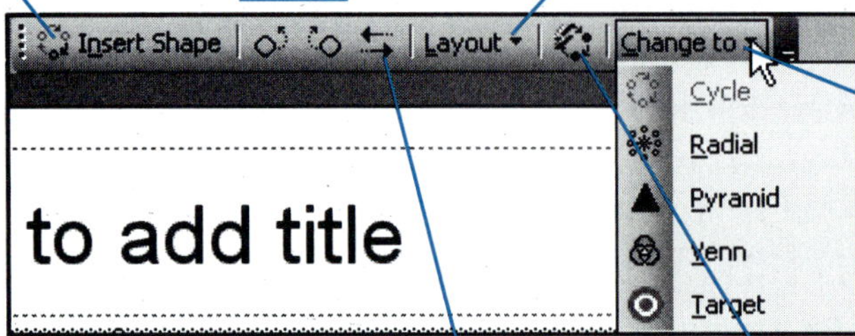

Organization Charts

Creating an organization chart is as simple as it is fun. Use the organization chart slide layout to place an organization chart in a slide. Examine the following illustration that describes the Insert Shapes section of organization chart toolbar.

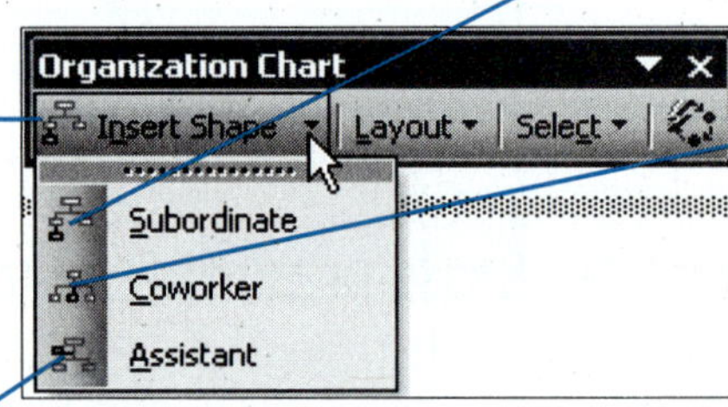

Hands-On 5.10 Set Up an Organization Chart

In this exercise, you will create an organizational chart in PowerPoint, adding text to the various levels of the chart. Then you will save the presentation in RTF (rich text format) to use in Word.

Insert the Organization Chart

1. Select the Revenue Details slide and click the New Slide button to insert a new slide.
2. Scroll toward the bottom of the Layout list and choose the Title and Diagram or Organization Chart layout.
3. In the Title placeholder, type **`Our Management Team`**.
4. Double click the Organization Chart icon in the diagram placeholder to display the Diagram Gallery.

5. Take a moment to examine the various diagram types.
6. Choose the Organization Chart diagram and click OK.
   A sample organization chart will be inserted in the placeholder.

Add Text

7. Follow these steps to add text to the organization chart:

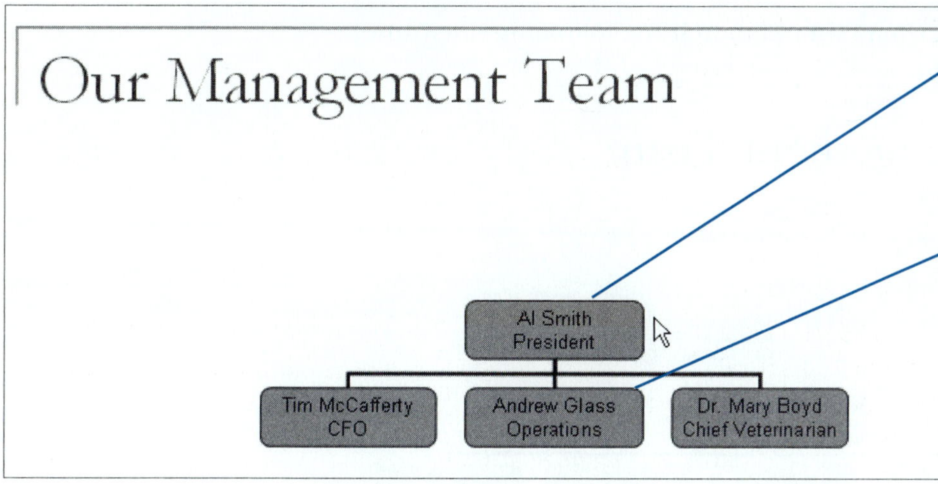

A Click in the single box at the head of the chart and type **`Al Smith`**. Tap [Enter] and type **`President`**. The single box represents the head of this organization.

B Enter the text shown in the three boxes below Al Smith. Each of these boxes, called subordinates, are placed below the head of the chart. They report to the head of the organization.

Add a Coworker Box

8. Click in the Andrew Glass box in the organization chart.
   This selects the appropriate box so you can add another shape beside it.
9. Click the Insert Shape button on the Organization Chart toolbar and choose Coworker.
10. Type the name **`David Scott`** in the new box then tap [Enter] to move to a second line in the box and type **`Customer Service`**.

Add a Subordinate Box

11. If necessary, select the David Scott box by clicking in it.
    We will place a subordinate box below David Scott.
12. Click the Insert Shape button and choose Subordinate.
13. Type **`Alex Larkson`**, tap [Enter], and type **`Boarding Manager`** on the second line of the box.
14. Select the David Scott box.
15. Click the Insert Shape button and choose Subordinate
    David Scott should have two subordinate boxes below his name.
16. Type **`Cindy Marshall`**, tap [Enter], and type **`Training Manager`** in the second line of the box.

Add an Assistant Box

17. Select the Al Smith box (the head of the organization chart).
18. Click the Insert Shape button and choose Assistant.
    Notice that only two shapes are available—subordinate and assistant. The person at this level does not have a coworker.
19. Type **`Charlene Rousse`**, tap [Enter], and type **`Admin Assistant`**.
20. The Organization Chart should match the following illustration.

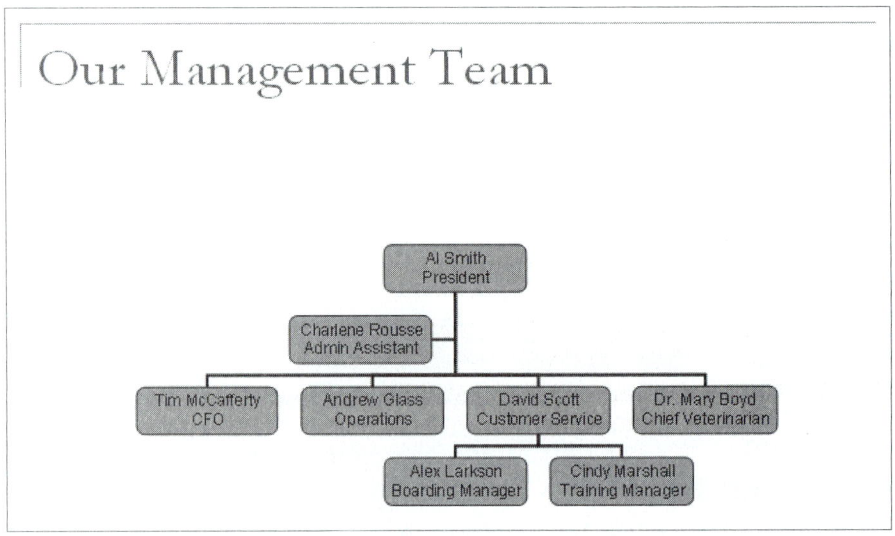

21. Feel free to experiment with options on the Organization Chart toolbar.
22. Save the changes to your presentation.

Save the Outline to Word as an RTF Document

23. Choose File→Save As from the menu bar.
24. Choose Outline/RTF from the Save as Type list at the bottom of the Save As box.
    The Outline/RTF option should be the last item on the list.
25. Navigate to your file storage location on the Save In list at top of the dialog box.
26. Enter the filename **`Pinnacle Pet Care RTF Outline`** and click the Save button.
27. Close the presentation and exit from PowerPoint.
28. Start Microsoft Word, click the Open button, and navigate to your file storage location.
29. Choose Rich Text Format from the Files of Type list at the bottom of the Open box.
30. Select the Pinnacle Pet Care RTF Outline document to open it.
31. Notice that PowerPoint formatted the paragraphs with Heading 1 and Heading 2 styles.
    The PowerPoint presentation has been saved as a Word outline.
32. Save the document and close the Word.
33. Save the presentation and close PowerPoint.

Concepts Review

True/False Questions

1.	Rich text format preserves all text and paragraph level formats.	TRUE	FALSE
2.	When importing Word outlines into PowerPoint, each paragraph formatted with Heading 2 style becomes a new slide in the PowerPoint presentation.	TRUE	FALSE
3.	Microsoft Graph is a program used to create organization charts.	TRUE	FALSE
4.	A Word table can be embedded into a PowerPoint slide using the Edit→Embed Object command.	TRUE	FALSE
5.	When you use Paste Special then change something in the source file, the change is automatically updated in PowerPoint.	TRUE	FALSE
6.	If a PowerPoint chart is linked to data in an Excel workbook, changes made to the workbook data are reflected in the PowerPoint chart.	TRUE	FALSE
7.	Organization charts cannot be modified once they have been inserted into a slide.	TRUE	FALSE
8.	The Format Painter can be used to copy formatting from one location to another.	TRUE	FALSE
9.	Data can be exported from Word to PowerPoint but never from PowerPoint to Word.	TRUE	FALSE
10.	A table created in PowerPoint and a table created in Word look exactly alike.	TRUE	FALSE

Multiple Choice Questions

1. Which command is used to import a Word outline into PowerPoint?
   - a. File→Import
   - b. Insert→Slides from Outline
   - c. Import→Word Outline
   - d. Edit→Outline
2. What happens when the Chart icon in the chart layout is double-clicked?
   - a. Excel is started
   - b. Microsoft Graph is started
   - c. A new presentation is created
   - d. An Organization Chart is started
3. Which command displays the Paste Special dialog box?
   - a. Insert→Paste Special
   - b. Edit→Paste Special
   - c. File→Paste Special
   - d. Format→Paste Special
4. Which keystroke moves the insertion point to the next cell in a PowerPoint table?
   - a. [Enter]
   - b. [Tab]
   - c. [Shift]
   - d. [Shift]+[Tab]

Skill Builders

Skill Builder 5.1 Create the Tropical Getaways Financial Overview

In this exercise, you will create a new presentation for Tropical Getaways from the AutoContent Wizard, link a Word table to a slide, and apply a new design to the presentation.

Use the AutoContent Wizard

1. Start PowerPoint and go to the New Presentation task pane. If your task pane is not visible, choose View→Task Pane→New Presentation.
2. Choose the From AutoContent Wizard option on New Presentation task pane.
3. This will open the AutoContent Wizard.
4. Click the Corporate category button in the second Wizard dialog box, choose the Financial Overview presentation type, and click the Next button.
5. Ensure that On-Screen Presentation is chosen in the third Wizard dialog box and click Next again.
6. In the Presentation Title box of the fourth Wizard dialog box, type **Tropical Getaways Financial Overview**.
7. Click in the Footer box and type **Tropical Getaways Financial Overview** for the footer text.
8. Click Next then click the Finish button.
   The AutoContent Wizard will build the presentation.

Create a Word Table

In the remainder of this exercise, you will create a table in Word and embed it in a new slide.

9. Choose the Stock Performance slide and click the New Slide button.
10. Scroll toward the bottom of the Slide Layout list and choose the Title and Table layout.
11. Click in the Title box and type the title, **Profitability by Division**.
12. Start Microsoft Word and follow these steps to insert a table:

A Click the Insert Table button on Word's Standard toolbar.

B Slide the mouse to highlight a 2×4 table, as shown here, then click to insert the table.

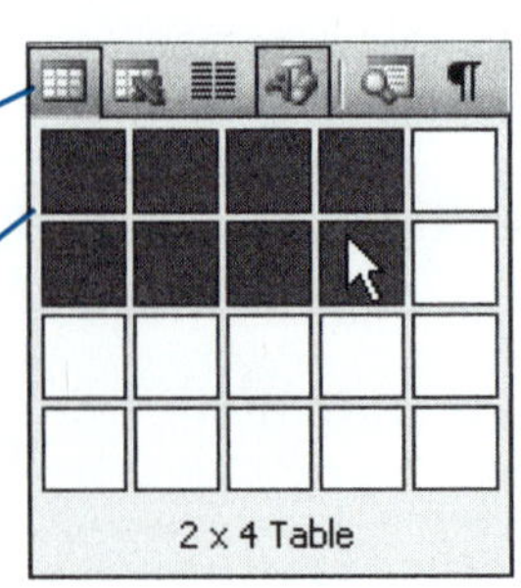

13. Type the following entries into the table:

Division A	Division B	Division C	Division D
19%	21%	42%	18%

14. Select the entire table and choose Table→Table AutoFormat from the menu bar.
15. Scroll through the list of table AutoFormats, choose the Table Contemporary format, and click Apply.
16. Click outside the table and notice the formats that have been applied.

Autofit Cells

17. Follow these steps to size the table and align the entries:

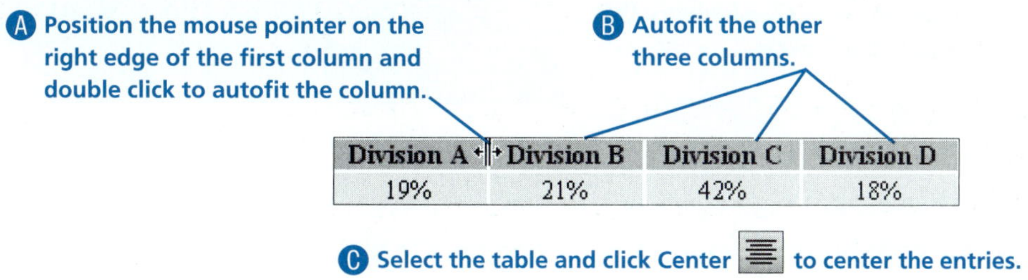

18. Save the Word document to your file storage location as **`Tropical Getaways Profitability Table`**.

Link the Table to the Presentation

19. Make sure the table is selected and click the Copy button.
20. Switch to PowerPoint by clicking the Microsoft PowerPoint button on the taskbar.
21. Click inside the table placeholder box to select it.
22. Choose Edit→Paste Special from the menu bar.
23. Choose the Past Link option and click OK to paste the Microsoft Word Document Object. *The table will appear quite small and off center on the slide.*

24. Follow these steps to size and position the table:

A Drag a corner sizing handle to increase the size of the table.

B Position the mouse pointer on the table and drag it to the desired position.

C Continue to size and move the table until it has the size and position shown here. The table's placeholder will appear too large for the slide, but that's okay.

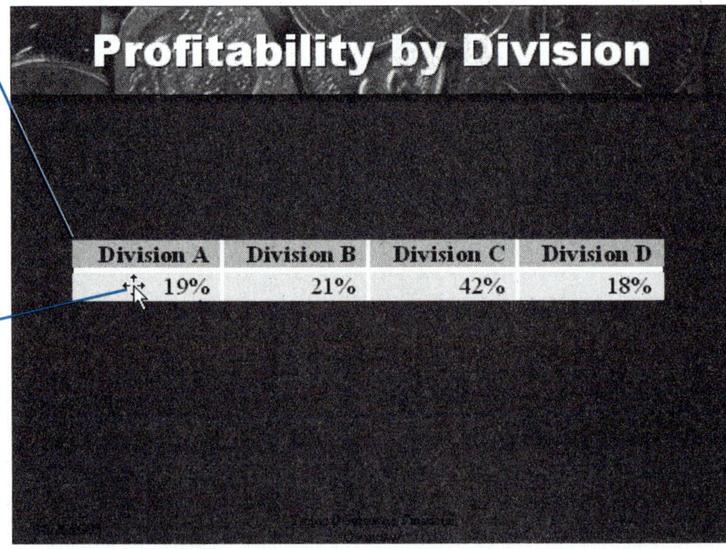

Update the Link

25. Switch to Word by clicking the button on the taskbar.

26. Change the Division A percentage to 50%.

27. Switch to PowerPoint to view the change reflected in the presentation.

Apply a Design Template

The design applied in the AutoContent Wizard is too dark. You will apply a more sedate design template in the next few steps.

28. Click the Design button on the Formatting toolbar to display the Slide Design task pane.

29. Scroll through the list of design templates and choose the Axis template.

30. Browse through the presentation and notice that the template has been applied to all slides. Feel free to make adjustments to any of the slides.

31. Select the <logo> marker on the Title page and tap Delete to remove it.

32. Select the Title placeholder and apply a bold format to the title, then change the font size to 28.

33. Delete the subtitle on the Title page so that only the Title is displayed.

34. Save the presentation as **Tropical Getaways Financial Overview**.

35. Switch to Word, save the document, and exit from Word.

Skill Builder 5.2 Add Chart Slides

In this exercise, you will add two chart slides to the presentation. You will change the chart type on one of the slides to a pie chart.

Add a Chart Slide and Enter Chart Data

1. Navigate to the Profitability by Division slide and click the New Slide button to insert a new slide.
2. Choose the Title and Content layout for the new slide. This is the third layout in the Content Layouts section.
3. Enter the title **`2004 Revenue Breakdown`**.
4. Click the Insert Chart icon in the content placeholder box.
5. Follow these steps to enter data in the chart worksheet:

A Enter the data in the eight cells shown here. The data you enter will replace the sample data already in these cells.

B Select the data in rows 2 and 3 by dragging the mouse pointer over the row headings. Press and hold the left mouse button as you drag.

C Tap Delete to delete the selected data.

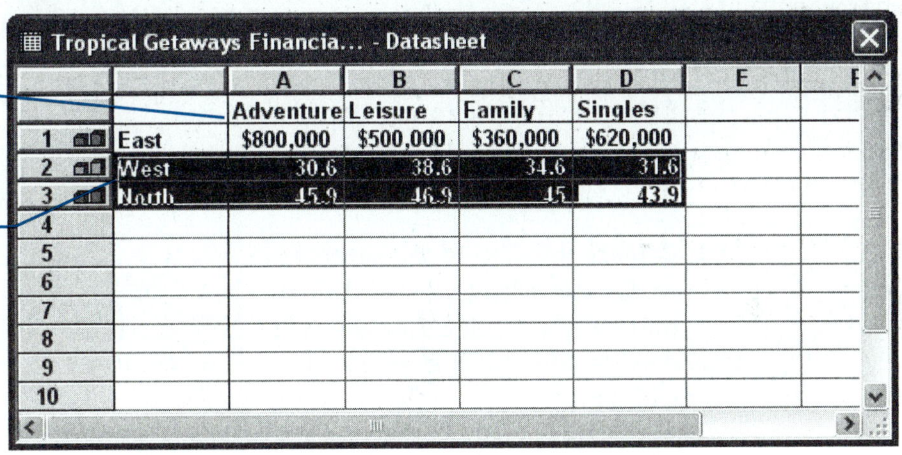

Convert the Chart to a Pie Chart

6. Choose Chart→Chart Type from the menu bar.
   Notice that the menu bar and toolbars are now those of the Microsoft Graph program.
7. Choose Pie from the Chart Type list on the left side of the dialog box.
   The first pie chart sub-type should be chosen on the right side of the dialog box.
8. Click OK and Graph will now display the data in a pie chart.

Format the Pie Chart

In the next few steps, you will remove the chart legend, display data labels, and remove the chart border.

9. Choose Chart→Chart Options from the menu bar.
10. Click the Legend tab and uncheck the Show Legend box.
11. Click the Data Labels tab, check the Category Name and Percentage boxes, and click OK.

12. Follow these steps to remove the border surrounding the pie chart:

A Click the thin, rectangular border surrounding the chart to select it.

B Now right-click the selected border (click the right mouse button).

C Choose Format Chart Area from the menu.

D Choose the None option and click OK. This will remove the border. Keep in mind that you can usually find a desired format option for an object by right-clicking the object.

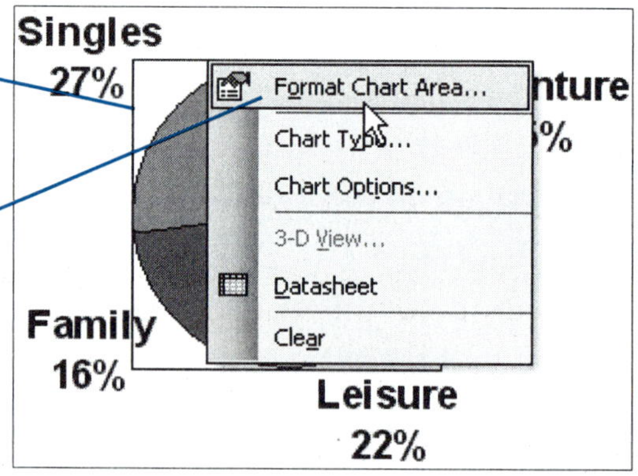

Add a Column Chart

13. Insert a new slide with the Title and Content layout. This is the third layout in the Content Layouts section.

14. Enter the title **`Revenue Projections`**.

15. Click the Insert Chart icon in the content placeholder box.

16. Replace the data in the sample worksheet with the data shown to the right. Notice that you will need to add a fifth row to the worksheet.

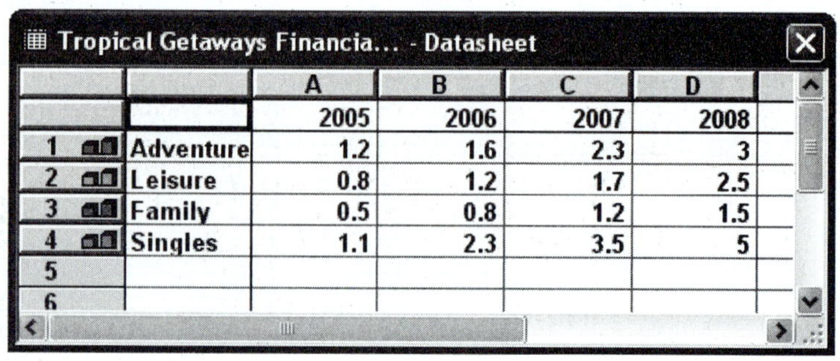
Tropical Getaways Financia... - Datasheet

		A	B	C	D
		2005	2006	2007	2008
1	Adventure	1.2	1.6	2.3	3
2	Leisure	0.8	1.2	1.7	2.5
3	Family	0.5	0.8	1.2	1.5
4	Singles	1.1	2.3	3.5	5
5					
6					

17. Choose Chart→Chart Options from the menu bar.

18. Make sure the Titles tab is chosen and type **`Millions of Dollars`** in the Value (Z) axis box.
This displays the title to the left of the vertical axis on the left side of the chart.

19. Click OK then click an open part of the slide to complete the chart formatting.
Your completed chart should match the example shown to the right.

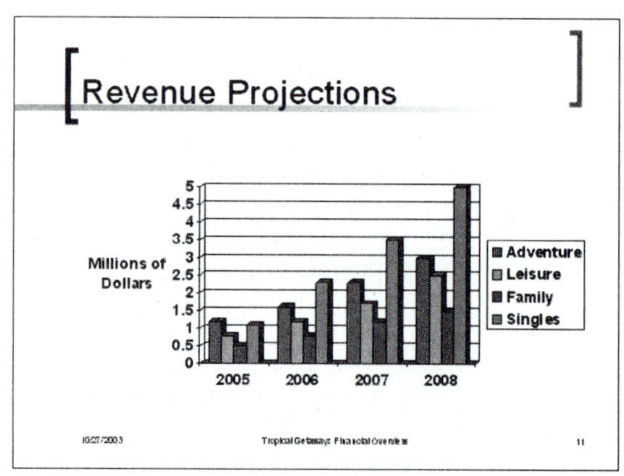

20. Save the changes to your presentation and continue with the next exercise.

Skill Builder 5.3 Add an Organization Chart and Closing Slide

In this exercise, you will add an organization chart to the Tropical Getaways Financial Overview presentation.

1. Navigate to the Revenue Projections slide.
2. Click the New Slide button to insert a new slide.
3. Apply the Title and Diagram or Organization Chart layout.
   This layout is located in the Other Layouts category, near the bottom of the slide layout list.
4. Type the title **`Our Team`**.
5. Double click the Organization Chart icon in the diagram placeholder.
6. Choose the Organization Chart diagram and click OK.
7. Enter the following text into the organization chart:

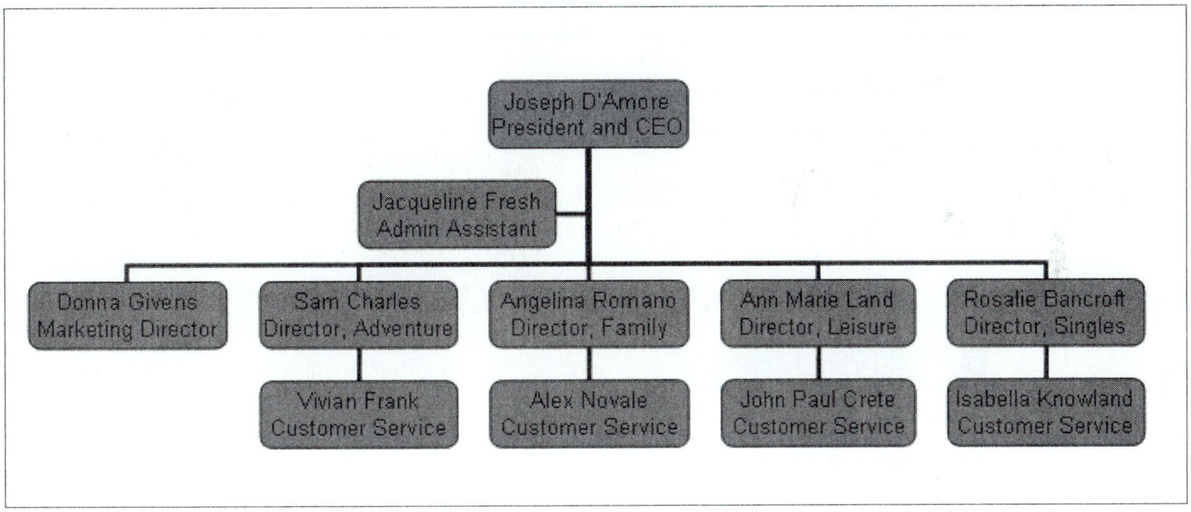

8. Add a closing slide, applying a Title slide layout, as shown in the illustration to the right.

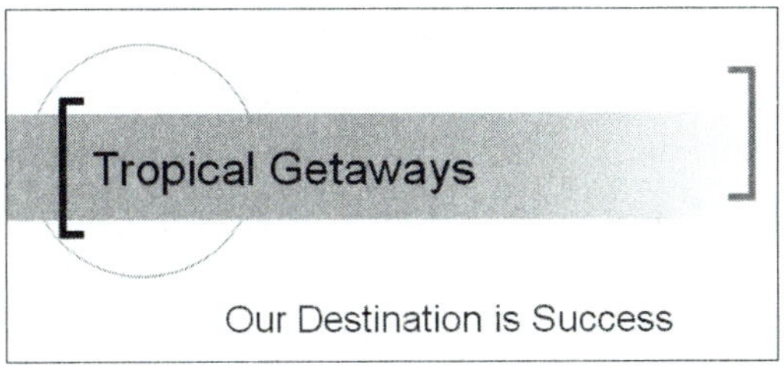

9. Choose the first slide in the presentation.
10. Click the Slide Show button on the View bar to start the presentation.
11. Work through the presentation by clicking on the various slides.
12. Save the changes to the presentation when you have finished then close it.

Assessments

Assessment 5.1 Work with Multiple Applications for a Presentation

In this exercise, you will add a chart, Word table, and PowerPoint table into the Classic Cars presentation.

1. Open the Classic Cars Tools presentation that you created in Lesson 4, Managing Presentation Tools.
2. Go to the Candidates for Election slide then click the New Slide button to insert a new slide.

Add a Chart

3. Apply the Title and Chart layout to the slide.
4. Type the title **`Classic Cars Financial Statement`**.
5. Click the Chart icon in the placeholder and create a datasheet with the entries shown at right.

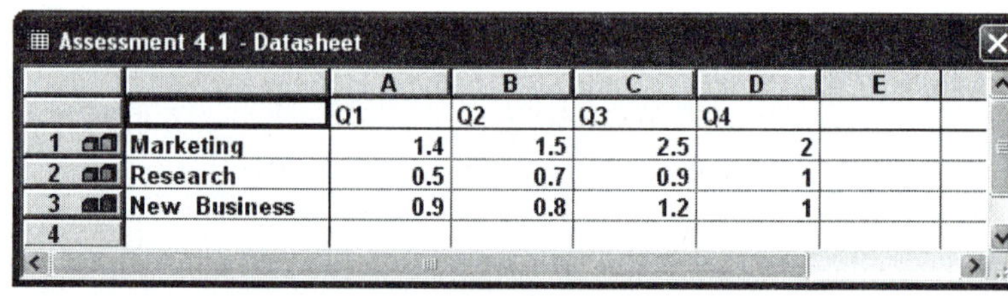

Assessment 4.1 - Datasheet

		A	B	C	D	E
		Q1	Q2	Q3	Q4	
1	Marketing	1.4	1.5	2.5	2	
2	Research	0.5	0.7	0.9	1	
3	New Business	0.9	0.8	1.2	1	
4						

6. After entering data, click the Chart Types drop-down button on the Formatting toolbar and select 3-D Column.

Add Data to the Chart Options dialog box

7. Choose Chart→Chart Options from the menu bar.
8. If necessary, click the Title tab and enter the Chart Title and Value (Z) Axis shown here.

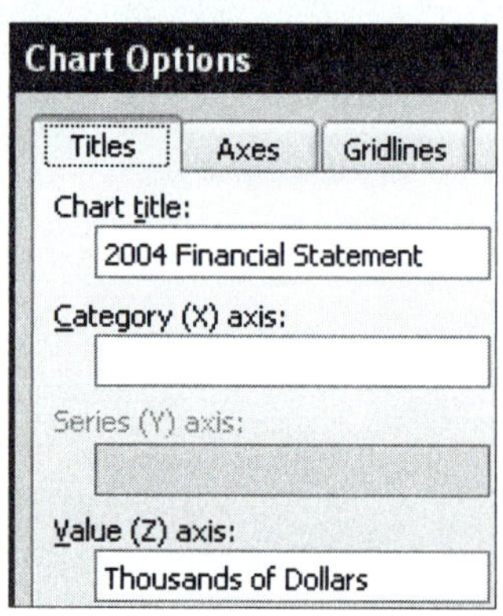

9. Click the Axes tab, choose Category as the Primary Axis, and check the Value (Z) Axis box.

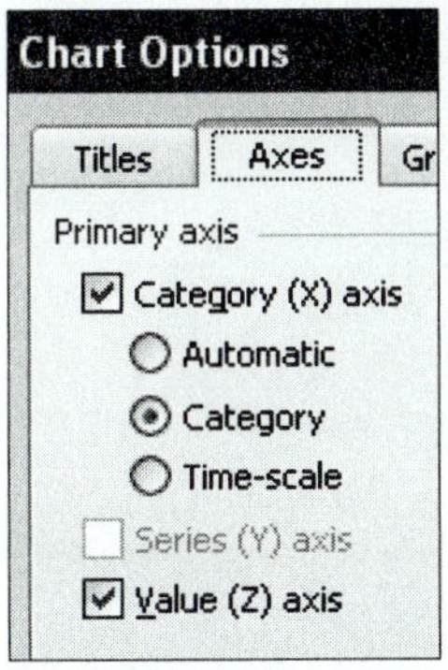

10. Click the Legend tab, if necessary check the Show Legend box, and choose the Bottom placement option.

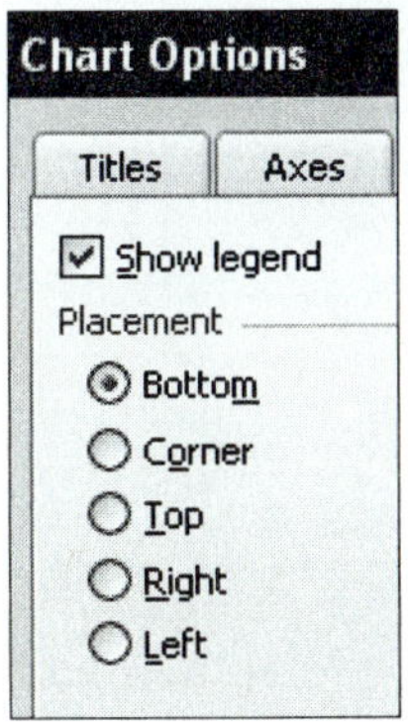

11. Click OK to apply the Chart Options.

12. Click anywhere outside of the chart and take a moment to examine the chart options you just set.

Add a PowerPoint Table

13. Go to the Candidates for Election slide (6th slide) and insert a 3×2 table.

14. Add the information shown in the following illustration:

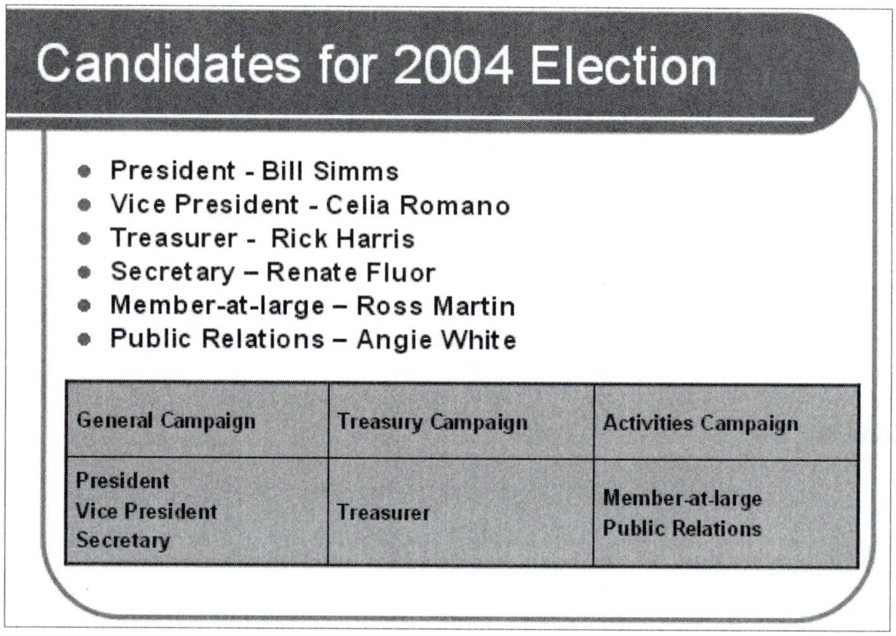

15. Select the table by double-clicking on the table border.

16. Add a fill color, change the font size to 18pt, and apply Bold formatting to the table text.

Add an Organization Chart

17. Insert a new slide below Candidates for Election and apply the Title and Diagram or Organization layout to the slide.

18. Add the title **`Management Status`**.

19. Develop the organization chart adding the boxes and text shown in the following illustration.

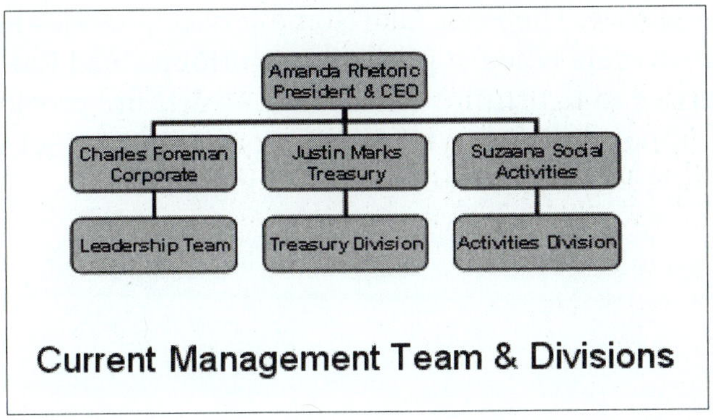

20. Save the presentation as Classic Cars Chart.

Critical Thinking

Critical Thinking 5.1 Integrate Word

Linda Holmes understands that houses sell better when they feel more like homes, so she develops the Feels Like Home service. The Feels Like Home service provides maintenance, cleaning, and other services to owners who list property with Homestead Realty. Linda subcontracts the Feels Like Home service to Hearthfire Enterprises. Hearthfire provides Linda with a Word outline so that she can import it into her PowerPoint presentation. Set up an outline in Word using the text and heading levels shown in the following table:

Outline Text	Heading Level
Feels Like Home Service Options	Heading 1
Sparkling Clean Rooms	Heading 2
Grandma's Apple Pie Service	Heading 2
Music to Sell By	Heading 2
Hearthfire Enterprises Employees	Heading 1
Days on Market	Heading 1
FAQs	Heading 1
How often will my home be checked?	Heading 2
Once per week if you use our Checkup plan.	Heading 3
What action is taken when you find a problem with my home?	Heading 2
We will contact you within 24 hours with an action plan.	Heading 3
How much do your services cost?	Heading 2
Each service option has a set fee schedule.	Heading 3

- Save your outline as **`Hearthfire Outline`**.
- Open the Homestead Realty presentation and import the Hearthfire outline into the presentation after the last slide. Once the outline is imported, move the Office Hours slide to the end of the presentation.
- Save the presentation as **`Homestead Realty Chart`**.

Critical Thinking 5.2 Work with Tables and Organization Charts

In this exercise, you will add an organization chart to the Homestead Realty presentation.

Change the slide layout of the Hearthfire Enterprises Employees slide to Title and Diagram or Organization Chart. Create the following organization chart on the slide:

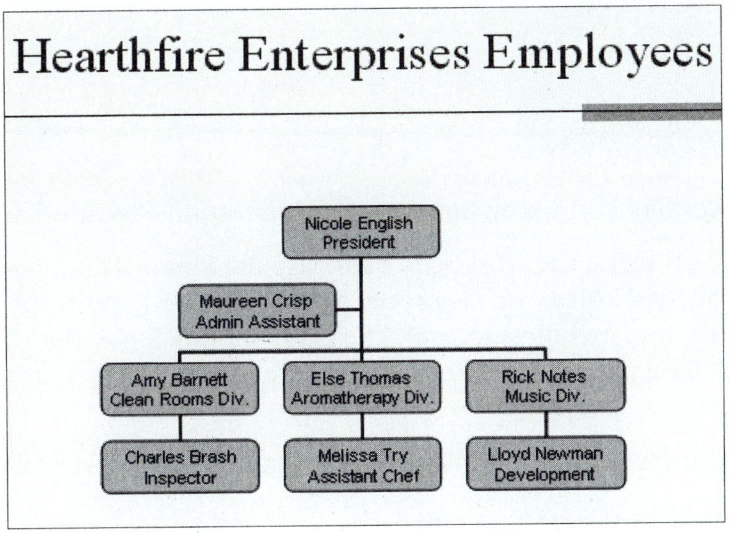

Save the presentation when you are finished.

Critical Thinking 5.3 Create Charts and Integrate Excel

In this exercise, you will import an Excel workbook into the Homestead Realty presentation. Change the slide layout of the Days on Market slide to Title and Chart. Enter the data shown in the following into the datasheet. The data specifies the number of homes in each price range that have sold within 0–30, 30–60, 60–90, and above 90 days:

	0–30	30–60	60–90	90&Up
0–100	3	5	2	1
100–200	2	6	3	0
200&Up	4	9	4	2

Change the chart options as described in the following table. Your completed chart will compare the number of homes in each price range that have sold within 0–30, 30–60, 60–90, and above 90 days. The chart should depict all three price ranges peaking around 30–60 days, indicating that most homes sell within that time period.

Chart type	**Stacked Area**
Chart title	Days on Market
Category (X) axis title	Days
Value (Y) axis title	Price Range

- Create the following workbook in Excel. Save it to your file storage location as **`CMA`**.
- Create an embedded chart using the workbook data. Use the Line with Markers Displayed at Each Data Value chart type. Also, use **`Days on Market`** as the X axis title, **`Selling Price`** as the Y axis title, and include a legend. The chart should depict the Highest, Average, and Lowest selling prices all declining as homes remain on the market for longer periods of time.
- Link the Excel chart into the chart placeholder on the CMA slide in PowerPoint.

	A	B	C	D	E
1		0-30	30-60	60-90	90&Up
2	Highest	$134,500	$134,900	$134,900	$133,000
3	Average	$126,850	$125,100	$124,600	$123,725
4	Lowest	$120,000	$119,000	$118,500	$117,000

- Apply the Descend animation scheme to all slides that were imported from the Word outline.
- Save your presentation then exit from PowerPoint.
- Exit from Excel.

LESSON 6

Working with Online Presentations

Although originally designed for presentations at traditional types of meetings and public speaking events, PowerPoint has evolved to include powerful capabilities for Internet-based communication. For example, you can save a PowerPoint presentation as a Web page to view in a Web browser window. PowerPoint also lets you insert hyperlinks from a slide to a Web page, a file, or another slide within a presentation. You can easily send a presentation as an attachment to an email message or broadcast a presentation online using a special add-in. In this lesson, you will learn various methods of transmitting your presentations online.

IN THIS LESSON

Microsoft Office PowerPoint 2003 objectives covered in this lesson

Objective Number	Skill Sets and Skills	Concept Page References	Exercise Page References
PP03S-4-1	Organize a presentation	182–183	183–184
PP03S-4-5	Prepare presentations for remote delivery	203–206	205–206
PP03S-4-6	Save and publish presentations	189–192, 194–197	192–195, 198–199

Additional learning resources are available at labpub.com/learn/pp03/

Case Study

Twilight Hollow Bank is impressed with the Pinnacle Pet Care Loan Statistics presentation and decides to make the $100,000 loan to Al Smith. They suggest that Al use the Internet to advertise his products and services. Buoyed by his success in securing the loan, Al decides to create a presentation that will be placed on the Pinnacle Pet Care Website. Al schedules a meeting with all of the department managers and, during the meeting, Al explains that he will send each of them a presentation via email. Al then calls Sarah, Pinnacle's Webmaster, to ask her if it is possible to add a hyperlink to a file or to link one presentation to another. Sarah explains with PowerPoint 2003 accomplishing this is a simple task. She also tells him that once the reviewed presentation has all of the desired links in it, she will publish it to their Web server so it can be accessed by anyone connected to the Internet. Al, thoroughly satisfied that Pinnacle Pet Care is headed in the right direction, strolls back onto his office to get the ball rolling.

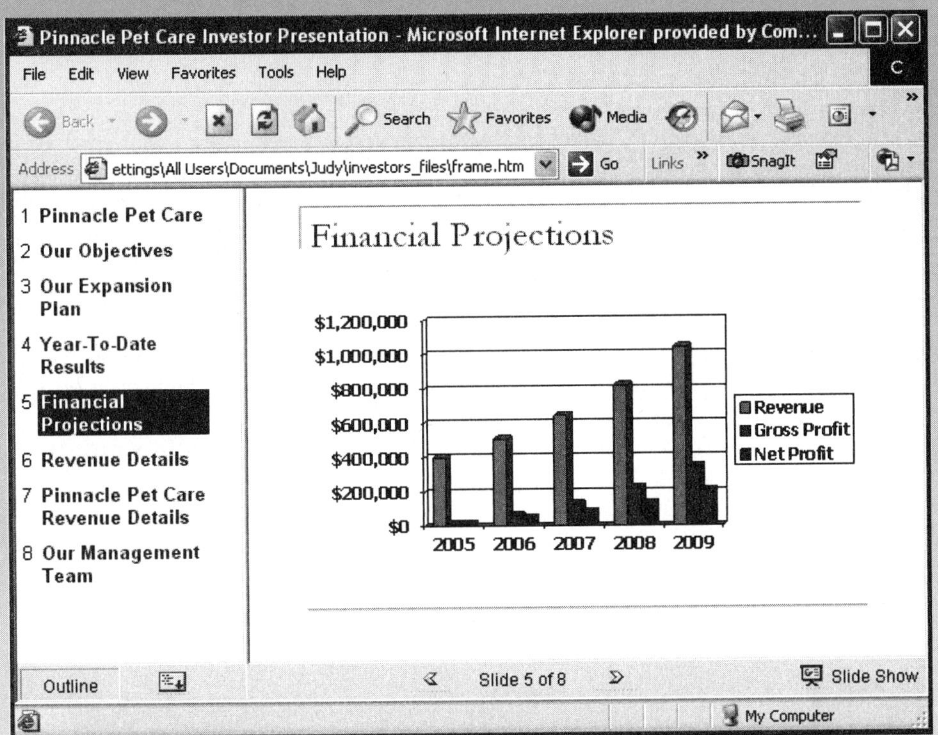

This is an example of an online presentation. Notice the hyperlinks on the left side of the screen.

Al likes how PowerPoint has transformed his presentation. However, it won't be available on the Web until it is published. Although he could ask Sarah for help each time he wants to revise the presentation and post them to the Web, it will be much easier for her to set up Al with a Web folder. Then, Al can revise the presentation and post it to the Web immediately—without the need for outside assistance. Al also wants to send presentations directly to potential investors via email. The Web folder allows him to deliver a presentation to others without depending on the speed of their Internet connections.

Using PowerPoint on the Web

The Web is an ideal medium to give others access to and for you to receive feedback on your presentation. You can publish the presentation to a Web server so others can view it in a browser while sitting at their own computers. In addition, you can email the presentation to others as an attachment or for review. You will learn about reviewing and collaborating on presentations in Lesson 7, Working with Online Collaboration.

Inserting Hyperlinks

Microsoft Office **Specialist**

A hyperlink is a command you can insert into your presentation that points to another slide in the same presentation, a different presentation, a custom show, a file in another program, or a Web page. A hyperlink can be a selected piece of text, another object on a slide, or an action button. For example, Al includes hyperlinks to Web pages on the Pinnacle Pet Care Website, allowing him to jump directly to those Web pages during a presentation. When he converts the presentation to Web page format, these hyperlinks will still function. There are three ways to insert hyperlinks:

- Click the Insert Hyperlink  button on the toolbar.
- Click Insert→Hyperlink on the menu bar.
- Right-click on a selection and choose Hyperlink from the pop-up menu.

FROM THE KEYBOARD

Ctrl+K to insert a hyperlink

There are numerous types of hyperlinks. The three most useful ones are described here.

- Hyperlinks to Web pages—These hyperlinks point to a page on the Web. When you click one of these hyperlinks, PowerPoint starts Internet Explorer and displays the Web page.
- Hyperlinks to slides—These hyperlinks point to other slides in a presentation. When you click one of these hyperlink, PowerPoint immediately displays the slide.
- Hyperlinks to files—These hyperlinks point to a file on your computer, such as a Word document or to another PowerPoint file. When you click one of these hyperlinks, Power-Point displays the document.

Updating Hyperlinks

Every time a presentation that contains hyperlinks opens, you may be asked to update the hyperlinks. PowerPoint does this to ensure the hyperlinks function properly. If a linked file is moved to a different location, the hyperlink will no longer work. It only takes a moment to update hyperlinks. However, you can also set PowerPoint to check hyperlinks manually using the Edit→Links command on the menu bar.

QR

QUICK REFERENCE: CREATING HYPERLINKS

Task	Procedure
Insert a hyperlink to a Web page	■ Select the text or object you wish to use as a hyperlink. ■ Click the Insert Hyperlink button and choose Insert→Hyperlink from the menu bar, or right-click the selection and choose Hyperlink. ■ Click Existing File or Web Page on the left panel then click Web Page on the right side of the dialog box. ■ Use the browser to display the desired Web page for your hyperlink then return to the PowerPoint window. ■ If desired, edit the Text to Display box and click OK.
Insert a hyperlink to a slide in your presentation	■ Select the text or graphic image you wish to use as a hyperlink. ■ Click the Insert Hyperlink button and choose Insert→Hyperlink the menu bar, or right-click the selection and choose Hyperlink. ■ Click Place in this Document on the left panel then choose the slide to which the hyperlink should point.
Insert a hyperlink to another file	■ Select the text or graphic image you wish to use as a hyperlink. ■ Click the Insert Hyperlink button and choose Insert→Hyperlink from the menu bar, or right-click the selection and choose Hyperlink. ■ Click the Existing File or Web Page button on the left panel then click the File button on the right side of the dialog box. ■ Navigate to the desired file and click OK. ■ Click OK again to create the hyperlink.
Remove a hyperlink	■ Right-click on the hyperlink and choose Hyperlink→Remove Hyperlink from the pop-up menu.
Update a hyperlink manually	■ Open the presentation that contains the hyperlinks. ■ Choose Edit→Links from the menu bar. ■ Click each link you wish to update manually and choose the Manual update option.

Hands-On 6.1 Insert a Hyperlink to a Web Page

In this exercise, you will insert a hyperlink that points to text on a slide in the Pinnacle Pet Care Online presentation to a Web page.

1. Open the Pinnacle Pet Care Online presentation.
2. Select the title on Slide 1.
   This tells PowerPoint that the title text will serve as the hyperlink you are about to create.
3. Click the Insert Hyperlink button on the toolbar.
   A dialog box appears, offering several options for inserting a hyperlink. In this case, you will insert a hyperlink to a Web page.

4. Follow these steps to create the hyperlink:

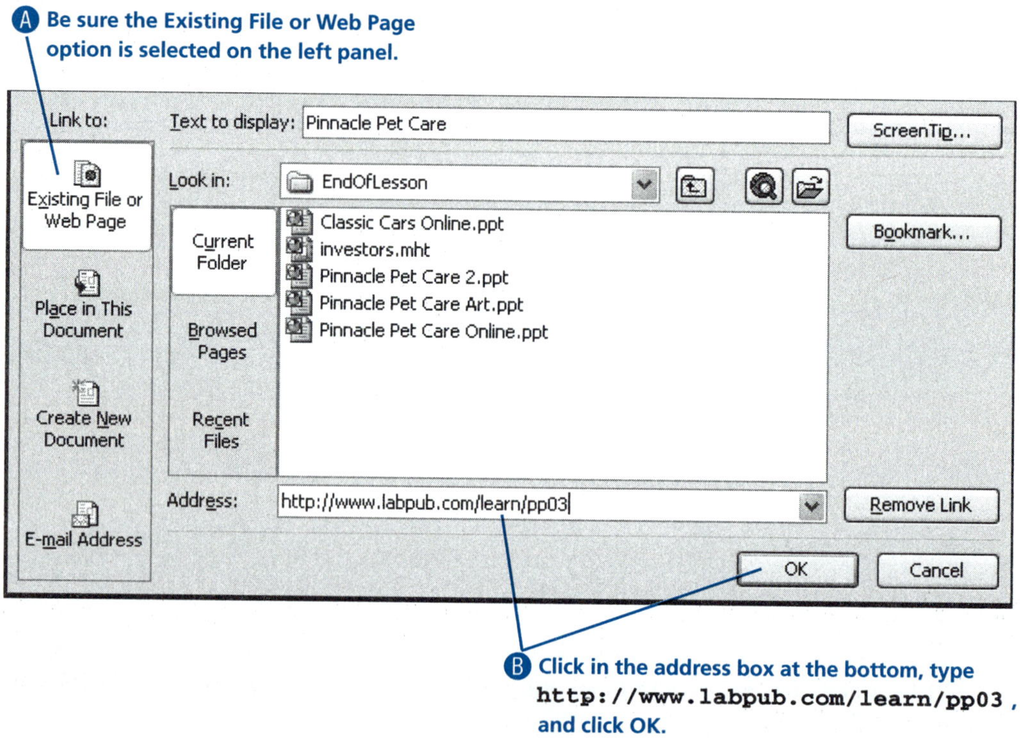

Notice that the title in Slide 1 is underlined, indicating it is now a hyperlink. The hyperlink is only active when the slide show is running.

Test the Hyperlink

5. Click the Slide Show button then point, don't click, to the new hyperlink.
   Notice that the mouse pointer changes to a hand and the URL of the hyperlink appears in a ScreenTip box. These are clues that the text is a hyperlink. You will learn how to create your own ScreenTips in Hands-On 6.2.
6. Click on the new hyperlink.
   This should start Internet Explorer and display the Web page you specified in step 4.
7. Click the Pinnacle Pet Care Promotion link on the Web page.
   After a pause, a Web page version of a PowerPoint presentation appears. You will learn how to create Web page versions of your presentations in the Saving the Presentation as a Web Page section.
8. Minimize the Internet Explorer window.
   You are returned to the slide show.
9. Tap [Esc] to exit the slide show.
10. Save the changes in the presentation.

Creating ScreenTips

A ScreenTip is text that appears when a pointer is over a hyperlink. For example, you can indicate the destination of the hyperlink in a ScreenTip if it's not obvious from some other feature on the slide. You can create a ScreenTip whenever you create or edit a hyperlink. If you don't create a custom ScreenTip, the default tip displays the complete path and filename to a file, the number and title to another slide, or the URL of a Website.

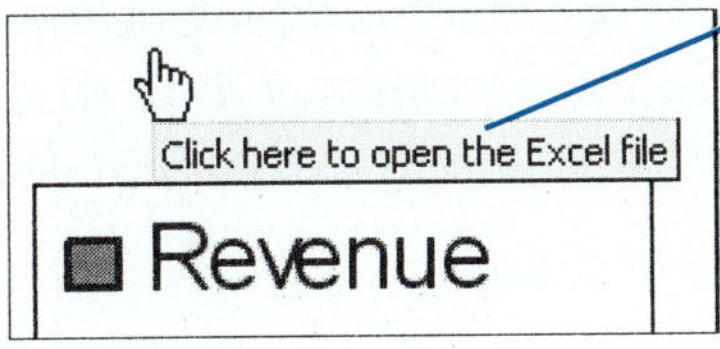

This ScreenTip indicates that this chart is linked to an Excel file.

Hands-On 6.2 Insert ScreenTips in Hyperlinks

In this exercise, you will insert two hyperlinks and create two custom ScreenTips.

Create a Hyperlink to a File

1. Display Slide 5, Financial Projections.
   This slide contains financial projections for the next few years. You will create a hyperlink from this chart so you can reference it during the presentation.
2. Select the financial projection chart so its handles are visible.
3. Click the Insert Hyperlink button.
4. Follow these steps to insert a hyperlink to another file:

A Be sure the Existing File or Web Page button is selected.

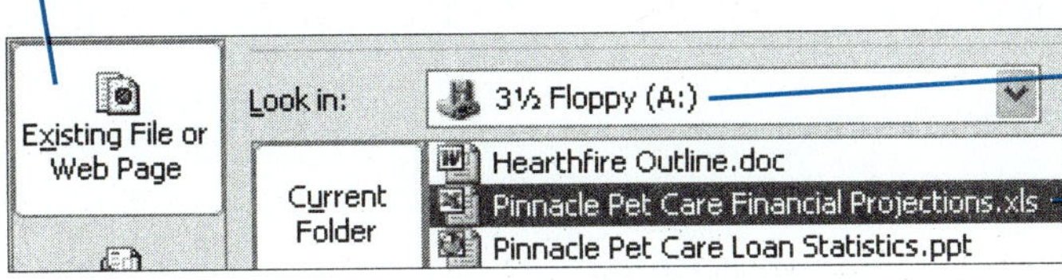

B Choose the 3½ Floppy (A:) drive from the drop-down list in the Look In box.

C Double-click to select the Pinnacle Pet Care Financial Projections Excel file.

Notice that the Text to Display box is grayed out with the words <<Selection in Document>>. This is because you are creating a hyperlink for an item on the slide rather than for a specific piece of text.

5. Follow these steps to create a ScreenTip:

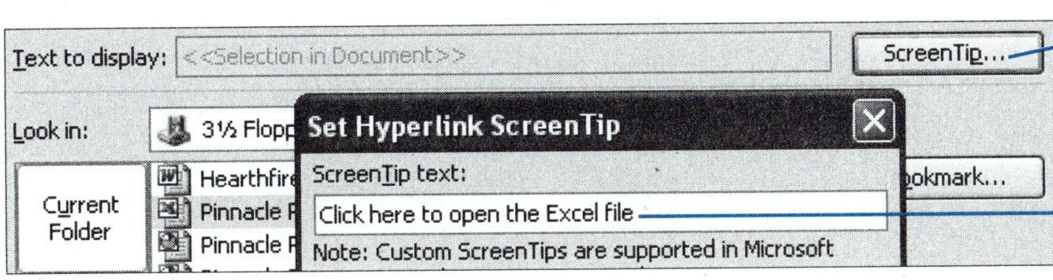

A Click the ScreenTip button in the upper-right corner of the dialog box.

B Type the ScreenTip message shown here and click OK.

6. Click OK to complete the hyperlink command.

7. Click the Slide Show button, move the mouse for about two seconds until the pointer appears, and point (don't click) over the chart.
Notice that when you point anywhere over the chart, a pointer hand appears. After a brief pause, the ScreenTip appears as well. The entire chart is now a hyperlink.

8. Click anywhere on the chart.
The Excel application will start and display the Financial Projections workbook. As a presenter, you could now manipulate figures on the spreadsheet in response to a question or focus on specific details about the spreadsheet. As you can see, hyperlinks can start programs as well as open documents.

9. Close the Excel window then tap [Esc] to exit the slide show.

Create a Hyperlink to a Slide

Now you will create a hyperlink to a specific slide in the presentation.

10. Display Slide 4, Year-To-Date Results.

11. Position the mouse at the end of the last bulleted line and tap [Enter].

12. Click the Bullet button to turn them off for this new line.

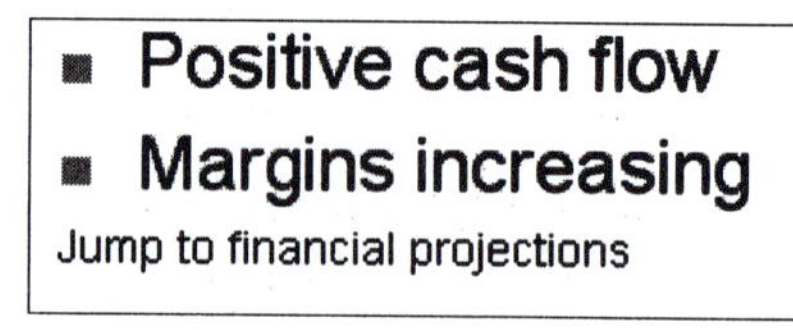

13. Change the font size to 16 then type **`Jump to financial projections`**.
The line should match this example. It will become the new hyperlink.

14. Be sure the new line is selected then click the Insert Hyperlink button.

15. Follow these steps to select a slide for the hyperlink:

Ⓐ Notice that the Text to Display matches the new line you typed on the slide.

Ⓑ Click Place in this Document.

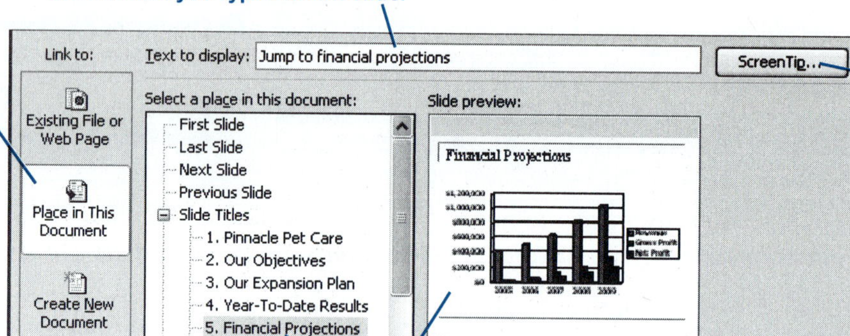

Ⓓ Click the ScreenTip button, type `Click here to view the financial projections chart`, and click OK.

Ⓔ Click OK to close the Insert Hyperlink dialog box

Ⓒ Click Slide 5 Financial Projections. Notice the preview of the slide to the right.

You are returned to the slide and, as you expect, the hyperlink text is underscored.

16. View the slide show and test the new hyperlink.
The hyperlink should immediately jump the presentation to Slide 5.

17. Tap [Esc] then save the presentation.

Inserting One Presentation within Another

If you want to connect two presentations, you have two options. Both can be equally effective.

- Create a hyperlink—You can create a hyperlink to another PowerPoint presentation file.
- Insert the presentation as an object—You can insert another presentation within a PowerPoint presentation slide. This uses Windows' Object Linking and Embedding (OLE) feature. You can insert an existing presentation or create a new one.

TIP! *You can also embed Word documents, Excel workbooks, and other types of files into a PowerPoint presentation.*

Object Linking and Embedding

To insert a presentation as an object inside another presentation, you have two options:

- Embedding—This places a copy of the presentation inside the PowerPoint presentation. Embedding increases the file size of the presentation.
- Linking—This method creates a link to the location of the embedded file without placing a copy of it in the presentation. Linking does not increase the size of the file; however, you must keep the two files in the same location for the link to work.

Displaying the Object

PowerPoint offers two ways of displaying inserted objects:

- As a miniature slide—This method places a smaller version of the object on the slide.
- As an icon—This method places an icon for the object on the slide.

A PowerPoint presentation object displayed as a miniature

A PowerPoint presentation object displayed as an icon

QR

QUICK REFERENCE: INSERTING A PRESENTATION AS AN OBJECT

Task	Procedure
Embed a presentation as an object within another presentation	■ Display the slide on which you wish to place the object. ■ Choose Insert→Object from the menu bar. ■ Choose the Create from File option, click Browse, and select the presentation to be inserted. ■ Place a checkmark in the Display as Icon box and click OK.
Link an existing presentation as an object within another presentation	■ Display the slide on which you wish to place the object. ■ Choose Insert→Object from the menu bar. ■ Choose the Create from File option, click Browse, and select the presentation to be inserted. ■ Place a checkmark in the Link box and click OK.

Hands-On 6.3 Insert a PowerPoint Presentation

In this exercise, you will place the Pinnacle Pet Care Art presentation as a linked object within the Pinnacle Pet Care Online presentation.

Insert the Presentation File as an Object

1. Tap [Home] to display Slide 1 then choose Insert→Object on the menu bar.
   The slide on which the object will be inserted must be displayed before you can insert it.

2. Follow these steps to insert a presentation:

A Click the Create from File option.

B Click Browse then choose the 3½ Floppy (A:) drive in the Look In box.

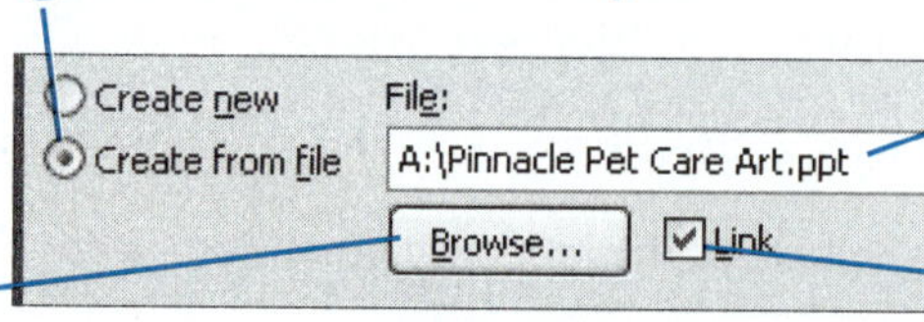

C Click the Pinnacle Pet Care Art file if it is available and click OK. If it's not available, choose any other PowerPoint presentation.

D Place a checkmark in the Link option box. Notice the Link description at the bottom of the dialog box.

E Click OK.

A miniature version of Slide 1 of the inserted presentation appears in the middle of the slide.

3. Follow these steps to change the size and location of the inserted object:

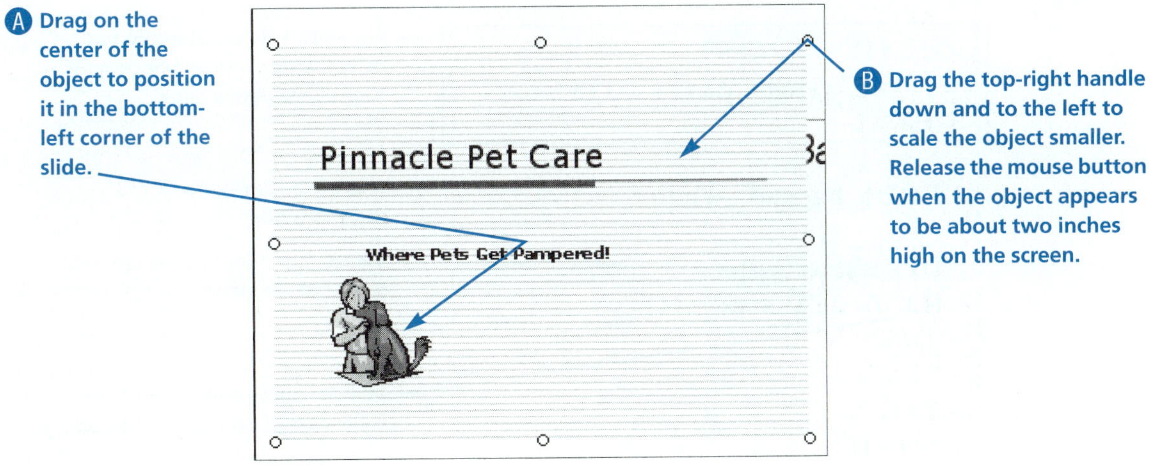

Test the Inserted Object

4. Click the Slide Show button and point (don't click) over the inserted object.
   Notice that a pointer hand appears, just as if the object were a hyperlink.
5. Click once on the object.
   The inserted presentation appears. In effect, you have opened this presentation from within the current presentation.
6. Tap the End key on the keyboard to view the last slide of the presentation. After the last slide has finished loading, click anywhere on the slide to end the presentation.
   You are returned to the original presentation. From here, you can resume the planned slide show.
7. Tap Esc to exit Slide Show mode and return to Normal mode.
8. Save the presentation.

Saving the Presentation as a Web Page

Microsoft Office Specialist

PowerPoint includes several features to help you communicate with others over the Internet. These features allow you to reach a wide audience, including users who do not have PowerPoint installed on their computers. In this section, you will learn to view and save a presentation on the Web and how to publish a presentation to a Web server so others can view it over the Internet.

About HTML

Web pages are programmed in a computer language called HTML (hypertext markup language). As computer languages go, HTML is straightforward. Many Webmasters program Web pages using HTML code. Following is an example of HTML code—what it means and how the page appears in a Web browser. However, when using PowerPoint, you do not have to know HTML code. Instead, PowerPoint writes the code for you when you convert a presentation to a Web page format.

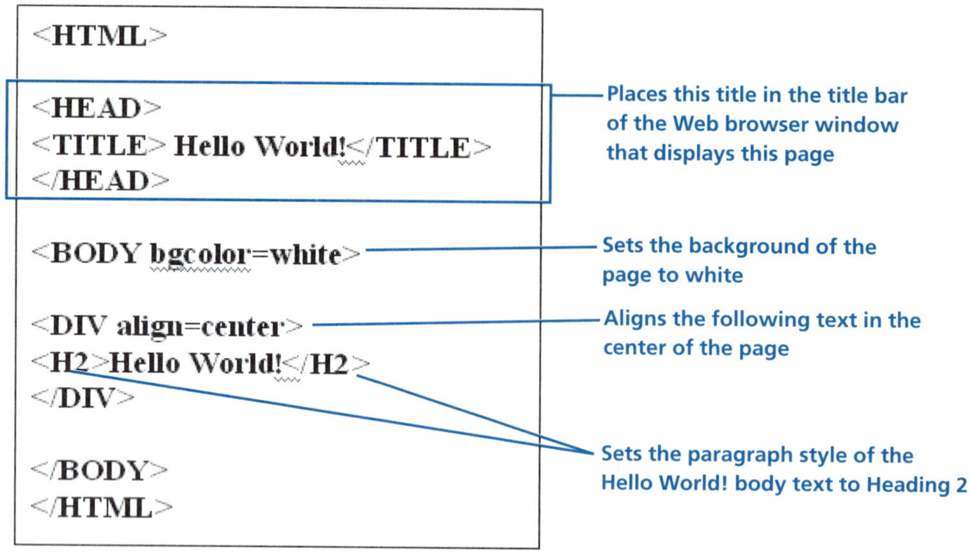

An example of HTML code and what it displays on a Web page

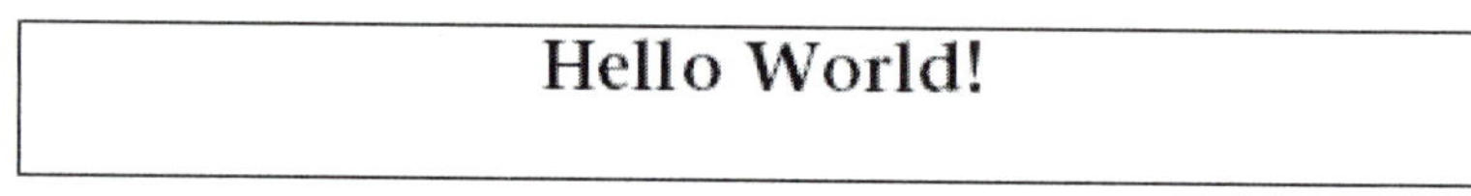

The Save as Web Page Command

The File→Save as Web Page command converts your presentation to an HTML file (along with many supporting files), allowing others to view it over the Internet. This command allows you to set many options to adapt and enhance the presentation when it is viewed over the Internet. For example, you can set the page name and opt to display speaker notes and navigation controls on the Web page.

Browser Support

There are several different Web browser programs in use on the Internet: Internet Explorer and Netscape Navigator are the two most popular browser programs for Windows and Macintosh. Both of these browser programs have various versions (such as 6.0, 7.0, etc.) and PowerPoint allows you to save a presentation in a form optimized for a specific type of browser. You can also choose to save a presentation in a format that accommodates a wide variety of browsers; however, this may result in a larger presentation that loads more slowly.

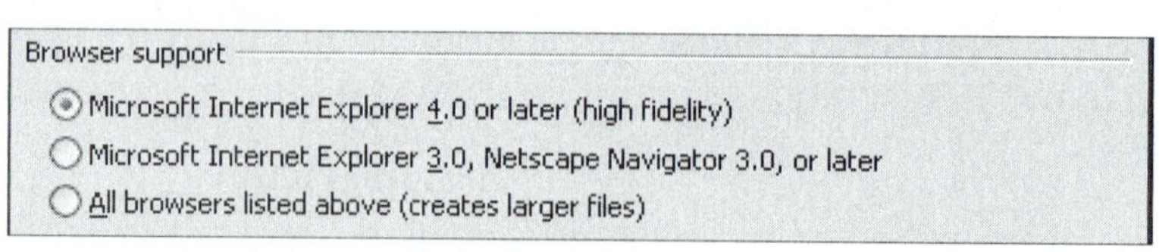

This section of the Publish dialog box lets you specify support for browser programs.

The following table outlines what happens when you save a presentation with support for a specific browser.

Browser	Notes
Internet Explorer 4.0 and later	PowerPoint can create a high fidelity Web page presentation for these browsers. This may not display clearly in other Web browser programs.
Internet Explorer 3.0 and Netscape Navigator 3.0 and older	Selecting support for these browsers results in a Web page presentation with less detail.
All browsers	This option supports a high fidelity presentation on the latest versions of Internet Explorer and will display clearly on other, older browser programs. However, this may result in files that are about 50% larger than the other options.

Display Options for Web Page Presentations

When you save a presentation as a Web page, PowerPoint gives you several options for displaying it. You can select specific options to display by default or allow users these options when they view the presentation in their Web browsers.

TIP! *You can make default settings to the Web Options in PowerPoint's Tools→Options dialog box. Click the General tab then click the Web Options button.*

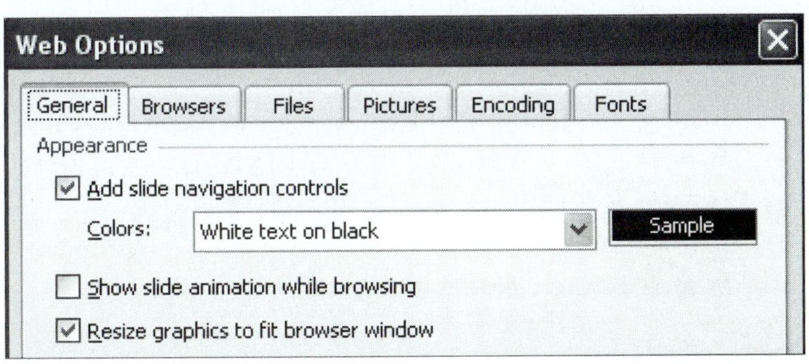

The Web Options dialog box allows you to set how the presentation will appear in a Web browser.

Setting the Target Monitor Size

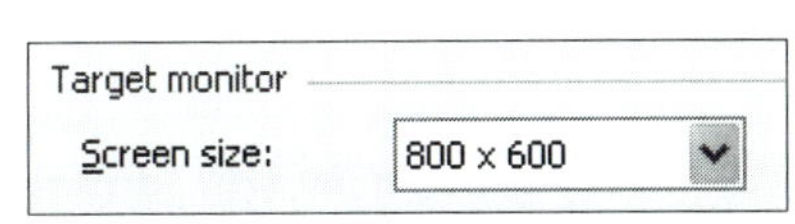

When you save a presentation as a Web page, PowerPoint saves all of the images in sizes it expects to display in a Web browser. You can indicate a target monitor size to help PowerPoint optimize image display for most of your target audience. This option is available under the Pictures tab of the Web Options dialog box.

TIP! *When in doubt, set the target monitor screen size for 800x600.*

Multiple Files for Web Pages

PowerPoint creates many supporting files when you save a presentation as a Web page. These files contain the images and data displayed by the Web version of the presentation. This is important to remember because if you move or copy a Web page to another location, you must also copy the folder with its additional files.

QR

QUICK REFERENCE: SAVING A PRESENTATION AS A WEB PAGE

Task	Procedure
Save a presentation as a Web page	■ Click File→Save as Web Page on the menu bar then click the Publish button. ■ Click the Web Options button, review the general options, and click OK. ■ Be sure you have set the desired browser support. ■ If desired, click the Change button to change the page title that will appear in the title bar of the Web browser. ■ Click the Browse button then choose the destination of the Web page and its files. If desired and available, you can save the Web page to a Web folder. (See the Using Web Folders section on page 197.) ■ If desired, place a checkmark in the Open Published Web Page in Browser option box. ■ Click the Publish button.
Make default settings for presentations saved as a Web pages	■ Choose Tools→Options from the menu bar. Click the General tab then click the Web Options button. ■ Make the desired default settings and click OK. These settings will appear the next time you save a presentation as a Web page.

Hands-On 6.4 Save a Presentation as a Web Page

In this exercise, you will save the Pinnacle Pet Care Online presentation as a Web page.

Save the Web Page Presentation

1. Click File→Save as Web Page on the menu bar then click the Publish button.
   Although you can save the presentation as a Web page without clicking Publish, you would not be able to review many of the save options.
2. If necessary, clear the checkmark from the Display Speaker Notes option in the top section of the dialog box.
   It is usually unnecessary to take up valuable screen space with speaker notes.
3. Click the Web Options button.
   This dialog box allows you to set many options. Usually, the default options are sufficient. However, in this case you will make some adjustments.

4. Follow these steps to adjust the Web options:

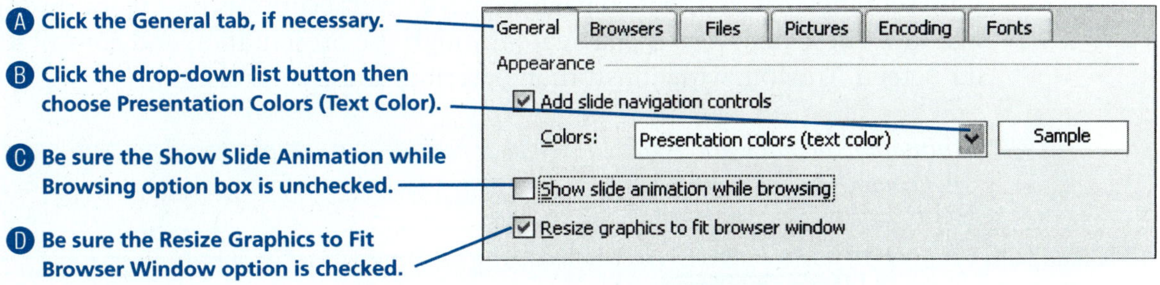

5. Click the Pictures tab and set the Target monitor screen size to 800x600.
Most computers now use the 800x600 screen size.

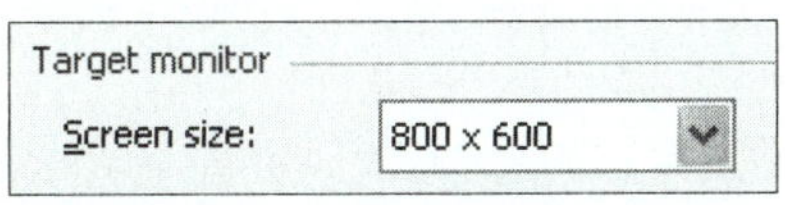

6. Click OK to close the Web Options dialog box.
7. Make sure the Browser support option is set for Microsoft Internet Explorer 4.0 or Later (High Fidelity), as shown here.

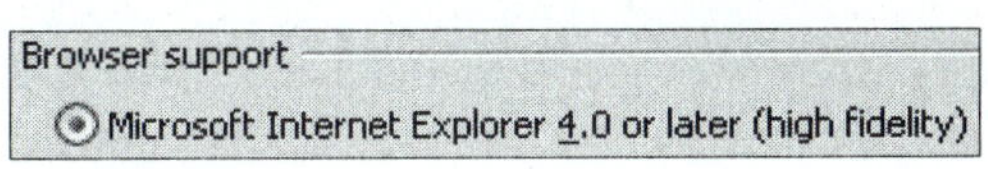

8. Click the Change button near the bottom-right corner of the dialog box, change the title to **`Pinnacle Pet Care Investor Presentation`**, and click OK.
9. Click the Browse button then choose the 3½ Floppy (A:) drive in the Save In box. Taking care to type with lowercase letters, replace the filename with **`investors`** and click OK.
The Publish as Web Page dialog box displays.
10. On the bottom-left corner of the dialog box be sure the Open Published Web Page in Browser option is checked then click Publish.
It will take two or three minutes for the necessary files to be copied to the floppy drive. At the end of the save process, your Web page will appear in a new browser window. In the next section you will learn about navigating in a Web page.
11. Close ☒ the Internet Explorer window.
You are returned to the Pinnacle Pet Care Online presentation.

Viewing Presentations on the Web

Microsoft Office Specialist

A presentation saved as a Web page displays several controls that work through the browser window. These help viewers navigate through the presentation and control its appearance on the screen. The following illustration describes these controls.

TIP! *Animations do not work well on a Web page because most people would not think to click on a slide to make more of its content appear.*

The outline panel allows viewers to navigate through the presentation with the outline.

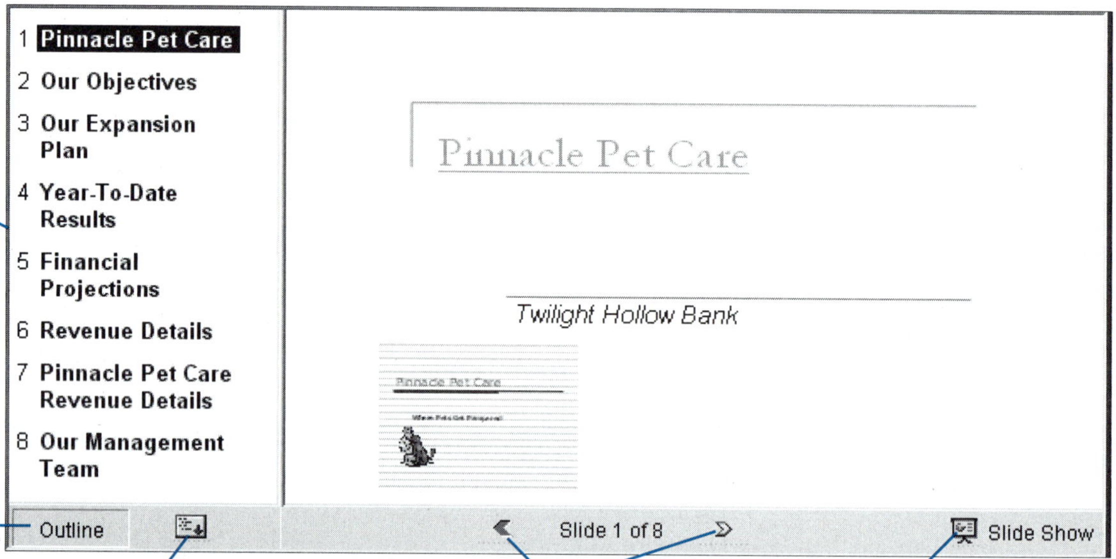

The Outline button switches the outline panel on and off.

The Expand/Collapse outline button toggles between showing only the titles and showing the titles plus the first-level bullets.

These Arrow buttons allow viewers to move forward and backward through the presentation.

The Full Screen Presentation button makes the presentation fill the screen.

Hands-On 6.5 Navigate a Presentation on the Web

In this exercise, you will navigate through a presentation saved as a Web page.

1. Run the Slide Show then click the Web page hyperlink on the title slide.
2. Click the Pinnacle Pet Care Promotion link.
3. Click Products Sold in the outline panel on the left side of the browser window.
   The outline panel works just as it does in the PowerPoint window. Notice that only the title of the slide is visible. This is because animation effects were added to display the bullets one at a time.
4. Click eight times on the slide to make all of the bulleted items appear.
   The animation effects created for this slide also work in the Web page version.
5. Point to either side of the text on the Outline button as shown at right (so the pointer arrow appears) then click.
   The outline panel disappears. This leaves more room for viewing the slides.

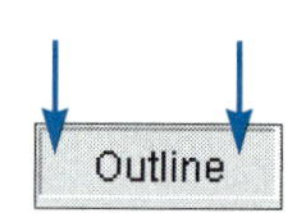

6. Click the Previous Slide button to view Slide 2. Click five times on the slide to make the bulleted items and image appear.

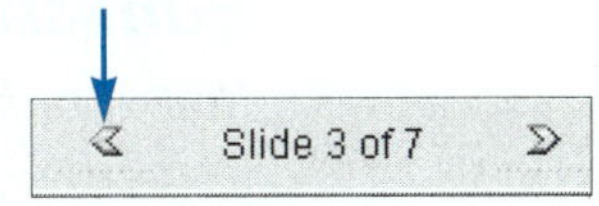

   This type of animation does not work well on a Web page and most people would not think to click on a slide to make more of its content appear. So, it's a good idea to remove animation effects on a presentation you save as a Web page. In Hands-On 6.4, you learned about an option in the Publish dialog box that allows you to remove animation effects.
7. Click the Next Slide button near the bottom of the window to return to Slide 3.
   Notice that you must click on the page to make the bulleted items appear again.
8. Click the Full Screen Slide Show button at the bottom-right corner of the window.
   The presentation now fills the entire screen. Notice that the presentation has returned to Slide 1 and that the Previous Slide and Next Slide buttons are gone.
9. Click once on the slide to advance to Slide 2.
   Whenever you click a completely displayed slide, you advance to the next slide. However, the animated bullet items and picture have disappeared again. You will have to click several times on the slide to make them reappear.
10. Tap the [End] key once.
    Notice that nothing happens. You cannot use the [Home] and [End] keys to navigate in a Web page slide show.
11. Click on the slides as necessary to reach the Monthly Events slide.
    All of this clicking is really getting tedious! This is an example of how a presentation proceeds if you don't turn off the Show Slide Animation While Browsing option you learned about in Hands-On 6.4.
12. Tap the [Esc] key to exit Full Screen mode then close the Internet Explorer window.
    You are returned to the PowerPoint window.

Storing the Presentation in a Folder

Microsoft Office Specialist

For others to view your presentation Web page over the Internet or an intranet, the pages must be hosted on a Web server. The act of placing your Web pages into a folder on a Web server is called publishing the pages. When you publish a presentation to a Web server, a copy of the presentation is saved on the server, making it accessible by anyone connected to the Web. The original presentation is stored on your computer. Most Internet service providers (ISPs) provide their subscribers with at least one megabyte or more of free Web space. Many ISPs have a variety of hosting plans and services to meet the needs of individuals, small businesses, and large corporations.

Publishing Methods

You can choose from several methods to publish your Web pages to a Web server. The method you choose depends on the capabilities of the ISP or corporate network system that hosts the Website. The most common methods are listed in the following table.

Method	When to Use It
Web folders	Use this method if your operating system supports Web folders. Windows 95, 98, NT 4.0, 2000 and Windows XP all support Web folders.
FTP (File Transfer Protocol)	Use this method if you do not have an automated method to publish the pages. An FTP utility allows you to send your pages manually to the folder/directory in the hosting service system that serves your pages.
ISP-provided utilities	Use this method if the ISP that hosts your Website provides a special utility for publishing Web pages.

Naming Web Pages

When you create your own Web pages, you should pay careful attention to their names. Many Web servers run on an operating system called UNIX that has rules for naming files that differ from Windows. The following points will help you create file names compatible with most Web server systems:

Rule	Reason
Never use spaces in the filenames of Web pages and graphics	UNIX systems do not allow spaces in filenames. Use underscores instead. For example, my_web_page.
Give the primary page on your Website the name index.htm	If someone enters the URL of your Website but does not include a specific a filename, most Web servers will display the index.htm page. If this page does not exist, browsers to your site may receive an error message.
Try not to use uppercase letters in filenames	Web page filenames are case-sensitive. On UNIX servers for example, MyHomePage.htm and myhomepage.htm represent different filenames. If you consistently use lowercase letters when naming Web pages, you can decrease the chances that a browser will receive an error message.

Using Web Folders

Web folders allow you to publish Web pages and graphics with drag-and-drop ease. Web folders on your computer are associated with folders on a Web server system. When you move or copy files to a Web folder, the files are automatically copied to the associated folder on the Web server system. If you delete files from a Web folder, they are also deleted from its associated Web server folder.

A Web folder on your computer

QR

QUICK REFERENCE: SAVING A DOCUMENT TO A WEB FOLDER

Task	Procedure
Publish to a Website with a Web folder	■ Choose File→Save as Web Page from the menu bar and click the Publish button. ■ Click the Browse button then click the Web Folders button on the left side of the dialog box. ■ If you are running Windows 2000 or XP, click the My Network Places button. ■ Double-click to open the desired Web folder. Click OK if you are asked to supply a password. ■ Taking care to follow the naming rules described in the Naming Web Pages section on page 196, enter the name for the Web page and click Open. ■ Click Publish to save the Web page to your Web folder.
Copy a published presentation to a Website with a Web folder	■ Navigate to the drive and folder where the Web page version of the presentation is stored. Make sure your Web page and its folder have Web-compatible names. ■ Select both the presentation file and its associated folder and choose Edit→Copy from the menu bar or use [Ctrl]+[C] from the keyboard. ■ Navigate to the Web Folders icon (Windows 95/98/NT) or to My Network Places (Windows 2000/ME/XP) and open the desired Web folder. Click OK if you are asked to supply a password. ■ Choose Edit→Paste from the menu bar or use [Ctrl]+[V] from the keyboard. ■ After the transfer is complete, the pages can be viewed over the Internet.
Delete files from a Website with a Web folder	■ Open a My Computer or Exploring window, open the Web folders folder, and open the Web folder from which you wish to delete files. ■ Select any files you wish to delete then click the Delete button on the toolbar.
Send the URL of published presentation via email	■ Open your Web folder then double-click the file (not the folder) for your presentation. This displays your presentation in a browser window. ■ If you are using Internet Explorer, choose File→Send Link by E-mail from the menu bar. This creates a new email message containing the URL of your presentation Web page. ■ Address, edit, and send the message.

Hands-On 6.6 Publish the Presentation in a Web Folder

In this exercise, you will save the Pinnacle Pet Care Online presentation in Web page format to a Web folder. You will then open the page in the Web folder to view the presentation over the Internet.

NOTE! *If your computer does not have a Web folder installed, skip this exercise.*

Before you Begin: *If you have a Web folder, enter your username and password required to access it.*

Web Folder Name: ______________________________

Username: ____________________________________ (optional)

Password: ____________________________________ (optional)

Publish the Presentation to a Web Folder

1. Save the presentation.
   It's always a good idea to perform a normal save before you save the presentation as a Web page to a Web folder.
2. Choose File→Save as Web Page from the menu bar and click the Publish button.
   The options you set in Hands-On 6.4 are still in force. Now you will navigate to your Web folder.
3. Click the Browse button.
4. Follow these steps to save the presentation to a Web folder:

A Click My Network Places (for Windows 2000 and XP) or the Web Folders button.

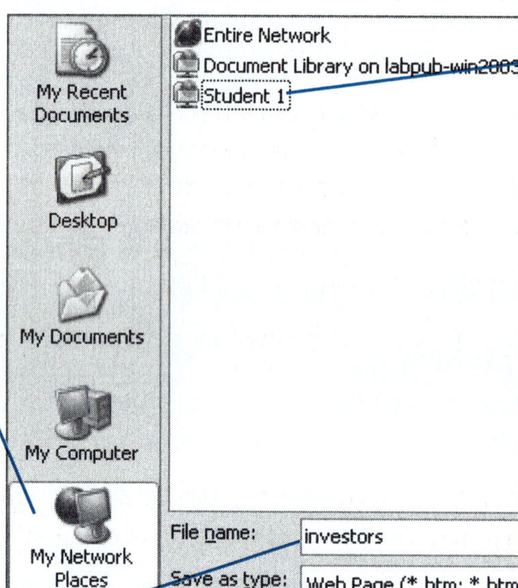

B Double-click on the Web folder you have been assigned.

C Click OK if you are asked for a network password. If the dialog box is empty, enter your username and password and click OK.

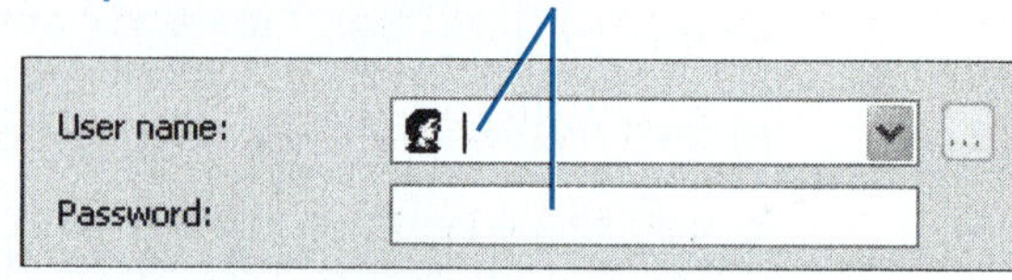

D Change the Save as Type to Web Page.

E Be sure the filename is in all lowercase letters and click OK. Click Yes if you are asked to replace an existing version of the file with the new one you are publishing.

5. Click the Publish button.
   A Transferring File dialog box may appear to show the progress of the transfer as the Web page files are transmitted to the associated Web server folder. Depending on the speed of your Internet connection, this transfer may take up to two or three minutes. When the transfer is completed, your presentation will appear in a new browser window. Notice the URL of your presentation in the Address bar. If this were a real Website, your presentation is now available over the Internet!
6. Navigate through your online presentation to verify that all of its features and hyperlinks function as expected. (Exception: The linked PowerPoint presentation at the bottom-left corner of Slide 1 will not function in the Web page version.)
7. Close Internet Explorer.

Sending the Presentation via Email

PowerPoint allows you to send a presentation to an email recipient. In fact, you can create the email message directly from PowerPoint or your email program. When you give the command to send a presentation by email, PowerPoint gives you two choices:

- Send the presentation as an attachment—This option creates an email message using Outlook or Outlook Express and automatically attaches the presentation to the email message.
- Send the presentation for review—This option creates a new email message with the presentation attached to it. It also places a copy of the presentation in a Document Workspace if your company has a special Web server.

The Email Button

The PowerPoint 2003 toolbar contains an Email (as Attachment) button that makes it easy to send any document attached to an email message. When you click the Email button on the toolbar, PowerPoint immediately displays a message box ready for you to address and choose attachment options. You have two attachment options from which to choose:

- Regular attachment—each recipient gets a separate copy of the presentation
- Shared attachment—each recipient gets a copy of the presentation and it is available in a Document Workspace

The Send To Command

PowerPoint's Send To command lets you choose whether the presentation should be sent as an attachment or for review. You simply choose File→Send To on the menu bar then choose the method of transmission.

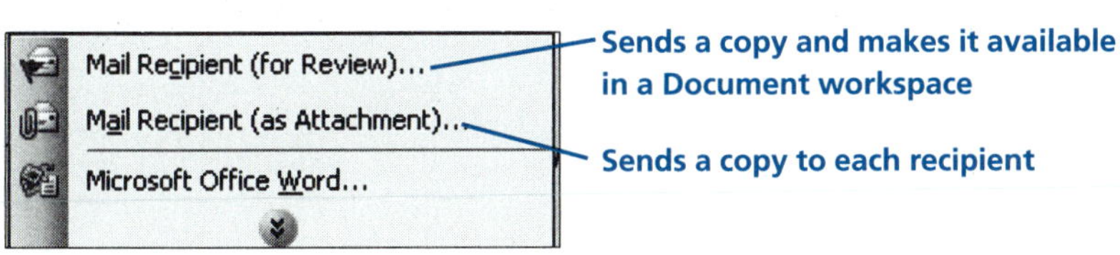

Selecting an Email Program

PowerPoint works with any email program or Webmail service that you select from the Internet Options menu in Internet Explorer or in the Windows Control Panel. If you want to change the email service, you should make this selection before starting PowerPoint.

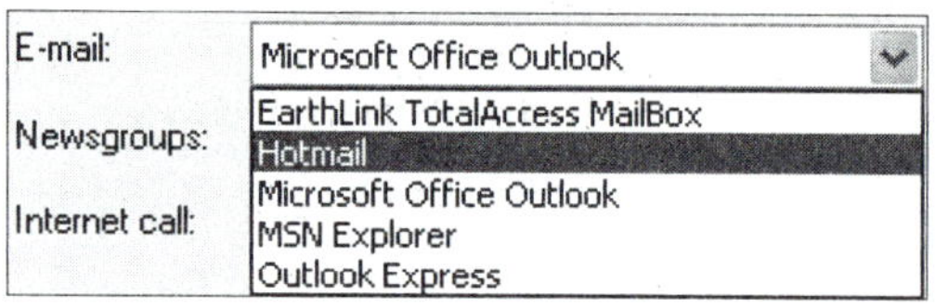

The Internet Explorer Programs tab allows you to select from among the email programs and/or Webmail services installed on your computer.

QR

QUICK REFERENCE: SENDING A PRESENTATION VIA EMAIL

Task	Procedure
Set up the email service PowerPoint uses to send presentations	■ Close the PowerPoint program window if the program is running. ■ Start Internet Explorer then choose Tools→Internet Options from the menu bar and click the Programs tab. ■ Choose the desired service/program from the Email drop-down list (e.g., Outlook or Hotmail) and click OK. ■ PowerPoint will use the selected email program the next time you give the command to send a presentation via email.
Send a presentation via email	■ Open or create the presentation to be sent. ■ Click the Email button on the PowerPoint toolbar or choose File→Send To→Mail Recipient (as Attachment) from the menu bar. ■ Enter the recipient's email address and, if desired, revise the subject line. ■ Click the Attachment Options button and choose the desired option. ■ Click the Send button on the message window toolbar.

Email Addresses

When you enter an email address for a message, you must follow certain rules and make sure that all parts of the email address are typed correctly. The following figure shows the primary parts of an email address.

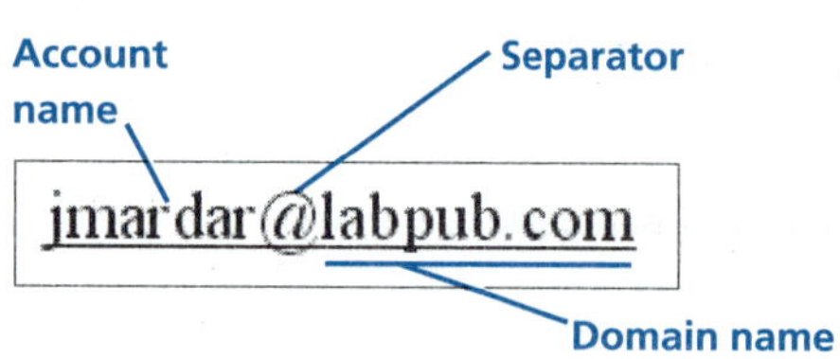

TIP! *As is the case with Web page URLs, email addresses cannot contain spaces.*

The following table outlines the rules for email addresses.

Element	Rule
@	Email addresses **always** contain the @ symbol to separate the account name from the domain name.
Space Characters	An email address **cannot** contain space characters.
Punctuation Characters	An email address **can** contain certain punctuation characters, such as dashes and periods.

Email Attachments

An attachment is a file you include with an email message. Some types of information are not as easy to work with in the form of an email message. For example, although you could send the outline of a PowerPoint presentation in the body of an email message, some of the formatting and all of the images on the slides would be lost. It is much more efficient to send the entire presentation as an attachment in this case.

An attachment can be any type of file, including Word documents and Excel workbooks. You can even attach Word and/or Excel documents to the same message with a PowerPoint presentation.

NOTE! *Hands-On 6.7 gives basic instructions for sending and receiving attachments with Outlook 2003. For detailed information on this topic, see* Microsoft Office Outlook 2003: Essentials Course.

Hands-On 6.7 Send a Presentation via Email

In this exercise, you will send a presentation as an email message then open the attachment after it is received.

Select an Email Program

NOTE! *Depending on how the computer lab is configured, you may have access to email via Outlook 2003, Outlook Express, or a Webmail service (i.e., Hotmail).*

1. Close the PowerPoint window. Click Yes if you are asked to save changes to the presentation.
   Your new email service selection will not work unless you start PowerPoint after the selection is made.
2. Start Internet Explorer with Start→(All) Programs→Internet Explorer.
3. Choose Tools→Internet Options from the menu bar then click the Programs tab.
4. Use the E-mail drop-down list to select the appropriate email service or program, such as Outlook or Hotmail.

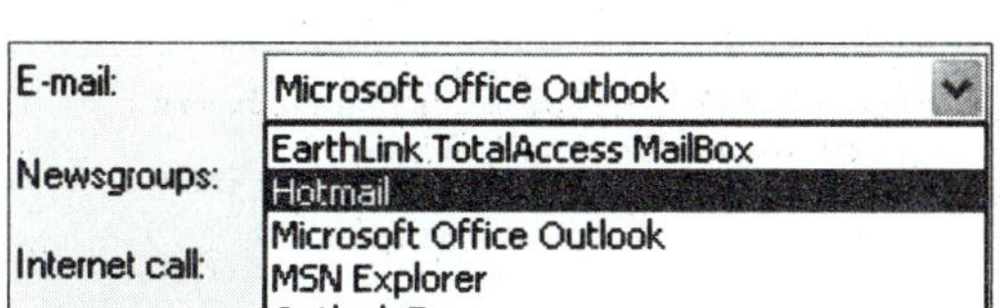

5. Click OK then close the Internet Explorer window.
You should now be viewing your presentation in the PowerPoint window.

Send a Presentation as an Attachment

6. Start PowerPoint and open the Pinnacle Pet Care Loan Statistics presentation. Click the Update Links button if you are asked to update the hyperlinks in your presentation.

7. Choose File→Send To→Mail Recipient (as Attachment) from the menu bar.
There will be a pause as a new message is created with the selected email program or Webmail service. Notice that the presentation appears as an attachment in the message box. The subject of the message has also been filled in for you.

NOTE! *The instructions for the rest of this exercise are specific to Outlook 2003. If you are using Hotmail or Outlook Express, adapt your interpretation of the instructions accordingly.*

8. Follow these steps to address the message:

Ⓐ Enter your email address in the To box. You can enter a Hotmail account address or an email address assigned to your computer.

Ⓑ Type the body of the message as shown here.

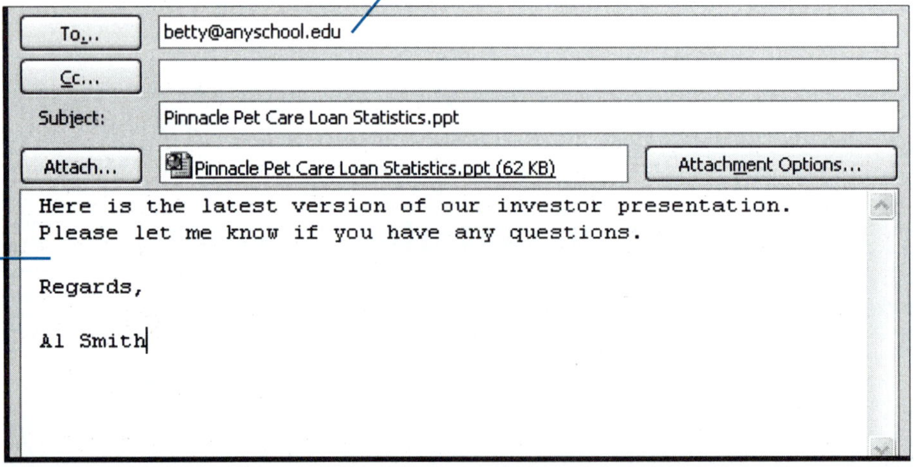

9. Follow the applicable bulleted step:
   - If your computer can send and receive email: click the Send button on the message toolbar.
   - If your computer cannot send and receive email: close the message window. Click No when you are asked if you wish to save the message. Skip the rest of the exercise—you will not be able to open the attachment since you cannot send it.

Open the Attachment

10. Click File→Close on the menu bar. Click Yes when you are asked to save the changes to the presentation.
This closes your presentation so it will open from the attachment.

11. Start your email program.

12. Follow these steps to open the attachment:

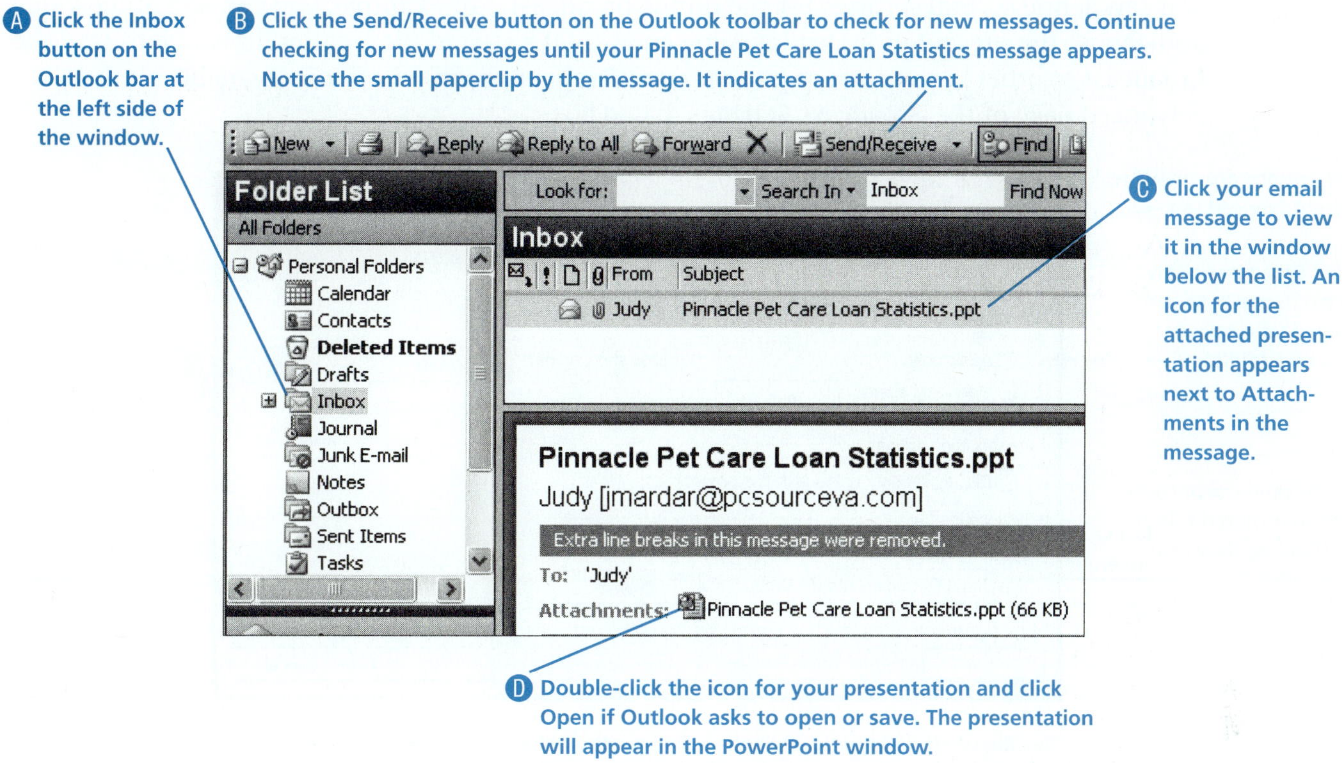

13. Click the Update Links button if PowerPoint asks to update the hyperlinks in your presentation.

14. Click the Outlook message button on the taskbar then close ☒ Outlook.

Broadcasting Presentations Online

Microsoft Office Specialist

You can use PowerPoint to schedule an online broadcast of a presentation over the Internet or a private network. The presentation can even include audio and video. For example, the broadcast can include your voice narrating points in the presentation. As the presentation is broadcast, you can save it to a folder for access by anyone who missed the original broadcast.

An add-in called Presentation Broadcast is required in order to broadcast a presentation. The free add-in is available from the Microsoft Office Online Website, which then places an Online Broadcast command on the Slide Show menu item.

Defining Settings for a Broadcast

You can define several settings for the online broadcast. For example, you can add audio/video and choose the presentation display. You can also set a shared file location in which to save the broadcast so others can have access to it later. There are browser options available on the Advanced page of the Broadcast Settings dialog box.

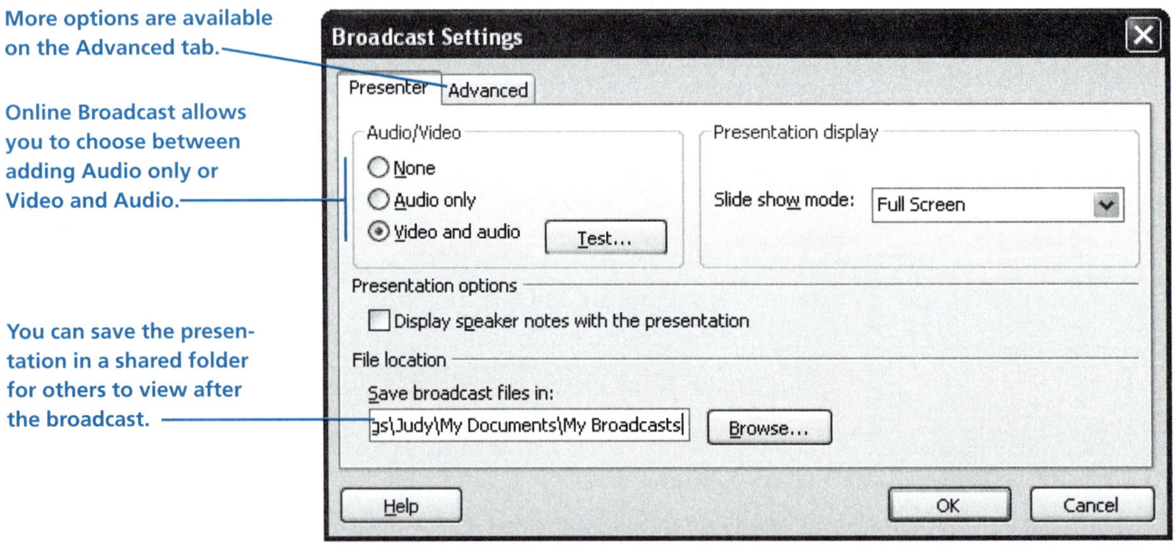

This dialog box allows you to set options for the online broadcast of the presentation.

Microsoft Windows Media Server

If you are sending the broadcast to more than 10 people, you must use a Microsoft Windows Media Server, a digital media platform that supports streaming media. If you work in a corporate environment and are unsure about the availability of a Windows Media Server on your network, ask your network administrator.

The following Quick Reference table describes broadcast settings as well as installing the presentation broadcast add-in.

QR

QUICK REFERENCE: DEFINING SETTINGS AND INSTALLING ONLINE BROADCAST

Task	Procedure
Define online broadcast settings	■ Start PowerPoint and open the presentation you wish to broadcast. ■ Click Slide Show→Online Broadcast→Settings from the menu bar. If Online Broadcast is not in the list, you must install the add-in. ■ Choose the desired Presenter options. ■ Choose the desire Advanced options. ■ Click OK.
Install the online broadcast add-in to PowerPoint	■ Click Help→Microsoft Office Online. ■ Click Downloads in the left pane. ■ Type **broadcast** in the Search box and click Go. ■ Click the Presentation Broadcast Add-in link then click the Download button. ■ Follow the online download instructions.

Hands-On 6.8 Define Settings for an Online Broadcast

WebSim *In this exercise, you will run a simulation of defining broadcast settings for the Pinnacle Pet Care Loan Statistics presentation. Because many computer classrooms do not allow programs to be downloaded from the Internet, this simulation will run from a Web page. (See Skill Builder 6.5 for a guided exercise in downloading and installing the Presentation Broadcast Add-in if your personal computer allows downloads.)*

1. Click Slide Show→Online Broadcast→Settings.
2. Follow these steps to define the broadcast settings:

Ⓐ Ensure the Video and Audio option is selected.

Ⓑ Click the Browse button and select the My Broadcasts folder then click the Select button. This specifies where the broadcast files will be saved for later viewing.

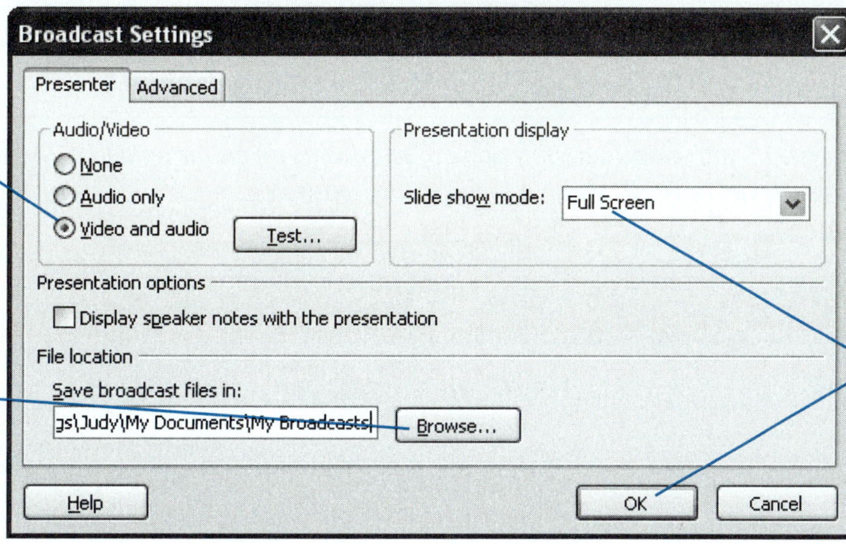

Ⓒ Verify that Full Screen is selected in the Slide Show Mode box and click OK.

3. Take a few minutes to view the other options available on the Advanced tab.
4. Click OK.

Schedule an Online Broadcast

Microsoft Office Specialist

When you schedule a broadcast, you can send an email message to all desired attendees, inviting them to view it. Attendees receive a hyperlink that connects them to the broadcast. Outlook 2003 users will also receive a reminder message with a button they can click to launch Internet Explorer and view the broadcast.

QR

QUICK REFERENCE: SCHEDULING AN ONLINE BROADCAST

Task	Procedure
Schedule an online broadcast	■ Open the presentation you wish to broadcast. ■ Click Slide Show→Online Broadcast→Schedule a Live Broadcast from the menu bar. ■ Enter a description for the broadcast then click the Schedule button. ■ Your email program opens automatically for you to send a message to the desired attendees. If using Outlook, you can use its group meeting tools. ■ Click OK to acknowledge the confirmation message that displays.

QUICK REFERENCE: SCHEDULING AN ONLINE BROADCAST (CONTINUED)

Task	Procedure
View a broadcast using Outlook for email	■ Be sure Outlook has scheduled an appointment for the meeting with a reminder setting. ■ When the reminder message for the broadcast appears, click the View this Broadcast button.
View a broadcast using another program for email	■ Open the email invitation to the broadcast. ■ Click the URL for the broadcast in the body of the message.

Hands-On 6.9 Schedule an Online Broadcast

In this exercise, you will run a simulation of scheduling an online broadcast. Because many computer classrooms do not have the required broadcasting software installed, this simulation will run from a Web page.

1. Be sure the Pinnacle Pet Care Loan Statistics is still open.
2. Click Slide Show→Online Broadcast→Schedule a Live Broadcast from the menu bar.
3. Follow these steps to schedule the broadcast:

(A) Enter the description shown here.

(B) Click the Schedule button. Your email program opens automatically for you to send a message to the desired attendees. If using Outlook, you can use its meeting tools.

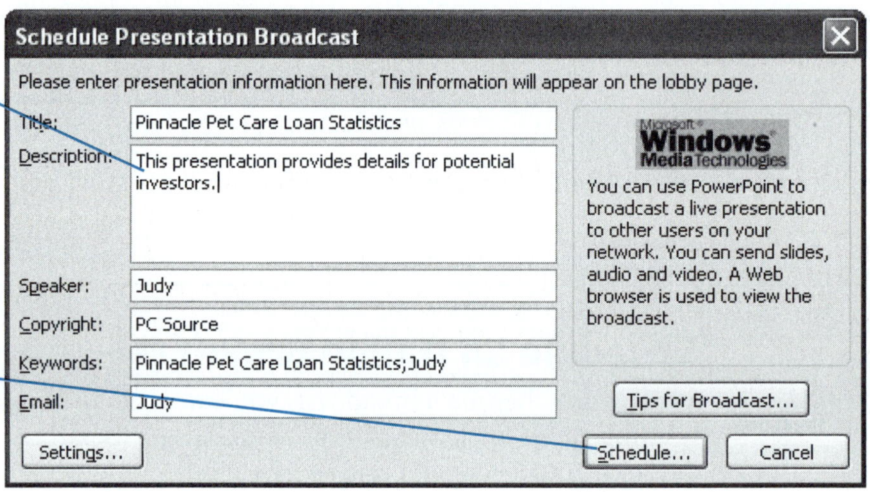

4. Send the email message giving the broadcast details and click OK to in the confirmation message.
5. Save the presentation and close it.

Concepts Review

True/False Questions

1.	A presentation saved as a Web page displays almost identically to the way it appears in PowerPoint.	TRUE	FALSE
2.	You can create hyperlinks to Web pages on PowerPoint slides.	TRUE	FALSE
3.	You can create hyperlinks on a slide to files on a hard drive or floppy disk.	TRUE	FALSE
4.	You can create multiple hyperlinks from the same object to jump to different places.	TRUE	FALSE
5.	When you save a presentation as a Web page, it is automatically available for viewing over the Internet.	TRUE	FALSE
6.	You can insert one PowerPoint presentation inside another.	TRUE	FALSE
7.	PowerPoint always uses the Outlook program to generate an email message with a presentation attached to it.	TRUE	FALSE
8.	PowerPoint allows you to deliver a presentation to other viewers over the Internet.	TRUE	FALSE
9.	PowerPoint can help you schedule an online broadcast of a presentation.	TRUE	FALSE
10.	Animation effects won't work on a presentation saved as a Web page.	TRUE	FALSE

Multiple Choice Questions

1. When you save a presentation as a Web page ________.
   a. a single PowerPoint presentation file is created
   b. a single HTML file is created
   c. an HTML file and a folder containing additional files are created
   d. All of the above

2. Which types of hyperlinks can you create on a slide?
   a. To Web pages
   b. To other files
   c. To slides within the presentation
   d. All of the above
   e. Both a and c

3. What is a Web folder?
   a. A folder on the computer with a direct connection to a Web server
   b. A standard Windows folder that only contains Web pages
   c. A method to publish files directly to the Internet
   d. Both a and c

4. Which of the following statements about sending a presentation via email is true?
   a. You can only send a presentation if you first save it as a Web page.
   b. You can send an entire presentation as an attachment to an email message.
   c. You can send several selected slides as an attachment to an email message.
   d. All of the above

Skill Builders

Skill Builder 6.1 Insert Hyperlinks

In this exercise, you will insert a hyperlink to another presentation file. This hyperlink will function much like the Insert→Object command you used in Hands-On 6.3.

1. Open the Pinnacle Pet Care 2 presentation.
2. Display Slide 3, select New Products and Services at the bottom of the bulleted list, and click the Insert Hyperlink button.
3. Follow these steps to select the file for the hyperlink:

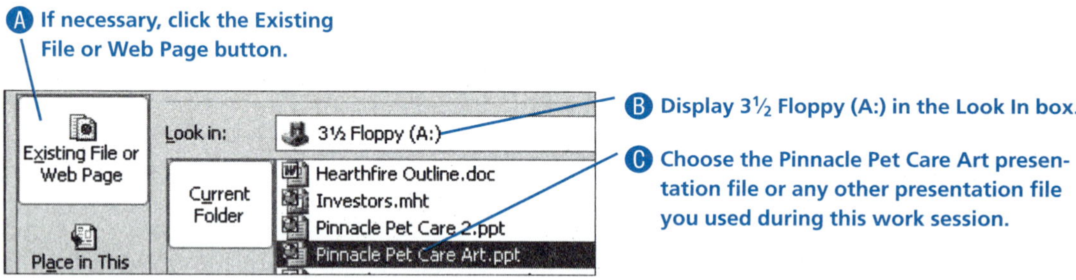

4. Click the ScreenTip button, type **`Click here to open the Pinnacle Pet Care Art presentation`**, and click OK.
5. Click OK to complete the Insert Hyperlink command.
   Notice the underscore below the text you selected in step 2.

Test the Hyperlink

6. Click the Slide Show button and point (don't click) over the hyperlink.
   The mouse pointer should change into a small hand and your ScreenTip should appear; this indicates the destination of the hyperlink.
7. Click the hyperlink.
   The linked presentation will be displayed. You could now navigate through this presentation normally; in this case, you will close it.
8. Tap the Esc key to exit the linked presentation.
   Now you are back to your original presentation, and could continue from where you left off.
9. Tap the Esc key again to exit the original presentation then save and close it.

Skill Builder 6.2 Send a Presentation via Email

In this exercise, you will open another presentation and send it as an attachment to an email message.

1. Open the Tropical Getaways Online presentation.
2. Follow the appropriate step below to send the presentation:
   - Click the Email (as Attachment) button if you use Outlook or Outlook Express.
   - Click File→Send To→Mail Recipient (as Attachment) from the menu bar if you use a web-based email program like Hotmail.
3. If your computer cannot send and receive email messages, perform the following bulleted items. If your computer can send and receive email, move on to step 4.
   - Close the message.
   - Click No when you are asked if you wish to save the message.
   - Skip the remaining steps of this exercise.

Send the Message

NOTE! *The instructions for the rest of this exercise are specific to Outlook 2003. If you use Hotmail or Outlook Express, you should adapt your interpretation of the instructions accordingly.*

4. Address the message to yourself.
   If you are in a classroom, feel free to also send this message to a classmate; if you do, he or she should email you their presentation as well.
5. Enter **`from [your name]`** at the end of the subject line.
6. Click the Send button.
   The message is placed in the Outlook 2003 Outbox for delivery.
7. Close the presentation.
8. Start Outlook (or your selected email program) and display the Inbox.
9. Click the Send/Receive button until you receive your email message (or a message from your classmate); this may take a minute or so.
10. Double-click to open the newly arrived message then open the presentation file attachment.
11. Close the presentation, message, and Outlook windows.

Skill Builder 6.3 Save a Presentation as a Web Page

In this exercise, you will open a presentation and save it as a Web page.

1. Reopen the Tropical Getaways Online presentation.
2. Choose File→Save as Web page from the menu bar then click the Publish button.
3. Be sure the Display Speaker Notes option is not checked.

Set the Web Options

You will vary some of the options so you can compare their effect with the settings you used in Hands-On 6.4.

4. Click the Web Options button and make sure the General tab is selected.
5. Set the Colors for the slide navigation controls to a color scheme that is easy to read. (White text on black is often the easiest to read.)
   Optional: If you wish, clear the checkmark from the Add Slide Navigation Controls option to see how this affects your presentation display.
6. Click the Pictures tab then ensure 800×600 is chosen as the Target Monitor Screen Size.
   This allows you to see the effect of sizing images on the slides for monitors set at low resolution. You may have to design a Web page for the lowest resolution among your target audience.
7. Click OK to close the Web Options dialog box.

Save and View the Web Page

8. Click the Change button next to the Page Title setting. Change the name to **Getaways** and click OK.
9. Click the Browse button. Save the Web page to your file storage location as **tropicalgetaways**, change the Save as Type to Web Page, and click OK.
10. Be sure the Open Published Web page in Browser option is checked then click Publish.
11. It may take two or three minutes for the Web page to save and display in a browser window.
12. After the page is displayed, navigate through the presentation. Try using the various controls to switch the outline panel on and off, expand the outline, and use the full-screen presentation mode.
13. Close ☒ Internet Explorer.
14. Save the presentation and close the PowerPoint window.

Skill Builder 6.4 Publish a Presentation to the Web

In this exercise, you will take the presentation you saved as a Web page in Skill Builder 6.3 and copy it into a Web folder. Then you will open the presentation page from the Web folder to view it over the Internet.

TIP! *You should skip this exercise if your computer does not have a Web folder.*

Publish the Presentation

1. Open a My Computer window and display the 3½ Floppy (A:) drive.
2. Click to select the presentation tropicalgetaways_files Web page folder.
3. Hold down the [Ctrl] key and click the tropicalgetaways Web page file then release the [Ctrl] key.
   The [Ctrl] key allows you to select noncontiguous items in the My Computer window. Both items must be copied in the next step for your Web page to display properly.
4. Click Edit→Copy on the menu bar.
   This copies information about the Web page file and its folder. In a moment, you will paste these items into the Web item.

Windows 95/98/NT 4.0

Windows 2000/XP

5. Click the Up One Level  button until you see the icon appropriate to your version of windows then double-click to open that item.
6. Double-click to open your assigned Web folder. Click OK if you see a prompt to enter a network password.
7. Choose Edit→Paste to copy the Web page and its folder onto the Web server. Click Yes to All if you are asked to replace existing files with these new files.
   A transfer status box may appear to display the progress of the file transfer to the Web server connected to your Web folder.

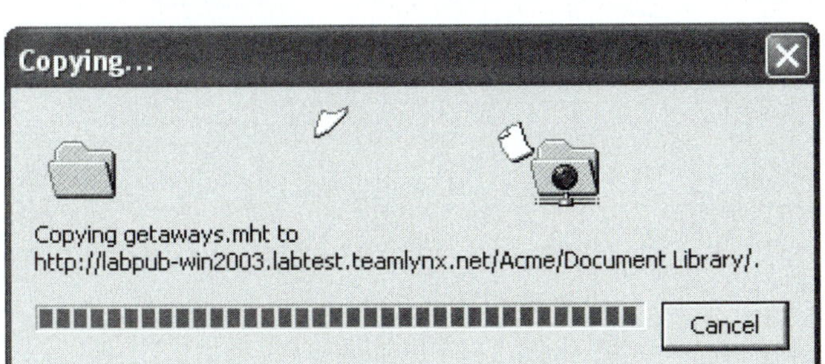

View the Presentation over the Internet

8. Wait for the transfer to finish then double-click the HTML file (not the folder) for the presentation you just copied. Tap the [F5] key to refresh the view, if necessary.

   There will be a pause as Internet Explorer starts and loads the presentation. Notice the URL in the Address bar near the top of the browser window. Anyone entering this URL in their Web browser can view your presentation.

9. Take a moment to view the presentation. The various controls should work just as they did when you viewed it from your file storage location.

10. Close [X] the Internet Explorer and My Computer windows.

Skill Builder 6.5 Install the Presentation Broadcast Add-In

In this exercise, you will download and install the Presentation Broadcast Add-in feature.

NOTE! *If you are at a computer that does not allow downloading from the Internet, skip this exercise and continue with Assessment 6.1.*

1. Open PowerPoint and click Help→Microsoft Office Online on the menu bar.
   The Microsoft Office Online Web site displays on the screen.

2. Follow these steps to install the add-in:

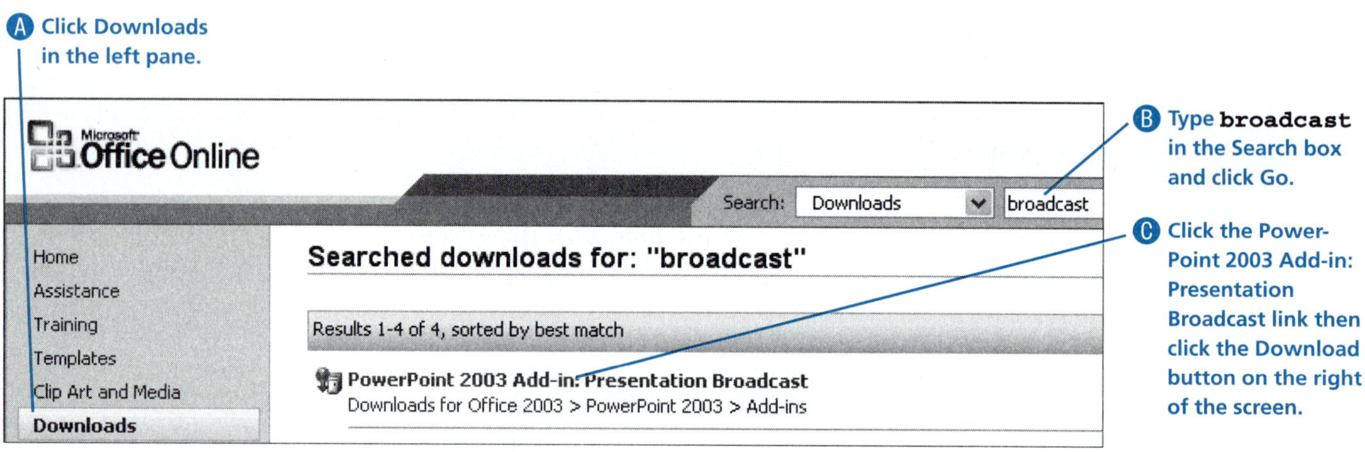

   The File Download dialog box appears.

3. Follow the onscreen instructions to download the file.
   When the download process is completed and you have restarted your computer, the Online Broadcast command will appear on the Slide Show menu drop-down list.

4. Close ☒ the Internet Explorer window.
   You are returned to the PowerPoint window.

Assessments

Assessment 6.1 Insert Hyperlinks in a Presentation

In this exercise, you will insert a hyperlink to a Web page in a PowerPoint presentation to a Word file.

1. Open the Classic Cars Chart presentation.
2. Display Slide 4, Door Prizes and create a hyperlink on the Las Vegas Vacation bullet text that jumps to http://www.lasvegas.com/.
3. Display Slide 5, Agenda For The 2004 Convention and create a hyperlink on Popular Road Trips that jumps to the Tropical Getaways Online presentation.
4. Run the slide show and test the hyperlinks.
5. Save the presentation as **`Classic Cars Online`**.

Assessment 6.2 Save a Presentation as a Web page

In this exercise, you will save the Classic Cars Online presentation as a Web page. The presentation should still be on the screen.

1. Save the presentation as a Web page to your file storage location with the following settings:
   - Do not display speaker notes
   - Set browser support for Internet Explorer 4.0 or later
   - Page title: **`Classic Car Web [Your Name]`**
   - Navigation Controls: Set Colors to Black text on White
   - Target Monitor screen size: 800x600
   - filename: **`classiccarwebyourname`**
2. Click the Print button on the Web browser's toolbar to print the Title page of the presentation.

Assessment 6.3 Publish a Presentation to the Web

In this exercise, you will publish the Classic Cars Online presentation to a Web folder.

NOTE! *Do not perform this assessment unless your computer is equipped with a Web folder.*

1. Save your presentation as a Web page according to the instructions in Assessment 6.2, with the following exceptions:
   - filename: **assessmentlastnamefirstname**
   - Destination: Save as a Web page to your assigned Web folder
2. Print the Web page.
3. Close the Internet Explorer window.

Assessment 6.4 Send a Presentation via Email

In this exercise, you will create an email message with the Classic Cars Online presentation as a regular attachment.

1. Create an email message to yourself, sending the Classic Cars Online presentation as a regular attachment.
2. Enter **[your name]** at the end of the subject line of the message.
3. If your computer cannot send and receive email with Outlook 2003 (or some other email program), perform the following steps. Otherwise, skip to step 4.
   - Choose File→Print from the message window toolbar. Print the message and retrieve the printout.
   - Close the message window. Click No when you are asked if you wish to save the message.
4. If your computer can send and receive email messages, perform these steps:
   - Address the message to yourself and click Send.
   - Choose File→Print from the message window toolbar. Print the message and retrieve the printout.
   - Start your email program.
   - Display the Inbox then click the Send/Receive button on the toolbar to ensure the message was sent.
   - Close the email program window.

Critical Thinking

Critical Thinking 6.1 Embed and Link Presentations

Your manager, Christina Diamond, knows of your PowerPoint expertise and asks you how the Homestead Realty Art presentation can be shared with agents. She would also like the Tropical Getaways Online presentation to be embedded into it. She wonders if there is a way to have the CMA chart jump to the CMA Details Excel file and if it could be sent by email to all the agents. You tell her not to worry, that yes, you can satisfy all of her requests and will have it done by the end of the day. When finished, save the presentation as **`Homestead Online`**. Close the presentation when you are finished. Later, run the presentation for your co-workers, friends, or relatives.

Critical Thinking 6.2 Insert Hyperlinks and Publish to the Web

Brittany Cleaver is the office manager of Tropical Getaways, Homestead Realty's sister company. Brittany is so impressed with what you did for the Homestead presentation that she asks Christina if she can borrow you to do a similar task for her presentation. Brittany would like you to modify the Tropical Getaways Online presentation to link the popular destinations to their Websites. For example, link Tahiti to tahiti.com. In addition, she would like to have the presentation viewed over the Internet by all the agents across the United States, rather than emailed to them as an attachment. You tell her this will be a cinch and you'll be happy to accommodate her wishes. When finished, save the presentation as **`Tropical Getaways Online`** then close it.

LESSON 7

Working with Online Collaboration

PowerPoint has been taken to a new level with Internet integration. With PowerPoint 2003, we are no longer constrained by geographical limitations that hinder us from working with our team members across the country. PowerPoint 2003 allows you to collaborate on presentations by adding and tracking, then merging changes from multiple sources. In this lesson, you will learn how to use the collaboration tools that PowerPoint 2003 offers.

IN THIS LESSON

Microsoft Office PowerPoint 2003 objectives covered in this lesson

Objective Number	Skill Sets and Skills	Concept Page References	Exercise Page References
PP03S-3-1	Track, accept, and reject changes in a presentation	220–222, 226–229	222–223, 228–231
PP03S-3-2	Add, edit, and delete comments in a presentation	224	225–226
PP03S-3-3	Compare and merge presentations	231–232, 235	232–235

Additional learning resources are available at labpub.com/learn/pp03/

Case Study

In Lesson 6, Working with Online Presentations, Al sent a presentation via email to all managers, asking that each of them review the presentation. He has since learned that PowerPoint offers some very powerful collaboration tools. Al's learned that his managers can review the presentation online, insert comments and make changes directly to a presentation. He can then track the changes and, when finished, he can compare and merge the reviewer's copies into his master file. With these newfound tools at his fingertips, Al is excited to get started with the review process of his latest presentation. An example of sending a presentation from PowerPoint through Microsoft Outlook is shown in the following illustration. Also shown is a sample slide with changes from multiple reviewers that will be compared and merged with the original presentation.

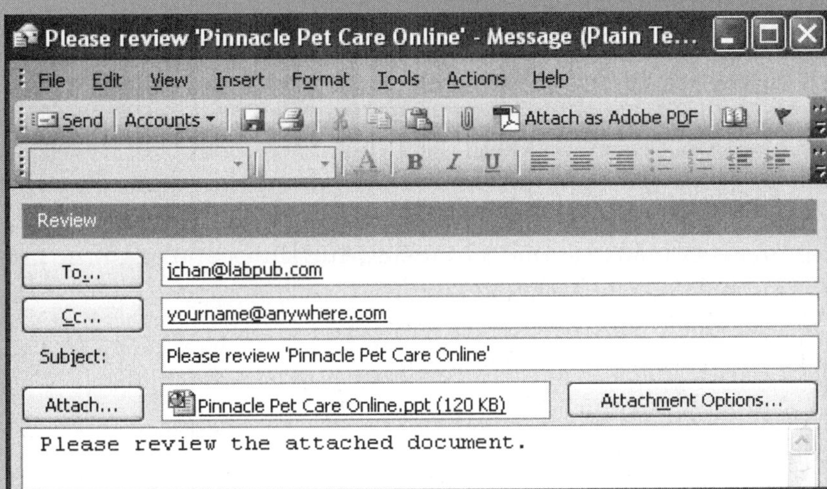

Sample Microsoft Outlook message window sending a presentation for review using PowerPoint's Send To command

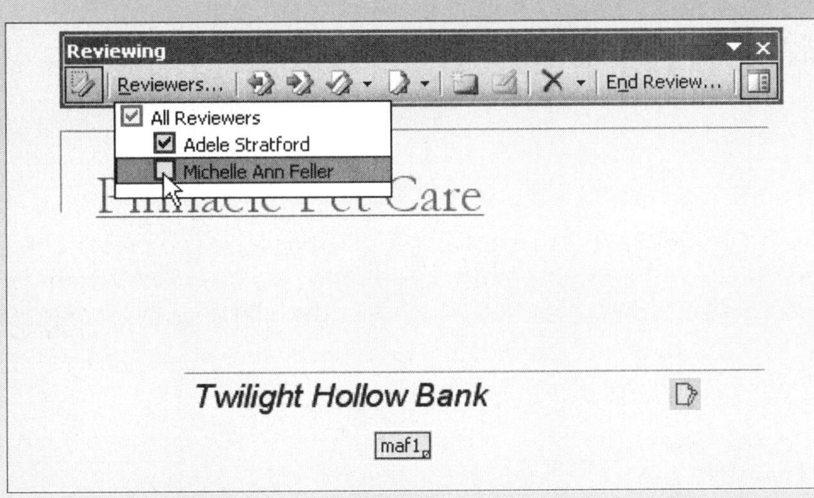

Example of a slide with changes indicated from multiple reviewers

Collaborating Online

Microsoft Office Specialist

If you have ever worked on a team presentation project, you know the havoc created as a presentation is passed from person to person for review. PowerPoint 2003 now has an integrated reviewing process that is automated to track changes, merge the changes, and create one final presentation.

There are many ways to collaborate online, from sending the presentation through email, placing it on a shared server, and handing reviewers a copy of the file on a CD. The reviewers make appropriate suggestions and changes then return the reviewed copy to you so you can merge them with the original. You'll be able to track the changes and view who made what change.

Setting Up a Review Cycle

The first steps in setting up a review cycle are to decide how you want to receive feedback from the reviewers and what your goals are. For example, do you want reviewers to make actual changes to the presentation or to simply write comments? You indicate your preference in the email message that accompanies the presentation. If you want to request the reviewers to make changes directly in the presentation, you can use PowerPoint's Revisions task pane and tracking features or instruct team members to review the slides and send the presentation back to you with comments in an email message.

Review Cycle Process

Regardless of the method you choose to collaborate, there is a standard review cycle process, which is shown in the following table.

Process Step	Performed By
Send the presentation for review	Original author
Review the presentation, making changes or adding comments	Reviewer(s)
Return the presentation to the original author	Reviewer(s)
Compare, merge, and finalize the reviewed presentation	Original author

Sending a Presentation for Review

You can use Microsoft Outlook or another email program to send the presentation for review. This allows the reviewers to make changes directly to the presentation. When you receive the feedback from the reviewers, you, as the owner of the original presentation, can accept or reject the changes then compare and merge the reviewed copies into your original. You initiate the process from the opened PowerPoint presentation.

Using Outlook to Send a Presentation

There are advantages to using Microsoft Outlook to send a presentation. Outlook automatically adds a message to the text area of the message box. You can also use Outlook's Follow up button to set a due date and time as a reminder to the reviewer.

After issuing the Send To→Mail Recipient (for Review) command in PowerPoint, Microsoft Outlook displays a message box already containing the subject, the attached file, and a "Please review" message. All you have to do is enter the recipient(s) email address(es).

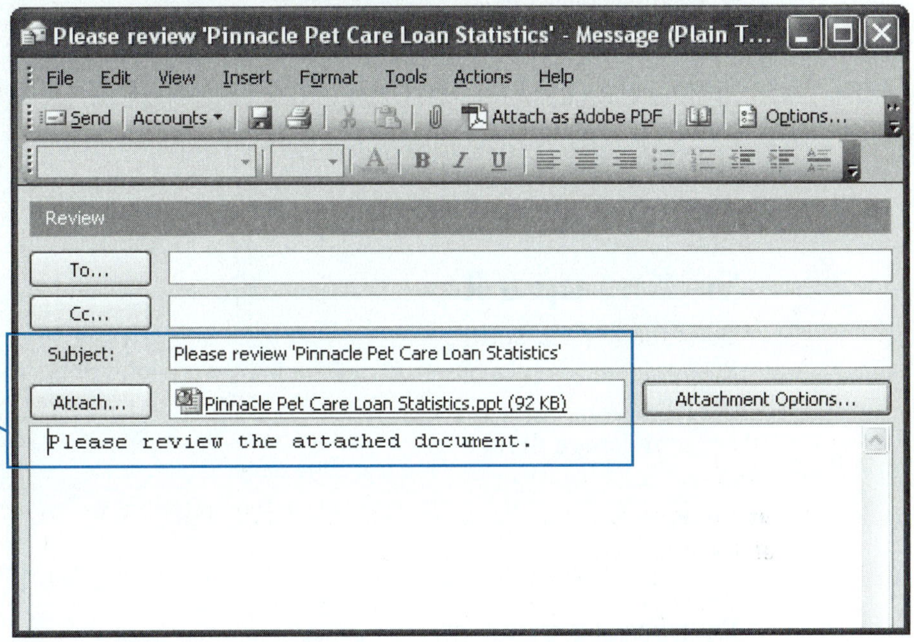

Using Other Email Programs or Drives to Send a Presentation

Programs other than Outlook do not provide the same automatic tracking services. For example, you have to track the changes manually and stay on top of the review cycle.

Setting a Due Date for the Review

You can flag a message for follow up when you send it with Outlook. For example, you can flag a message to set a due date for the review. When the due date passes, the message in the reviewer's Inbox and in your Sent Items box turns red to alert both parties.

You can select a flag message from the drop-down list or type your own custom message.

You can set a due date and time for the flag. The message turns red when it is past due.

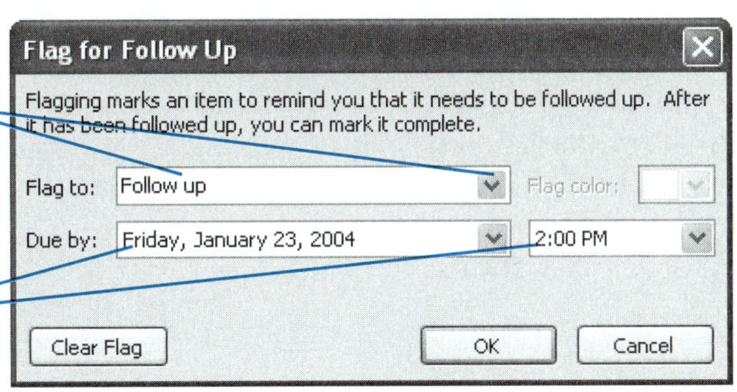

The following Quick Reference table describes the procedures for sending a presentation for review.

QR

QUICK REFERENCE: SENDING A PRESENTATION FOR REVIEW

Task	Procedure
Send a presentation for review using Microsoft Outlook	■ Open the presentation in PowerPoint. ■ Click File→Send To→Mail Recipient (for Review). ■ Enter the email addresses of the reviewers. ■ Optional: Click the Follow up Flag button to set a deadline, reminder, or other option. ■ Click the Send button.
Preparing the presentation to send for review	■ Open the presentation in PowerPoint. ■ Click File→Save As. ■ Rename the presentation, indicating which reviewer is to review this copy. Do this for each reviewer. ■ Click the Save as Type box, select Presentation for Review, and click Save. ■ Close the presentation.
Send a presentation for review using another email program, network server, or on disc	■ Open your email program and address a message for the first reviewer. ■ Use your email program's procedure to attach the saved copy of the file and click Send. Or, ■ Send an email message to all reviewers telling them the name of the shared network folder in which you placed their copy. Be sure to tell them in the message to only review the copy with their name on it. Or, ■ Save each copy to a disc then distribute to the appropriate reviewer.

TIP! *Save all reviewer copies in a special folder to keep them together.*

Hands-On 7.1 Send a Presentation for Review

In this exercise, you will send the Pinnacle Pet Care Online presentation for review using the Send To command. You will also set a due date for the review.

NOTE! *The instructions for this exercise are specific to Outlook 2003. If you are using Hotmail or Outlook Express, adapt your interpretation of the instructions accordingly.*

Use the Send To Command

1. Open the Pinnacle Pet Care Online presentation.
2. Click File→Send To→Mail Recipient (for Review).
   There will be a slight pause as a new message is created with the selected email program or Webmail service. Notice that the message box only requires you to enter the recipient's email addresses; all other boxes are complete. You may add additional text to the subject and message body if desired.

3. Follow these steps to fill in the message box:

A. Notice that the title bar of the message box displays "Please review…".

B. Enter this email address in the To box. You can also enter a Hotmail account address or an email address assigned to your computer.

C. Enter your personal email address in the Cc box.

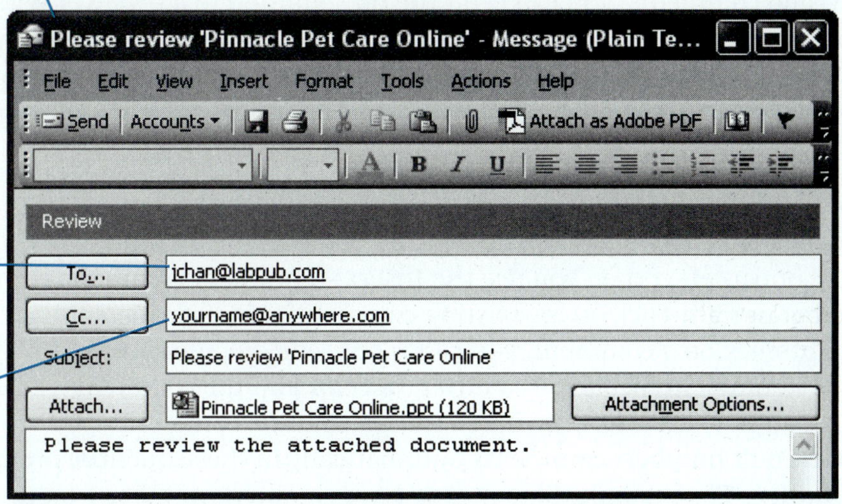

D. Notice the body text that was entered automatically when you used the Send To→Mail Recipient (for Review) command. Add **`Please provide feedback by making changes directly in the presentation or adding comments`** after the first sentence.

Set a Due Date

4. Click the Follow Up button on the toolbar.
   A Flag for Follow Up dialog box appears.

5. Follow these steps to set the due date and time:

A. Be sure Review is displayed in the Flag To box; if it isn't, select it from the drop-down list.

B. Click the drop-down arrow next to Due By and select today's date.

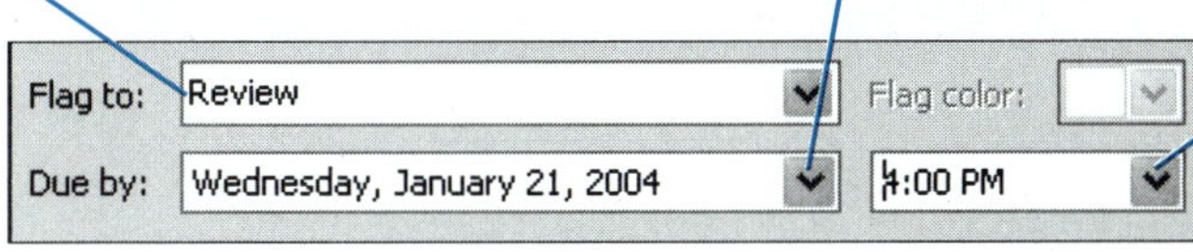

C. Click the drop-down arrow next to the time box and choose the time one-half hour from now.

D. Click OK.

6. Click the Send button.

7. Close Microsoft Outlook.
   The presentation displays on the screen.

8. Save and close the presentation.

Working with Comments

Microsoft Office Specialist

A PowerPoint comment inserted in a presentation is the electronic equivalent of passing a printed copy of the presentation to a team member with a yellow sticky note on it asking for a response. Using comments, you can send the presentation to a reviewer with your notes, questions, or concerns regarding individual slides and have them add their own comments and return the presentation to you for review. With this method, reviewers do not make changes directly to the slides.

Adding, Editing, and Deleting Comments

Comments can be inserted anywhere on a slide; however, the default location is the upper-left corner. You use the Insert→Comment command on the menu bar or right-click on an existing comment to insert a new one. When you right-click on a comment, you can insert, edit, copy, or delete it. Each reviewer's comment displays in a different color and the comment indicator (a small box) indicates the user's initials and the comment number. PowerPoint numbers comments automatically in the sequential order they are placed in the presentation. For example, Slide 8 may have comment number 1 on it, while Slide 1 may have comment number 15 on it.

TIP! *You can read a comment simply by pointing to it. You do not have to click on it.*

QR

QUICK REFERENCE: USING COMMENTS IN A PRESENTATION

Task	Procedure
Insert a comment	■ Display the slide to receive the comment. ■ Click Insert→Comment on the menu bar. ■ Type the comment then click outside of the comment box. Or, if there is an existing comment on the slide: ■ Right-click on the comment. ■ Choose Insert Comment from the pop-up menu. ■ Type the comment then click outside of the comment box.
Edit a comment	■ Right-click on the comment. ■ Choose Edit Comment from the pop-up menu. ■ Revise the comment as desired then click outside of the comment box.
Delete a comment	■ Right-click on the comment. ■ Choose Delete Comment from the pop-up menu.

Hands-On 7.2 Insert, Edit, and Delete Comments

In this exercise, you will insert, edit, and delete comments in the PPC Comments 1 presentation.

Insert Comments

1. Open the PPC Comments 1 presentation.
2. Click Insert→Comment on the menu bar.
3. Follow these steps to insert a comment on Slide 1:

Ⓐ Notice that the small box in the upper-left corner contains your initials and the comment number. This box will remain on the slide when you are finished typing the comment.

Ⓑ In the comment box type **Create a hyperlink here on the title to jump to the Pinnacle Pet Care Website** then click outside the box.

4. Display Slide 2.
5. Point (don't click) to the small comment box.
   After a couple seconds, the comment pops up on the screen so you can read it.
6. Follow these steps to insert a comment from the existing one:

Ⓐ Right-click on the existing comment box and choose Insert Comment from the pop-up menu.

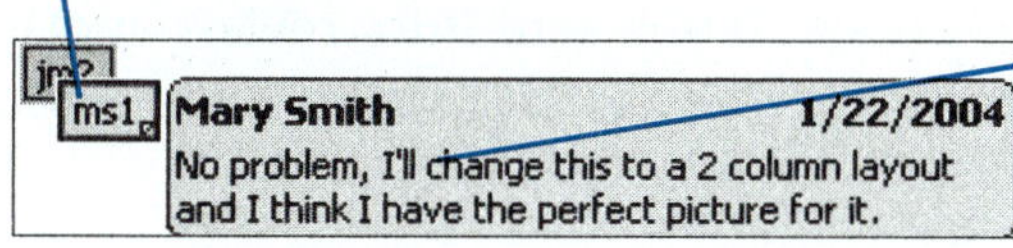

Ⓑ Enter this text for the new comment then click outside the box. Notice that the comment has your initials on it.

Notice that there are now two comments: the original one and the one you just inserted. You will delete the original comment later in this exercise.

Edit Comments

7. Follow these steps to edit the comment:

Ⓐ Right-click on the comment you just inserted and choose Edit Comment from the pop-up menu.

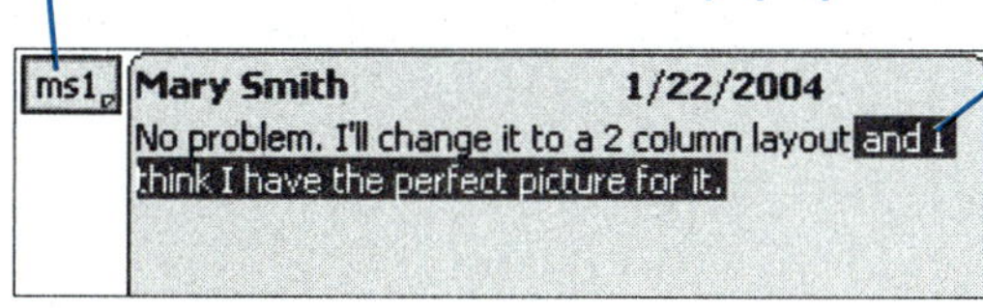

Ⓑ Select the highlighted text here and type a period. Notice the selected text is deleted and a period is inserted.

Ⓒ Replace the deleted text with **Do you know if there is a VISA logo somewhere I could use?** When finished, click outside the box.

Notice that the comment number does not change in the small box. Numbers are only given to new comments.

8. Display Slide 1, right-click on the comment in the lower-right section of the slide, and choose Edit Comment from the pop-up menu.
9. Select the text in the comment and tap [Delete].
10. In the comment box type **`Check with corporate and have them email you the bank's logo file, then insert it here.`**
11. When finished typing, click outside the box.

Delete Comments

12. Display Slide 2.
13. Follow these steps to delete the original comment on this slide:

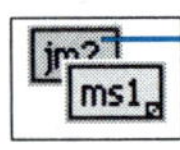

Ⓐ Right-click on the original comment box. Be sure you right-click on the original box underneath yours.

Ⓑ Choose Delete Comment from the pop-up menu.

14. Save the presentation and close it.

Tracking Changes in a Presentation

Microsoft Office Specialist

When reviewers send their copies of the presentation back to you, you will open them in PowerPoint, review and decide on the changes, then finalize the original presentation. If you sent the presentation using the File→Send To command, it will come back to you as an email attachment and you will open it from Outlook. If you sent it for review another way—for example, you put it on a shared network drive—you must use the Tools→Compare and Merge command on the menu bar.

There are several types of changes that PowerPoint 2003 tracks. The types are categorized in levels beginning at the presentation-level down through the text-level. The following table outlines the various types of changes that PowerPoint tracks.

Type of Change	Description
Presentation Level	Slide size
	Content and list of named shows
	Headers and footers for slides, title slides, and notes
Slide Level	Color scheme
	Animation
	List of shapes
	Slide master
	Slide master list of color schemes, default text styles, backgrounds, and objects
	Slide transition
	Slide layout
	Headers and footers
Shape Level	Action settings
	Recolor information
	External objects
Paragraph Level	Bullet typeface, color, and size
	Bullet animation schemes
	Bullet margins and tabs
	Paragraph indent, alignment, and direction
	Paragraph margins and tabs
	East Asian word wrap and alignment settings
Text Level	Font typeface, color, and size
	Languages
	Hyperlinks

The Reviewing Toolbar

The Reviewing toolbar contains buttons to let you easily work with changes and comments in a presentation. The buttons and their descriptions are described in the following table. The Reviewing toolbar displays automatically at different times throughout the review cycle. Thus, depending on the stage of the review cycle, certain buttons may not be available for use.

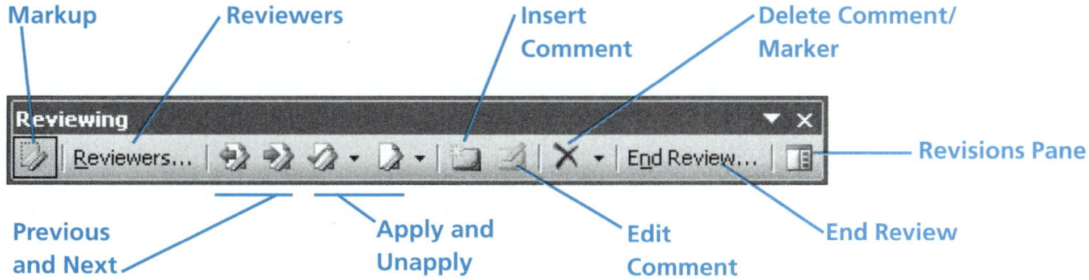

Review Button	Function
Markup	Turns the tracking feature on and off
Reviewers	Lists the names of reviewers from which to choose
Previous Item	Moves to the previous tracked change or comment
Next Item	Moves to the next tracked changed or comment
Apply	Accepts a single change, all changes on a slide, or all changes in the presentation
Unapply	Rejects a change, all changes on a slide, or all changes in the presentation
Insert Comment	Inserts a comment on the displayed slide
Edit Comment	Opens the comment text box to allow editing
Delete Comment/Marker	Deletes a change or comment or all changes and comments (the name of the button changes to either Delete Comment or Delete Marker depending on the type of revision selected)

Hands-On 7.3 Examine the Reviewing Toolbar

In this exercise, you will examine the buttons on the Reviewing Toolbar.

1. Open the Sample Changes presentation.
   The presentation opens and displays change markers, the Reviewing toolbar, and the Revisions task pane. You will work with the task pane in Hands-On 7.4.
2. Follow these steps to choose a specific reviewer:

Ⓐ Click the Reviewers button on the Reviewing toolbar.

Ⓑ Click this checkbox to hide Michelle's changes and view only Adele's.

Ⓒ This was Michelle's comment. It is simply hidden on your screen because you just removed the checkmark from her name. Notice also that the change markers are a different color for each reviewer.

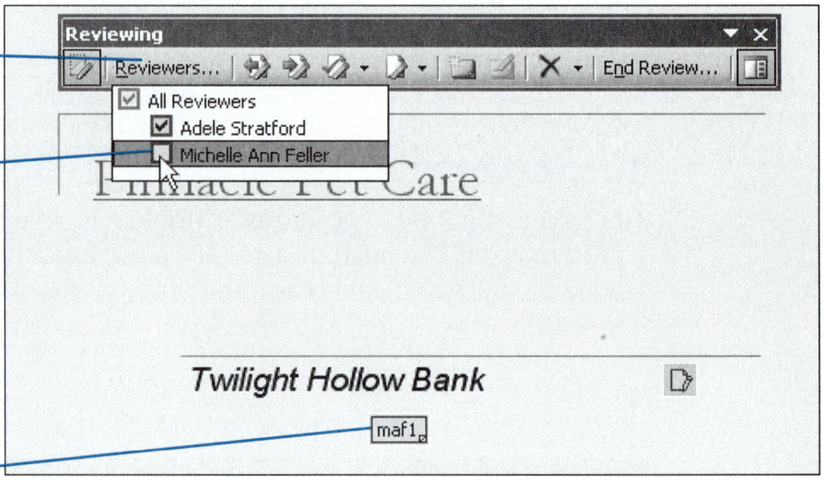

3. Click the Reviewers... button again, click the checkbox next to Michelle's name, and click outside the drop-down list.
   Michelle's marker appears on the screen again.

4. Follow these steps to add a comment:

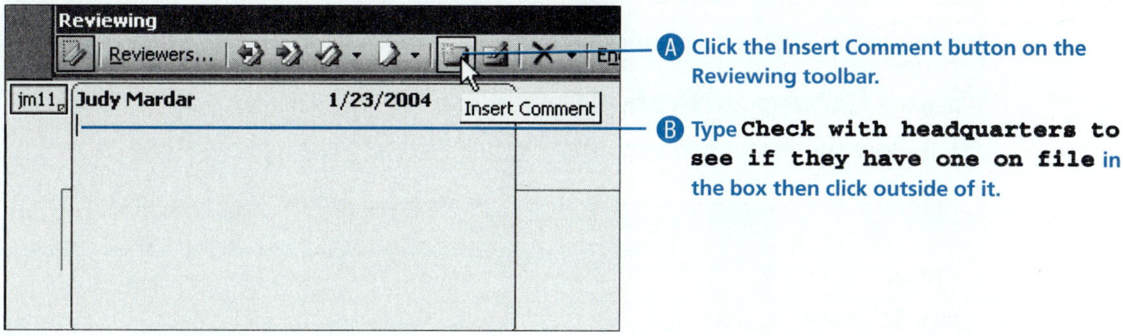

5. Take a few minutes to acquaint yourself with the other buttons on the toolbar, referring to the preceding table for the description, if needed.
6. When finished, save the presentation then continue with the next topic.

The Revisions Task Pane

Microsoft Office Specialist

The Revisions task pane tracks all the changes made by the reviewers. The top half of the List page displays all changes made to the selected slide, while the bottom half of the task pane displays all changes made to the presentation level. The Gallery page displays thumbnail views of the changes for you to view before deciding to accept or reject them.

WARNING! *If you click directly on a slide in the Gallery, you are accepting all the changes made by that reviewer. If you do click on a slide, you can use Undo to reverse the action.*

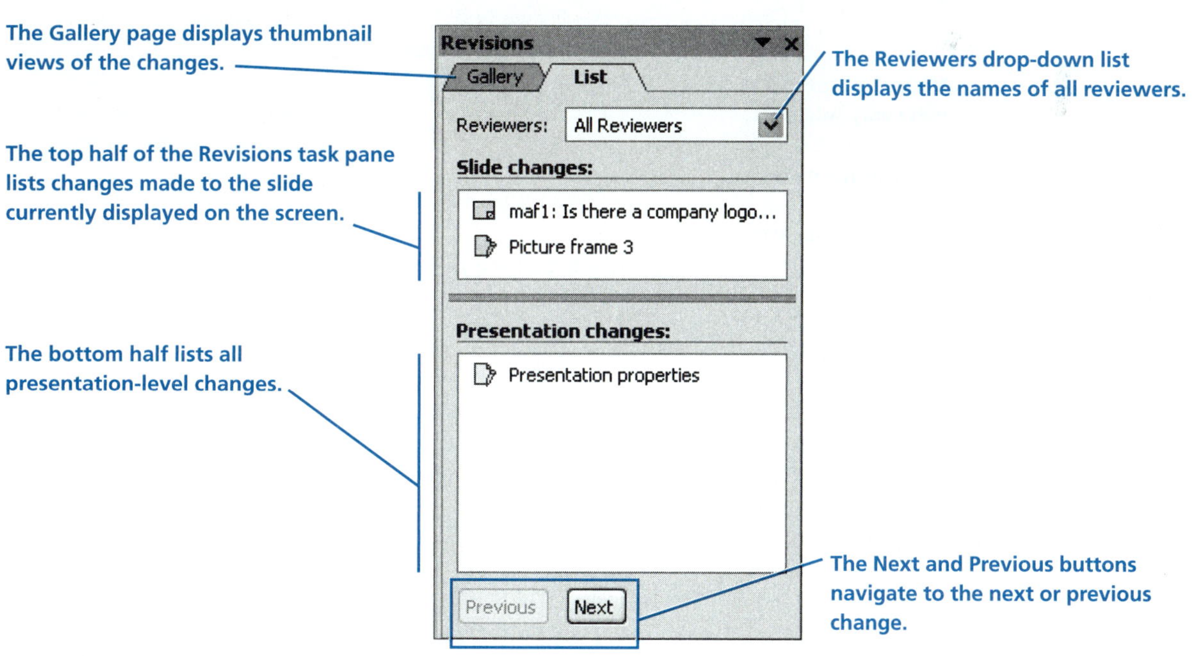

Hands-On 7.4 Examine the Revisions Task Pane

In this exercise, you will examine the sections of the task pane in the Sample Changes presentation.

View a Change with the List Page

1. Follow these steps to view the Picture Frame 3 change on Slide 1:

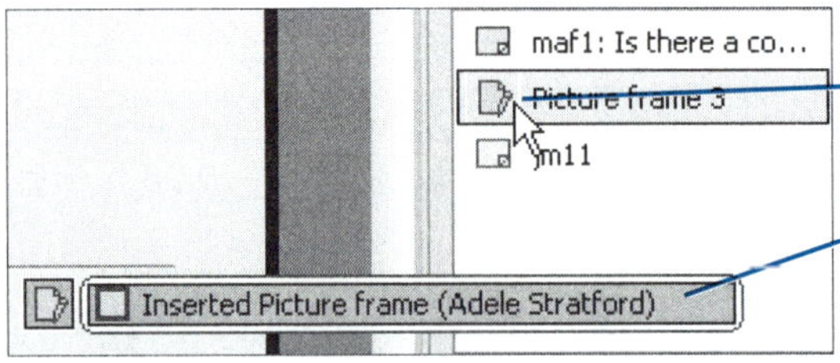

A Click the Picture Frame 3 item in the task pane List page.

B Notice a description of the change displays next to the change marker.

C Click a blank space on the slide.

No changes were accepted since you clicked in a blank area of the slide. You will learn how to accept or reject changes in Hands-On 7.5.

View Changes with the Gallery Page

2. Display Slide 2.
Notice the different colored change markers, which indicate that two different reviewers made the changes.

3. Follow these steps to view the changes made to this slide using the Gallery page:

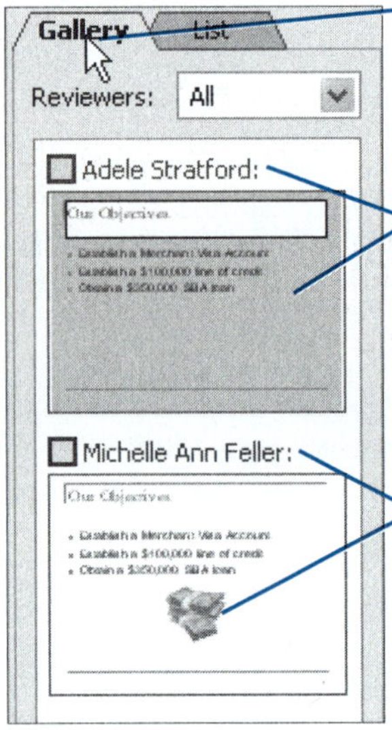

A Click the Gallery tab at the top of the Revisions task pane.

B Adele changed the slide background color.

C Michelle added a piece of clip art.

Because these are two completely different changes, they do not conflict with each other so they could potentially both be accepted. When two changes conflict, you must decide which one to accept. Again, you will learn about accepting and rejecting changes in Hands-On 7.5.

4. Point (don't click) on the top slide in the task pane.
A drop-down arrow appears on the right side of the thumbnail picture.

5. Click the drop-down arrow to view its contents.
   Notice that you could choose to apply all the changes that this reviewer made to the presentation. This is a very quick way to update the presentation, but only use it if you are certain you would want all of the changes.

6. Feel free to view other slides in the presentation using the Gallery page or the List page.
7. When finished, close the presentation. If you are asked to save the changes, click No.

Comparing and Merging Presentations

Microsoft Office Specialist

When you receive reviewed presentations back, you will compare them to the original and either accept or reject the changes. There are two methods of opening the reviewed files. The method you chose depends on the method you used to send the original for review. If you used the Send To command in PowerPoint and sent it through Microsoft Outlook, you will open the presentation from the attached file in the email message. If you used another way to distribute the presentation, you will use the Tools→Compare and Merge Presentations command.

Using the Compare and Merge Presentations Command

As mentioned previously, using any method other than PowerPoint's Send To command to send the presentation requires you to use the Compare and Merge Presentations command to review the changes. You must first open the original presentation file in PowerPoint before you begin the merging procedure. Other methods of sending a presentation for review include storing it in a shared folder, sending copies of it using a different email program, and saving it onto discs then distributing them to reviewers. Once the reviewed presentations are open, they are reviewed as one file. When finished accepting and rejecting the changes, you will save the finalized version and end the review cycle. The following Quick Reference table outlines the procedures for the Outlook method versus all other methods.

TIP! *You can accept multiple changes from different reviewers as long as the changes do not conflict with each other. If they do, you must choose one change to accept.*

QR **QUICK REFERENCE: REVIEWING CHANGES**

Task	Procedure
From an email attachment	■ Open Outlook and display the message with the attachment. ■ Double-click on the attached reviewed presentation. ■ Click Yes in the alert box and PowerPoint will automatically combine the reviewed presentation with your original presentation. ■ Click on a marker or on an item in the Revisions task pane. ■ Click Apply or Unapply to accept or reject the marker. ■ Click Next Item to advance to the next marker. ■ Continue navigating through the changes until all are accepted or rejected. ■ Save the presentation and close it.

QR QUICK REFERENCE: REVIEWING CHANGES (CONTINUED)

Task	Procedure
From a medium other than email	■ Open the original presentation in PowerPoint. ■ Click Tools→Compare and Merge Presentations on the menu bar. ■ Display the appropriate drive/folder in the Look In box and select the file(s) to merge. ■ Click the Merge button. ■ Click on a marker or an item in the Revisions task pane. ■ Click Apply or Unapply to accept or reject the marker. ■ Click Next Item to advanced to the next marker. ■ Continue navigating through the changes until all are accepted or rejected. ■ Save the presentation and close it.

Hands-On 7.5 Use Compare and Merge Presentations

In this exercise, you will compare and merge files in your file storage location that were not sent originally using the Send To command. You will also accept and reject changes.

Merge Reviewed Copies of a Presentation

1. Open the Pinnacle Pet Care Online presentation.
2. Click Tools→Compare and Merge Presentations on the menu bar.
   The Choose Files to Merge with Current Presentation dialog box displays so you can select which files to compare and merge with the original.
3. Follow these steps to merge two reviewed files with the original presentation:

Ⓐ Display the 3½ Floppy (A:) drive in the Look In box.

Ⓑ Click the PPC Comments 1 file, hold down the Ctrl key, and click the PPC Comments 2 file.

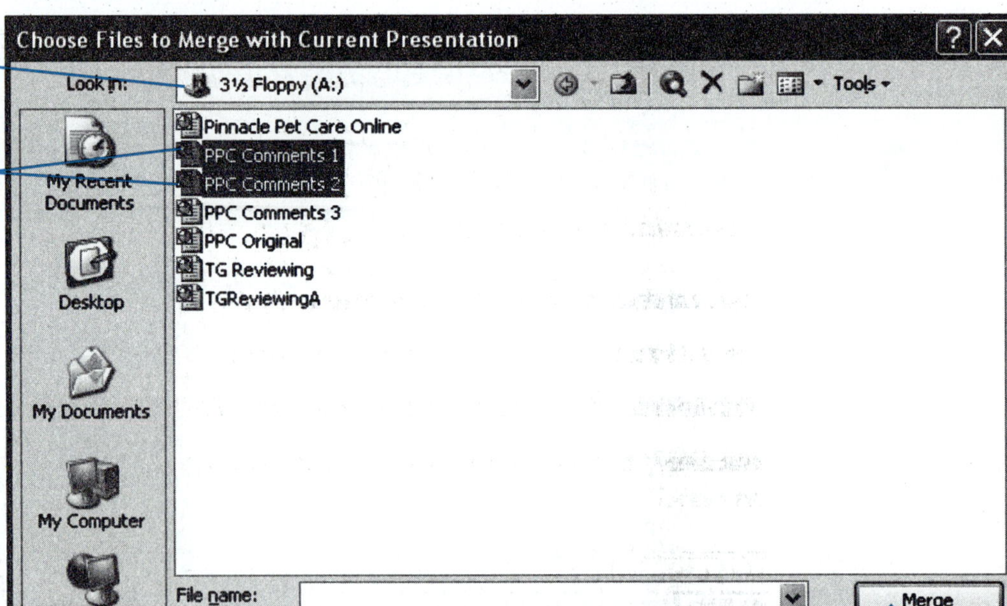

Ⓒ Click the Merge button.

A message displays stating that some files were not sent originally with the Send To command. If these files were sent through Microsoft Outlook using the File→Send To command in PowerPoint, you would not see this message.

4. Click the Continue button.
   Both files merge with the original Pinnacle Pet Care Online presentation. The change markers indicate differences in the three files. Also, notice that the Reviewing toolbar and the Revisions task pane displayed automatically.

Review the Merged Presentation

5. Follow these steps to review the merged presentation:

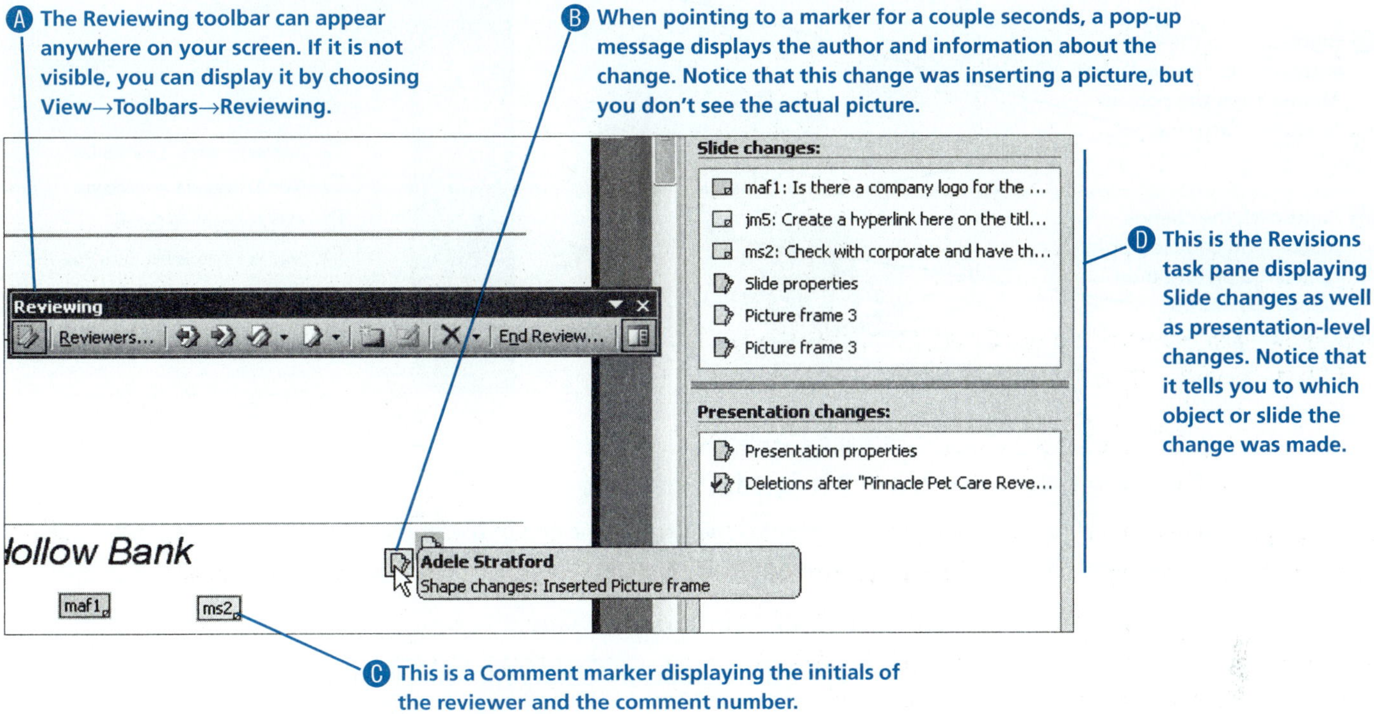

Accept and Reject Changes

6. Click the maf1 change marker.
   The comment text displays.
7. Click the Delete Comment button on the Reviewing toolbar.
   The comment disappears.

8. Follow these steps to view the details and choose actions for markers:

A Click Slide Properties in the Revisions task pane. The change marker displays a description of the change when it is selected in the task pane or when you click on the marker itself.

B Click the Apply button on the Reviewing toolbar to accept the change. Notice that this change applied a new design template only to the selected slide. You must accept the change for each slide since the change was not made in Slide Master.

C Right-click on these two markers and choose Delete Marker from the pop-up menu for each one.

D Right-click the change marker and choose Apply to insert a picture then delete the marker.

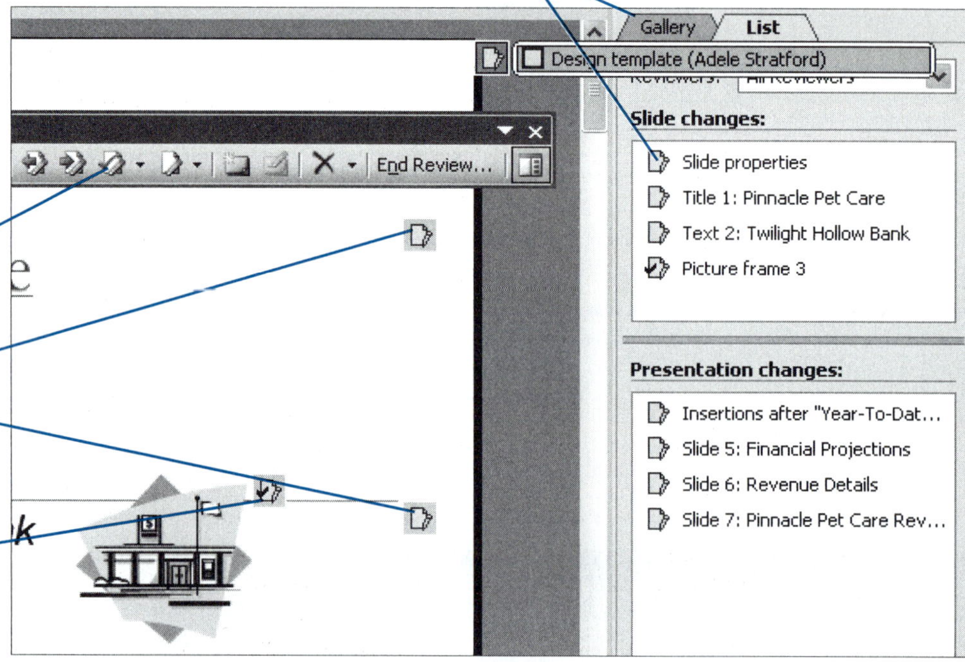

Review Changes from Multiple Sources

There could be numerous individuals making changes or one individual making multiple changes to the same object. When one conflicts with the other, you must choose which change to accept.

9. Display Slide 4 then click Chart 3 in the task pane.

10. Follow these steps to accept the appropriate change to the chart object:

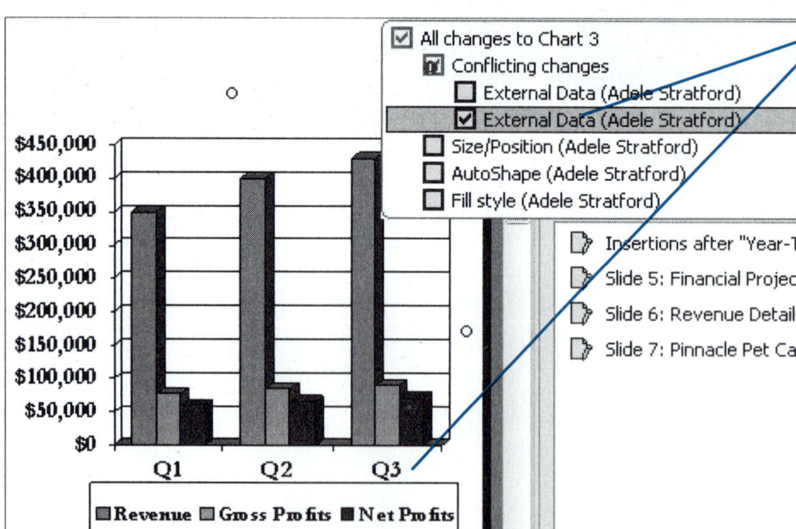

A Take a few seconds to click each checkbox and view the different changes then click this one. Notice that this change placed the legend below the chart, making it the easiest to read of all the changes.

B Click the change marker then click the Delete Marker button.

11. Feel free to go through the presentation and experiment with accepting, rejecting, and deleting markers.
12. When finished, click Save and close the presentation.

Reviewing Changes Sent Through Microsoft Outlook

Microsoft Office Specialist

When you receive the presentation back as an attachment to an email message, you open the presentation from Outlook. You open each attachment and answer Yes to a confirmation message asking if you want to merge the presentation with the one on your computer. Once you've opened all the attachments from each reviewer's email you begin the review process, accepting or rejecting the changes.

Hands-On 7.6 Review Presentations Sent by Outlook

WebSim

In this exercise, you will run a simulation of opening two separately reviewed presentations attached to Outlook messages. The exercise will also simulate accepting and rejecting changes in the reviewed versions. Because you may or may not have others you can send the presentation to and actually receive feedback from, this simulation will run from a Web page. Also, these instructions are written especially for Microsoft Outlook. If you are running a different email program, you will use the Tools→Compare and Merge method, which you learned earlier.

1. Open Microsoft Outlook.
   Notice the two Pinnacle Pet Care Online "review" messages.
2. Double-click the Pinnacle Pet Care Online1 attachment and click Yes to confirm that you want to merge this file.
   PowerPoint automatically combines the reviewed copy with your original presentation. Also, notice the Reviewing toolbar and the Revisions task pane that appear.
3. Click the Outlook button on the taskbar then double-click on the Pinnacle Pet Care Online2 attachment and click Yes to confirm the merge.
   Both files are compared to the original presentation sent out and change markers display on slides where changes or comments have been made.
4. Navigate through the presentation using the Reviewing toolbar and the Revisions task pane, accepting or rejecting changes and comments you like.
5. When finished, save the presentation as **`Merged PPC Online`** then close it.

Concepts Review

True/False Questions

1. You can send a presentation through any email program. **TRUE** **FALSE**
2. Reviewers can put comments in a presentation but cannot actually change anything on a slide. **TRUE** **FALSE**
3. Using Microsoft Outlook to send a presentation for review has many advantages. **TRUE** **FALSE**
4. You can set a due date and time for the review. **TRUE** **FALSE**
5. When you click on a slide in the Gallery page of the Revisions task pane, all changes are accepted for that particular reviewer. **TRUE** **FALSE**
6. Once you add a comment to a slide, you cannot delete it. **TRUE** **FALSE**
7. More than one person cannot review a presentation at the same time. **TRUE** **FALSE**
8. PowerPoint can track changes from multiple reviewers. **TRUE** **FALSE**
9. The Revisions task pane lets you see what the change is before you accept it. **TRUE** **FALSE**
10. You must use Compare and Merge Presentations if the file was not sent with the File→Send To command in PowerPoint. **TRUE** **FALSE**

Multiple Choice Questions

1. Which of the following actions can be accomplished with comments?
   - **a.** Inserting
   - **b.** Editing
   - **c.** Copying the text
   - **d.** All of the above
2. Where do you find the Compare and Merge Presentations command?
   - **a.** Insert
   - **b.** File
   - **c.** Tools
   - **d.** Window
3. When you receive reviewed presentations via Microsoft Outlook, how do you begin the merging process?
   - **a.** Open the original presentation in PowerPoint then open each reviewed copy.
   - **b.** Double-click the file attachment in each received message.
   - **c.** Open the original presentation in PowerPoint then use the Tools→Compare and Merge.
   - **d.** None of the above
4. Which of these is not a change level?
   - **a.** Paragraph
   - **b.** Shape
   - **c.** Graphic
   - **d.** Text

Skill Builders

Skill Builder 7.1 Add Comments

In this exercise, you will add comments to the Tropical Getaways Online presentation.

1. Open the Tropical Getaways Online presentation.
2. Click View→Toolbars→Reviewing on the menu bar.
3. Display Slide 6, titled Travel Now and Save.
4. Click the Insert Comment button on the Reviewing toolbar and create the comment shown to the right.

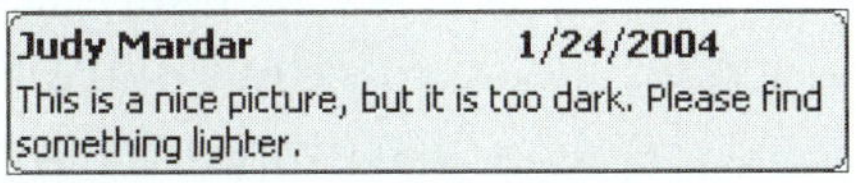

5. Display the last slide, Tropical Getaways.
6. Insert the comment shown in the illustration to the right.

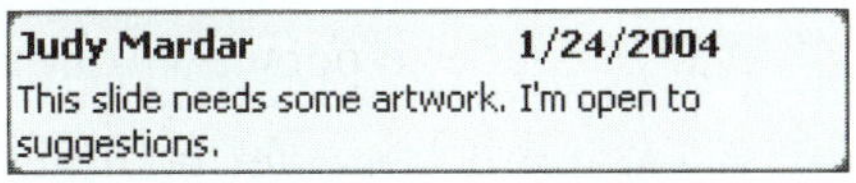

7. Save the presentation and continue with the next exercise.

Skill Builder 7.2 Edit and Delete Comments

In this exercise, you will edit and delete comments in the Tropical Getaways Online presentation. The presentation should still be open.

Edit a Comment

1. Display Slide 6.
2. Right-click on the existing comment and choose Edit Comment from the pop-up menu.
3. Select the second sentence in the existing comment and tap [Delete].
4. Replace the deleted sentence with the following text: **Try to find a piece of clip art instead of a photograph**.
5. Add a new comment: **That's a great idea. But I don't have much clip art on my computer. Do you have a specific image in mind?**

Delete a Comment

6. Right-click on the original comment box and choose Delete Comment from the pop-up menu.
7. Feel free to experiment adding, editing, and deleting comments.
8. When finished, save the presentation as **TG Reviewing1** and leave it open for the next exercise.

Skill Builder 7.3 Send a Presentation for Review

In this exercise, you will send the TG Reviewing1 presentation for review using Microsoft Outlook.

1. Click File→Send To→Mail Recipients (for Review).
2. Follow these guidelines to complete the email message:
   - Address the message to yourself and two others.
   - Set today as the due date and set the time due for the next half-hour from now using the Follow Up flag button.
   - Insert the sentence at the end of the message as shown here:

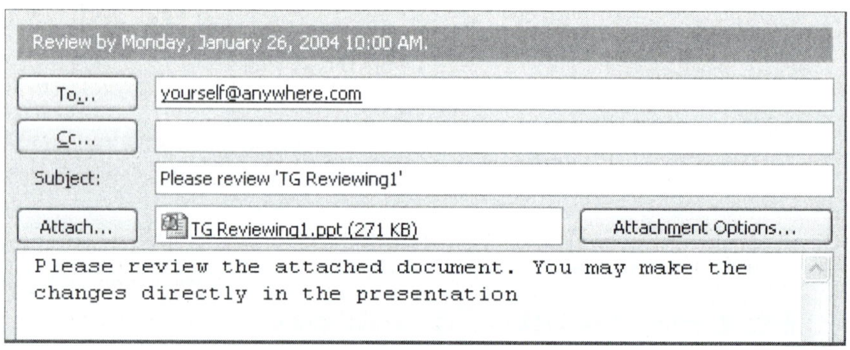

3. Click Send Send.
4. Save and close the presentation.

Skill Builder 7.4 Compare and Merge Reviewed Presentations

In this exercise, you will accept and reject changes using Compare and Merge Presentations.

1. Open the TG Merging1 presentation.
2. Click Tools→Compare and Merge Presentations.
3. Switch to your file storage location.
4. Select the TG Merging2 and TG Merging3 files, click Merge then click Continue.
   Notice the two different color change markers on Slide 1. This indicates that two different reviewers made changes.
5. Point to each marker and read the pop-up messages to see that both reviewers inserted pictures on this slide.
   Notice that the Revisions task pane also tracked the changes and now displays them in the list.
6. Click the Gallery tab on the task pane so you can see the picture each reviewer inserted.
   Now you see the pictures and can decide which one to accept and which one to reject.
7. Click the change marker for Stephanie's insertion.
8. Click the Apply button on the Reviewing toolbar to accept the change.
   The clip art is inserted on the slide, but notice that the change marker remains. Next, you will delete the change marker.
9. Click the marker then click the Delete Marker button on the Reviewing toolbar.
10. Delete the marker for the remaining change on Slide 1.
11. Continue through the presentation, accepting and rejecting the remaining changes as you see fit.
12. When you are finished, there should be no markers for changes or comments left in the presentation.
13. Save the presentation as **Merged TG** then close it.

Assessments

Assessment 7.1 Use Comments

In this exercise, you will add, edit, and delete comments in the Classic Cars1 presentation.

1. Open the Classic Cars1 presentation.
2. Read then delete the comment on Slide 4.
3. Add a comment to Slide 3, asking if anyone has a picture of a Corvair.
4. Edit the comment you just added to include Thunderbirds also.
5. Add a comment to Slide 5 asking if anyone knows of any car club Websites. Tell them to make a hyperlink to the URL from the ...Car Club bulleted text.
6. Add, edit, or delete any other comments you feel appropriate.
7. Save the presentation but don't close it; you will use it in the next exercise.

Assessment 7.2 Send a Presentation for Review

In this exercise, you will send the Classic Cars1 presentation for review. The presentation should still be open.

1. Use the Send To command in PowerPoint to send the presentation to yourself and two others for review.
2. Use today's date and a half-hour from now for a due date.
3. Add to the standard body message: **`You may edit directly in the presentation`**.
4. When finished, send the message.

Assessment 7.3 Merge Reviewed Presentations

In this exercise, you will compare reviewed files and merge them with the original Classis Cars1 presentation. The presentation should still be open.

1. Use the Tools menu to compare and merge the Classic Cars2 and Classic Cars3 files with the original.
2. Navigate through the presentation viewing comments. Answer queries if required, and accept or reject the changes made by the reviewers as you see fit.
3. When finished, save the presentation as **`Merged Classic Cars`** then close it.

Critical Thinking

Critical Thinking 7.1 Review Presentations

The Automotive Association is gearing up for their annual convention. As a well-respected National Sales Manager for a major auto parts manufacturer, the association has asked you for some help with their presentation. You receive a copy of the presentation and make some comments on various slides. However, you want some of your colleagues to back you up on your comments and also see if they have others. You send the Classic Cars1 file to your colleagues from PowerPoint through email. You ask them to make comments and any changes they think are necessary. After the message sends, close the presentation.

Critical Thinking 7.2 Merge Reviewed Presentations

You have received the reviewed copies, AA Reviewed2 and AA Reviewed3, of the Automotive Association's presentation from your colleagues. Now it's time to see which changes, if any, you want to incorporate into the original presentation. To save valuable time, be sure to check out the changes before you actually accept them—otherwise you may be applying then unapplying needlessly. Before finalizing the presentation, run through it one last time to delete any left over change markers. To finalize the presentation with all the incorporated changes and comments, save it as **`Merged AA Presentation`** then close it.

LESSON 8

Managing Template Customization and Multimedia

In this lesson, you will focus on customizing templates in PowerPoint 2003. You will learn how to customize and save a design template as your own so you can reuse it as often as you like. In addition, you will apply multiple design templates to one presentation and customize the color scheme elements to your unique scheme. Lastly, you will learn how to incorporate action buttons and multimedia effects so you can include sound and animation in your presentation.

IN THIS LESSON

Microsoft Office PowerPoint 2003 objectives covered in this lesson

Objective Number	Skill Sets and Skills	Concept Page References	Exercise Page References
PP03S-1-5	Insert objects	257–259	259–262
PP03S-2-3	Format slides	244–245	246–249
PP03S-2-6	Customize slide templates	244, 249–250	246–252
PP03S-2-7	Work with masters	253, 255	253–257
PP03S-4-2	Set up slide shows for delivery	263–264	264–265

Additional learning resources are available at labpub.com/learn/pp03/

Case Study

Pinnacle Pet Care is planning to expand. In their quest to secure more funding to help the new Pinnacle branches flourish, Al and Charlene need to create multiple presentations to deliver to various boards, committees, and conferences. Charlene chooses one of their favorite presentations to customize and save as a Pinnacle Pet Care Template to help them establish a standard Pinnacle image. Although she thought it would be a chore, Charlene finds that customizing the template is easy. She changes the color scheme of the original design to match the colors most used by Pinnacle Pet Care in their advertisements.

Charlene plans to display their presentation at a kiosk during the upcoming National Pet World Trade Show. To make navigating through the slide show easy for the viewers, she adds attractive action buttons on each page. Charlene discovers that she can even add the action buttons to the Slide Master, saving herself tedious work. Finally, she and Al search the Web for appropriate sound files to complement the animation effects they have chosen.

Customizing Templates

Microsoft Office Specialist

Custom templates can be based on a blank presentation template, a design template, or an existing presentation. A design template contains pre-designed formats and color schemes you can apply to a presentation; however, you can customize any part of the template. When you save a customized template, it becomes part of the current presentation. You can also use the customized template to create new presentations with the File→New command.

Customizing PowerPoint Templates

There are several ways to customize a template, including changing the color scheme and slide background. The best presentation template design is simple, includes a minimal amount of fonts and background elements, makes good use of white space, and has a pleasant color scheme. Keeping the design simple ensures that the purpose of the slide is not lost.

Customizing a Color Scheme

A color scheme is comprised of eight individual colors for the background, text and lines, shadows, title text, and fills. It also contains three accent colors. You can customize an existing color scheme by changing one color or all of the colors. Once the desired color scheme is established, you can apply it to one slide or the entire presentation. You can add the new scheme as a Standard Color Scheme, making it available in the Slide Design task pane and under the Standard tab in the Edit Color Scheme dialog box.

Changing a Slide Background

Microsoft Office Specialist

Using Slide view or Slide Sorter view, you can change the background for one slide or the entire presentation. You might want to change the color, use an image, or add a textured look such as wood, marble, or fabric. You can also add color effects to vary the pattern and intensity of the color. For example, you can use a Gradient effect, which fades from dark to light across a slide, or use a variety of Texture effects.

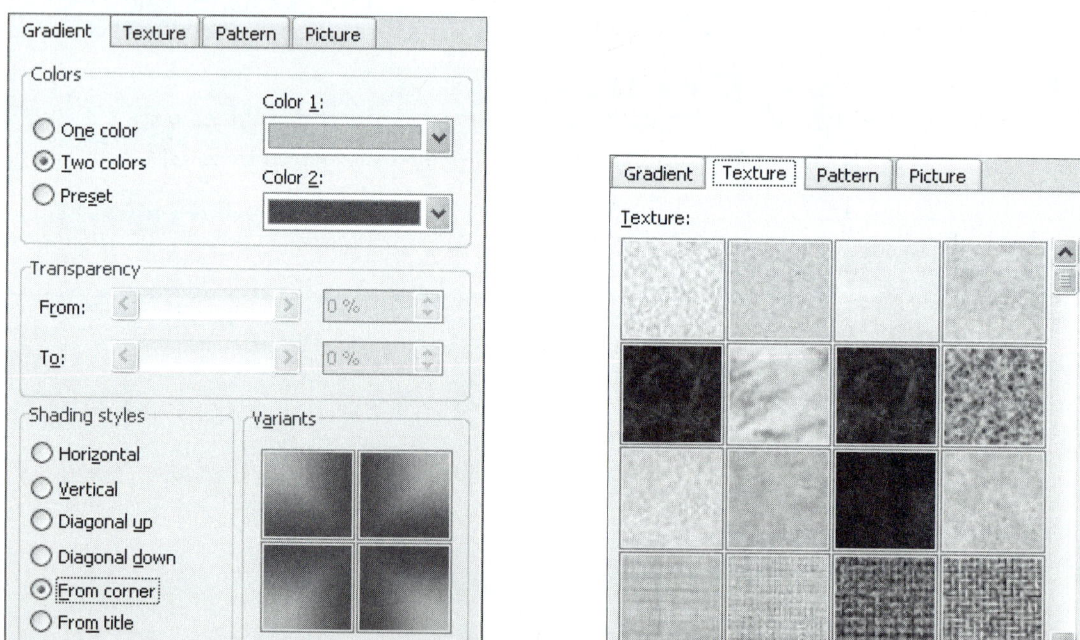

Sample Gradient and Texture options you can add as background effects

Both the Format→Background command and the Slide Design task pane can be used to change the slide background. However, it is important to understand that using the Format→Background method does not change the background color in the color scheme. This means that the background will always remain the chosen color, even if you apply a different template or change the background color of the template's color scheme. For example, imagine you decide to change the background color of Slide 1 to Blue using the Format→Background technique. Later you decide to change the template's color scheme background to Red using the Slide Design task pane. The result is that all the slides except Slide 1 change to red; Slide 1 remains the blue background.

The following Quick Reference table lists the Color Scheme and Background option procedures.

TIP! *The Apply option changes the background color of only the selected slide(s), while Apply to All changes the background color of the entire presentation.*

QR **QUICK REFERENCE: CUSTOMIZING THE COLOR SCHEME AND BACKGROUND**

Task	Procedure
Customize the color scheme	■ Choose Format→Slide Design, click the Color Schemes link in the Slide Design task pane, and click the Edit Color Schemes link at the bottom of the task pane. ■ Click the Custom tab. ■ Click the element you wish to change then click the Change Color button. Select the desired new color from the dialog box and click OK. ■ Click Apply to change the colors for the entire presentation.
Set a solid color as a slide background	■ Choose Format→Background from menu bar. ■ Click the drop-down arrow under the Background Fills box and select a color. ■ Click Apply or Apply to All.
Use a fill effect for the slide background	■ Choose Format→Background from the menu bar. ■ Click the drop-down arrow and select Fill Effects. ■ Click the Pattern, Texture, or Gradient tab, choose the desired effect from the samples, and click OK. ■ Click Apply or Apply to All.
Add a picture for the slide background	■ Choose Format→Background from the menu bar. ■ Click the drop-down arrow and select Fill Effects. ■ Click the Picture tab. ■ Click the Select Picture button and navigate to the location of your picture file. ■ Select the desired picture, click Insert, and click OK. ■ Click Apply or Apply to All.

Hands-On 8.1 Customize a Design Template

In this exercise, you will apply a different color scheme to the presentation then edit it. You will also change the slide background on selected slides.

Apply a Different Color Scheme

1. Start PowerPoint, open the Pinnacle Pet Care Onlinepresentation, and switch to Slide Sorter view.
2. Select Slide 2 then choose Format→Slide Design from the menu bar.
   The Slide Design task pane displays the list of available design templates.

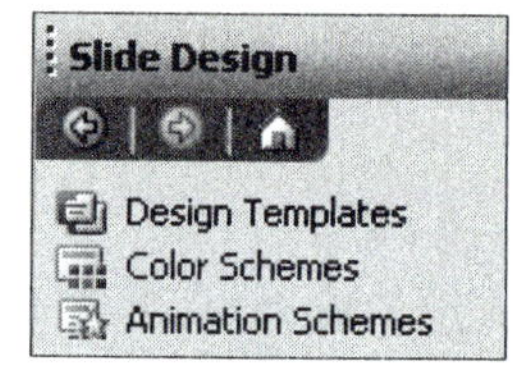

3. Click the Color Schemes link near the top of the task pane.
   The Slide Design task pane changes to display the list of available color schemes.
4. Follow these steps to apply a different color scheme to Slide 2:

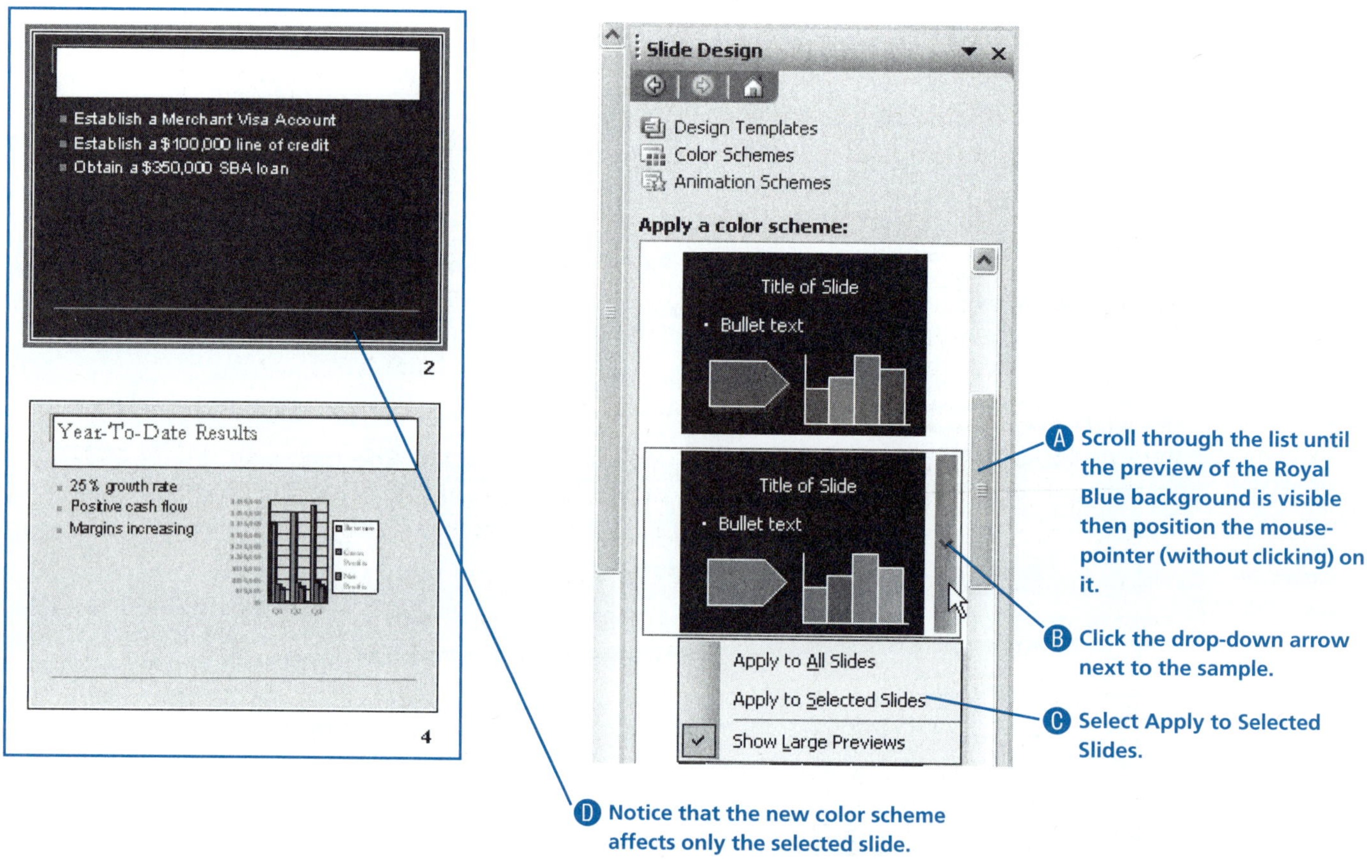

TIP! *To apply the color scheme to the entire presentation, simply click on the preview.*

Edit the Color Scheme

5. Click the Edit Color Schemes link at the bottom of the task pane.
   The Color Scheme dialog box displays the Standard color schemes and allows you to customize the colors. Notice that it displays the color scheme of the presentation, not the color scheme of Slide 2.

6. Follow these steps to customize the background color:

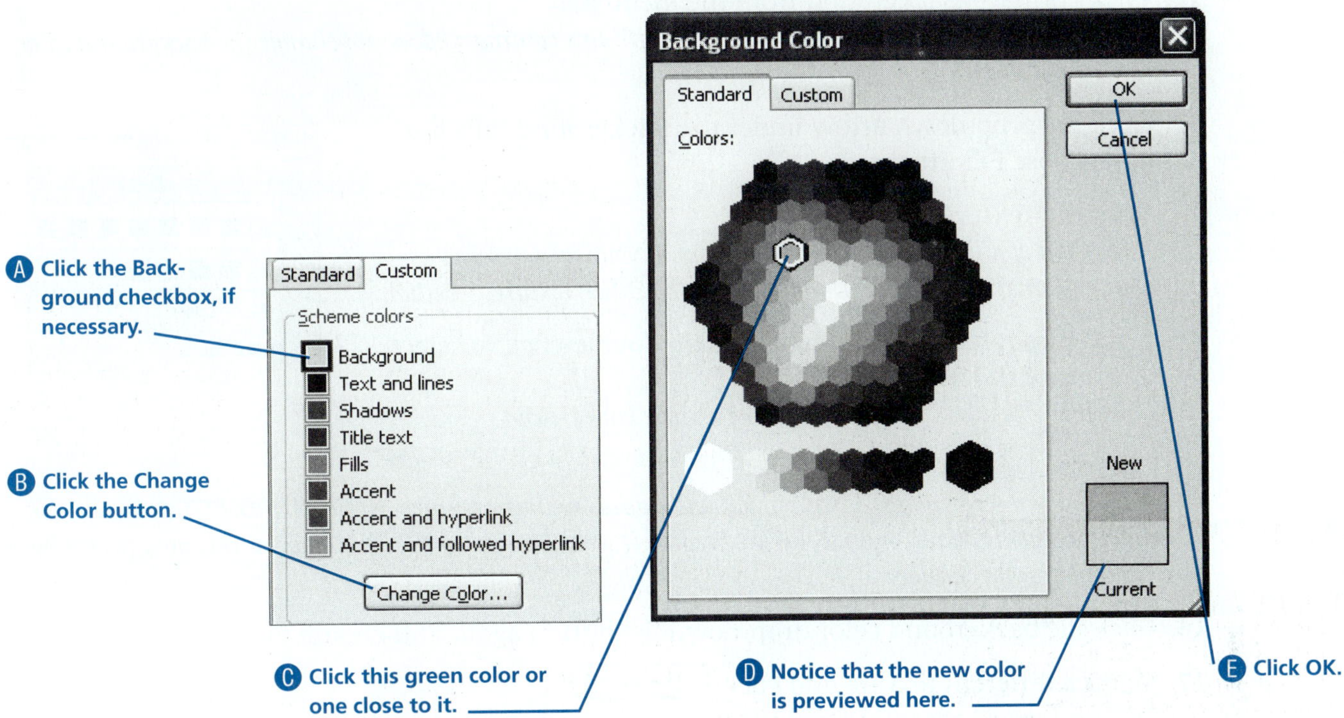

7. Click the Preview button.
You may have to wait several seconds while PowerPoint updates the colors on all the slides. Though all slides will display the new color, the change is not permanent until you click Apply.

8. Double-click the Title text checkbox.
Notice that double-clicking an item saves you from having to click the Change Color button because it displays that item's dialog box automatically. Notice also that because the last time the Title text color was set with a custom color, the Custom page displays when the dialog box opens.

9. Follow these steps to change the Title text color for the presentation:

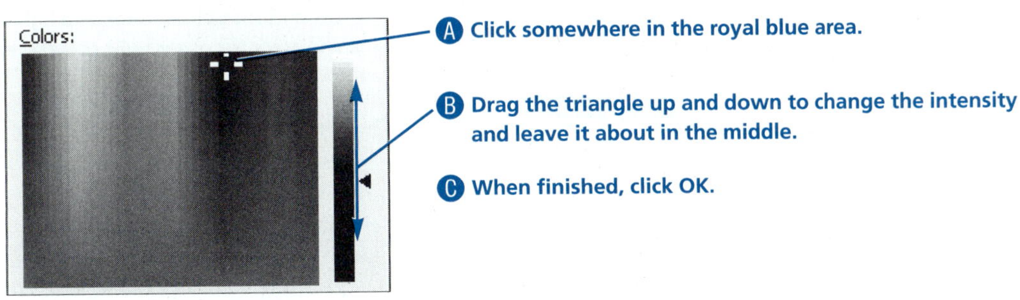

10. Click the Apply button.
Again, it may take several seconds to update all the slides. When it is finished updating, notice that all the slide backgrounds are green and the titles are now blue.

Edit the Slide Background with a Texture Effect

11. Click Format→Background from the menu bar.
Remember, changing the background color with this command does not change the background color of the color scheme.

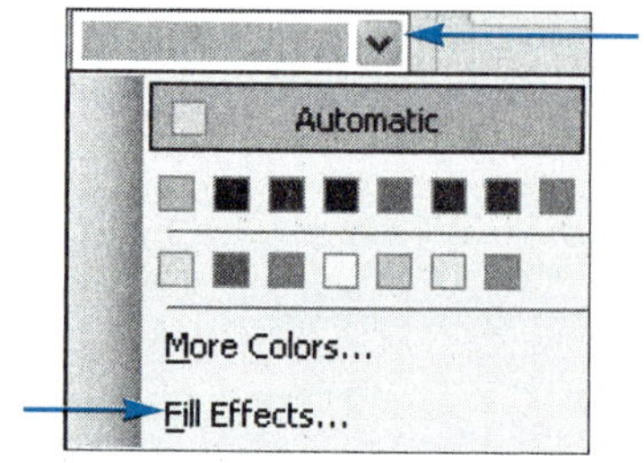

12. Click the drop-down arrow under the Background Fills box and choose Fill Effects.

13. Click the Texture tab.
A selection of all available textures appears. If you want to select a texture from a disk file or CD-ROM, click the Other Texture... button.

14. Scroll through the list of textures then double-click to select any one of them to preview.
PowerPoint displays an example of the texture background.

15. Click the Preview button.
Now you can see how one of your slides will appear with the texture. Notice that the Title placeholder and its contents do not change texture because it was changed in the Slide Master. It is not affected by the background change.

16. Click the background color drop-down list button again and choose Fill Effects.

17. Select a different texture and click Preview.
Textures can add attractive visual effects to your slides. Just make sure your text is clearly legible against this background.

Edit the Background with a Gradient Effect

Now you will create a gradient fill effect, which is often more dynamic than a solid color.

18. Click the drop-down arrow again, choose Fill Effects, and click the Gradient tab.

19. Follow these steps to define a Two-Color, From Corner gradient effect:

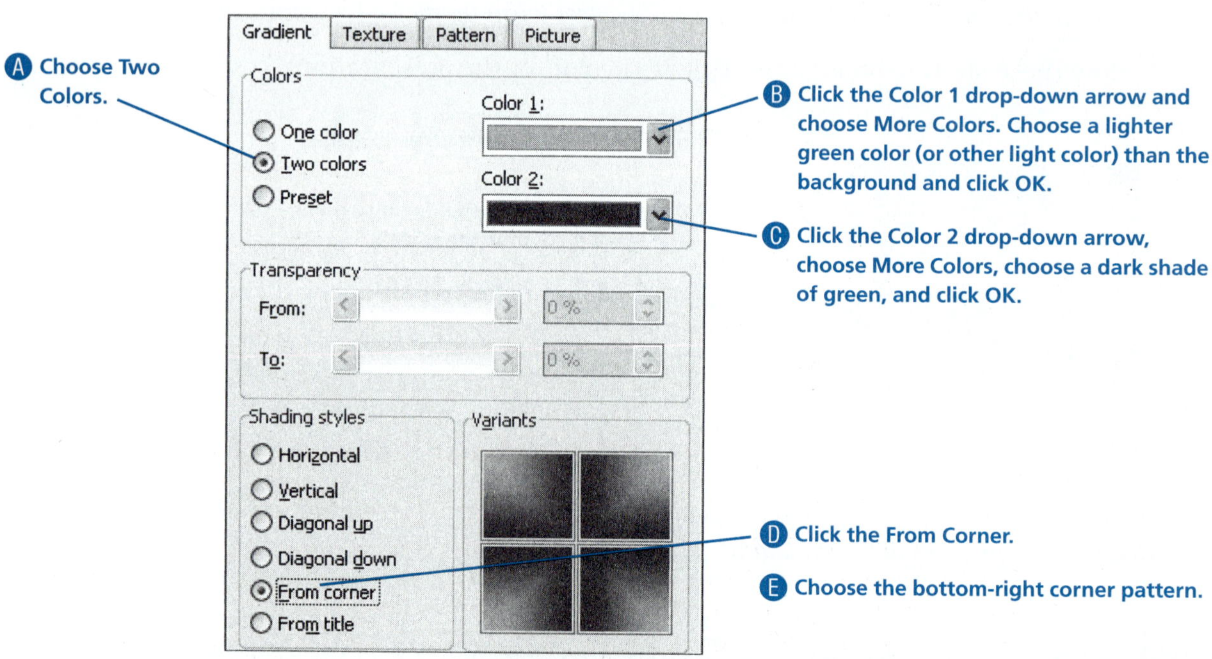

20. Click OK to close the dialog box then click the Preview button.
The new background pattern appears on the current slide.

21. Use the Fill Effects command one more time. Set a new gradient color scheme or texture—whichever you prefer. Preview the new fill effect on the current slide. Feel free to try other gradient fill effects then proceed to step 22.

22. Click Apply then click the Slide Show button to view the slide.
Fill effects can be very effective slide backgrounds.

23. Tap [Esc] to return to Normal view. Save the presentation but leave it open.

Saving the Customized Design Template

Microsoft Office Specialist

The easiest way to create a template is to create a presentation based on an existing design template; customize it with the formatting, graphics, and other settings you desire; and save the presentation as a template.

Template Location

The Templates dialog box display whenever you choose the On My Computer link from the New Presentation task pane. The Templates box reflects the path to the C:\Documents and Settings\[user_name]\ Application Data\Microsoft\Templates folder. Any custom templates you save in the Templates folder will appear under the General tab of the Templates box. Any folders located in the C:\Documents and Settings\[user_name]\Application Data\Microsoft\Templates folder will appear as additional tabs in the Templates box. You may want to add tabs to the Templates box to organize your custom templates. The following Quick Reference table describes several procedures for creating templates.

NOTE! *Many computer labs prevent students from accessing the C: drive; therefore, you may need to save the template to an alternative file storage location. If so, you must use the Save the Template to a Diskette or other Location method outlined in the following Quick Reference table to apply the template to a presentation.*

QR

QUICK REFERENCE: CREATING TEMPLATES

Method	Procedure
Save a template to the default location	■ Create the presentation and choose File→Save As. ■ Choose Template from the Save as Type box. ■ Type a filename and click Save. The template will appear in the General tab of the Templates box whenever you choose On My Computer from the New Presentation task pane.
Save the template to a diskette or other location	■ Create the presentation and choose File→Save As. ■ Choose Template from the Save as Type box. ■ Choose a storage location from the Save In box and type a filename. ■ Click Save. ■ To access the template, use Windows Explorer to navigate to the diskette or other storage location where the template is located. ■ Double-click the template and a new presentation based on the template will appear.

QR **QUICK REFERENCE: CREATING TEMPLATES (CONTINUED)**

Method	Procedure
Create a new tab in the Templates box and save there	■ Create the presentation and choose File→Save As. ■ Choose Template from the Save as Type box. ■ Click the New Folder button on the Save As dialog box. ■ Type a name for the new folder and click OK. ■ Type a name for the template and click Save. The next time you display the Templates box, a new tab will appear with the same name you assigned to the folder. Your template will appear in the new tab.

Hands-On 8.2 Save and Use a Custom Design Template

In this exercise, you will make the Pinnacle Pet Care presentation generic so it can be used for different purposes. Then you will save the presentation as a template in the default folder.

Make the Presentation Generic

1. Double-click Slide 1 to switch back to Normal view.
2. Click the Normal view button to display the Slides panel on the left.
3. In the slides panel, select Slides 2–8 and tap [Delete]. Click OK when you are asked to confirm the deletion.

TIP! *You can click the first slide (Slide 2), hold down the [Shift] key, and click the last slide (Slide 8) to select them all.*

Since these slides won't necessarily be used for future presentations, you can delete them from the custom template. This does not affect slides on the presentation file itself.

4. Click the New Slide button and choose the Title layout. In the subtitle placeholder, type **Type ending subtitle here**.
5. Copy the Title text from Slide 1 to the Title placeholder in Slide 2.
   You are setting up the template so it will always have a Title slide at the beginning and ending of the presentation.
6. Change the Twilight Hollow Bank subtitle to **Type subtitle here**.
   This will remind you to add a subtitle to the slide when you create a new presentation.

Save the Presentation as a Template

7. Choose File→Save As from the menu bar.
8. Follow these steps to save the new design template:

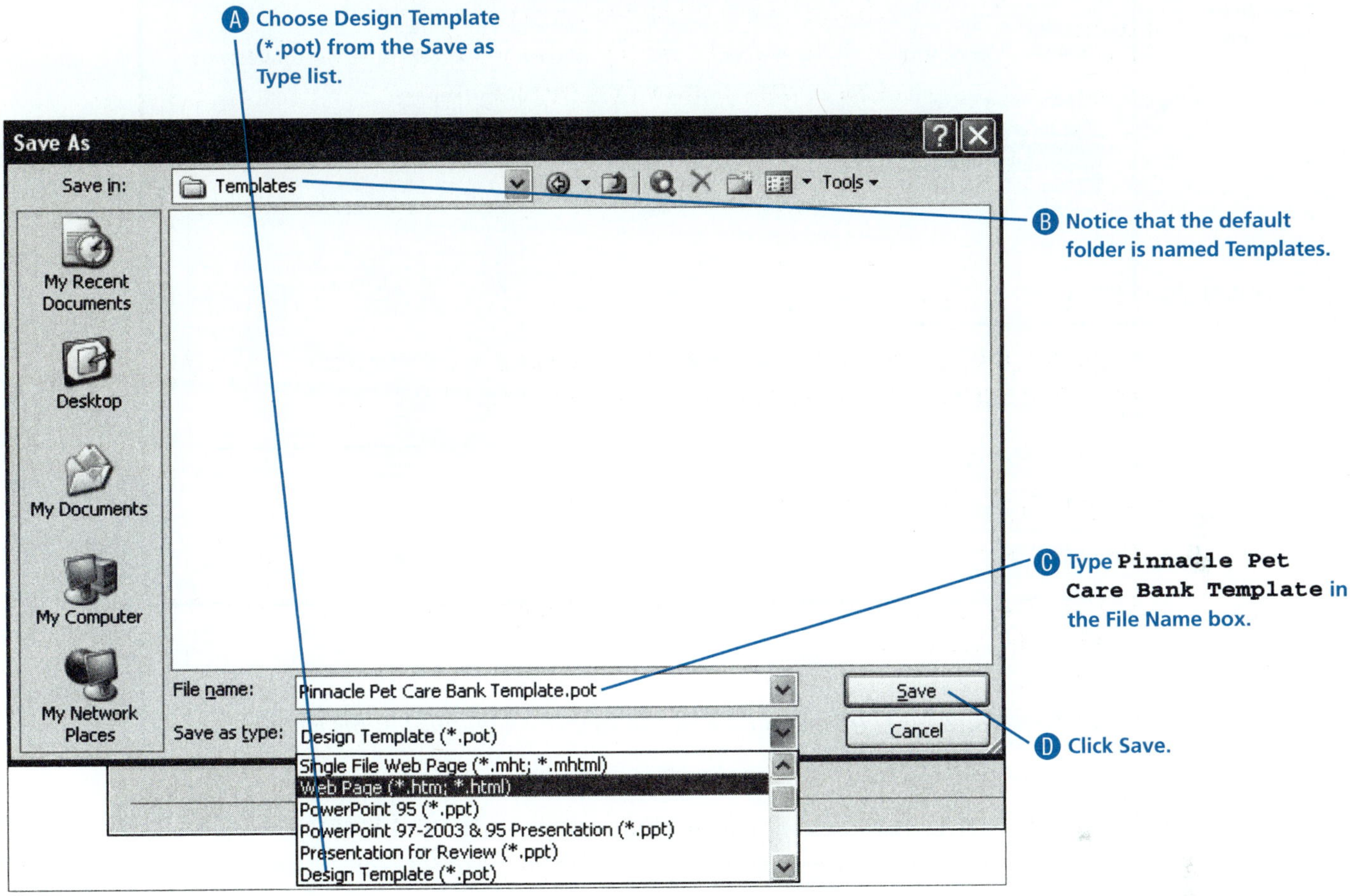

9. Choose File→Close from the menu bar to close the template.

Base a New Presentation on the Template

10. Click File→New.
    The New Presentation task pane displays, as shown to the right.
11. Click the On My Computer… link on the task pane.
    The New Presentation dialog box displays. Notice that the custom template you just saved is in the window on the General page.

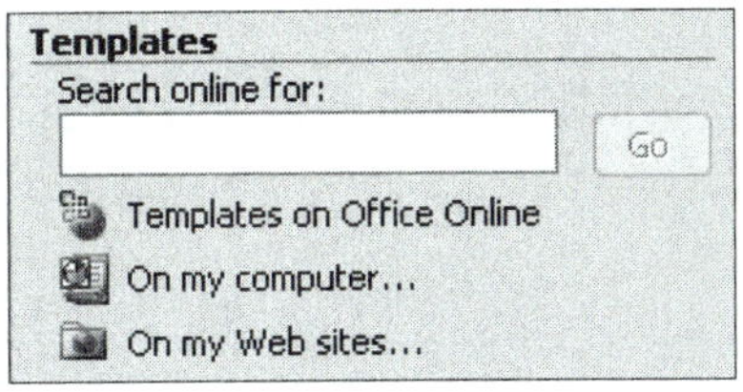

12. Follow theses steps to create a new presentation based on the custom template you saved in step 8:

Ⓐ Click once on the Pinnacle Pet Care Bank Template.

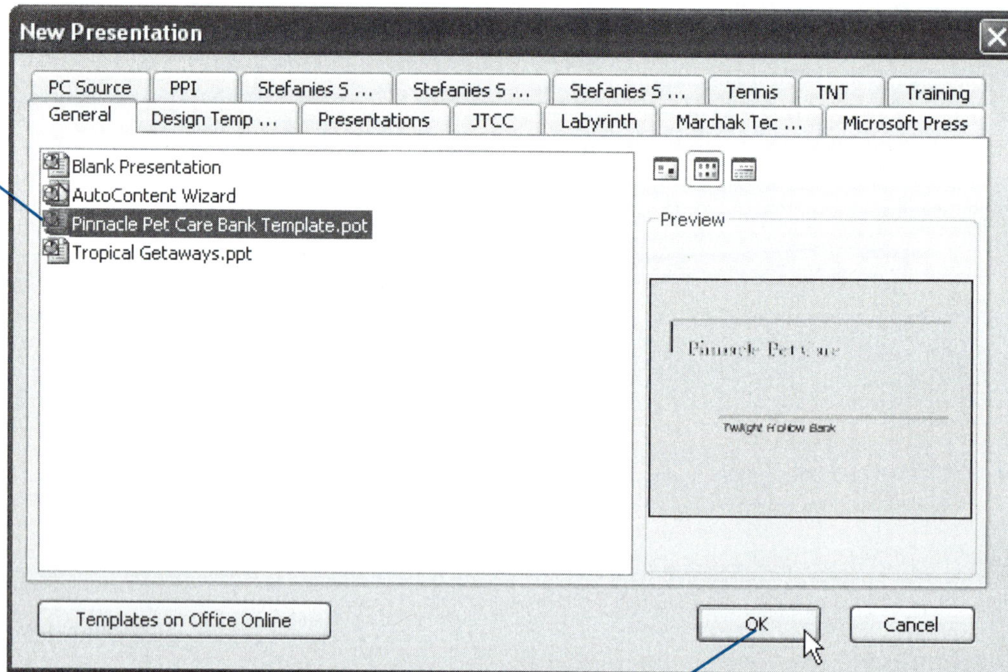

Ⓑ Click OK.

A new presentation displays with all the design elements contained in the template.

13. Change the subtitle on both slides to **`Newark Bank`**.
14. Insert a new Title and Text slide after Slide 1.
    Notice how your custom template background and color scheme appears on the new slide.
15. Click File→Save As from the menu bar.
16. Save the presentation as **`Newark Bank`** to your file storage location then close it.

Managing Multiple Slides

Microsoft Office Specialist

PowerPoint files are based on master files. The masters store all of the design elements, including the font styles and sizes, placeholder sizes, background design, and color schemes. You can view masters using the View→Masters command on the menu bar.

When you apply a design template, PowerPoint duplicates the information from the template masters to the presentation masters. You can also apply multiple design templates to presentations.

Applying Multiple Design Templates

When you apply multiple design templates, it is usually less time-consuming to do it in Slide Sorter view. You simply display the Slide Design task pane and, after selecting the desired slide(s) and template, choose to apply the template only to the selected slide(s).

WARNING! *Be careful when applying multiple designs. Make sure the different designs do not interfere with the flow of the presentation.*

Each template typically contains a title master and a slide master, aptly called slide-title master pairs. When you apply multiple design templates to a presentation, multiple slide-title master pairs appear in Master view.

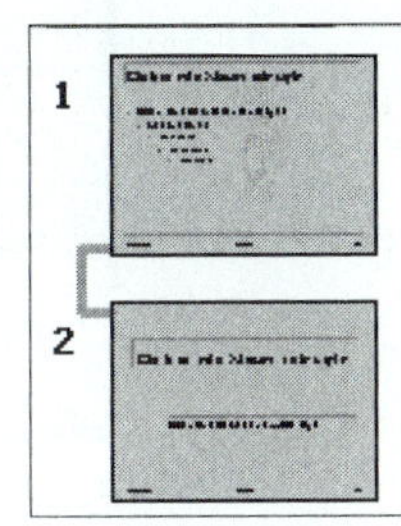

Sample slide-title master pair in Master view

TIP! *If you don't like the effect of a new design template, click the Undo button to revert to the previous design template.*

Hands-On 8.3 Apply the Design Template

In this exercise, you will add your custom design template to an existing presentation. Then you will select a group of slides in the presentation to which you will apply a different design template.

Apply the Custom Template to the Entire Presentation

1. Open the Pinnacle Pet Care Twilight Bank presentation.
2. Choose Format→Slide Design on the menu bar.
   The Slide Design task pane appears, displaying the available design templates.
3. Scroll down the list and click the Ocean template.
   Again, it may take several seconds to update all the slides to the new template.
4. Scroll through the slides to confirm the new design template has been applied to the various slide types.

Apply the Custom Template to the Presentation

5. Click the Browse link at the bottom of the task pane.
   The Apply Design Template dialog box displays.

6. Follow these steps to apply the custom design template:

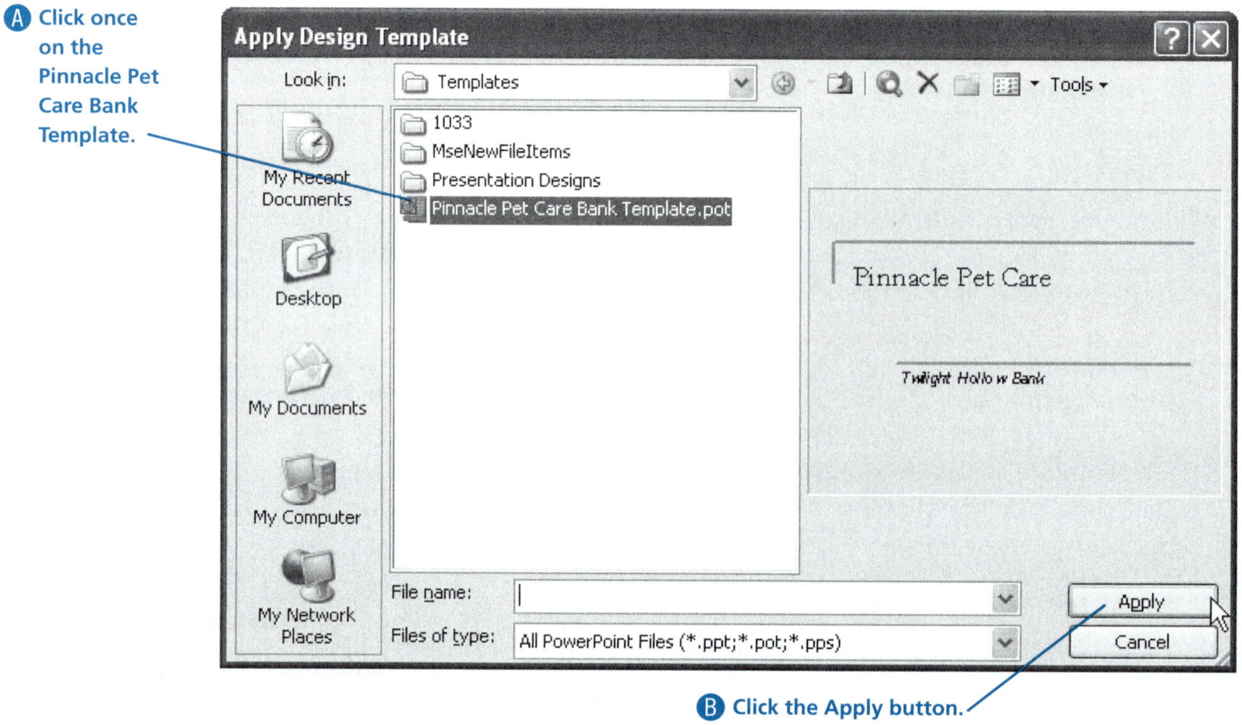

The entire presentation changes to the look of your custom template.

Apply a Different Template to Selected Slides

7. Switch to Normal view.

8. Add three new Title and Text slides to the presentation after Slide 1. Type the following titles into the slides:
   - Slide 2: **`Pet Corner`**
   - Slide 3: **`Adopt-A-Pet Day`**
   - Slide 4: **`Community Outreach`**

9. Switch back to Slide Sorter view; select Slides 2, 3, and 4; and display the Slide Design task pane.

10. Scroll down the list of design templates to view the Watermark template in the task pane, but don't click yet.

11. Follow these steps to apply a different template to the selected slides:

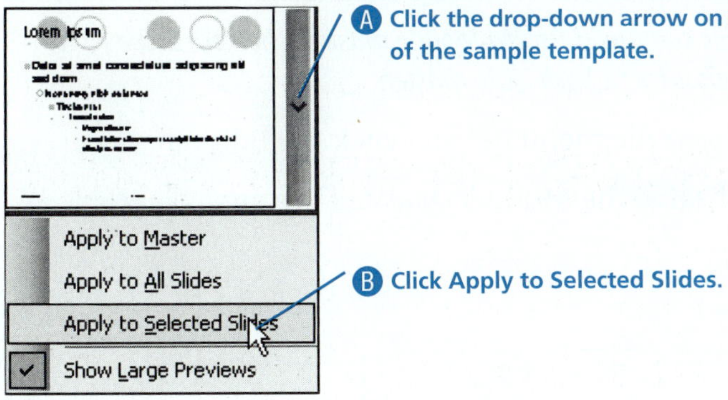

The Watermark design template is applied to Slides 2, 3, and 4 only.

12. Feel free to scroll through the presentation to view the difference in templates.
13. Save the presentation as **`Pinnacle Mixed Designs`** and continue with the next topic.

Creating and Managing Multiple Slide Masters

Microsoft Office Specialist

You can use the Tools→Options dialog box to control the use of multiple masters in a presentation. Under the Edit tab, you can check the box next to Multiple Masters to disable the feature or uncheck the box to allow multiple masters in presentations. When you apply a different design template to selected slides, PowerPoint automatically inserts new title and slide masters.

Multiple masters in a presentation require special attention when you want to change a placeholder. For example, to change the font for the Title placeholder, you must remember to change it in both Title masters. The same is true if you want to change the bullet style: you must change it in both slide masters.

Hands-On 8.4 Manage Multiple Masters

In this exercise, you will disable the use of multiple slide masters then turn the feature back on. You will also change the Title text placeholder in both Title masters.

1. Click Tools→Options from the menu bar and click the Edit tab.
2. Follow these steps to disable the Multiple Masters feature:

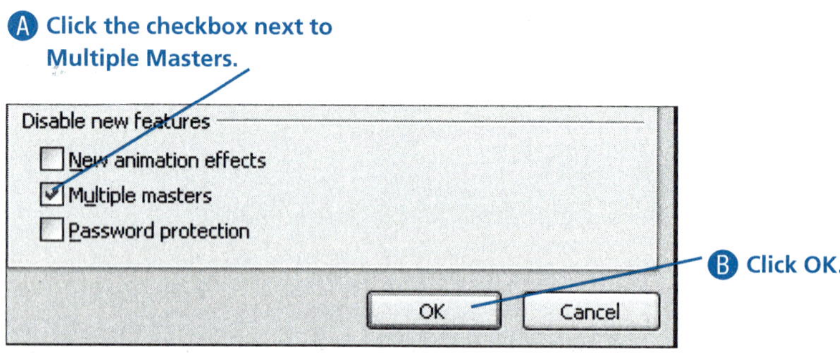

The feature is now disabled.

3. Click the drop-down arrow next to the Watermark or any other template.
Notice that Apply to Selected Slides option is no longer available. You can now only apply a new design to all of the slides.
4. Choose Tools→Options→Edit.
5. Click the checkbox next to Multiple Masters to clear it.
The Multiple Masters feature is now enabled and you can use the Apply to Selected Slides option again.
6. Switch to Normal view. Double-click the Normal view button again on the bottom-left corner of the screen to display the Slides panel on the left if it's not already displayed.
7. Click View→Master→Slide Master.
Notice the two slide-title master pairs. There are two because you applied a different design template to Slides 2, 3, and 4 in Hands-On 8.3. Also, notice that a special Slide Master View toolbar appeared on the screen.

8. Follow these steps to change the font style, color, and size of the Title text:

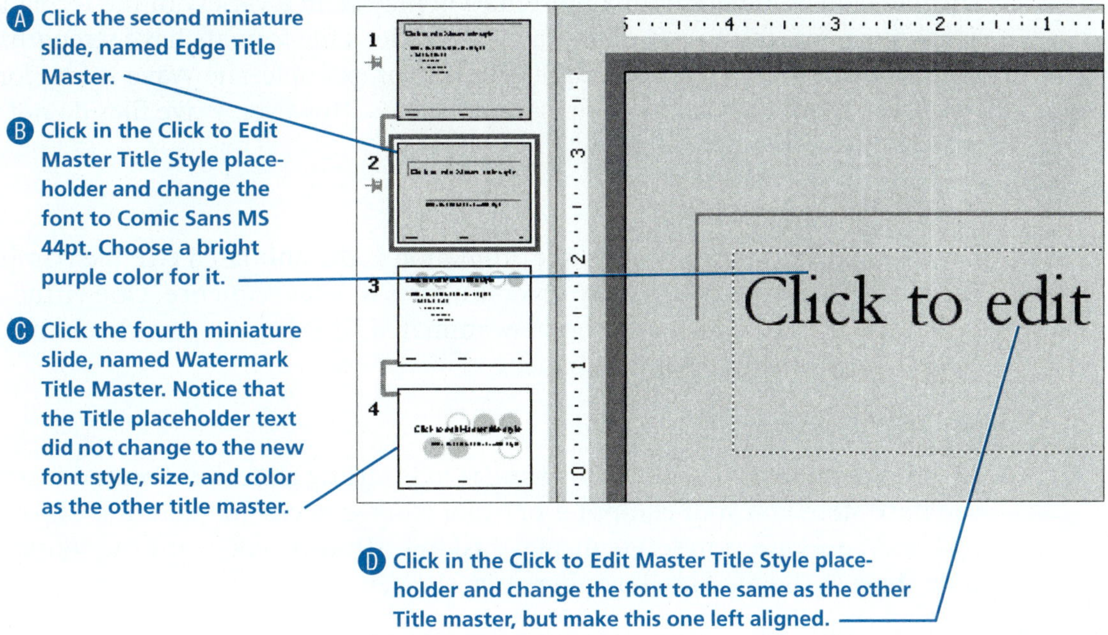

Notice that both title masters now have the same formatting. Any slides based on these masters will be uniform.

9. Feel free to modify the Title placeholder for the Slide Master using formatting of your choice.

10. Click the Normal view button.

11. Save the presentation and continue with the next topic.

Incorporating Multimedia

Microsoft Office Specialist

PowerPoint allows you to include various types of multimedia in a presentation. For example, you can add animated clip art and sound to any slide. Adding a multimedia file to a slide is similar to inserting a picture. The Insert command allows you to locate and select the type of media or desired file.

TIP! *Although multimedia can add dynamic elements to your presentation, it is best used in moderation. For example, a sound set to play when each slide is opened soon loses its novelty and becomes a distraction. Sometimes less is more.*

Multimedia Effects

The media files you use with a presentation may be in a variety of file formats. A file format is a technique for storing computer data. The various file formats have strengths and weaknesses that may suit them for specific applications. For example, the Wave sound format requires more disk space than many other sound formats. However, Wave files do not require any special software to play properly.

Animation Formats

The most popular format for simple animation is the animated GIF file (Graphics Interchange Format). Animated GIFs display several frames in a set sequence. One virtue of this file format is that it is very compact. Finding new animated GIFs is easy; just check the Clip Art on Office Online link in the Clip Art task pane.

Sound Formats

Adding sound to a presentation is similar to inserting a picture. You can insert it from a file you have stored on your computer or other storage device, or from the Clip Organizer. When you insert a sound, a message displays asking, "How do you want the sound to start in the slide show?" The message box offers two choices:

- **Automatically—**plays the sound file when the slide is first displayed.
- **When Clicked—**plays the sound file when you click on it during a presentation.

When you insert a sound file onto a slide, a small image appears. It can be moved anywhere on the slide. You can test the image while in Normal view by double-clicking on it.

TIP! *You can drag a sound image off the slide into the gray area so it is not visible when you run the slide show.*

Most sound files for windows will be in one of two file formats:

- **Wave** (.wav)—This is an older, uncompressed audio format. Most Windows computers can play wave files without any additional software.
- **MPEG** (.mpg)—Motion Pictures Experts Group is a highly compressed audio format that is popular on the Internet. To play an MPEG file, your computer must be equipped with an MPEG player program, such as the Windows Media Player.

TIP! *Movie files are inserted using the same command as sounds.*

Downloading New Media from the Web

Microsoft has several Web pages devoted to PowerPoint. These pages frequently feature new templates, media and other useful items to include in your presentations. For example, there may be interesting sounds or animations available to download. Downloading is the process of saving a file from a remote Web page to your local computer system.

QR QUICK REFERENCE: INSERTING MOVIES AND SOUNDS

Task	Procedure
Insert a sound file onto a slide	■ Display the slide on which you wish to insert the sound file. ■ Choose Insert→Movies and Sounds→Sound from File ■ Navigate to the sound file and click OK. ■ Click Automatically or When Clicked according to your preference.
Insert a move file onto a slide	■ Display the slide on which you wish to insert the sound file. ■ Choose Insert→Movies and Sounds→Movie from File ■ Navigate to the movie file and click OK. ■ Click Automatically or When Clicked according to your preference.

Hands-On 8.5 Use Animated GIFs and Sounds from the Web

In this exercise, you will view a variety of online media and insert them in your Pinnacle Mixed Designs presentation.

Save a Picture from a Web Page

1. Start Internet Explorer and enter the URL labpub.com/learn/pp03/ in the Address bar.
2. Click the Animated GIFs hyperlink.
   There may be a pause while the images load into the browser. This page contains examples of animated GIF files, most of which are shareware animation and are available for personal—but not commercial—use.
3. Follow these steps to save the Pinnacle Pet Care animated GIF file:

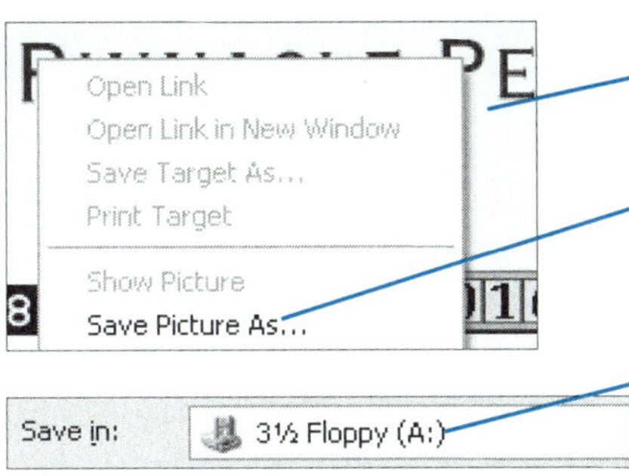

(A) Right-click anywhere on the Pinnacle Pet Care picture.

(B) Click Save Picture As... on the pop-up menu.

(C) Click the drop-down arrow on the Save In box, choose your file storage location from the list, and click Save.

   The picture is saved to your file storage location.

Download a Picture from a Web Page

4. Display the Adopt-A-Pet Day slide.
5. In the Text placeholder, type **`Tabby & Calico Cats`**, press [Enter], type **`Beagles, Golden Retrievers and Other Dogs`**, and click outside the Text box.
6. Click the Insert Clip Art button on the drawing toolbar.
   The Clip Art task pane displays.

7. Click the Clip Art on Office Online link at the bottom of the task pane to find an animated GIF from the Office Online Website.

8. Follow these steps to download two pictures from Office Online:

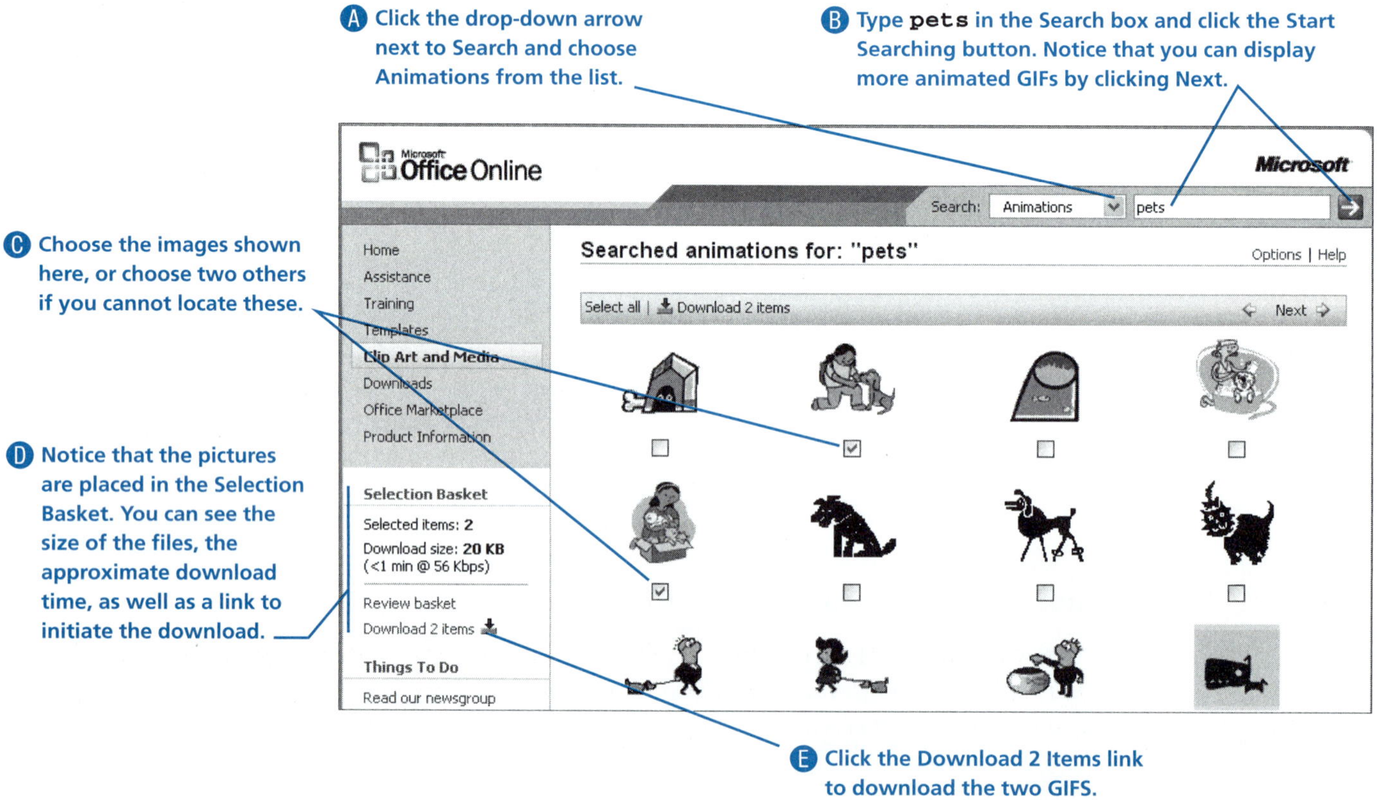

NOTE! *A dialog box may appear asking you to install an ActiveX control. Ensure that Microsoft Corporation is the distributor before clicking Yes to complete the download.*

Insert to the Clip Organizer and Copy to the Presentation

9. Follow these steps to download the pictures into the Clip Organizer:

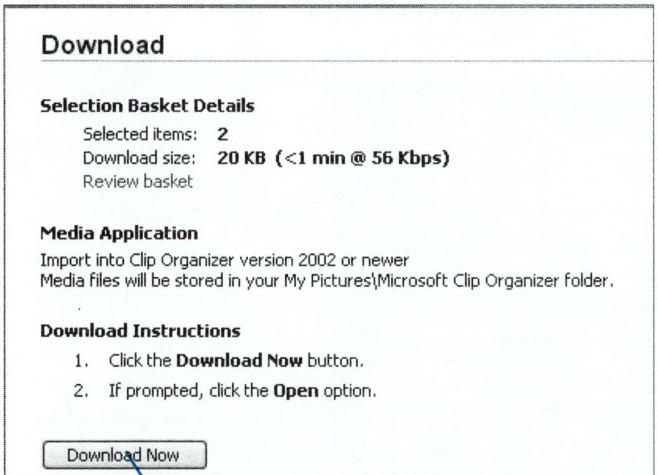

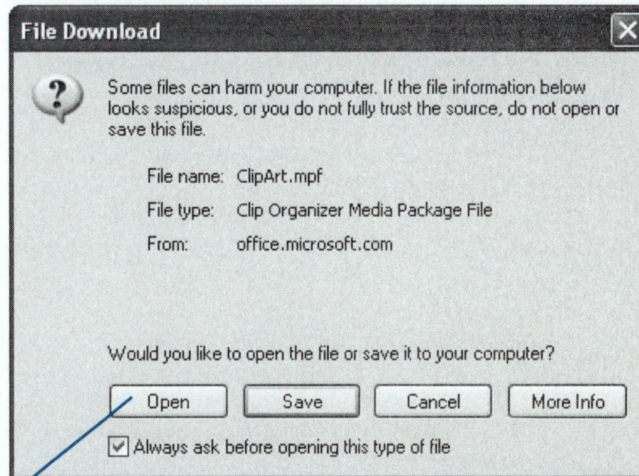

A Click the Download Now button. Notice that the File Download dialog box displays with a warning message.

B Click the Open button. A progression box appears as the clips are downloaded to the Clip Organizer. Note that you may need to "replace" the image if a message indicates that it already exists.

The download progression box remains on the screen until the download is complete. Then, the Clip Organizer displays the two downloaded pictures.

10. Follow these steps to copy the two images:

A While holding down the [Ctrl] key, click on both images then right-click on either one.

B Click Copy from the pop-up menu.

11. Click the PowerPoint button on the taskbar.
The presentation displays the Adopt-A-Pet Day slide.

12. Click the Paste button.
Both pictures are pasted on the middle of the slide so you will need to move and resize them. Notice that the pictures are not animated in Slide view; you must run the slide show to view the animations.

13. Drag the top image to the left and the bottom one to the right then resize both images.

Add Sound from the Clip Organizer

14. Click Insert→Movies and Sounds→Sounds from Clip Organizer.

15. Follow these steps to insert a sound file from the Clip Art task pane:

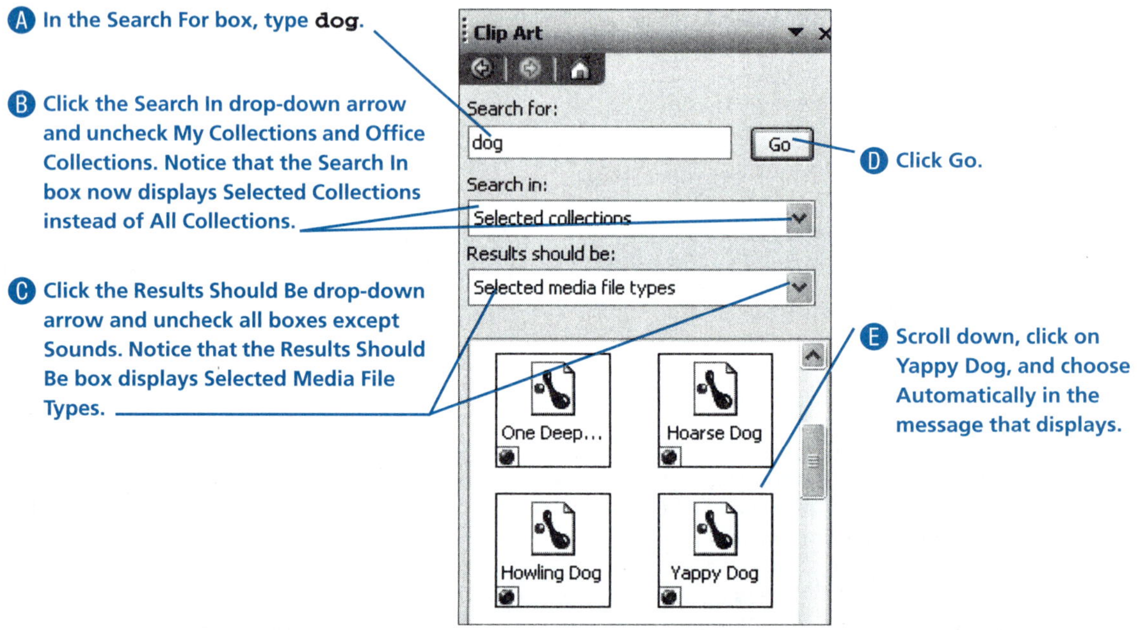

16. Feel free to click the Slide Show button to view the animation and sound. When finished, tap [Esc].
Remember, you can move the sound file just like any image. If you don't want the sound image to display when your run the slide show, drag it off the slide and it will be heard—but not be seen.

17. Save the presentation and close it.

Using Action Buttons

Microsoft Office Specialist

Action buttons allow you to add navigation controls to your presentations. Action buttons contain widely recognized symbols for navigation and information commands, such as Next, Previous, Information, Document, and Sound. Action buttons are especially useful for creating a self-running presentation that will be controlled by others, such as a presentation running on a sales table at a conference.

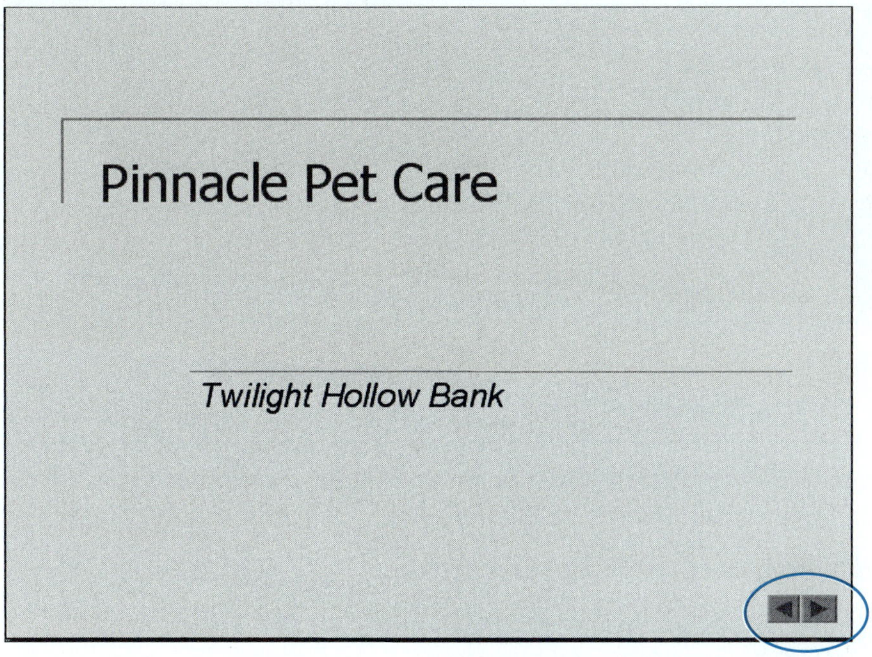

The Next and Previous Action buttons offer intuitive controls to anyone who wants to navigate through a presentation.

Identifying Action Buttons

All Action buttons, except Custom, have built-in functions that run whenever that button is clicked in Slide Show mode. ScreenTips make it easy to identify the function of an Action button when you choose it from the menu.

A ScreenTip displays when you rest the mouse pointer on an Action button for a couple seconds.

TIP! *To quickly add Action buttons to all slides in your presentation, place them on the Slide and Title Masters.*

QR

QUICK REFERENCE: CREATING ACTION BUTTONS

Task	Procedure
Insert an Action button on a slide	■ Display the slide (or Slide Master) on which you wish to place the Action button. ■ Choose Slide Show→Action Buttons on the menu bar. ■ Click the desired button. ■ Position the crosshair pointer where you would like to place the button then drag to the desired size. ■ Edit the button function or click OK to accept the default function.
Reposition an Action button	■ Point at the button until the mouse pointer changes to a four-headed arrow. ■ Drag the button to the desire new location. ■ Click on the button then drag the sizing handles to change the size.

Hands-On 8.6 Create Action Buttons

In this exercise, you will insert Action buttons in the Slide Master to control movement forward and backward in your presentation. You will also copy the Action buttons to the Title Master.

1. Open the Pinnacle Pet Care Online presentation.

Insert Action Buttons on the Slide Master

2. Click View→Master→Slide Master on the menu bar.
   Remember, anything you place on the Slide Master appears on all of the slides in the presentation, except those that used the Title Slide Layout.
3. Be sure you are viewing the Slide Master and not the Title Master then click Slide Show→Action Buttons on the menu bar.
   A menu of all the available Action buttons appears. You can also create custom buttons when needed.
4. Follow these steps to place the Forward or Next button on the Slide Master:

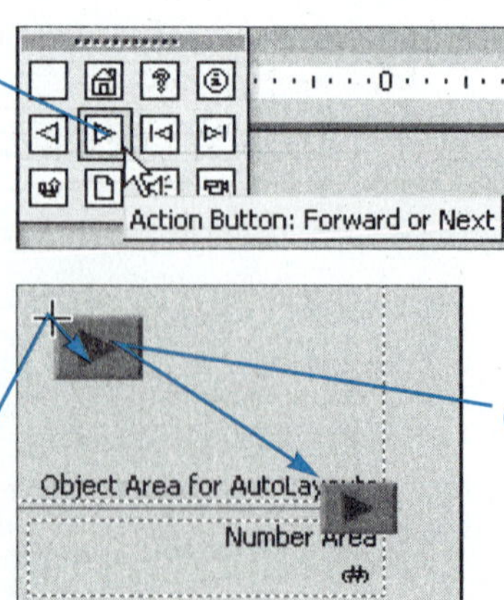

Ⓐ Click the Forward or Next button.

Ⓑ Position the crosshair mouse pointer next to the bottom-right corner of the slide then drag down and to the right to create a small button. When the Action Settings dialog box displays indicating the action is to Hyperlink to the next slide, click OK.

Ⓒ Point to the center of the button until the mouse pointer becomes a four-headed arrow then drag the button down to the position show here.

5. Insert a new Action button using the Back or Previous button. Place this button as shown at right. Try to make the button approximately the same size as the Forward or Next button.

TIP! *Temporarily place one button above the other to size them identically, or turn on the Snap to Grid feature from the Drawing toolbar.*

6. Adjust the size and location of the buttons on the bottom-right corner of the slide master until they match the figure to the right.

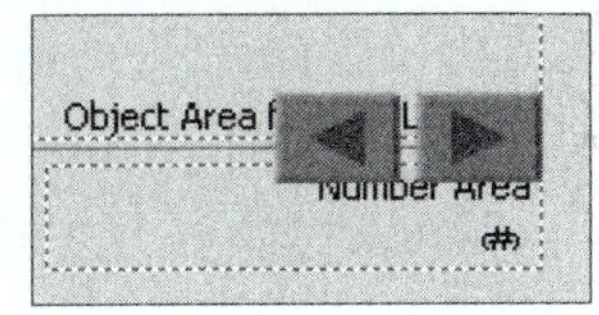

Copy the Buttons to the Title Master

7. Follow these steps to copy the buttons:

A Click the Back or Previous button.

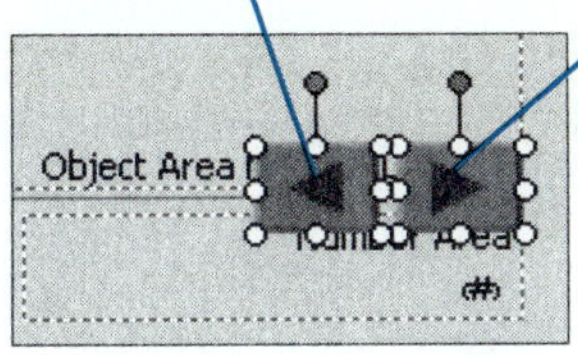

B Hold down the [Shift] key then click the Forward or Next button. When you release the [Shift] key both buttons should have sizing handles around them.

C Click the Copy button on the toolbar.

8. Click the Edge Title Master: Preview on the Slides panel.
   Notice that the Action buttons are not on the Title Master.
9. Click the Paste button.
   Notice that the buttons are automatically pasted in the same place on the Title Master as they are located on the Slide Master.
10. Click the Normal view button.

Test the Buttons

11. Click the Slide Show button.
12. Click the new Forward or Next button on that slide.
    As you would expect, you advance to the next slide. Of course, you could also advance to the next slide by clicking on the slide itself. However, someone unfamiliar with PowerPoint may not think to do this. The Action buttons give users unfamiliar with PowerPoint intuitive control over the presentation.
13. Click the Back or Previous button on the next slide. Without this arrow, moving back would be more difficult for users unfamiliar with PowerPoint.
14. Click the Forward arrow to advance to the animated slide.
    You should now be enjoying the animated GIFs and sounds on the Adopt-A-Pet Day slide.
15. Tap the [Esc] key to exit Slide Show view.
16. Save the presentation, close it, and continue with the end-of-lesson exercises.

Concepts Review

True/False Questions

1.	You can change the background color of a presentation.	TRUE	FALSE
2.	You can create your own design template from a presentation you have customized.	TRUE	FALSE
3.	Design templates are normally saved on the floppy drive.	TRUE	FALSE
4.	You cannot apply a different design template to a presentation after it has been created.	TRUE	FALSE
5.	The color scheme of the design template cannot be changed.	TRUE	FALSE
6.	You are limited to finding clip art or sound files on your hard drive.	TRUE	FALSE
7.	The most common file format for Windows sound files is GIF.	TRUE	FALSE
8.	Action buttons help a viewer navigate through a slide show.	TRUE	FALSE
9.	Slide design affects the tone of the presentation.	TRUE	FALSE
10.	You can add a textured look to the background.	TRUE	FALSE

Multiple Choice Questions

1. Which of the following is a multimedia file you can insert into PowerPoint presentation?
   a. Animated .GIF file
   b. .WAV Wave sound file
   c. .AVI Movie file
   d. All of the above

2. Why would you want to add Action buttons to a presentation?
   a. To allow the display of multimedia content
   b. To permit the use of different color schemes
   c. To make it easier for users to navigate an unattended slide show
   d. To allow the use of a custom design template

3. Why would you want to create a custom design template?
   a. To display a presentation on the Web
   b. To quickly create new presentations based on a custom design
   c. To display multimedia in a presentation
   d. None of the above

4. You can add texture, gradient, or color to the presentation by choosing ________.
   a. File→Texture
   b. Format→Add Gradient
   c. Slide Design→Color Schemes
   d. New Presentation→Templates

Skill Builders

Skill Builder 8.1 Customize a Template

In this exercise, you will create a new presentation then customize its color scheme and background.

Change the Color Scheme

1. Click File→New to create a new presentation and base it on the Capsules design template. In the Title placeholder, type **`A New Design Template`**. Type **`[Your Name]`** as the subtitle.
2. Choose Format→Slide Design and choose Edit Color Scheme at the bottom of the task pane.
3. Click Accent in the Scheme Color list and click Change Color. Choose a new color then click the Preview button to view the effect of the change.
   If you don't like the color change, choose a different color.
4. Try changing at least two other colors in the color scheme, such as Text and Lines and Shadow. When you are finished, click the Apply to All button.

Change the Background

5. Choose Format→Background from the menu bar then click the drop-down list button and choose Fill Effects.
6. Click the Texture tab then choose a new texture from the list and click OK and Preview.
   Depending on the design template you selected, the background texture may or may not be apparent.
7. Choose the Fill Effects command again then click the Gradient tab.
8. Choose the Preset option in the Colors section then use the Preset Colors drop-down list to review several of the fills. Select and preview a preset fill you think will coordinate with your existing color scheme.
9. Choose the Fill Effects command once more. Apply either a gradient fill or a texture as a final change to the slide background. After you preview the background, click Apply to All.

Add a Title and Text slide

10. Create a new Title and Text slide and title it **`Customizing a Template`**. Perform the following steps on the slide:
    - Put **`Your Name`** in the Subtitle object
    - Change the Color Scheme
    - Apply a texture to the background
    - Add a bulleted list slide with the text of your choice
11. Save the presentation to your file storage location as **`Color Schemes`**.

Skill Builder 8.2 Add Action Buttons

In this exercise, you will add Action buttons for navigation to the slide and title masters and other Action buttons to a single slide.

Add Action Buttons for Navigation

1. The Color Schemes presentation should still be open.
2. Open the Slide Master.
3. Use the Slide Show→Action Buttons command to create Forward or Next and Back or Previous Action buttons on the lower-right corner of the Title placeholder. The design will vary depending on your choices, but it should be similar in structure to the following illustration.

4. Click the Normal view button.
5. Run the slide show to test the Action buttons.
6. Save the changes and continue with the next exercise.

Skill Builder 8.3 Save a Template

In this exercise, you will save your newly developed presentation as a template then use it to create a new presentation.

1. The Color Schemes presentation should still be open.
2. Click File→Save As from the menu bar and select Design Template from the list.
3. Save the template as **`Capsules Template`** then close it.
4. Click File→New from the menu bar.
5. Select your new template from the Recently Used Templates list.
6. Display Slide 2 of the presentation.
   Notice the Action buttons appear on this slide.
7. Close the presentation without saving.

Edit the Design Template

8. Display the Open dialog box and change the Files of Type to Design Templates.
9. Double-click the Capsules Template design template.
   Unlike the File→New command, the Open command opens the original template, not a copy, which allows you to make changes to the template. This way, you do not have to create a new presentation based on the template.
10. Display Slide 2 and choose Edit→Delete Slide from the menu bar.
11. Save the changes and close the file.

Assessments

Assessment 8.1 Create Action Buttons

In this exercise, you will add Action buttons to the slide masters.

1. Create a new presentation based on the template of your choice.
2. Enter **`Action Buttons`** as the title and **`[Your Name]`** as the subtitle of the presentation.
3. In the Slide Master, create Forward or Next and Back or Previous Action buttons on any area that is appropriate to the presentation design.
4. Create a new Title and Text slide and entitle it **`Different Action Buttons`**.
5. Place a Sound Action button on the slide, choose the sound of your choice from the dialog box that opens automatically, and click OK.
6. Save the presentation as **`Action Buttons`**.

Assessment 8.2 Customize the Color Scheme and Background

In this exercise, you will change the name of your presentation then customize the color scheme and background.

1. The Action Buttons presentation should still be displayed on the screen.
2. Click File→Save As to save the presentation as **`[Your Name] Custom`**.
3. Customize the background of this new slide using a gradient fill or a texture of your choice.
4. Edit the color scheme, including either the Title or Text and Lines color, and at least one other color scheme item, such as Accent or Shadows.
5. Create a new Title and Text slide in the presentation. Title the slide **`Customization`**. Create bullet items that describe each custom setting you applied to this presentation. For example:
   - Background: two-color gradient fill, diagonal down
   - Title color: orange
   - Accent color: light blue
6. Save the presentation and continue with the next exercise.

Assessment 8.3 Create a New Design Template

In this exercise, you will create a new design template and save it to your file storage location.

1. Save the [Your Name] Custom presentation with the following instructions:
   - Template Name: **`[Your Name] Template`**
   - Save the template to your file storage location (not to the Templates folder on the hard drive).
2. Close the presentation.

Critical Thinking

Critical Thinking 8.1 Web Research: Insert Clip Art and Sound Action Buttons

As the advertising manager for a small but quaint village in New England, you are asked to create a kiosk-style presentation that will be set up at a national Bed & Breakfast Hospitality trade show. Choose an appropriate design and save it as a template. Search the Internet for appropriate clip art, sounds, and research information. Create your presentation with the following elements:

- The presentation will contain a Title slide and four Title and Text slides using the titles shown in the following table.

Slide	Topic
Slide 1	**Welcome to New England**
	Subtitle: Your Name
Slide 2	**Cape Cod**
Slide 3	**Penobscot Bay**
Slide 4	**Colonial New England**

- All slides should contain navigation buttons.
- Slides 1–3 should all have clip art and related sounds.
- Slide 4 will have three bulleted items:

  Freedom Trail

  Paul Revere

  Places to Visit

- Search the Internet to find information for each of the three topics and add it to the slide.

Save your presentation as **New England** and close it.

Critical Thinking 8.2 Create a New Customized Template

Brenda Johnson has some extra time on her hands and is anxious to enhance her PowerPoint knowledge. She enlists your help in customizing an existing design template and saving it as her own template. She explains that she likes the simplicity of the Eclipse design template, but needs you to show her how to make certain changes. The changes need to affect the design of all the slides except the Title slide. Help Brenda do the following:

- Change the background color to a dark color.
- Change the text, text and lines, and accent colors to coordinate with the background color.

- Add a texture to the background. Try at least three textures before settling on the final texture.
- Add two directional Action buttons so each slide contains navigational arrows in the title.

Save the template as **`Template Design`** then run the slide show to see your hard work before saving and closing the file.

Critical Thinking 8.3 Web Research: Research Animated GIFs

Sally Lee was so successful in her first presentation for MicroChip Sales that she has asked to create a kiosk-style presentation for the MicroChip Sales department to show in a national trade show.

Open the MicroChip Sales presentation and use the following guidelines to customize the presentation:

Slide Title	Insert Animated GIFs, Action Buttons
	Insert the Forward or Next button so it is replicated throughout the presentation.
Title Slide	Research the Internet for an animated GIF that portrays computers working together in a network. Insert it in an appropriate place on the slide.
Meeting the Needs (Slide 4)	Add the Chip categories in text boxes to the Pyramid Autoshape in order of their performance.
Cost Analysis (Slide 5)	Add a layout that will support title, text, and content. Then, insert animated GIFs in the content layout that are appropriate for this presentation.
Our Strengths (Slide 6)	Add a text box containing **`Flexibility`** in the center of the Speed, Clarity, and Honesty process.
Key Benefits (Slide 7)	Add clip art that summarizes the presentation's strengths, services, and product line.
Next Steps (Slide 8)	Insert an appropriate sound file to mesh with the Next Steps goals.

Save the presentation as **`MCS Template`** and close it.

LESSON 9

On the Road Again: A Case Study Workshop

In this lesson, you will learn about transporting presentations from your computer to another computer. This lesson also addresses other vital components of a successful presentation, such as setting up the meeting room and preparing everything from the lights to the hardware and software. The checklists and guides presented in this lesson will assist you with these all-important tasks in addition to helping you target your audience. Lastly, a practice workshop requires you to create and deliver a presentation to a live audience, which will undoubtedly provide you with essential presentation skills.

IN THIS LESSON

Microsoft Office PowerPoint 2003 objectives covered in this lesson

Objective Number	Skill Sets and Skills	Concept Page References	Exercise Page References
PP03S-4-5	Prepare presentations for remote delivery	276–277, 280	277–279, 281

Additional learning resources are available at labpub.com/learn/pp03/

Case Study

The date of the National Pet World Trade Show has finally arrived! Al Smith and Charlene Rousse travel together to Chicago, getting there a day early so they can check out the conference center where Al will be giving the Pinnacle Pet Care workshops. Charlene contacted the trade show officials earlier to review details such as computer setup, the amount of time allotted to Al for the presentation, and the estimated number of participants.

Charlene used PowerPoint's amazing Package for CD feature to create a CD containing the complete presentation. When they arrive at the conference center, Al inspects the computer projection system while Charlene unpacks the CD, handouts, and speaker notes for Al. Charlene reviews the Presentation Setup checklist while Al readies himself to run through the presentation. Before he utters a word, Al runs through the PEER-LESS guides that Charlene created for him. As Charlene lowers the lights, Al steps up to center stage to practice the presentation.

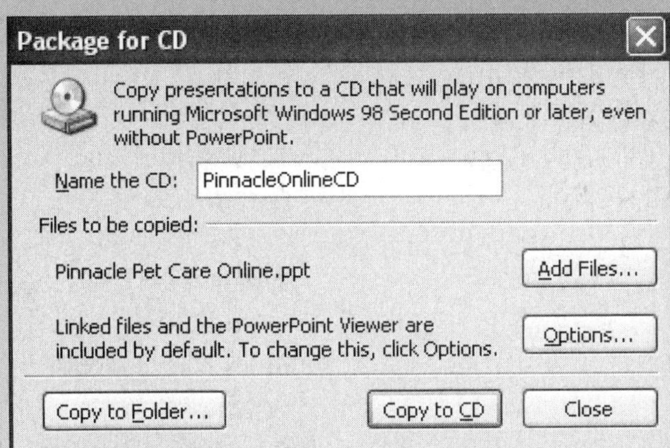

Package for CD dialog box

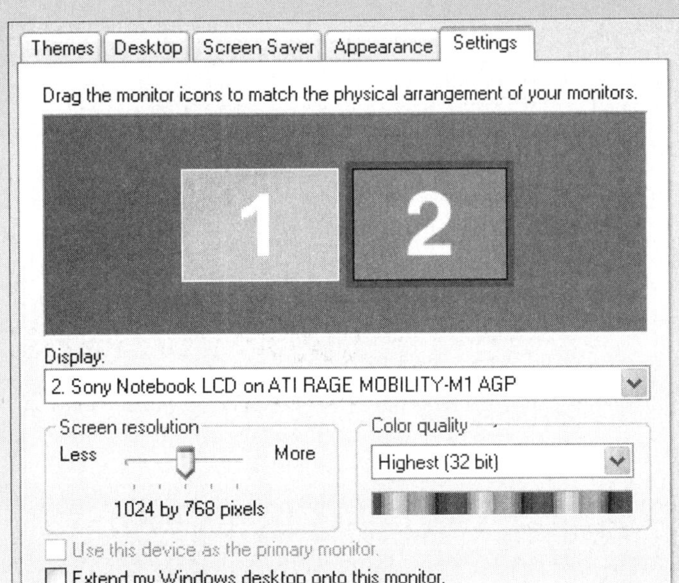

Screen Settings dialog box

Transporting the Presentation

Microsoft Office Specialist

If you are using a notebook computer to create and deliver your presentation, you have a self-contained unit that contains the PowerPoint application, images, fonts, and all linked files for the presentation. However, if you need to deliver the presentation on a computer other than the one on which it was created, those essential files will not be present. For example, you may be presenting at a conference, a school, a client site, or another branch of your office. To be sure you have all the files you need, you can store the presentation and accompanying files on a compact disc (CD) to use at the site of the presentation using the Package for CD feature.

TIP! *Another convenient way to transport a presentation is on a USB Flash drive—a small, compact device that plugs into the USB port of any computer. See page 303 of the appendix for a description of USB Flash drives.*

How Package for CD Works

The Package for CD feature collects all of the elements required for your presentation to run smoothly. These elements include the presentation file, any linked files, fonts, and any special program files PowerPoint needs. In addition, you can include the PowerPoint Viewer, a program that allows a presentation to run on a computer that does not have PowerPoint installed. After all options are set, Package for CD places all the files in a folder and compresses them to save onto a CD, diskette or other removable media, or a hard drive.

TIP! *The PowerPoint Viewer cannot be included if you are copying the presentation to a diskette.*

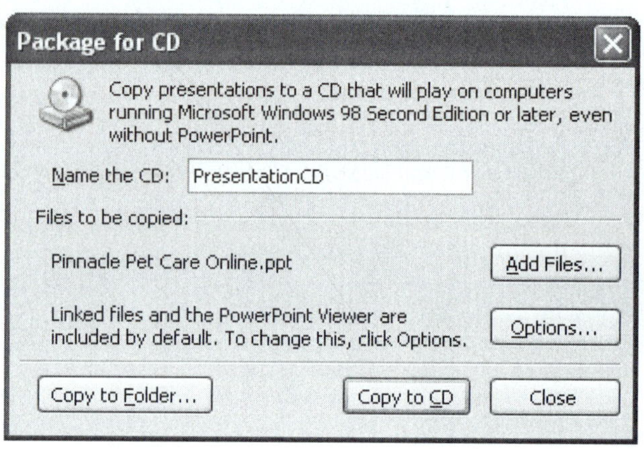

Package for CD dialog box

Using the PowerPoint Viewer

Once you have copied your presentation onto a CD using the Package for CD command, you can take it to any computer to run it—whether that computer has PowerPoint installed on it or not. When you view the contents of the CD in a My Computer or Explorer window, you will notice a file in the list named pptview. This is the file used to open the PowerPoint Viewer. Each time you want to run a presentation through it, you must open the PowerPoint Viewer.

The first time the viewer is used, it prompts you to accept the License Agreement. Upon accepting, the program is installed automatically. Thereafter, each time you open the pptview file, the viewer opens immediately and displays a list of presentations stored on the CD.

When to Use Font Embedding

You should be aware of potential problems with fonts if you are going to run a presentation on a computer other than your own. If a font specified in your presentation is not available, PowerPoint will substitute the closet match it can find. However, even fonts that appear quite similar may differ in width and relative height. This could make your lines wrap incorrectly and cause other problems with the display of your presentation. Embedding the fonts is one of the options in the Package for CD feature.

In the following example, both lines are identical except for the font. Notice how much longer the lower line is.

Both of these lines contain the same text. — **This line uses the 12pt Times New Roman font.**

Both of these lines contain the same text. — **This line is set in 12pt Georgia font.**

TIP! *Always embed fonts if you will present on a different computer.*

QR

QUICK REFERENCE: TRANSPORTING A PRESENTATION

Task	Procedure
Pack a presentation for transport to another computer using Package for CD	■ Click File→Package for CD on the menu bar. Be sure there is a compact disc (CD) in the CD-RW drive. ■ Select the desired options and click Copy to CD.
Unpack the presentation at the destination computer	■ Open a My Computer window and display the CD drive. ■ Double-click the presentation folder then double-click the presentation filename. ■ Depending on the options you set on how to play the presentation, it will begin running immediately or you will be prompted to run it.

Hands-On 9.1 Pack the Presentation for Transport

In this exercise, you will use the Package for CD feature. Since many classrooms are not equipped with a CD-RW drive, which you need to burn a CD, you will use the Copy to Folder option and place the presentation in a new folder. In Hands-On 9.2, you will simulate burning a CD.

1. Open the Pinnacle Pet Care Online presentation.
2. Click File→Package for CD.

3. Follow these steps to name the CD—this also names a folder containing all the presentation files:

A In the Name the CD box, type `PinnacleOnlineCD`.

B Notice that the File to be Copied section already indicates the Pinnacle Pet Care Online presentation because you opened the file prior to selecting the Package for CD command.

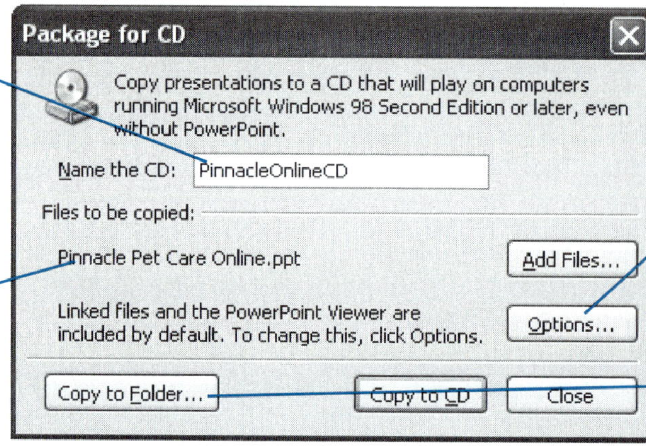

C Click the Options button, check the checkbox next to PowerPoint Viewer, Linked Files and Embedded TrueType fonts, and click OK.

D Click the Copy to Folder... button. A dialog box displays, allowing you to choose where to copy the presentation.

4. Click the Browse button on the Copy to Folder dialog box to choose a location to save the presentation.

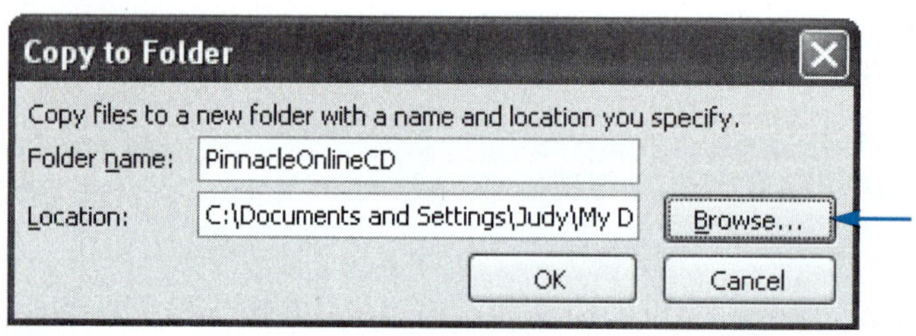

5. Follow these steps to create a new folder in My Documents and copy the presentation into it:

A Notice that the My Documents folder is the default folder.

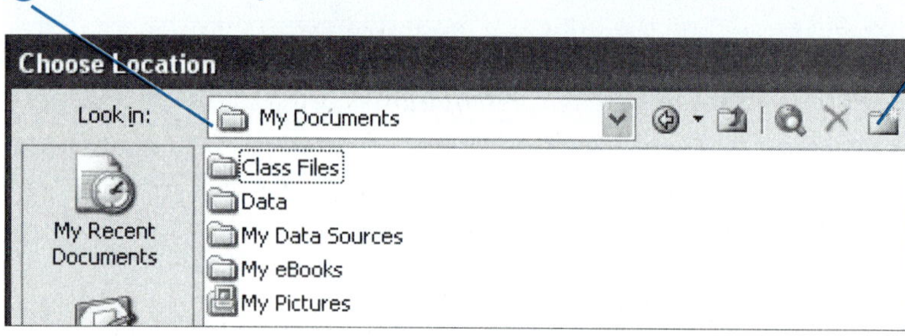

B Click the Create New Folder button on the dialog box toolbar and name the folder **`Class Files`**. There may already be a folder named Class Files on the computer you are using. If so, you can type a different name.

C Click the Select button at the bottom-right corner of the dialog box then click OK in the Copy to Folder dialog box. Notice that a progress box displays while the presentation is being copied.

6. Click the Close button on the Package for CD dialog box.
The presentation is now in the selected folder and ready for unpacking.

Unpack the Presentation

In this section of the exercise, you will unpack the presentation to the PinnacleOnlineCD folder in the My Documents folder. Imagine instead that you are unpacking the presentation to the hard drive of the presentation computer.

7. Close the PowerPoint program. Click Yes if prompted to save the presentation.
8. Minimize all open windows to display the Desktop.
9. Follow the applicable bulleted step below to open a My Computer window:
   - If you are using Windows 2000, double-click the My Computer icon on the Desktop.
   - If you are using Windows XP, click the start button then click My Computer.
10. Double-click the Class Files folder inside the My Documents folder.
11. Double-click the PinnacleOnlineCD folder.
    Notice that all the files in this folder included with your presentation file. These are your supporting files required to run the presentation.
12. Double-click pptview in the file list to open the PowerPoint Viewer.
    The viewer must be opened in order to run the presentation through it. If the viewer is not installed on your computer, you will be asked to accept the License Agreement to install it. Once you click Accept, it will install automatically.

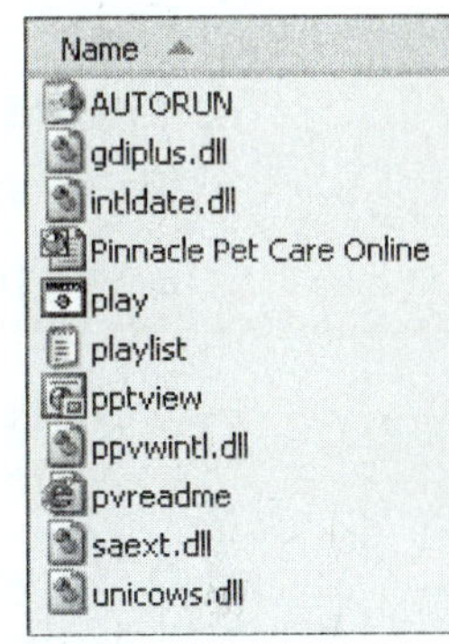

The list of required files included by the Package for CD command

13. Follow these steps to run the Pinnacle Pet Care Online slide show:

A **Verify that the PowerPoint Viewer dialog box is open.**

B **Double-click the Pinnacle Pet Care Online presentation in the PinnacleOnlineCD folder. The slide show begins playing immediately.**

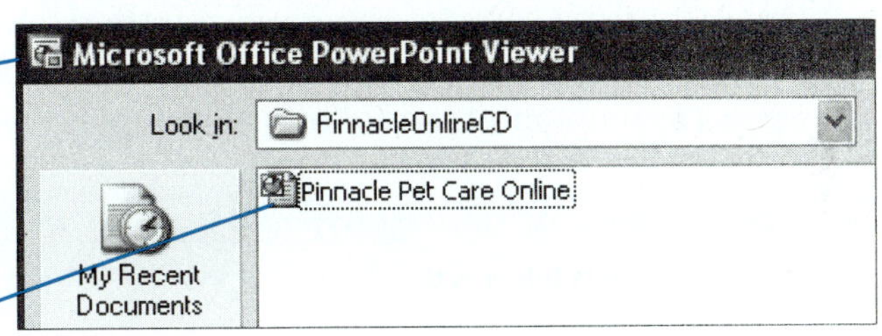

Notice that you do not see the PowerPoint window because the presentation is being played through the PowerPoint Viewer and not the application. Notice also that the Pointer or Navigation toolbar options are not available when running the show through the viewer. Therefore, navigating through the slide show must be done with the mouse. You can click on a slide to advance to the next slide or right-click to access a pop-up menu that allows you to navigate to anywhere within the presentation.

14. Continue clicking and advancing through the entire presentation then click the Close button on the PowerPoint Viewer dialog box.
    Notice that when you clicked on the last slide, you were returned to the PowerPoint Viewer dialog box. Therefore, during a live presentation, do not click on the last slide so the audience won't see the dialog box.

TIP! *Always end the presentation with a Title Layout slide with the title End of Presentation or some other indicator that the presentation is completed.*

Writing Files to a CD

Microsoft Office Specialist

Most new computers being sold today include a CD-RW (Compact Disc-Read/Write) drive. Windows XP includes the software necessary to write files to a compact disc with a CD-RW drive. (Previous versions of Windows required you to install additional software to perform this task.) Since CDs can hold up to 650 MB of data safely and durably, they make an ideal long-term storage medium.

NOTE! *Although you can also write files to a recordable CD in Windows 2000, this requires the installation of special software. Virtually all CD-RW drives come bundled with this software. However, there is quite a variety of software available for this task. This topic will only address the basic capabilities built into Windows XP.*

Types of Writeable CDs

There are two types of compact discs to which you can write files:

- **Write Once (Standard)**—These CDs allow you to write files to discs but not erase files from them. Although you can write files to a standard CD on several occasions, each file uses up more of its storage capacity. Once the storage capacity is reached, you can no longer write new files to the CD. Files written to a standard CD can last up to 30 years or more.
- **Rewritable CDs (Erasable)**—These CDs allow you to erase files as well as write to them. In general, writing files to a rewritable CD is slower than writing files to a standard one. However, you can erase individual files from the CD or reformat it to erase all files. This type of CD makes a useful short-term backup medium.

Example

Once Charlene completes her presentation, she decides to create a backup copy of it on a CD. Since she wants a permanent copy, Charlene chooses a write once CD (CD-R). She uses the Send To command then follows the steps to record this copy to the CD.

QR

QUICK REFERENCE: WRITING FILES TO A CD

Task	Procedure
Write files and/or folders to a CD	■ Select the files and folders in the Open dialog box then right-click and choose Send To→[CD-RW drive letter]. ■ In a My Computer window, display the CD-RW drive. (Windows displays all files and folders ready to be written to the CD-RW drive.) ■ Place a writeable CD disc in the CD-RW drive. ■ Click the Write these Files to CD command in the CD Writing Tasks panel on the left. ■ Follow the on-screen prompts to complete the task.

Hands-On 9.2 Write Files to a Compact Disc

WebSim *In this exercise, you will run a simulation of writing files to a CD. Because many computer classrooms lack the CD-RW drives required to burn a CD, this simulation will run from a Web page. (See Skill Builder 9.1 for a guided exercise in writing to a CD if your computer has a CD-RW drive.)*

NOTE! *Windows 2000 users can run this WebSim, too.*

Package the Presentation

1. Launch Internet Explorer then enter the URL http://labpub.com/learn/pp03 in the address bar.
2. Click the Presenting on the Road link on the Web page then click the Writing Files to a CD link.
   You start in the My Documents folder. Now you will select a file to copy to the CD.
3. Click the PinnacleOnlineCD folder.
4. Click the Copy the Selected Items link in the task panel on the left.
5. Choose the CD drive letter from the list then click the Copy button at the bottom of the dialog box.
   Windows copies the selection to a special location on the hard drive. When the files are copied, a prompt at the bottom-right corner of the Desktop indicates that files are ready to be written to the CD.

6. Click the balloon to view the file to be written to the CD.
   Windows displays the file you copied. Here, you can add more files and folders to this list. For now, let's assume that you only need to write this file to the CD.
7. Click the Write these Files to CD command in the task panel.
   The CD Writing Wizard appears to guide you through the process of writing the CD.
8. Click the CD Name box to erase the default name then enter the new name **`Backup Presentation`**.
9. Click the Next button near the bottom-right corner of the dialog box.
   Windows begins writing the files to the CD. The estimated time remaining for the task displays as the task proceeds. When the task is completed, Windows ejects the CD.
10. Click the Finish button to complete the task.
    Windows displays the now empty window for drive letter you indicated in step 5.
11. Close the Internet Explorer window.

Preparing the Meeting Room

When you take a presentation on the road, you may have limited control over many details. It is important to specify clearly all of the equipment and room setup requirements for your presentation ahead of time. Several critical details are described in the following topics.

Setting Up a Slide Show

PowerPoint allows you to set up variations on a slide show. Now that you have developed your PowerPoint skills, examine the Set Up Show dialog box once more in the following illustration. The Slide Show→Set Up Show command display a dialog box with several adjustable settings.

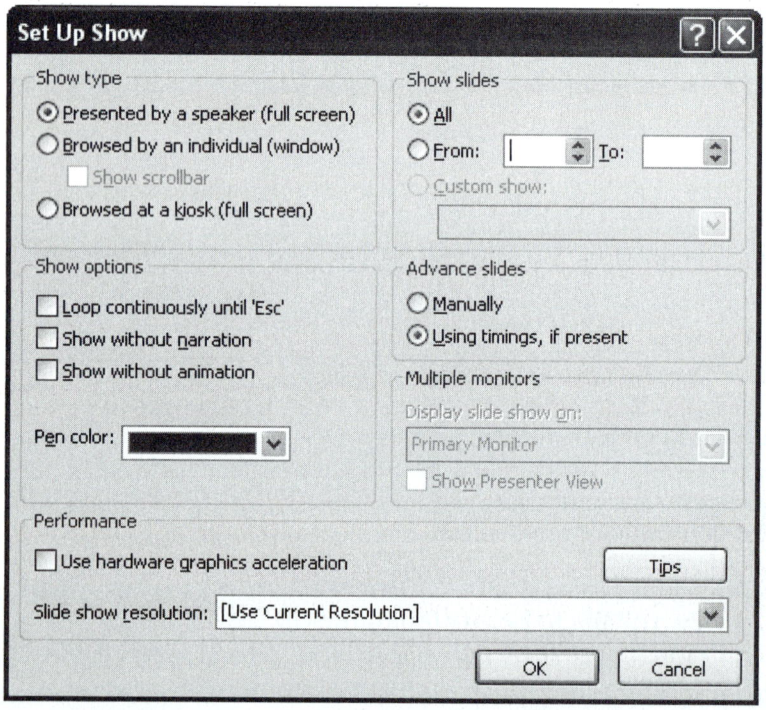

The Set Up Show dialog box allows you to control the display of a slide show.

Specifying the Equipment Setup

It is always a good idea to know as much as possible about the equipment that will be available in the presentation room. Telephone the owner of the computer or send them an email to ask questions and verify that the available equipment meets your needs.

Sound Amplification and Speakers

If you are making a presentation to a large audience, or if you have some audio content in the presentation, you will need some sort of amplification system and speakers. You should not count on notebook computer speakers being loud enough for an audience greater than two or three. Likewise, if you will have a self-running presentation at a vendor table or kiosk, you should use external speakers to provide good sound quality—something few notebook computers can provide unassisted.

Projection Displays

Unless your audience is quite small, you will need a way to project the presentation on a screen, wall, or large computer monitor. Most computer screen projection systems fit one of the following descriptions:

- **Computer projection display—**These are projectors designed to project computer video from the computer directly to a screen or wall. These units usually offer a bright picture that is visible in a variety of lighting conditions.
- **Overhead projection display—**You use this older style of display in conjunction with a standard overhead projector. These displays tend to be far less bright than projectors. The room must be completely dark for the audience to see the presentation. If the room has many windows, make sure they have curtains or shades to block out any direct sunlight.

TIP! *Every motion you make on the presentation computer is displayed on the big screen, which the participants will see. There are no secrets from the participants!*

Screen Size

An important consideration for successful projection is the resolution (screen size) of the projector and the presentation computer. If you will present on your own notebook computer, be sure to check the capabilities of the projection display you will use. Older projection displays may only be able to project a 640×480 pixel screen. This means you may not be able to display as much material legibly on the screen. Also, many notebook computers will not display their screen satisfactorily at a size of 800×600. However, most projection displays can display a 1024×768 screen.

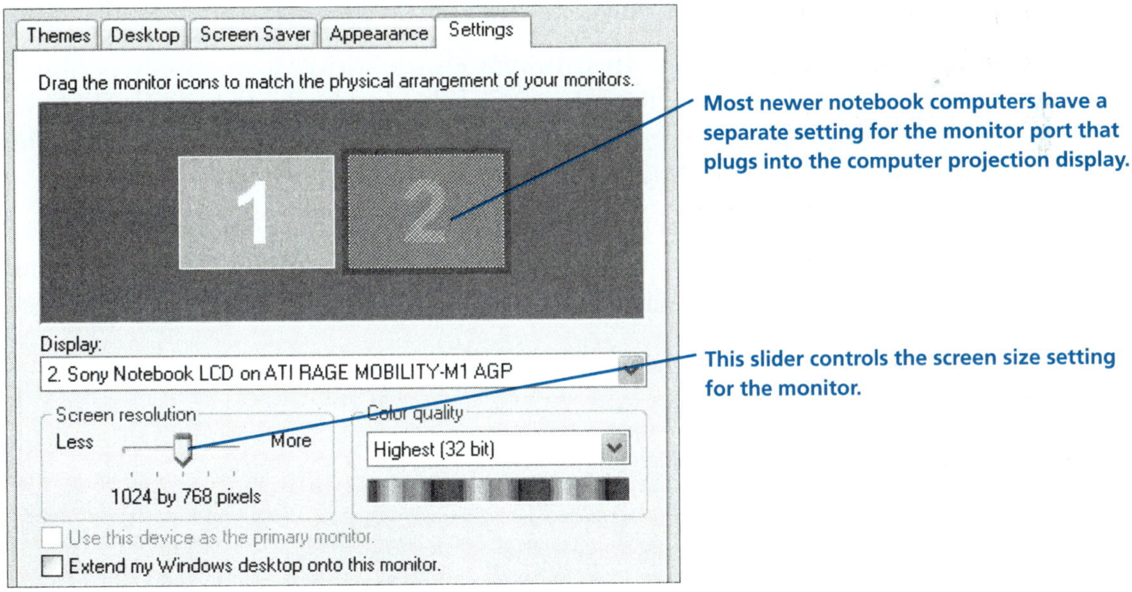

WARNING! *Be certain that the presentation computer and projection display are set for the same screen size—otherwise, the projection display will not work. See the following Quick Reference table for more information.*

QR

QUICK REFERENCE: SETTING UP A SLIDE SHOW

Task	Procedure
Set up a slide show	■ Click Slide Show→Set up Show on the menu bar.
Set the screen size on the presentation computer	■ Right-click on a clear area of the Windows Desktop and choose Properties from the context menu. ■ Click the Settings tab to check the current screen size. ■ If necessary, use the slider control to adjust the screen size then click Apply.
Check the screen size setting on a projection display (generic steps only)	■ Obtain a copy of the instruction manual and check the features page, the index, or the specifications page. ■ The screen size setting is commonly referred to as the resolution of the projection display. ■ Find the menu button on the body of the projection unit or its remote control. Search for a resolution setting on the control menu.

TIP!

If there is no resolution setting on the menu, the unit is probably only capable of projecting a screen size of 640×480 pixels.

The Presentation Computer

If you will not make the presentation on your notebook computer, you should ask several questions regarding the computer you will be using:

- **Does the computer have PowerPoint 2003?** If not, you should use the Package for CD feature that includes the PowerPoint Viewer program so you can display your presentation.
- **Does the computer have the fonts I need?** If not, be sure to use the Package for CD feature that will automatically include all of the fonts used in the presentation.
- **Does the computer have an Internet connection?** If you use hyperlinks to Web pages in your presentation, be sure to verify that the computer you will use has a working Internet connection. If you are delivering the presentation in a college or school, ask if you can connect to the Internet.
- **Do I need a password or ID to open PowerPoint?** Many company and school computers require a username and password. Be sure you know the password for the computer you will use and for the computer your participants will use (if this is a hands-on presentation).

Presentation Setup Checklist

Make a copy of the following checklist and use it to help prepare for your next presentation.

Presentation Computer Software

_____ Computer has PowerPoint 2003 installed

_____ Set Package for CD to include the PowerPoint Viewer

_____ Computer has any other programs I need to run installed (for example, Word and Excel)

Setting Up the Computer Display Projector/Panel

Projection Display Screen Size	Presentation Computer Screen Size
___ 640×480	___ 640×480
___ 800×600	___ 800×600
___ 1024×68	___ 1024×768
___ Other __________	___ Other __________

_____ The focus is clear and can be seen from any area of the room

_____ The projector is stable and balanced (if it is not a ceiling mount) so the slide show will not be skewed

_____ The audio equipment for the projection unit is active and not muted

Room Lighting

_____ Room can be darkened completely for the presentation

_____ Dim lights available for attendees to take notes during presentation

_____ Projection display is powerful enough to be easily visible at time of day planned for the presentation

Audio

_____ ■ Computer can play sound files

_____ ■ Computer can play MPEG files

_____ ■ Presentation computer can be connected to an audio system

_____ ■ External speakers are available for presentation computer

_____ ■ Computer can play movies with sound

Switching Programs during Slide Shows

Windows allows you to switch between various programs with the [Alt]+[Tab] keys. This technique can be quite useful when you need to switch to other programs during a PowerPoint slide show. Simply hold down the [Alt] key, tap the [Tab] key until a box appears around the desired program icon, and release the [Alt] key.

This selection window pops up when you hold down [Alt] then tap the [Tab] key.

Preparing for Success

With the projection unit ready, your presentation and the computer you will use synchronized for screen resolution and effects, don't forget to run through a checklist of your own. Traditionally, if you are narrating the presentation and delivering it to an audience, you will have created handouts for them and speaker notes for yourself. Use the following checklist to ensure that you are fully prepared so that the minute the first participant enters the room you can give them your full attention.

Checklist Prior to Leaving Your Office

Before leaving your office, check that you have with you:

_____ A CD with your presentation and all accompanying files and fonts

_____ Handouts you prepared for the participants (be sure you have enough handouts so you don't have to scurry to a copier at the last moment—be prepared!)

_____ Speaker notes that you can use as a guide as you deliver the presentation

_____ Media that you want to give to the participants (such as a business card CD that contains a copy of the presentation)

NOTE! *Business Card CDs are compact discs the size of a business card. They are easier to carry than regular CDs yet can hold more information than a 3½" floppy diskette.*

_____ Clean tablet, pens, and business cards to use after the presentation

Allow Yourself Time

Always arrive at the meeting site at least one-half hour before the presentation begins. If this is the first time you have used the computer or been to the meeting site, allow one hour to give yourself time to find the location and make any adjustments necessary before the participants arrive. Traditionally, participants arrive 15–20 minutes before the presentation is scheduled to begin.

Prepare for the Workshop

When you arrive at the meeting place:

_____ Unpack the files on the CD to the computer you will be using.

_____ Step through the checklists.

_____ Run the presentation in its entirety.

_____ Note where the light switches are located so you can smoothly turn them on and off. Check to see if there is a remote control unit to do this for you.

_____ Bring a laser pointer with you or check if the projection remote control is also equipped with a pointer feature.

_____ Place the handouts on a table nearby for easy access.

_____ If you are displaying a resource table, lay out the resources so participants can browse through them.

_____ Be generous in supplying resources whether they are handouts, CDs, or souvenirs that will remind them of presentation.

_____ Bring candy or souvenirs to give out for participation rewards.

Greet the Participants

_____ Greet participants with a smile and take the time to talk with each of them.

_____ Explain a general timeline so they know what to expect; for example, that you'll be letting them out sometime in the morning and afternoon for a break and if they're "really good" you might even let them out for lunch. Finally, let them know that they will be out of there, no later than…

_____ Ask questions of the participants and reward answers.

_____ Request that they ask questions and explain that there are "no dumb questions," so ask away.

_____ Devise and use an "ice-breaker" for introductions if the group is small.

TIP! *There are plenty of books and Websites devoted to giving creative presentations, including icebreakers, energizers, and other tips and tricks.*

Targeting Your Audience

It is important to know whom your audience will be when creating the PowerPoint presentation. Finding out the day of the presentation is too late. For example, you would create two completely different presentations if your audience were managers versus clerical staff. Let's quickly review the delivery tips that were introduced in Lesson 1, Creating and Delivering a Presentation.

PEER Guidelines

How you present the information on each slide makes the difference between an engaging and an unsuccessful presentation. Lead your audience. Help them focus on the message of your presentation, not on you as the presenter. Give a presentation using the following **PEER** guidelines to deliver an effective presentation:

- **Pace.** Maintain a moderate pace. Speaking too fast will exhaust your audience and speaking too slowly may put them to sleep.
- **Emphasis**. Pause for emphasis. As you present, use a brief pause to emphasize your points. The pause you take will give your audience time to absorb the message.
- **Eye Contact**. Address your audience. Always face your audience while speaking. A common mistake is to speak while walking or facing the projection screen. If you are speaking from a lectern or desk, resist the temptation to lean on it. Stand tall and make eye contact. Use the three-second rule: look somewhere different after three seconds—any longer than that is staring. At the same time, don't dart your eyes around continuously.
- **Relax**. You are enthusiastic and want to convey that tone to the audience. When you speak, avoid fast movement, pacing, or rushed talking because your audience will be drawn to your movements and miss the point. So speak clearly and maintain a steady pace.

LESS Guidelines

In addition to the PEER guidelines, consider the following **LESS** guidelines to help you deliver your presentation **PEERLESS**ly.

- **Limit questions**. This depends on the type of presentation you are giving. If the presentation is just that—a presentation versus a training session—limit the audience to asking many questions until after the entire presentation. However, if it is a particularly long presentation and you're not allowing questions, you must have energizers prepared to keep your audience with you. Nothing is more boring that just sitting and listening hour after hour. If the presentation is a training session, invite questions—if the question is not relevant, you can say you'll address it later in private. Or, if the question is coming up on the next slide, just say something like, "Oh I'm so glad you asked, that's coming next," and continue.
- **Engage your audience**. An interactive presentation is not a free-for-all for the audience, but includes you asking a brief question or two during and after the presentation to be sure the audience understands your points. Do something different every 20 minuets or you risk "losing" your audience. For example, lecture, ask a hypothetical question, lecture, give a "pop quiz" on the material, lecture, ask for a question, and so forth.

- **Stay focused**. If you are given 20 minutes to deliver your presentation, do not go over your allotted time! Even if you have an unlimited amount time to deliver, don't presume that the audience has nothing else to do but listen to your presentation. As captivating as the presentation may seem, be considerate of their time constraints.
- **Seek feedback**. After the presentation is over but before the audience leaves the room, ask for feedback from them. Use their feedback to improve the presentation the next time it is delivered.

A Practice Workshop

As the sales representative for Pinnacle Pet Care East, you are requested to give a series of presentations to various vendors throughout the Northeast to promote the new branch. Beth Newland, your manager, schedules you as the speaker at trade shows and conferences that will be held in Boston, New York City, Philadelphia, and Atlantic City over a two-week span of time. Beth tells you will have approximately 30 participants in the audience and will have 20 minutes to deliver your presentation before the next presenter is scheduled. She cannot give you the details of the computer setup on each computer you will be using since it will vary from state to state. However, the computers will be set up in the conference room of each hotel at which you will stay for each visit. Beth emphasizes that there will be banking, advertising, and newspaper reporters in your audience. She asks that you stack the presentation with facts about Pinnacle's financial projections and impress the audience with the rise of Pinnacle's success through customer testimonials. With airline tickets in hand, you head to your office to create the presentation and prepare for four presentation events.

Create the Presentation

Create a PowerPoint presentation using the Pinnacle Pet Care Online presentations or a Pinnacle template. Enhance the presentation appropriately. Add a Word table that features t projected income of Pinnacle Pet Care East. Be generous in appropriating statistics for a po tive cash flow for the branch over a five-year span. Feel free to be creative. Add clip art, sou and animation as you deem appropriate. Save the presentation as **`PPC East`** and copy it t My Documents folder using the Package for CD feature.

Research Room and Computer Specifications

Use the Internet to research the phone number for each hotel that will host the confere

Imagine you are asking the conference official the following questions and make pract notes of the answers:

- How many participants are enrolled in the presentation?
- What type of projection unit is used in the room?
- Will I have access to an easel with notepaper or a whiteboard?
- Does the computer I will be using have PowerPoint 2003 installed in it? If not, v is installed? Determine the specifications of the computer.

Plan

Plan accordingly by creating a presentation with handouts so the audience can take notes throughout the presentation. Add 10 to this count so you will have more than enough in case there are last-minute registrations for your workshop.

Go over the checklists that Charlene has distributed to all of the sales representatives at Pinnacle:

- Determine the screen resolution
- Remember delivery guidelines for a slide show
- Prepare the meeting room
- Remember delivery tips and PEERLESS guides

Practice, Practice, Practice

Practice the presentation using the speaker notes and pointer arrow tools as though you were delivering it to a live audience. Practice installing the PowerPoint View and running through the presentation

Pack Your Bags

Assemble each part of the presentation event you will need in an area small enough for you to carry, such as a briefcase. Use the checklist to ensure that the CD, supporting material, handouts, and souvenirs are represented in the right amounts and for all scenarios.

On the Road Again...

As you travel to each conference, use the Internet to find out the local news in Boston, New York City, Philadelphia, and Atlantic City so you will be able to talk with the participants about their cities.

Concepts Review

True/False Questions

1.	The PowerPoint Viewer will run on any Windows operating system.	TRUE	FALSE
2.	You can only use the Package for CD feature to store a presentation on external media.	TRUE	FALSE
3.	The Package for CD feature automatically includes files that are linked to the presentation.	TRUE	FALSE
4.	You can set the screen resolution of the presentation computer using the Set Up Dialog box.	TRUE	FALSE
5.	Checking the meeting room before the presentation is for amateurs.	TRUE	FALSE
6.	You can switch programs during a presentation using the Slide Show toolbar.	TRUE	FALSE
7.	A drawback to the PowerPoint Viewer is that the Slide Show toolbar is not accessible.	TRUE	FALSE
8.	Using Embedded TrueType fonts is important to correctly display the presentation.	TRUE	FALSE
9.	An interactive presentation is a free-for-all so the audience can take control.	TRUE	FALSE
10.	Seeking feedback on the presentation will help you deliver it more effectively.	TRUE	FALSE

Multiple Choice Questions

1. What is a CD-RW?
   a. Compact disc
   b. Rewritable compact disc
   c. Compact data
   d. Overgrown 3½" floppy diskette
2. The Package for CD Feature contains ________.
   a. the presentation you add to the Package for CD folder
   b. any linked files for the presentation
   c. the PowerPoint Viewer
   d. All of the above
3. Using Embedded TrueType fonts is only important if ________.
   a. you don't have PowerPoint installed on the presentation computer
   b. you are just using the PowerPoint Viewer
   c. you want the sizing and style of the presentation to display as you created it
   d. you have hyperlinks in the presentation
4. Which of the following statements describes a limitation of the PowerPoint Viewer?
   a. It does not support the function of the Slide Show toolbar when you run the presentation.
   b. You can only navigate through the presentation using the shortcut menu after right-clicking.
   c. You do not have access to the Pointer Arrow button on the Slide Show toolbar so you cannot use the pen tool.
   d. All of the above

Skill Builders

Skill Builder 9.1 Pack a Presentation for Transport

In this exercise, you will use the Package for CD feature to pack a presentation on a CD.

Pack the Presentation

1. Open the Tropical Getaways Online presentation from your file storage location.
2. Click File→Package for CD from the menu bar.
3. Name the CD **`Tropical Online`**.
4. Click the Options button and be sure the PowerPoint Viewer, linked files, and Embedded TrueType fonts are checked then click OK.
5. Open the CD Drive and insert a CD-RW disc.
6. Click the Copy to CD button to write the file to the CD.

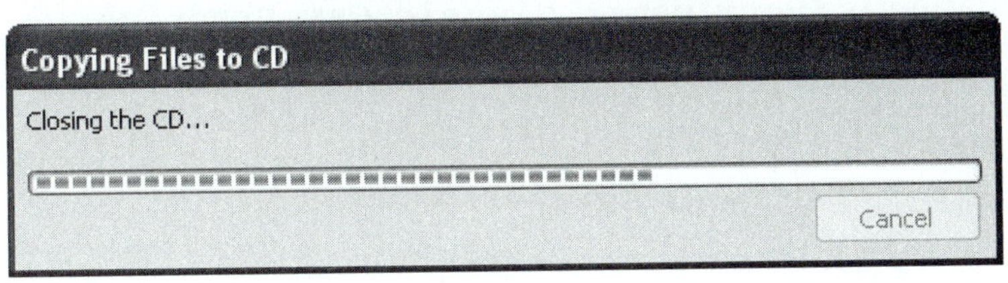

A progress box displays while the file is being copied.

7. When the file is finished copying onto the CD, be sure to label it appropriately.
When it is finished, the CD will eject automatically.

Check the CD

8. Re-insert the CD into the drive.
The presentation should start up immediately. You may need to accept the PowerPoint Viewer License Agreement if this is the first time you've used it. If the PowerPoint View does not start up automatically, you must perform steps 9–11. If it does start, skip to step 12.
9. Open a My Computer window.
10. If necessary, install the PowerPoint Viewer by double-clicking on the pptview file then accept the license agreement.
11. Double-click the Tropical Getaways presentation.
12. Navigate through each slide by clicking through the slides, including the last one that ends and closes the presentation.

Skill Builder 9.2 Deliver the Classic Cars Presentation

In this exercise, you will deliver the Classic Cars presentation before a live audience by using a computer that has the PowerPoint application installed on it.

Create Handouts and Hyperlinks

1. Open the Classic Cars Online presentation.
2. Create a new slide with information found on buying, insuring, and displaying the classic car of your choice using one of the following Websites: www.google.com, www.myclassiccar.com, or www.classic-car-directory.com.
3. Create a set of handouts that are three on a page and include space for note-taking.
4. Insert at least two hyperlinks in the presentation that point to resources on the Web for maintaining and insuring the classic car.
5. Save the presentation as **`[your name] Classic Car Practice`**.

Prepare the Presentation

6. Copy the presentation and its related files to a CD drive or, if you don't have one, copy it to the Class Files folder in My Documents.

Practice the Presentation

7. Practice the presentation alone before presenting it to the live audience.
8. Step through the PEER-LESS guidelines to ensure that your presentation style is effective.
9. Check the projection unit to be sure that it is in focus and displays the slides so they do not appear crooked.
10. Run the slide show and use the speaker notes as a guide.

Real-Time Delivery

11. Ask several classmates, co-workers, or friends to be your audience for this trial presentation. If you are in a classroom, deliver it to your class.
12. Greet the participants of your audience as though it were the first time you met them. Introduce yourself and your subject.
13. Dim the lights and throw yourself into presenting this slide show as though it were for a real company!

Assessments

Assessment 9.1 Pack and Unpack a Presentation

In this exercise, you will pack and unpack a presentation.

1. Open the Chicago presentation.
2. Change the presentation title to **`Touring Chicago`** and the subtitle to **`[Your Name]`**.
3. Use Package to Go to pack the presentation in the My Documents\Class Files folder.
4. Close the PowerPoint program on your computer.
5. Unpack and run the presentation from the Package to Go file in the Class Files folder.

Assessment 9.2 Burn a CD

In this exercise, you will burn a CD of the Pinnacle Pet Care Online presentation. You will also play the presentation from the CD. (If you don't have a CD-RW drive in your computer, you can save the presentation in the Class Files folder in My Documents.)

1. Open the Pinnacle Pet Care Online presentation.
2. Create a CD of the presentation or save it to an alternative file storage location.
3. Run the slide show from the CD.
4. Ask your class, co-workers, or friends to participate in the presentation as your audience.
5. Deliver the presentation and, afterward, ask for feedback on your style and performance.

Critical Thinking

Critical Thinking 9.1 Create a Presentation about Chicago

As a newcomer to the exciting city of Chicago, Nicole is intrigued by the history and folklore she has learned. She goes to the Chicago Public Library and spends whole afternoons researching facts about Chicago's historical foundation. Although Chicago is noted for great restaurants and lively Blues hall, she learns that Chicago is also steeped in a cultural history that encompasses art, music, and politics. When she has gathered the key events in Chicago history, she enthusiastically calls the Chicago Historical Society and offers to give the presentation at their next Annual Meeting.

Search the Web using standard search engine such as www.google.com to find out information about Chicago, Illinois. Accumulate enough data for a six-page presentation. Include slides with data about art museums; Chicago architects; tourist attractions; and areas such as the Sears Tower, Navy Pier, and Wrigley Field. End the presentation with your favorite aspect of the city. Add hyperlinks to the attraction you chose. Save the presentation as **Chicago Info**. Present the presentation to a live audience, whether it is fellow students, your family, or a civic group.

Critical Thinking 9.2 Create a New Hire Orientation Presentation

As the new Human Resources manager for the American Museum of Natural History in New York City, Ann Marie DeSantos is determined to provide the newly hired staff with the necessary tools to help run this world-famous museum. She knows how important it is for them to understand the history of the museum in addition to museum policies and procedures. Ann Marie decides that the museum needs a standardized New Hire Orientation presentation. She knows that PowerPoint has a feature called the AutoContent Wizard that includes an Employee Orientation presentation. She thinks this would be a good start and asks you to customize it for her. Ann Marie asks you to make all of the design and content decisions. When finished, save the presentation as **New Hire Orientation**.

Practice your presentation as though you had PowerPoint installed on the computer you will use in the live setting. Give your presentation before a live audience of friends, family, or fellow students. When finished, close the presentation.

Critical Thinking 9.3 Create a Presentation for the Blue Hill Agency

The Blue Hill Agency, a small but thriving real estate agency, has recently hired you. Joseph Kindle, your manager, knows of your PowerPoint expertise and asks you to create a PowerPoint presentation to present at the National Real Estate Association's Annual Meeting. He tells you that the presentation should outline the company's marketing techniques and follow-up services. There also needs to be slides listing the staff and their positions, and an organization chart showing the hierarchy of the agency. Include slide for extra services, frequently asked questions, and the office hours. Use a template design, clip art, animation, and sounds of your choice. Save the presentation as **Blue Hill Agency**. Run the presentation for your classmates, friends, or relatives.

When you are finished, close the presentation and exit from PowerPoint.

ENDIX

Using File Storage Media

You may wish to use storage media besides the floppy disk referred to in most of the lessons. This appendix contains instructions for downloading and unzipping the exercise files used with this book, and an overview for using this book with various file storage media.

In This Appendix

The following topics are addressed in this appendix:

Downloading the Student Exercise Files

The files needed to complete certain Hands-On, Skill Builder, Assessment, and Critical Thinking exercises are available for download at the Labyrinth Website. Use the following instructions to copy the files to your computer and prepare them for use with this book.

Hands-On A.1 Download and Unzip Files

Follow these steps to download a copy of the student files necessary for this book:

1. Launch Internet Explorer.
2. Enter **labpub.com/students/fdmso2003.asp** in the browser's address bar and tap [Enter].
   A list of books in the applicable series appears. If you don't see the title of your book in the list, use the links on the left side of the Web page to display the list of books for your series.
3. Click the link for your book title.
   A prompt to open or save a file containing the student exercise files appears.
4. Click the Save button.
5. Choose your file storage location and click Save.
   After a pause, the exercise files will begin downloading to your computer. Continue with the next step after the download is complete.
6. Click the Open button on the Download Complete dialog box. Or, open your file storage location and double-click the newly downloaded file if the dialog box closed automatically.
7. Click OK, and then follow the step for your file storage location:
   - **Floppy Disk:** Click the Browse button, choose the 3½ Floppy A: drive, click OK, and then click the Unzip button.
   - **USB Flash Drive:** Click the Browse button, navigate to your USB flash drive, click OK, and then click the Unzip button.
   - **My Documents Folder:** Click the Browse button, navigate to the My Documents folder, click OK, and then click the Unzip button.
   - **Network Drive Folder:** Click the Browse button, navigate to your assigned folder on the network drive, click OK, and then click the Unzip button.
8. Click the Close button after the files have unzipped.

Working with File Storage Locations

New technologies continue to expand the variety of available computer storage media. The $3\frac{1}{2}$ inch floppy disk has been around since about 1983. That's incredibly ancient in the fast-moving field of computers. It's easy to use other storage media with this book. Potential alternative storage locations include:

- The My Documents folder
- A USB flash drive
- A folder on your local hard drive
- A folder on a network drive

Using Alternative File Storage Locations

Depending on the file storage media you select, some steps you perform in the Hands-On exercises will differ from what you see illustrated. However, with a little practice you should find it easy to interpret the instructions for use with your file storage media.

Example: Using a USB Flash Drive

You are performing an exercise in which you create and save a new file. If you are using a USB flash drive, simply substitute the drive letter for your flash drive for the $3\frac{1}{2}$ Floppy (A:) drive shown in the figure instruction.

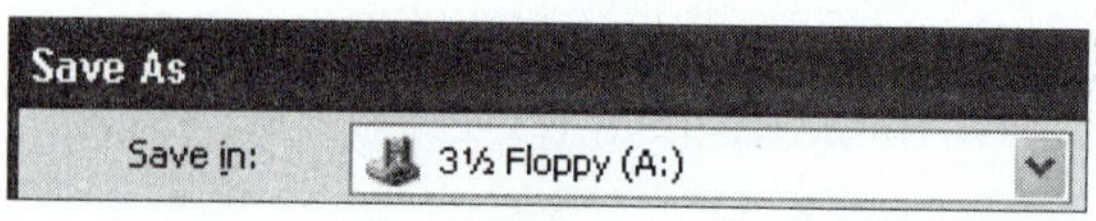

The storage location as it appears in the book

The storage location as you perform it on the screen

Using a Floppy Disk

If you use a floppy disk to store your exercise files, you should be aware of space limitations. This section explains how to keep track of the available space on a floppy diskette, and how to delete unnecessary files to conserve space.

Storage Limitations of Floppy Disks

As you work through the exercises in this book, you will create numerous files that are to be saved to a storage location. A floppy diskette may not have enough storage capacity to hold all files created during the course (particularly if you perform all of the Skill Builder and Critical Thinking exercises). Thus, you may want to use an alternate storage location for all files accessed and created during the course.

Checking Available Space on a Floppy Disk

If you choose to use a floppy disk as your storage location, you may reach a point at which the disk fills up and no additional files can be stored on it. However, if you regularly check the available space on your floppy disk, this problem should not arise.

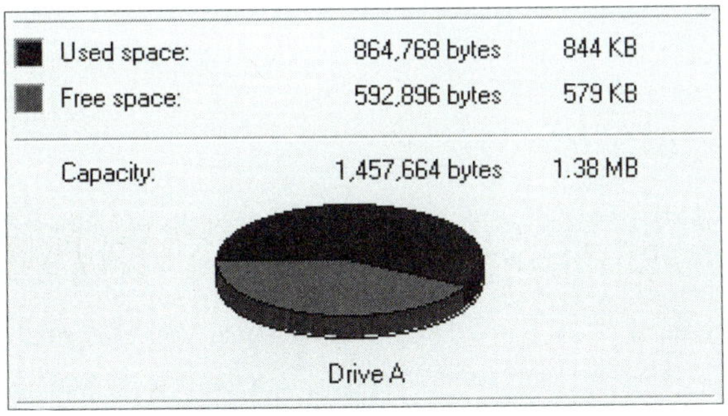

Windows can display a pie chart of the available space on your floppy disk.

Freeing Up Space on the Floppy Disk

If your floppy disk runs short of space, you will need to selectively delete files from it. You should delete files from lessons already completed, freeing up space for exercises in the current lesson.

TIP! *Use the following procedure to check your available floppy disk space before you begin work on a new lesson. If you have less than 100 KB remaining on the disk, delete some files to free up space.*

Hands-On A.2 Check Free Space on a Floppy Disk

1. Open a My Computer window.
2. Right-click the 3½ Floppy (A:) drive and choose Properties from the context menu.
   Windows displays a pie chart with details on the used and available space on the floppy disk.
3. Examine the Free Space information and click OK.

Used space:	1,379,840 bytes	1.31 MB
Free space:	77,824 bytes	76.0 KB

4. Follow the step for the amount of disk space remaining:
   - **Close** the Properties window. Close the My Computer window if there is more than 100 KB of space remaining on the disk. Skip the remaining steps in this procedure. You are finished and ready to proceed with the next lesson.
   - **Close** the Properties window. Continue with the remaining steps in this exercise if there is less than 100 KB of space remaining on your floppy disk.

Delete Unnecessary Files

5. Double-click to open the 3½ Floppy (A:) drive.
6. Choose View→List from the menu bar.
   The My Computer window displays your files as a compact list.
7. While holding down the [Ctrl] key, select files for lessons that precede the one you are working on now and tap the [Delete] key on the keyboard. Choose Yes if you are asked to confirm the deletion of these files.
   Windows deletes the selected files.
8. Close the My Computer window.
   You now have plenty of space for your work in the next lesson.

TIP! *If you accidentally delete an exercise file needed for a later lesson, don't worry. You can repeat the procedure outlined in Hands-On A.1 to download and unzip the student exercise files as many times as necessary.*

Using a USB Flash Drive

A USB flash drive stores your data on a flash memory chip. You simply plug it into a USB port on any computer and Windows immediately recognizes it as an additional disk drive. USB flash drives can store 32 megabytes (MB) or more of your data files. Large capacity USB flash drives can store 512 MB or more.

Most USB flash drives are about the size of your thumb and plug into any available USB port on your computer.

USB Flash Drive Letter

When you plug in a USB flash drive to a Windows computer, Windows automatically assigns it the next available drive letter. Windows uses drive letters to identify each drive connected to the computer. For example, the primary part of the hard drive is always identified as the C: drive. The CD/DVD drive is typically the D: or E: drive.

This USB flash drive is the F: drive.

TIP! *Your USB flash drive may receive a different drive letter on different computers. This does not affect any files stored on the drive.*

Hands-On A.3 Rename Your USB Flash Drive

You may find it convenient to rename your USB flash drive to make it easier to recognize when you save or open files.

TIP! *Some Windows systems may not give you renaming privileges for drives.*

1. Plug the USB flash drive into an available USB port.
2. Open a My Computer window.
3. Right-click your USB flash drive and choose Rename from the context menu.

NOTE! *In the next step, Windows may display a prompt that you cannot rename this flash drive. You have not done anything wrong! You can use the drive with its current name. You may also want to try renaming it later using a different login.*

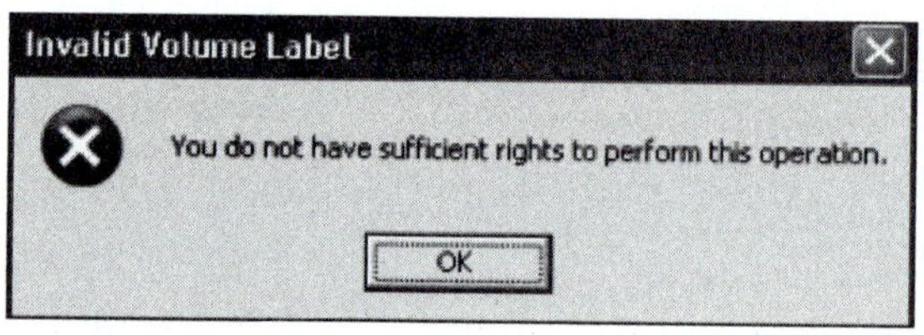

4. Type **`FlashDrive`** as the new drive name and tap [Enter]. Click OK if you receive a prompt that you do not have sufficient rights to perform this operation.

If you were unable to rename the flash drive, don't worry. Renaming the flash drive is a convenience for recognition and has no other effect.

Using the My Documents Folder

Windows creates a unique My Documents folder for each login. This folder resides on the main system drive (usually the C: drive). The Office 2003 application programs provide a My Documents button in their Open and Save As dialog boxes to make navigation to this folder convenient.

The My Documents button in the Word 2003 Save As dialog box

Using a Network Drive Folder

You may use a system connected to a network. There may be a folder on a network server computer in another location that is dedicated to storing your work. Usually, you will find this folder within the My Network Places folder of your computer. The Office 2003 application programs provide a My Network Places button in their Open and Save As dialog boxes to make navigation to this folder convenient. You may have to navigate deeper into the folder to locate your personal network drive folder.

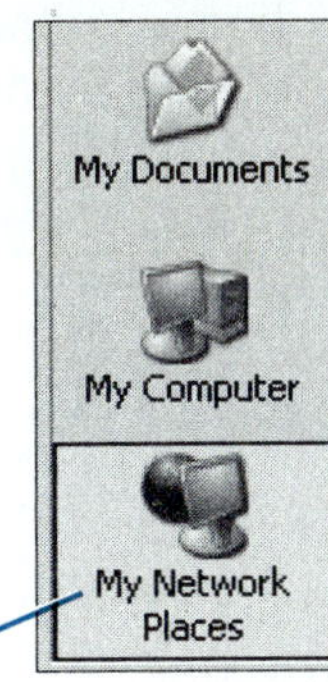

The My Network Places button in the Word 2003 Save As dialog box

Index

L

M

N

O

P

T

U

V

W

Notes